The British Canoe Union

Canoe and Kayak Handbook

Edited by Franco Ferrero

With contributions by:

Duncan Winning, Graham Mackereth, Rob Cunnington, Lara Tipper,
Ray Goodwin, Keith Hampton, Bill Taylor, Leo Hoare, Ian Coleman,
Suresh Paul, Richard Harvey, David Halsall, David Taylor, Richard Ward,
Gerry McCusker, Claire Knifton, Keith Morris, Gordon Brown, Matt Berry,
Loel Collins, Andy Maddock, Melissa Simons, Martin Streeter,
Paul O'Sullivan, Ken Hughes, Pete Astles

Illustrations by:

Carol Hughes

Pesda Press - Wales

First published 1981
Second Edition 1989
Third Edition 2002

ISBN   0-900082-04-6

ISBN   0-9531956-5-1

Published in Great Britain 2002

by Pesda Press
'Elidir'
Ffordd Llanllechid
Rachub
Bangor
Gwynedd
LL57 3EE

Copyright © 2002 BCU Coaching Service

ISBN   0-9531956-5-1

Printed in Great Britain by

Cambrian Printers - Wales

Foreword

You do realise, of course, that if you have got to the stage of thinking enough about paddling to pick up this book you are probably already damaged forever as a human being! Buried deeply inside your psyche is an urge to spend totally unreasonable amounts of time in the often uncomfortable surroundings of a small boat. Take heart in the fact that you are not alone, and that the number of your fellow paddlers continues to grow steadily.

The sheer size of this book is evidence of the progress that has been made in canoeing and kayaking, from the distant days when the boats all looked very much the same and the official manual was but a sliver. Through development of equipment and evolution of technique we have discovered many different ways to enjoy and negotiate the waters of our little planet. The range of boat shapes and performance is staggering, and the differing types of paddling available to us are incredibly diverse.

The cynic might say that modern canoeing/kayaking has become a collection of totally unrelated sports – that the flat water sprinter has nothing whatsoever in common with the white water free-style star, and that the rambling sea kayaker shares nothing at all with the competitive slalom racer. But this is not so. As we sit or kneel in this small craft, which we have carried to the water's edge under our own steam and give it life through the way we grab hold of the water and pull on it, we are united. There are easier ways to travel through water but none has the simple, delightful and fluid appeal that comes when a paddle blade gripped by the bare hand translates itself into movement of the boat. A canoe or kayak in expert hands is a true delight to watch.

The BCU Canoe and Kayak Handbook, as well as providing invaluable information on specific areas, serves as an important reminder that we are part of one great paddlesport family. There is a huge amount of knowledge, experience and tradition to be passed on in these pages. Some of this information lies within the area of teaching and coaching. Here again, paddling is quite unique in being a sport where great emphasis and value has been placed on helping people to learn and develop safely and efficiently. Coach education has evolved no less rapidly than the rest of the sport and anyone endorsed as a coach, at any level, can be proud of their efforts.

Unlike many other forms of recreation, our sport continues to be harmless to the natural environment in which it happens. In the future we must continue to preserve the tradition of care for the environment and wildlife - this handbook provides an important instrument to that end. Leaving nothing but the fading wake from our boats and the spinning eddies from the paddles must be the tenet for all.

No one could possibly think that you could become an expert paddler by reading a book. There isn't any short-cut to getting on the water and gaining experience. What this very special book does is draw on the countless years of experience of the expert authors, and condense this background knowledge into a single, unique publication.

Enjoy your paddling.   Ray Rowe

Dedication

This book is dedicated to the memory of

Geoff Good

BCU Director of Coaching (1979-1999)

A gentleman and a scholar

Acknowledgements

I would like to thank the numerous people who have supported the contributors and the editor and made this book posssible. Supportive roles have ranged from proof reading to providing or even posing for photographs. They are:

John Anderson, Pam Bell , Will Behenna, Howard Blackman, Chris Charlton, Lisa Coe, Ally Collett, Ian Cave, Heather Corrie, Louise Dawkin-Jones, Tom Desbruslais, Desperate Measures, Ian Duffy, David Enoch, David Green , Huw Evans of White Water Consultancy, JJ Canoeing and Rafting, Joan and Lisa Ferrero, Murdo Fraser, Paul 'Skinny' Jones, Kevin East, Karen Harvey, Mark Hickman, Kate Howlett, Carol Hughes, Roger Huyton, Colin Johnstone, Karen Johnstone, Darren Joy, Colin Kempson, Viv Kendrick, Dave Luke, Mad River Canoes, Morag MacLean, Dave Manby, Dave McEneaney, Peter Mitchell, Carroll O'Dolan, Fran Pothecary, Alistair Randall, Paul 'Cheesy' Robertson, Jorgen Samson, Geoff Smedly, Paula Syred, Ruth, Joseph and Hanna Taylor, Steven Train, John Vogler, Barney Wainwright, Swifty, Dale, Emily, Eric, Mike, Mitesh and Nualla.

A particular vote of thanks is due to Mike Devlin, our Director of Coaching, for his unstinting support and hard work.

Photographic Acknowledgements

Cover
Main photo: Popp & Hackner
Sea kayak: Franco Ferrero
Open canoe: Ray Goodwin
All other photos: BCU Library

Chapter 1
Title photo: Hugh Kerr
1.4 Henderson family, 1.5 Loch Lomond Sailing Club, 1.6 Good Family, 1.7 Jones family, 1.8 Loel Collins, 1.10 Franco Ferrero
Portrait: Gordon Brown
All other photos: Hugh Kerr

Chapter 2
2.2 Franco Ferrero,
All other photos: Graham Mackereth

Chapter 3
Title photo: Mike Devlin
Portrait: Rob Cunnington
All other photos: Ian Cave

Chapter 4
All photos: Lara Tipper

Chapter 5
All photos: Ray Goodwin

Chapter 6
Title photo: BCU Library
6.1, 6.2, 6.3 Franco Ferrero, 6.4 BCU Library
Portrait: Keith Hampton

Chapter 7
Title photo: BCU Library
All other photos: Bill Taylor

Chapter 8
All photos: Ian Cave or Leo Hoare

Chapter 9

Title photo: Pete Astles
Portrait: Ian Coleman
All other photos: Ian Cave

Chapter 10
All photos: Suresh Paul

Chapter 11
All photos: Richard Harvey

Chapter 12
12.1, 12.2 Joan Ferrero, 12.3-12.5 Franco Ferrero
All other photos: David Halsall

Chapter 13
Title photo: Sue Ottoline
13.1 Sue Hornby, 13.2, 13.7 BCU Library, 13.4 Franco Ferrero
All other photos: David Taylor

Chapter 14
14.1 Barney Wainwright, 14.2, 14.6 Dave Enoch, 14.3 BCU Library, 14.4, 14.6, 14.7 John Anderson, 14.14 Sue Hornby,
All other photos: Richard Ward

Chapter 15
Portrait: Gerry McCusker
All other photos: BCU Library

Chapter 16
16.1 Richard Godfrey, 16.2, 16.3 Loel Collins, 16.7, 16.11 Franco Ferrero, 16.12 Stephen Macdonald
All other photos: Claire Knifton

Chapter 17
All photos: Ray Goodwin

Chapter 18
Title photo: Franco Ferrero
All other photos: Keith Morris

Chapter 19

Portrait: Graham Mackereth
All other photos: BCU Library

Chapter 20
20.3 Brian Wilson
All other photos: Gordon Brown

Chapter 21
Portrait: Ian Coleman
All other photos: Helen Metcalfe

Chapter 22
22.12 Franco Ferrero
All other photos: Matt Berry

Chapter 23
Title photo: Peter Hollingsworth
All other photos: Ian Cave

Chapter 24
Portrait: Andy Maddock
All other photos: BCU Library

Chapter 25
Portraits: Melissa Simons and Martin Streeter
All other photos: BCU Library

Chapter 26
Title photo: Waghi Kayak Expedition
26.9a-c and portrait: Paul O'Sullivan
All other photos: Ian Cave

Chapter 27
All photos: Ken Hughes and Ian Duffy

Chapter 28
28.7, 27.8 Sue Ottoline
All other photos: Pete Astles

Contents

Information

Yearbooks (free to members) - for information, calendar of events, contact details for specialist committees and access officers.

BCU Coaching Directory, BCU Coaching UK - for details of the Coaching Scheme and syllabuses for the tests and awards. Information from these publications is available for free from the BCU website.

Clubs

One of the best ways to get involved in paddlesport is to join a club. Details of clubs and how to contact them are available from the yearbooks or by contacting one of the governing bodies.

Individual and Family Membership

Join your association and help us to promote and defend the interests of canoeists and kayakers throughout the UK. (See contact details below.)

The Governing Bodies

The British Canoe Union represents the interests of canoeists and kayakers at UK and international level. It is also responsible for coordinating all matters of a federal nature that affect all of the Home Countries.

British Canoe Union,
John Dudderidge House,
Adbolton Lane,
West Bridgford,
Nottingham,
NG2 5AS

Tel 0115-9821100 - Fax 0115-9821797
E-mail info@bcu.org.uk - Website www.bcu.org.uk

The Home Countries are represented by the following associations which represent paddlers at local, regional and home country level:

Canoe Association of Northern Ireland,
c/o The House of Sport,
Upper Malone Road,
Belfast, BT9 5LA
Tel 02891-469907
E-mail cani@clara.net - Website http://home.clara.net/cani

English Canoeing Association, *The ECA is being formed at the time of writing, contact the BCU on English matters.*

Scottish Canoeing Association,
Caledonia House,
South Gyle,
Edinburgh, EH12 9DG
Tel 0131-317-7314 - Fax 0131-317-7319
E-mail scaadmin@dircon.co.uk - Website www.scot-canoe.org

Welsh Canoeing Association,
Canolfan Tryweryn,
Frongoch,
Bala,
Gwynedd, LL23 7NU
Tel 01678-521199 - Fax 01678-521158
E-mail welsh.canoeing@virgin.net - Website www.welsh-canoeing.org.uk

Introduction

This book is designed to be read by different people at different levels. For the newcomer it is an introduction to the breadth of the varied aspects of canoeing and kayaking available. To experienced paddlers it is a chance to learn more about the areas of the sport they are less familiar with, and to update their knowledge of those they have already embraced. To the coach, who is expected to be a 'font of all knowledge' it is the essential reference book.

Someone once described the task of being the governing body of all aspects of canoeing and kayaking as the equivalent of being responsible for all team games played with a ball. BCU Coaching UK has put together this book so that we can all have access to knowledge of the many different facets of canoeing and kayaking. Each chapter will give an overview of its aspect of the sport and cover as much detail as is feasible in a book of this nature. In addition most chapters will provide a further reading list, and where appropriate, a list of available videos and websites so that the reader can explore further.

The Handbook will be updated much more regularly in future. Nonetheless, for the information that needs updating annually I will refer you to the yearbooks produced by the governing bodies. For information on the star tests and coaching awards you should consult the BCU Coaching Directory, available direct from the BCU.

The Coaching Service also administers a network of national association contacts and Regional and Local Coaching Officers. The contact details for these people can be found on the BCU website or in the BCU Yearbook. Alternatively, whether you wish to know more about the work of the coaching service, wish to contact coaching officers for their support, or wish to offer your support to the network, please contact the BCU directly.

Editing this book has been an 'interesting' experience that has made me some new friends and taught me far more than I would have expected. I hope it has a similar effect on all those who read it. If you have any comments or suggestions for improvements for future editions, please send them to me via BCU Coaching.

Franco Ferrero

Franco is a Level 5 Coach (Inland and Sea) and now divides his work time between freelance coaching, writing and publishing. He was formerly the head of the canoeing department at Plas y Brenin, and was honoured with the Geoff Good Coach of the Year Award (coaching adults category) in 2000.

His main paddling interests are white water and sea touring, though he occasionally 'dabbles' in other aspects of paddlesport and is also a keen mountaineer. He has paddled throughout Britain and the European Alps, as well as in Norway and Nepal.

1 A Short History of Paddlesport in Britain

One bright, sunny day in the 1950's Alex Davidson, of the Scottish Hostellers' Canoe Club, was paddling north on Loch Lomond heading for the club's boathouse at Rowardennan. On rounding one of the many islands on the loch, he thought he had gone through a time warp; before him was a scene that seemed to have been transported from the previous century. An elderly gentleman was sitting in a Rob Roy canoe, its prow resting gently on the shingle beach while he enjoyed his sandwiches in idyllic surroundings. As they chatted, the ninety year old paddler enthused about canoeing. Alex began to appreciate the antiquity of the sport, and the fact that it could be enjoyed by all kinds of people and practised in a variety of craft at all levels. As a young sea paddler, he had not realised this before. The nonagenarian's craft was called 'Maisa', and was reputed to have come ashore from a submarine with a German saboteur in the First World War... but that's another story.

Introduction

It is generally accepted that in Britain canoes are based on the birch-bark and dugout canoes of the North American Indian and the kayak of the Inuit. However, canoeing in the British Isles goes back into prehistory. Many dugout canoes have been recovered from the margins of rivers, lochs and lakes. The ubiquitous skin-covered curraghs and coracles of the ancient Celts were widely used on ocean and river. Records exist reporting several visits to the Orkney Isles by 'finnmen' in their skin boats, the

earliest known to the writer being from 1682. The descriptions of the craft are reminiscent of Greenland kayaks.

All these were working boats and native peoples throughout the world have used such craft for occasional recreation. However, it is only in relatively recent times that purpose-built, recreational craft have appeared. In 1830 the 'Jersey Loyalist' reported that a Mr Canham from London, had crossed from Cherbourg to Alderney in a canoe, "much like an Icelander's caiak, consisting of a light wooden framework some ten feet by two feet, covered with tarred canvas. At one end was a receptacle for containing provisions and at the other, one for holding Congrave rockets, to be used in case of shipwreck. Each gunwale had attached to it a long thin bag filled with bladders, to aid stability. The owner, sitting in the centre was protected from spray by a covering of tarred canvas". Mr Canham's declared intention was to continue his voyage to Jersey, thence to Portsmouth.

Well-off Victorians were an adventurous lot and there is no doubt that some of them took to canoeing. However, the credit for popularising the sport must go to a remarkable Scot, John MacGregor. He adopted the nom de plume 'Rob Roy' after the Scottish folk hero of his clan and used the name for each of his seven canoes.

Rob Roy's first thoughts on a canoe were in 1848; however it was not until 1865, after seeing the native canoes in North America and the Kamschata, that he had his first canoe built by Searle's of Lambeth. She was fifteen feet long, planked in oak, clinker fashion with a deck of broad cedar boards. An unfeathered seven-foot paddle was provided, and a lug-sail and jib could be set on a small mast.

MacGregor documented his first epic voyage in the best selling book 'A Thousand Miles in the Rob Roy Canoe on Rivers and Lakes of Europe'. For an early portion of the voyage he was accompanied by the Earl of Aberdeen whose canoe was a foot longer than the 'Rob Roy', its planking being of fir rather than oak. Such was the impact of MacGregor's book that canoeing became instantly popular among his peers, and a number of these early paddlers undertook committed trips. The Earl's younger brother, the Hon. James Gordon, is credited with the first crossing of the English Channel in a Rob Roy canoe. Following his success on European waters MacGregor undertook major canoe tours in Scandinavia, the Middle East, Holland and the Shetland Isles. He wrote about the first two in 'Rob Roy on the Baltic' and 'Rob Roy on the Jordan', both best sellers.

In July of 1866 MacGregor conceived the idea of the 'Canoe Club'. The Prince of Wales became the Commodore that year and in 1873 Queen Victoria bestowed upon it the title 'Royal'. Branches were formed in Cambridge, on the Humber and the Mersey. Unhappy with this arrangement, the

Mersey canoeists formed their own club in 1873. Other early clubs were formed at Bradford, Carlow, Castle Troy, the Clyde, the Forth and the Trent.

Photo 1.1   The 'Lark', a 'Clyde' type paddling/sailing kayak built in the 1870s

With the expansion of interest in the new sport, other canoe designers entered the field; W. Baden-Powel, C.G.Y. King, E.B. Tredwen, and many more builders became involved. Meanwhile however, factories producing open canoes were established in Canada. Many of these beautiful, cedar-planked craft were imported, hence open canoes in Britain became known as 'Canadian Canoes'.

Photo 1.2   The 'Maisa', built in Germany in 1913 for a trip to the West of Scotland

1887 saw the formation of the British Canoe Association, which lasted about thirty years. Revived in 1933, it merged with the recently formed Canoe Section of the Camping Club of Great Britain. This was not a practical arrangement; as a section of a club whose main activity was not canoeing, the Association could not gain acceptance as a national governing body. So in March 1936, representatives of the Canoe Section of the Camping Club, Clyde Canoe Club, Manchester Canoe Club and the Royal Canoe Club formed the British Canoe Union, which quickly affiliated to the international body of the day, the IRK. This was completed just in time for

British paddlers to compete in the 1936 Olympic Games, the first to include canoeing.

Three years later, in July 1939, members of the Canoe Section of the Camping Club, Clyde Canoe Club, Forth Canoe Club (1934) and Scottish Youth Hostels Canoe Club founded the Scottish Canoe Association. In 1944 it was agreed that, without prejudice to its independence, the Association would act as the Scottish Division of the Union. Not until April 1964 did the Union formally recognise the Association as the governing body of the sport in Scotland.

Photo 1.3   A canvas 'Loch Lomond' design from the late 1940s, designed by Hugh Stevenson and paddled by his widow Carrie

Organised paddling in Northern Ireland goes back to about 1949, the Canoe Association of Northern Ireland being formed in 1961. Isolated as it was from mainland paddling by the Irish Sea, as interest in competitive paddling grew, CANI events were integrated into the Irish Canoe Union calendar.

After a third BCU/SCA agreement in 1972, the Association began to take a more active role in the management of the Union. However, after a period it was obvious that the system was not working. In 1976 a working party recommended a move to a federal structure. There followed a year of work preparing the details to be put to the members. The 1978 AGM of the Union decided unanimously that a federal structure be implemented from the first of November 1978 and that a Special General Meeting be held in September to agree the details.

The Scottish Canoe Association adopted its new, federal compatible Constitution on 14th September 1978. Sixteen days later at the SGM of the Union the members rejected the detailed proposals laid before them by their Council and by one vote reversed the decision of the AGM held earlier in the year. Both Councils agreed that something had to be

done to overcome the existing unworkable arrangement. Early in 1979 both parties signed a working agreement, to take effect from 1st November 1979. It became known as 'the federal agreement', and was used as the basis for subsequent agreements with the Canoe Association of Northern Ireland and the newly formed Welsh Canoe Association, and defined the constitutional structure of British canoeing for the next twenty years. At the time of writing, this structure is again in a state of flux with the formation of an English Canoe Association and a new federal British Canoe Union Limited, made up of the four National Governing Bodies.

Sprint Racing

The Canoe Club's first regatta was held in April 1867. The Paddling Challenge Cup, long acknowledged as the oldest paddling trophy in the world was first competed for in Rob Roy canoes in 1874. However the Ardencaple Cup, presented to the winner of the Rob Roy Canoe Race at the Gareloch Regatta in 1868, has recently been discovered.

Specialist racing canoes appeared, longer and narrower, including Rob Roy fours. 'Single Streaks' emerged, these were built to suit the size and weight of the paddler and had one very light 'strake' or plank on each side. Unfeathered spoon-bladed paddles were adopted.

Paddle racing remained a fairly low-level activity. It was much more popular on the continent and was incorporated in the 1936 Olympic Games in Berlin. The British were not prepared for such an event but, after intense training in what craft they could muster, produced a team. In Berlin they competed in borrowed folding kayaks. G. W. Lawton came eighth, with A. R. Brearley and J. W. Dudderidge coming ninth in the single and double 10,000 metre events respectively.

John Dudderidge brought a German coach to run courses. The Royal Canoe Club purchased three K1s and three K2s from Austria. However, activities were brought to a halt by World War Two.

The first Olympic Games after the war were held in London in 1948 and found British paddlers no better prepared than before. There were no boats, no team and little finance. Jicwood of Weybridge built twelve kayaks and Wolverstone Shipyard produced two canoes. Once selected and equipped, the team had only six months left to train. Our performance was not great, but the Games did play an important part in the promotion of sprint paddling in this country. Jicwood donated the kayaks to the Union, and at the World Championships at Copenhagen in 1950 our team manager bought all the second-hand kayaks he could get. These were distributed so as to allow training at local level.

Photo 1.4   A W Simmons and Jack Henderson in Jicwood K1s, May 1948

1953 saw the first West European Championships at Duisburg in Germany in which we gained a second place, and the International Regatta at Namur in Belgium produced a first in the K4. This win was the first time a British crew had won an international canoeing event on the continent. Also in this year the first annual Sprint Championships were held on the Serpentine in London.

In an effort to encourage more participation, in 1956 the Union introduced the specification for the National Chine Kayak. This plywood craft, in single and double versions, could be produced at home relatively easily and cheaply and be used for racing and touring.

By 1957 the numbers involved in sprint were very low, and as a temporary measure handicap events with Juniors and Seniors competing together were introduced, resulting in a record number of junior paddlers. The British Open Youth Championships were established in 1961. Heats were held in different parts of the country, were open to members of youth organisations such as the Scouts, Guides, Sea Cadets, and organised through the offices of the CCPR and the SCPR in Scotland the following year.

The advent of glass-fibre construction put relatively good craft on the market at far cheaper cost than the veneer boats considered necessary for top level competition.

The opening of the National Water Sports Centre at Nottingham, in the centre of England, in 1972 was a tremendous addition both for hosting Internationals and training.

Sprint racing in open canoes was never the strongest aspect of British paddling. However after the 1973 World Championships it started to grow. Two names particularly associated with this development are Train and Fladbury. David Train founded Fladbury Canoe Club in 1973 and started to develop his placid water philosophy. His sons Stephen and Andrew were and are a particularly successful C2 crew. In winning the Silver Medal for C2 10,000m at the 1985 World Championships they were the first non-Eastern block Europeans to win an open canoe medal.

The 1980's brought more competition, sponsorship, a full time coach, enhanced Sports Council funding and increasing success in international competition. In the 1990's the National Lottery brought more funding into sport and to support individual top class competitors. However, an Olympic medal was not attained till 2000 when Tim Brabants achieved Bronze in the K1 1000m event at Sydney, Australia.

Sailing

MacGregor's first 'Rob Roy' was fitted with a small lug-sail and jib, and at least one other of his canoes was yawl rigged. After his trip to Sweden in 1869 Warrington Baden-Powell decided much better use could be made of sail. He designed many sailing canoes called 'Nautilus' and was one of the prime movers in the development of the early sailing canoe.

For cruising, canoes divided into paddling canoes that could be sailed in favourable conditions and sailing canoes that could be paddled when there was no wind. The latter type were developed further by the Humber Yawl Club, the Mersey Canoe Club and the Clyde Canoe Club, increasing in size and sailing capability at the expense of any pretence of paddling. The culmination of this development was the Clyde Canoe Club's 1934 class of five-ton centreboard canoe yawls; all connection with canoeing had gone. This branch of canoeing gave birth to small yacht cruising.

However, in 1985 John Bull resurrected the concept by fitting a simple sailing rig to a standard open canoe and designing easily constructed plywood open sailing canoes. He also founded the

Open Canoe Sailing Group. The use of a small aux-
iliary sail on a paddling canoe continued in regular
use by sea paddlers up until the 1960's.

On the racing front, the Royal Canoe Club presented the Sailing Challenge Cup in 1874, one of
the oldest sailing trophies in the world. Clyde Canoe
Club and the Humber Yawl Club compiled their
own classes to suit their local waters. The Clyde
classes were still being raced into the 1950's. Competition with the Americans promoted advances in
design. They started sitting out on their side decks
to counterbalance the effect of the wind. In 1887 an
American designed the sliding outrigger seat which
was not at that time adopted in Britain.

*Photo 1.5   From the original hanging in the
premises of the Loch Lomond Sailing Club,
founded as the Clyde Canoe Club*

In 1933 Uffa Fox built two very novel canoes
which met both American and Royal rules. He
and Roger de Quincy challenged for the New York
Canoe Club International Trophy, which Roger
won. This prompted the American Canoe Association and Royal to get together and agree new rules.
Meanwhile, the rest of Europe raced to different
rules. In 1946 when the International Canoe Federation was set up, the Anglo-American rules were
adopted and the International 10 square metre Sailing Canoe was born.

The advent of glass-fibre, coupled with the adoption of a standard hull for the 10 square metre class

reduced costs and boosted the numbers of participants. Ever pursuing improvements in performance,
some of the class now compete in a subsection fitted
with a retractable bowsprit flying a spinnaker.

Slalom

Franz Schulhoff, later known as Frank Sutton, came
to Britain from Austria in the mid 1930's. Credited
with the first descent of seven Alpine rapid rivers,
he joined the Royal Canoe Club, led members on
French Alpine rivers, taught them Eskimo rolling
including the 'put-across' method invented by him,
and founded the BCU Rolling Circus.

Two members of the Ista Canoe Club in Vienna
are believed to have run the first Canoe Slalom in
1934. Frank Sutton organised the first British slalom
at Trevor Rocks on the Dee in 1939. A second was
held on the Teme, then the war intervened. A slalom
held on the Tay in 1947 heralded a return to peace-
time activities.

Attendance at World Championships indicated
that we were well behind in both technique and
equipment. Oliver Cock was appointed British Team
Coach in 1953. Around the same time Milo Dufek,
a Czechoslovakian open canoe paddler, adapted the
specialised canoe strokes to the kayak, (in North
America the stroke we know as the 'bow rudder'
is still known as the 'dufek stroke'). Top competition took place in folding kayaks and we lacked the
specialised designs. In the early 1950's after careful
observation of the opposition boats, suitable British designs appeared. It is generally acknowledged
that the J. S. Mk. 6 was the ultimate Folding Slalom
Kayak. Success came in 1959 at Geneva when Paul
Farrant won the F1 World Championship.

Glass-fibre, hard shell kayaks replaced the folders
and hull shape changed to accommodate new techniques, like end dipping. Canoes, C1 and C2
became more popular, following a similar development process to kayaks. Technique continued to
improve and in 1980 Martyn Hedges became European C1 Champion.

The dam-controlled site on the river Tryweryn
in Wales was developed to International competition standard, becoming a valuable training facility. Slalom became an Olympic event for the 1972
Games at Munich with a purpose-built artificial
course at Augsburg. The advantages of such a course
for competition and training were considerable, but

it was fourteen years later before the first British artificial course was opened at Nottingham.

1981 was a memorable year. The World Championships were held at Bala on the Tryweryn, Richard Fox became World K1 Champion, the Men's K1 Team and C2 Team both won Gold and the Ladies K1 Team won Silver. The first Commonwealth Championships were run by the SCA at Grandtully, with England taking all the first places.

These were boom years for slalom but the introduction of plastic playboats heralded a decline in the numbers taking up the activity. Nevertheless the performance at the top remained good with, for example, Gareth Marriott taking Silver in C1 at the Barcelona Olympics in 1992 and Paul Radcliffe taking Silver in K1 at the Sydney Olympics in 2000.

Wild Water Racing

In the early days of slalom it was quite common to have a race down a longer stretch of the same river being used for slalom, and the Leven Wild Water Test series in the Lake District was very popular.

With growth in numbers, specialist craft were developed and modern wild water kayaks have more in common with sprint craft than the slalom boats once used. With specialised boats came specialist paddlers and the Union established a new committee to cater for this aspect of the sport, previously handled by the Slalom Committee. The first international success came at Skopje in 1975 with the GB Women winning the team event and the individual Silver and Bronze.

Marathon Racing

Originally known as Long Distance Racing, Marathon seems to have a number of roots. An English Channel race was proposed as far back as 1874. In the late 1940's the Scottish Hostellers' Canoe Club instituted a sixty-mile time trial for sea kayaks involving loch, river and sea.

Two crews from Devizes Rover Scouts paddled from Devizes to Westminster at Easter 1948 in 90 hours. At Whitsun two crews from the Chippenham Sea Cadets did it in 77 hours. The following year twenty-two crews competed. Responding to the growing interest, Frank Luzmore of Richmond Canoe Club set up an organising committee and the first formal Devizes to Westminster Race ran at Easter 1950.

To cater for the increased interest in Long Distance Racing, the BCU set up a LDR Committee in 1958. Early on, various handicap systems were used and for some years all the Scottish LDR's were held on the sea.

Over the years a great variety of classes have been used to suit the conditions of the day. Today competitions are predominately run in International K and C classes. LDR became Marathon Racing in 1978 to make it more acceptable to the ICF who recognised it officially in 1979. The first World Championships in Marathon were held at Nottingham in 1988.

Lloyd's of London presented the Royal Marines with a magnificent Trophy in 1957 to commemorate their anti-shipping raid on Bordeaux by kayak during the Second World War. The Marines placed the Trophy in the care of the BCU. Named the Hasler Trophy, after Major 'Blondie' Hasler, who led the raid, it is competed for annually by clubs on a points system at ranking events and is the premier marathon trophy.

Canoe Polo

The 'Graphic' of 18th September 1880 reported a canoe polo match at Hunter's Quay on the Firth of Clyde. Polo has long been played in a very informal way as a fun event.

However, its introduction as a competitive discipline in Britain seems to have been sparked by a demonstration event at the Crystal Palace Canoe Exhibition in 1970, the first National Championships being held at the next exhibition. A National League was formed in 1979.

Most competitions were held in swimming pools and specialised kayaks were soon developed. Special paddles, helmets and face guards quickly followed. As the sport developed, swimming pool availability proved a difficulty in some areas and many competitions are now held in the open.

Surf

Old BCU film library material shot by Frank Sutton in the late 1930's shows surfing in Greenland style kayaks. Oliver Cock started annual surfing weeks at Polzeath in Cornwall in 1952. In 1964 the location shifted to Bude where the first National Championships were held in 1967. The rules were adapted from malibu board competition and the craft used were mostly slalom kayaks.

However, in 1970 the specialised surf kayak appeared, requiring the establishment of additional classes. That year also saw interest expand to the North East of England with the first local championships being held there. Surf activity in Britain now extends from the north coast of Scotland to the Channel Islands and is competed for in International K1s and high performance classes open to any design. The World Championships have been hosted twice by the SCA at Thurso and in the 2001 'Worlds' at Santa Cruz, Scotland's Tracy Stewart won the Ladies and Jersey were first in the team event.

Freestyle

The introduction of short, plastic playboats capable of gymnastic manoeuvres promoted this latest type of competition on standing waves, on river or tidal overfalls. Paddlers in either kayak or canoe demonstrate a variety of moves at rodeo events. Now established internationally, Britain won 3 Gold and 5 other medals at the 1999 World Championships in New Zealand and had a clean sweep at the 2000 European Championships.

Lifeguards

Rear Admiral D. J. Hoare is credited with conceiving the idea of training canoeists to go to the assistance of people in distress. He set up the Canoe Lifeguards of the London Federation of Boys' Clubs in the late 1950's. When the Council of the Union agreed to the formation of the Corps of Canoe Lifeguards in 1960, three of the Federation's Canoe Lifeguards were invited to form the nucleus of the new operation.

By 1970 a specially developed rescue canoe, based on the KW7 and coloured in broad red and yellow bands, was in production as was the first Canoe Lifeguard Manual. The Corps was renamed the British Canoe Union Lifeguards in 1991 and a full Specialist Committee of the Union was set up to accommodate it. Some of the Corps awards were adopted by the Coaching Scheme and they were responsible for compiling the first sea proficiency tests.

Despite aspirations of becoming a UK wide service, Lifeguard registered clubs are currently confined to the south coast plus a couple in Wales.

Coaching Scheme

The Coaching Scheme has its roots back in 1947, when a small group of paddlers had the idea of establishing a set of proficiency tests based on their experience in the skiing world. Two years later they produced the syllabus for the first proficiency tests.

Some ten years on John Dudderidge, now a member of the renamed Proficiency Committee, was asked to compile canoeing standards for the Duke of Edinburgh Award Scheme. This gave impetus to produce a syllabus for advanced tests. John journeyed widely during 1959 and 1960, selecting people to organise coaching, based on the Central Council of Physical Recreation's regional structure.

Thus the scheme was born and became the responsibility of the National Coaching Committee under John's Chairmanship. Oliver Cock was appointed the first full-time National Coach in 1962. However, the Scottish Canoe Association did not start its Coaching Scheme until 1965, signing an agreement in 1967 to maintain common standards for tests and awards throughout the UK.

Photo 1.6   Geoff Good, Director of Coaching 1979-1999

Over the years the Scheme has grown both in size and complexity, and is held in high regard in many countries. Indeed many foreign paddlers seek to become BCU Coaches, particularly in North America, which has led to some controversy.

Touring and Expeditioning

Touring has always been the backbone of the sport. It is recorded that at the first meeting of the Canoe Club in 1866, trips were already proposed for that year in England, Ireland, Scotland and Wales, and to Denmark, Norway and Sweden.

Development of the folding canoe opened up even more possibilities. For example, in the 1930's Major Raven-Hart undertook voyages in America, Burma, Dalmatia, Egypt, France, Germany and wrote about his exploits in 'Canoe Errant on the Nile' and 'Canoe Errant on the Mississippi' among others. Tripping in this type of craft continues and led Peter Salisbury to found the 'International Long River Canoeist Club' in 1975. Among other trips, Peter and his wife Jane paddled their folder down 300 miles of the Kwai Yai in Thailand in 1984.

Improvements in air travel, coupled with the evolution of glass-fibre, thermosetting plastics and advances in kayak design, opened up a whole new world to white water paddlers. Many expeditions to demanding rivers in previously unpaddled and remote areas were undertaken. In response to this upsurge in activity, the BCU set up an 'Expeditions Committee' to consider applications from paddlers for recognition, grant aid and patronage for their adventure.

This modern form of expeditioning seems to have started when Chris Hawkesworth took a party of twenty kayakers, three canoeists and nine rafters to the Grand Canyon of the Colorado in 1971. The party included a number of well-known names in British paddling and even had its own photographer for the 224 mile trip. Two firsts were claimed for the adventure, Pauline Squires being the first lady singles paddler on the river with John Goodwin and Albert Woods in the first C2 to make the trip.

Photo 1.7 Mike Jones on the Orinoco

The following year one of the Colorado paddlers, Mike Jones, teamed up with Mick Hopkinson, Dave Burkinshaw and Steve Nash to paddle 200 miles of the Blue Nile. They had to contend with attacks from crocodiles and gunfire from local tribesmen in addition to laden kayaks, which were difficult to control in the heavy water. Mike Jones was in action again in 1976 when, with five other paddlers he descended the Dudh Kosi, the river of Everest. Launching at a record 17,500 feet above sea level they faced 80 miles of Grade 5 to 6 very cold glacier-fed water. Perhaps attracted by the warm water, three of the Dudh Kosi team and two others jour-

neyed to Venezuela in 1977 to paddle the 50 mile Maipure rapids on the Orinoco. Again attacked by crocodiles and bitten by mosquitoes, Mike Jones considered the rapids the biggest and most dangerous he had ever been on.

An epic 3,000 mile source to sea expedition to the Nile in 1978/1979 was led by Marcus Bailey.

In September 1979 a group of eight British paddlers and one Canadian, organised by Peter Knowles, paddled the lower part of the Grand Canyon of the Stikine in British Columbia. The Stikine has twice the volume of the Colorado, half the width and a fall of up to 400ft per mile. The canyon is 4,000ft deep with 2,000ft cliffs dropping sheer to the river in places. Having completed this first descent, the group then turned their attention to the Stikine's southern neighbour, the Iskut, where they were all looped in loaded boats, spent four days on a six and a half mile portage and suffered night time visits from grizzly bears.

Expeditions grew in complexity. In 1980 a desire by Chris Hawksworth and Alan Barber to paddle the Marsyandi, rising in the Annapurna range of Nepal, rapidly expanded to a team of twenty-six. This was augmented in Nepal by two guides, one liaison officer, one hundred and twenty-two porters, seven cooks and five sherpas. The carry-in to the start point was a ten day walk and the river required numerous portages in the difficult terrain. In contrast, a much smaller expedition to the Niger delta that year covered 200 miles in a locally hired dugout.

A source to sea expedition of note, staged in 1981 and led by Pete Knowles, took a party of five men and a woman 800 miles from the Rockies to the Pacific on the Fraser River in Canada, a local paddler joining them at Moran Canyon. Three canyons, two high falls and "Hells Gate" were all negotiated successfully, only Bridge River Rapid being portaged. This was the first kayak group to do "Hells Gate" without raft support and the first time a woman paddler had even attempted it.

1982 saw Jim Hargreaves and three others paddling on the lower Rio Bio in Chile. Although not a long river by New World standards, it has a high volume and a spectacular series of canyons and rapids, heavier and more difficult than those of the Grand Canyon of the Colorado.

Expedition fever reached such a pitch that in 1986 fifteen were scheduled to leave the UK for areas outside Europe, including one to the Zambezi where Alan Fox and Guy Reeve paddled the gorge from the foot of Victoria Falls to Lake Kariba. Crocodiles and minefields proved to be as big a hazard as the rapids.

Peter Knight, James Morris, Ian Huntsman and Jason Buxton tackled the gorges of the Turikho and Yarkhun rivers, headwater tributaries of the Indus, in 1990. Marcus Bailey, Phil Blane, Loel Collins, Colin Hill, Geoffrey Lennon and Paul O'Sullivan ventured even further afield in 1994 when they paddled very demanding water on the rivers of Papua New Guinea.

Photo 1.8   New Guinea 1994

Not all expeditions were filled with experienced paddlers. In 1984 Guy Baker took a team, including four youngsters from London Youth Clubs, down the Zanskar in India from its highest navigable point to its confluence with the Indus. A Yorkshire School Exploration Society group, comprising three leaders and seven pupils led by Alan Elsworth, in 1988 paddled the world's highest sea, Chinghai Hu in China at an altitude of 10,450 feet.

The last quarter century can be described as the golden era of white water exploration, with many firsts on big water rivers, deep gorges or source to sea paddles. There has been an excellent safety record on BCU approved expeditions, often involving joint participation with young people and local paddlers and establishing friendships in many lands.

Sea Paddling

In 1866 while MacGregor journeyed on his second 'Rob Roy' in Scandinavia, he lent the first to his friend Mr Lawton who took her on his yacht to Norway. There, in company with the canoe 'Rollo', she was paddled and sailed among the fjords and finally round the North Cape. In 1872 he undertook a cruise in the Shetlands in his seventh 'Rob Roy'.

Clyde Canoe Club, founded in 1873 quickly became established as the one most active in sea canoeing, with several cruises to the Western Isles on record. The club is also credited with introducing the technique of feathering paddles in the 1880's.

Robert Louis Stevenson started his paddling on the sea at Granton on the Firth of Forth. In 1876 H. W. Eaton of the Mersey Canoe Club crossed solo from Douglas, Isle of Man to Llandudno in Wales, a distance of 56 miles in twenty-two hours. Mr John Ross Brown spent his annual holidays, in the late 1880's & 1890's, canoeing round successive sections of the Scottish coast, covering some 3,500 miles in his meanderings.

Most craft prior to the First World War were wooden planked, relatively heavy and designed for sailing as well as paddling. Between the wars, in the wake of the introduction of folding canoes, there was an upsurge in sea touring on the west coast of Scotland. Canvas covered, rigid designs suitable for sea paddling appeared. Scottish students hired canoes and organised cruises, which were attended by their peers from universities in two continents and six countries.

In 1930 Gino Watkins, already an acknowledged explorer although only in his twenties, led a group of fourteen young men on an expedition to East Greenland. Kayaks were obtained from the Inuit who also taught them paddling skills. A second expedition in 1932 had much reduced resources; Gino planned to obtain food for the group by hunting from his kayak and met an untimely death doing so. As a result of these expeditions, a number of kayaks were brought to Britain and some replicas were built. However, it was not until the advent of glass-fibre sea kayaks that Inuit craft appear to have had a major influence on the design of recreational kayaks in the UK.

Canadian John Nolan, joint holder of the World Record Distance for Inland Water at 3,450 miles, set out from London on June 2nd 1933 to paddle right round the coast of Great Britain, sponsored by "The Wide World" magazine. Much to his annoyance, a young German woman shadowed him. Fraulein Fridel Meyer had paddled from Bavaria to London the previous year. Neither made it; Fridel retired at Montrose some 600 miles into the trip due to serious injuries received in a car accident. Nolan managed to make Aberdeen, a further 36 miles, before heart problems forced him to give up. Fridel Meyer made another attempt the following year, this time in a clockwise direction. How far she got is not known, but it appears she successfully rounded Lands End and headed north.

After the Second World War canoes were scarce, continental craft were unobtainable and British builders suffered from severe shortage of materials: ideal conditions for the emergence of the amateur builder utilising whatever materials could be found. Many sea paddlers ventured forth in one of Percy Blandford's PBK designs. There were club based designs, like the 'Loch Lomond' from the board of Hugh Stevenson. It was one of the first recreational canoes developed in the UK specifically for sea touring. Joe Reid followed with the 'Clyde' single and double, based on West Greenland kayak lines.

Photo 1.9   Replica West Greenland Kayak

During the 1950's and 1960's British sea paddlers were ambitiously expanding their area of activity. Typical trips were a double crossing of the Northern Irish Sea in 1958, cruises to the West of Ireland in 1959 and 1961, Lofotens in 1964, crossing to St Kilda in 1965, crossing the Pentland Firth in 1966, West Norway in 1967 and crossing the Southern Irish Sea in 1969. During this period, names like Joe Reid, Dougie Gilchrist, Hamish Gow and Andrew Carnduff were much to the fore.

In 1959 a Glasgow student, Kenneth Taylor, undertook an expedition to the village of Igdlorssuit in Western Greenland. He brought back a sealskin-covered kayak. As a follow-on Chris Hare expeditioned there in 1966. He also returned with a kayak.

The 1960's and early 1970's were a period of great development. The Coaching Scheme was growing.

The introduction of outdoor activities in schools, coupled with the improved economic situation, gave rise to an explosion in the number of paddlers and a demand for kayaks suitable for sea paddling. Glass-fibre craft appeared. The 'Wessex Sea Rapier' was developed from the 'Seaway', drawn in 1942 by the prolific Norwegian designer Hoel. Derek Hutchinson produced his first sea kayak design inspired by a picture of a Mackenzie Delta kayak. Geoff Blackford built a plywood version of Ken Taylor's Igdlorssuit kayak, about 25 centimetres longer with a higher deck and larger cockpit to accommodate a European paddler. He called her the 'Anus Acuta' and the design was taken up commercially by Frank Goodman. Chris Hare's Igdlorssuit kayak influenced the 'Lindisfarne' produced by Northern Kayaks. The new material made it easier to incorporate bulkheads and hatches into the designs, adding to the seaworthiness of the craft.

With this new-found availability of suitable kayaks, the golden age of Nouveau Sea Kayaking began. Many more paddlers took up the activity, some engaging in long and demanding trips and expeditions to foreign shores. Just a few examples include: the crossing of the North Sea, led by Derek Hutchinson; a trip to Spitzbergen led by Sam Cook; a circumnavigation of Iceland by Nigel Foster and Geoff Hunter; Jersey Canoe Club's circumnavigation of Ireland and trip to Spitzbergen; Paul Caffyn and Nigel Dennis's circumnavigation of mainland Britain; David Mann's solo paddle from Norway's border with Russia to Lindesnes, the country's most southerly point; the rounding of Cape Horn by Frank Goodman, Nigel Matthews, Barry Smith and Jim Hargreaves; the Falkland Islands by Mike Devlin, Andy Forsyth, and Tim Gunn; Brabant Island, Antarctica led by Clive Waghorn and the crossing from Weymouth to Jersey in a sea double by Andy Stamp and Nigel Hingston.

John Ramwell, who instigated the formation of the BCU Sea Touring Committee in 1973 and runs the International Sea Kayak Association, also ran trips for the British Schools Exploring Society, taking youngsters to Alaska, Greenland, Norway and Russia. In 1975 he organised a sea kayaking symposium and started a new phenomenon. Sea kayaking symposia are now held regularly in many locations around the British Isles.

Further Reading

A Thousand Miles in the Rob Roy Canoe, MacGregor J, 1866, London, Sampson Low
The Rob Roy on the Baltic, MacGregor J, 1867, London, Sampson Low
The Rob Roy on the Jordan, MacGregor J, 1869, London, Sampson Low
Canoe Travelling, Baden-Powell W, 1871
An Inland Voyage, Stevenson R L, 1878, London, Chatto and Windus
Yacht and Boat Sailing, second edition, Kemp D, 1880, London, The Field
Cruises in Small Yachts and Big Canoes, Fiennes Speed H, 1883, London, Norrie and Wilson
Canoeing with Sail and Paddle, Hayward J D, 1893, London, George Bell
John MacGregor (Rob Roy), Edwin Hodder, 1894, London, Hodder Brothers
Canoeing and Camping Adventures, Anderson R C, 1910, London, Gilbert-Wood
The Road to Rannoch and the Summer Isles, 1924, Edinburgh, Grant
The Heart of England by Waterway, Bliss W, 1933, London, Witherby
The Heart of Scotland by Waterway, Downie R A, 1934, London, Witherby
The Book of Canoeing, Ellis A R, 1935, Glasgow, Brown and Ferguson
Canoeing, Luscombe & Bird, 1936, London, Black
Canoes and Canoeing, Marshall J, 1937, Stirling, Mackay
Canoeing, McCarthy R H, 1940, London, Pitman
Quest by Canoe, Dunnett A M, 1950, London, Bell
Kayak to Cape Wrath, Henderson J L, 1951, Glasgow, McLellan
A Short History of Canoeing in Britain, Cock O J, 1974, London, BCU
Pleasure Boating in the Victorian Era, Vine P A L, 1983, Chichester, 0-82033-504-3
60 Years in Small Boats, Anderson R C, 1984, London, National Maritime Museum, 0-905555-76-7
The Little Kayak Book Part III, Brand J, 1988, Colchester, Brand
From the Rob Roy to the International Ten Square Metre Canoe, Eastwood A, 2001, Balfron, Eastwood

Duncan R. Winning, OBE

Duncan Winning was born in 1940 and started paddling on the Firth of Clyde in 1950. His main interest is sea kayaking, and since 1953 has never been without a kayak of his own design and build. In the late 1950s and 1960s he competed in slalom, white water racing, LD and sprint racing.

He was closely involved in introducing the Coaching Scheme in Scotland and is a Level 3 Coach (Sea).

Duncan joined the Scottish Canoe Association Council as Slalom Secretary in 1960. He served in turn as Secretary, Vice President and President, was an Honorary Vice President for four years and Honorary President since 1981. He served on the executive of the Scottish Sports Association and chaired their Outdoor Pursuits Group. In 1998 he was awarded the OBE for services to canoeing. He was appointed Honorary President of the Historic Canoe and Kayak Association in 2000.

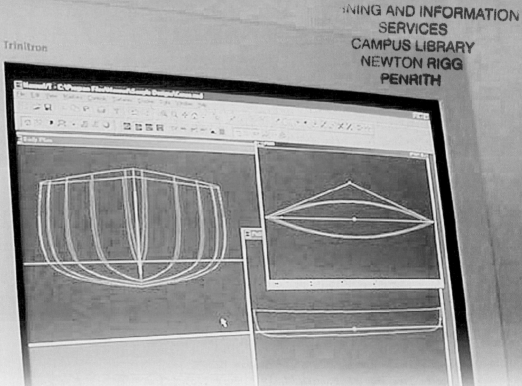

2 Canoe, Kayak and Paddle Design

To dream of improving a canoe, by making it faster, safer, more stable, more comfortable, prettier... To design in benefits and to see the benefits realised...
That's what design is about.

Introduction

The design of a canoe, kayak or paddle is part art and part science. The art aspect is usually fulfilled according to the old saying, "If it looks right, it probably is right".

Science aspects are an extremely complicated balance of many physical elements of performance, structure, and environment, and could mostly follow the phrase, "If it feels right, it's probably right for you!"

Some boats were designed to be paddled fast for long distances, some for surfing, some for spinning in circles and some to be always paddled in a swimming pool. The design criteria for each are very different, as are the needs of the paddlers.

A canoe, kayak or paddle that will suit one person probably won't be best suited to another. I hope the following chapter will make choosing or designing a canoe, kayak or paddle a little clearer, dispel myths, and help you look at equipment with a more discerning eye.

Terminology

In this chapter I will use the word 'boat' as a generic name for all paddled craft. Where I need to mention a more specific type, I will use the expression kayak, open canoe, etc. I will also avoid the technical language of naval architecture, unless absolutely necessary.

I touch upon shape, design, paddlers' needs, construction and material considerations; they are all interwoven elements in the design process.

The Boat

"There will never be a perfect canoe or kayak for all situations."

To get an understanding of the elements of a boat's design:

1. We'll look at a drawing of an open canoe and two different kayaks with some technical terms for certain parts of the craft, and its lines.

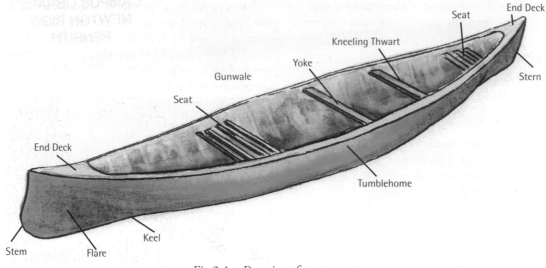

Fig 2.1 — Drawing of an open canoe

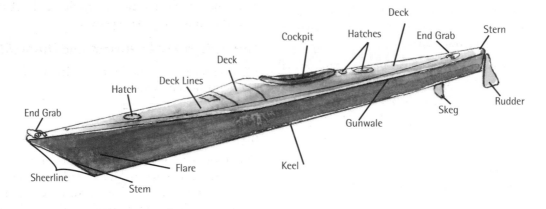

Fig 2.2 — Drawing of a sea touring kayak

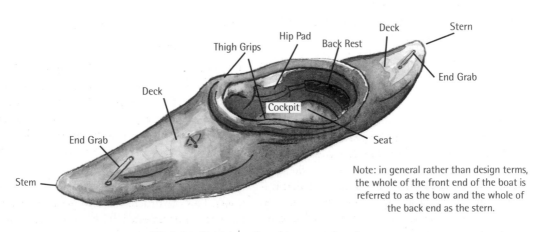

Note: in general rather than design terms, the whole of the front end of the boat is referred to as the bow and the whole of the back end as the stern.

Fig 2.3 — Drawing of a white water kayak

2. We will have a look at where canoe design has come from, so that we can better appreciate what we have today.

3. We'll look at design features and problems.

4. We'll look at setting your objectives so that you can find a design with benefits that will suit you.

History of Canoe and Kayak Designs

Good designs are usually evolutionary, that is they have evolved over several attempts, one step at a time. This is necessary because skill and paddling technique move at a similar pace.

Classic Designs

Classic designs have evolved from aboriginal beginnings. The shape of touring canoes and sea kayaks has been developed over thousands of years, because "necessity had to be the mother of invention". Some boats such as the sea kayak and the open canoe are designs that can hardly be bettered by shape alone; the development has mostly been in technology, for durability and lower cost.

These same design considerations are still very relevant today, after allowing for:

• Modern man's larger build.

• Paddling Environment.

• Paddler's skill.

• Requirement for creature comforts.

• The fact that evolution of these designs is now slow.

Modern Designs

These designs are for recreational and competitive paddling. The shape of such specialist leisure craft has been developed to optimise performance in their specialism, such as playboats, canoe polo, slalom, sprint and marathon racing.

Evolution of these designs is very fast and (in the case of playboats) fashionable features are related to new moves.

Design Origins

The earliest canoes were designed by experience and 'eye'. Later, when boat builders were commissioned to build canoes and kayaks for clients, it became necessary to build 'half models' so that features could be discussed and a decision made. In the 19th century designs were finally developed on paper with a traditional set of line plans.

Today, some boats are designed on paper, some are hand shaped, and some can be designed on a computer, with the fundamental shape being carved on a CNC Routing Machine. Please note that computers do not design; their use is merely to replace the process of drawing.

Photo 2.1   CNC Routing Machine

Today's designers are no different to aboriginal man; they use observation, experience, feedback from the users and more experience.

The Search for Lightness and Durability

All designs need to consider the limitation of available construction techniques.

Aboriginal

Dugouts, Birch-bark and Seal Skin

Developed over thousands of years these craft have taken advantage of locally available materials and environmental conditions. Although considered fragile by modern man, given the understanding of their limitations that the people who built them grew up with, they have been capable of incredible feats.

Recreational

Wood Era (after 1850)

The first wooden canoes and kayaks were built in Europe and in Canada. In Canada mass production was needed to supply the vast numbers that were required for exploration and wilderness travel. In Europe they were mostly custom-built for the wealthy Victorians to take advantage of their increasing leisure time.

Minimum building time was about 50 man-hours. This construction technique allowed a popular shape to be repeated, with canoes being built off moulds for the first time.

Folding (after 1908)

The first mass production of kayaks in Europe was in Germany. The development of the folding kayak enabled more people to buy a touring kayak, and to travel extensively (by train), and explore rivers. Thousands were built and exported worldwide.

Canvas and Wood (mostly after 1930)

This became more popular with the development of more affordable cars. It was no longer necessary to pack away your canoe, so costs came down again, as did the weight and ease of handling.

Stitch and Glue

During World War 2 waterproof glues were developed that allowed moulded, or stitch and glue ply canoes to be developed. Costs were about the same as wood and canvas, but they could be tougher and faster.

GRP and Advanced Composites

The use of Glass Reinforced Plastics (fibre-glass) started in the late 1950's, and by the mid 1960's all other methods were almost obsolete. This allowed the mass production of tough, light, and very long lived boats with almost no maintenance. Minimum building time is about 5 man-hours.

PE – Rotationally Moulded Polyethylene

This was developed in the mid 1970's and is today's most popular construction method, as the boats are extremely tough. A boat can be made in single or triple skin laminates, and a hull and deck can be produced in one piece, at very low cost. The materials are completely recyclable. Minimum building time is about 2 man-hours.

PE – Blow Moulded Polyethylene

This uses very expensive machinery and moulds for very fast moulding cycle times. Similar properties can be achieved as with rotationally moulded PE for single or twin skin mouldings.

Thermoform Plastics

These are single skin and vacuum formed, usually out of polyethylene or 'ABS'. This system has been used for the production of low cost open canoes, and a few kayaks.

Multi-Layer Sandwich

This method produces materials such as 'Royalex' and is mostly used for the production of light, rigid and tough open canoes.

These developments have continually brought down costs, so we now have paddlesport for all.

It's worth remembering that all these technologies remain useful today, each having unique benefits. It is also an interesting fact that the capabilities of advanced materials such as kevlar, carbon-fibre and epoxy resins were explored in the manufacture of canoes and kayaks long before they were used in such high-tech industries as aerospace and motor racing.

Design Performance Features and Problems

A canoe moves by forces acting on it. These consist of *active* forces such as from paddling or sailing, and *passive* and *external* forces such as from weight in the canoe or the effect of water or airflow on it.

Each force that acts upon a canoe causes some form of movement that can be a benefit, or a disadvantage. *All canoes are therefore a compromise*, being designed to optimise that compromise for the paddler's needs.

Hull Design

A hull will move in the following directions, either separately or (usually) jointly:

- Forwards.
- Backwards.
- Side to side.
- Up/downwards.
- Roll, which is its movement around its longitudinal axis.
- Pitch, which is movement around the transverse axis.
- Yaw, that is the rotation of the hull around its vertical axis.

"The ability to control these movements defines a design."

A boat turns as a result of the pressure on the hull being changed, such as by the paddler paddling harder on one side, or by the canoe being edged. A canoe or kayak doesn't turn as if on rails, its action is more like skidding, some boats more than others.

Speed

The forces opposed against you limit the speed you can paddle up to 'hull speed'.

Maximum hull speed (in knots) is up to 1.34 times the square root of the waterline, allowing for its shape, and the paddler's power. This is a rather arbitrary rule that was devised by Froude in the 19th century. Sprint canoes and sea kayaks that have a particularly high length to beam ratio can however exceed 'hull speed', as can play and surf boats whilst planing down steep waves. (N.B. 1 knot is 1.1515 miles per hour).

Photo 2.2   Sea kayak surfing

The limiting factors are:

- Skin friction on the canoe.
- Laminar Flow.
- Wave making drag on the canoe.
- Wind resistance on you and the canoe.
- Your strength and endurance.
- Weight of the canoe and its load (including you).

Skin Friction

At a cruising paddling speed, skin friction is the larger drag loss and is controlled by the total surface area of the boat. A playboat will out-sprint an Olympic sprint racing kayak for the first 2-3 strokes, because it has less wetted area and at low speeds skin friction has less effect than wave drag! At higher speed, the wave-making resistance/drag due to the playboat's short length limits speed up to 'hull speed', whilst the sprint kayak disappears into the distance.

Laminar Flow

It is extremely important to optimise the laminar flow of the water molecules on the craft's skin.

A very thin layer of water molecules will stick to the skin of a boat and move with it, effectively adding to the drag on the hull. Molecules attached to those move a little less quickly and others further away from the skin's surface less quickly still, until

the water is at rest. If the boat is badly scratched, is irregular in shape, or has a rough finish, the boundary layer will increase in size, and become turbulent. It will travel with the boat and effectively add its weight to the drag of the boat, slowing it down.

Speed Potential

An indication of the speed potential of a design can be sought by trying to reduce a design's Prismatic Co-efficient (Cp). This is found by dividing the displacement (cu metres), by a combination of the area of the widest point (sq metres), multiplied by the length (in metres).

SL Ratio

The ratio of S (Speed)/ Sq Root of the canoe/ kayak's length or S/L Ratio is a useful way to compare the speeds of different designs.

Therefore :

A K1 has a Speed-Length Ratio of 2.

A 3.5m touring kayak has a Speed-Length Ratio of .9.

A 5m sea kayak has a Speed-Length Ratio of 1.5.

Wave-making Drag

As speed increases, the waves that a canoe makes also increase, until at 'hull speed' the first wave is at the bow and the next transverse wave peaks in combination with the stern wave, adding additional resistance. Above this speed the canoe has to climb over its own bow wave, which with human power is unfortunately impossible. When a white water or slalom type of kayak is paddled hard on flat water with the bow lifted in the air, *it is not planing*. It is trying to get over its bow wave, with the stern being sucked down, due to the low-pressure area that is created with this type of hull shape.

A longer canoe or kayak will therefore go faster before this happens, so a long boat should always be faster than a short one.

The reduction of the bow wave is very important for high-speed canoes, so that modern racing canoes have a proportionally finer bow and fuller stern as a route to more speed.

Fuller ends typical in higher displacement canoes will push up bigger waves, by the water having to accelerate faster to move around the canoe, and sim-

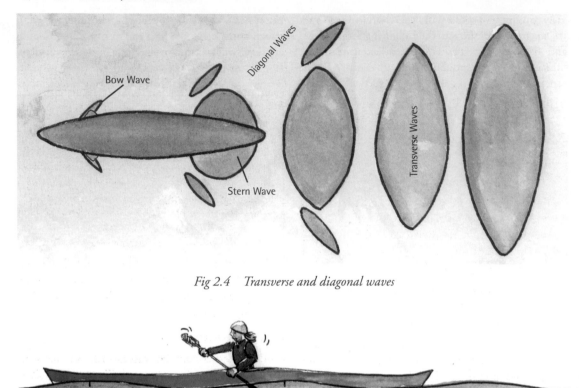

Fig 2.4   Transverse and diagonal waves

*Fig 2.5a   The **theoretical** max hull speed of a kayak with a 15' waterline length is Speed (in knots) = square root of the waterline length x 1.34. Therefore maximum theoretical hull speed is 5.19 knots.*

*   **Actual** speed is calculated using the wavelength created by the boat's passage. With a wavelength of half the waterline length of 15', Speed (in knots) = square root of the waterline length x 1.34. Therefore speed is 3.7 knots. The kayak is horizontal, easy paddling.*

Fig 2.5b   Sea kayak high speed cruising, wavelength almost the full waterline length of 14'. Speed is 5.02 knots. The kayak is starting to lift in the bow (2º off horizontal), and paddling effort is raised significantly.

Fig 2.5c   Sea kayak in a speed burst that can only be sustained for a short time. The bow is now lifting 5º off horizontal and the wavelength has increased to 18'. Speed is therefore 5.68 knots. Over very short distances some designs can exceed 'hull speed'.

ilarly at the stern of the canoe or kayak, the water has to accelerate where it is drawn back together. This will push up bigger waves, increasing drag and reducing speed potential.

Resistance to speed increases dramatically the higher the speed paddled. It is easily noted that low speed takes very little effort, but at higher speed it takes much more effort for a proportional increase in speed.

Length/Displacement Ratio

In a boat, its fineness and displacement is usually referred to as the Length/Displacement Ratio. This ratio is obtained by dividing the waterline length cubed, by the total displacement of the boat, which includes you and your load.

This ratio can range from .65 for long light boats to 2 for short heavy ones. A recreational touring kayak can average 1.5.

If you look at the height of waves and imagine the weight of water in them, then that weight represents the energy you are putting into paddling.

Length is however waterline length, not length overall. Some 5.2m (17') sea kayaks are effectively only a little over 4.5m (15'). In a surf or playboat you can take advantage of gravity to accelerate so that effectively you get the bow wave crest aft of the stern. The trough of your bow wave moves towards the crest of the stern wave and they start to cancel out, so that wave-making resistance is reduced while frictional resistance continues to increase. You are effectively surfing not only the wave you are riding, but also your own bow wave, which due to the

flatter hull form has dynamically lifted you to the water's surface.

Photo 2.3   Gravitational pull, combined with lift accelerates kayak

This is so dramatic that modern designs can plane whilst side-surfing, and so can now spin through 360 degrees so easily that it can be achieved using only body rotation.

Wind Resistance

Wind resistance can be substantial, and can be simply tested by choosing a windy day to paddle. Paddle with the wind, and then against it; you can feel a huge difference. The bigger the boat, and the higher you sit, the greater the effect.

Stability

Stability is your resistance in a boat against capsizing, and depends on the centre of gravity (CG), and the centre of buoyancy (CB). If the CG's vertical alignment falls far enough outside the CB you will capsize unless you support (provide additional force upwards) on a paddle stroke. Different types of canoe have varying tolerances to allow movement

Fig 2.6a-c   Figures a and b show a stable situation. C shows a paddler leaning into a wave to keep his CG over his CB, and using a bracing support to ensure he doesn't capsize.

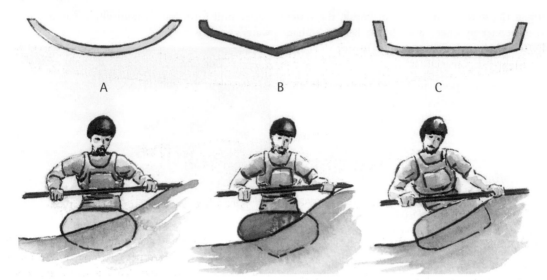

Fig 2.7   A: Round section kayak which has moderate progressive stability on flat water and in waves.

B: An extreme 'V' section kayak with poor initial stability on flat water and in waves.

C: A flat section kayak that has high stability on flat water, but is unstable in waves, as the hull tends to want to follow the contour of the waves. Freestyle boats exploit this to achieve remarkable moves.

NB: A semicircular shape is used for sprint racing canoes as it has the minimum wetted surface area, and is therefore fastest, but it also has least form stability of all shapes.

of your body and the canoe (CG), without causing a capsize risk. If you look at Fig 2.6c you will see a paddler about to capsize.

A canoe or kayak needs to be a platform from which you can comfortably apply your paddle strokes in the direction of your choice.

It should neither be unstable, so that you can't concentrate on what you are wanting to achieve, nor over-stable, as that will mean:

- It is wider and therefore slower both in speed and changing direction.

- If you capsize it will be harder to perform an Eskimo Roll, if it is possible, with your boat.

> ### CB and CG
> CB - Centre of Buoyancy is the centre of the displaced volume of water.
>
> CG - Centre of Gravity is the centre of the mass of the canoe and paddler.
>
> In an upright craft on flat water the CG is usually on the centre line of the boat immediately above the CB.

- It is also heavier.

- A flat-hulled boat will be stable on flat water, but unstable on waves.

(A boat with a low seat will be more stable than a boat with a higher seat).

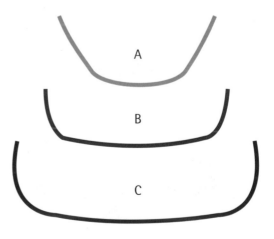

Fig 2.8   Profiles of a sprint kayak(A), a white water kayak(B) and an open canoe(C), all are stable enough, but not too stable

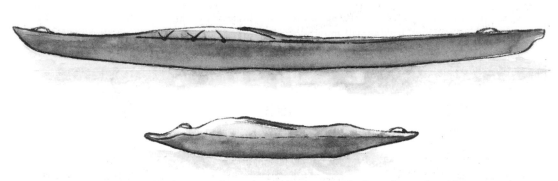

Fig 2.9   A side profile drawing of a sea kayak (top) and a playboat (bottom), to the same scale

Turning or Manoeuvrability

A boat's centre of effort and its centre of gravity will affect its turning. A canoe or kayak generally rotates about its CG, with the power of forces acting upon its form or shape that will determine the rate of turn. A long boat with a straight keel will have more resistance to turning than a highly rockered playboat.

For beginners, the first challenge will be to paddle the boat in a straight line. The ease with which a boat can be made to do this can be improved by:

- A moderate design with a longer and straighter keel.
- Stern-down trim or better still, a skeg.

A balanced design, with the hull shape being nearly symmetrical, front and back will be easier to control and more predictable than a design that is asymmetrical in hull shape.

Advantageous features for directional stability (anything that reduces manoeuvrability):

- Long straight keel.
- Well rounded hull cross-sections.
- Skeg or rudder systems.

Advantageous features for manoeuvrability:

- Short keel line.
- High rocker.
- Flat hull cross-sections with break-away edge.
- Foil shaped gunwales and low deck line.

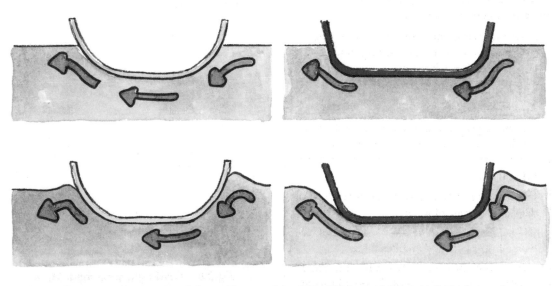

Fig 2.10   Cross-sectional drag at low speed (top), and high speed (bottom) for both round and square sections

However all good designs are never taken to an extreme, as even a racing kayak, or sea kayak has to turn sooner or later, so it must have a small amount of rocker. A boat without any rocker would feel dead.

A boat with too much rocker for the paddler's ability or experience would be uncontrollable.

It's all a compromise.

Paddling skills can be used to modify the design's natural characteristics. The paddler can lean to the side, forwards or backwards to change the hull shape presented to the water, to lower the boat's resistance to turning. A good design will be developed to take advantage of this.

If you trim a boat down at the stern (perhaps by the moving of the seat back or by the loading of heavier equipment), you will decrease the turn rate and increase the canoe's directional stability. This may be an advantage or disadvantage to you. If you trim the bow down, perhaps by leaning forward whilst paddling with a broad sweep stroke and also tilting the canoe away from the turn, you can reduce the keel's resistance and increase the rate of turn.

In Summary

Directional stability and manoeuvrability are direct opposites, which can be modified slightly by edging/ leaning and stroke, but you can't have the best of both. *A longer boat with a straighter keel will therefore turn more slowly than a shorter boat with a rockered hull shape.*

Different cross-sections can give a boat a very different feel and performance potential. Three extreme examples are:

Sprint Racing Kayaks

These have a semi-circular cross-section for minimum skin friction and resistance. This is very unstable, but very fast.

Open Canoes

These have broader and flatter cross-sections, which will show tendencies to be V'd, or a shallow arc. Whilst subtle, the difference in feel can be large.

White Water Playboats

These have an almost flat hull with very hard edges, for planing and spinning, and the deck is low profile so that it can move three dimensionally with the minimum force. Experts can use a harder sided but less forgiving shape, which has the bonus of carving better turns. Intermediate paddlers can choose slightly softer edges, which are less likely to catch, and are much easier to roll.

Skegs and Rudders

Wind and waves will exert a turning force on a boat (yaw); the more highly rockered the design, the more it will be turned by these forces. A sea kayak can be balanced on one heading whilst unbalanced on another. To counteract this problem with paddle strokes is extremely tiring, so it is usually necessary to have a method of trimming such kayaks.

Skegs

Some boats are fitted with fixed or lifting skegs. This is the nearest you can get to "having your cake and eating it."

Recreational paddlers use them to make their craft more directional, especially at the beginner's stage. Modern man needs to achieve quickly, and these give the easiest route to directional stability without learning to trim, lean or edge and apply advanced strokes.

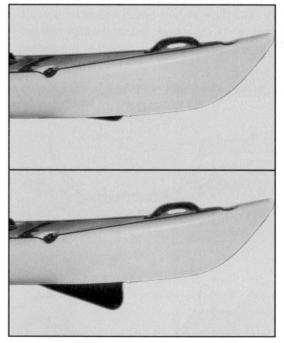

Photos 2.4a-b   Kayak with skeg up and down

Sea kayakers have found that lowering and trimming a skeg will substantially improve the directional stability and control of a kayak in stronger wind and waves. This happens when wind and wave action apply a force on the boat's centre of lateral resistance. The skeg shifts the centre of lateral resistance backwards and balances the boat's tendency to turn into wind.

The skeg needs to be positioned as far back as possible, but not so far that it comes out of the water when paddling over waves. The larger the open skeg box and the larger the cross-section of the skeg, the greater the drag will be.

Rudders

These are commonly used in sea kayaks, and always in sprint and marathon racing kayaks.

A rudder is however a more complex solution to a skeg, but more flexible. A rudder can be used to both trim the boat and change its direction. A rudder is more vulnerable to being damaged, as it is always exposed.

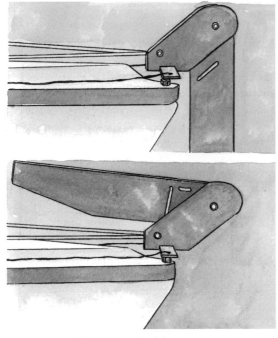

Fig 2.11   Rudder system

By changing its angle of attack to the water, the rudder generates a combination of lift and drag that turns the boat.

The paddler's feet operate a rudder. The steering mechanism is connected to the rudder's yoke by wire or rope. Sliding foot pedals are the simplest method of steering, but make good paddling technique difficult, whilst a 'T'-Bar and full width footrest is more efficient but less easy to adjust. Most rudder blades can lift if they hit an obstruction and,

in the case of sea kayaks, can be lifted up and parked on the deck.

There are great differences in quality in rudder systems. The better systems with airfoil-sectioned blades are highly engineered to be wobble free and immediately responsive. They are therefore relatively expensive due to their sophistication.

Less expensive rudder systems usually have flat aluminium blades and simple head systems and controls, which are fairly resilient against the knocks that a rudder will inevitably get.

Deck Design

A deck's shape is designed in combination with a hull shape, and should usually:

- Shed waves as quickly as possible.
- Catch the wind as little as possible.
- Provide the paddler with adequate foot space.
- Allow a kayak to complete an Eskimo roll easily by being well-rounded. (A flat deck would cause the paddler much more effort, as the kayak would want to rest upside down with the paddler acting as a keel.)
- Allow the paddler the closest possible paddle entry to the centre line of the boat to improve paddling efficiency.
- Take end grabs, hatches, deck lines or other performance and safety equipment as needed.
- Be shaped by the cockpit to deflect waves over the cockpit coaming edge, to help keep water from getting under a spraycover.

As with hull shape, all ideals have to be compromised. Perhaps one of the most complicated design types is the sea kayak, where all the above considerations are essential. The sea kayak overcomes this by having a high bow, due to the raised forward sheer line, which will :

- Break a wave and therefore help shed the wave quickly.
- Ride over a wave using dynamic (buoyancy and its flared shape) lift.

Aft of the bow, the deck drops away as much as possible, to reduce windage, with hatches and deck lines kept as low in profile as possible. The cockpit then peaks, with the deck rising a little more before it to drive waves over the cockpit edge to keep you dry inside, though at the cost of driving it into your chest if your lucky, in your eyes if not!

Photo 2.5   End Grabs and 'Shockbloc' footrest

White water expedition kayaks are usually shaped purely for shedding water, and keeping the cockpit dry.

Photo 2.6   'MicroBat' front deck

The latest playboats use volume around the centre of the kayak to support the paddler whilst 'cartwheeling', and to ensure that the kayak is retentive (stays in the stopper). Low volume and foil-shaped ends help the kayak slice predictably through the aerated water. The extreme contouring in the front and back provides dynamic lift in a 'loop' and other moves, that volume alone can't achieve, to get the paddler airborne.

Photo 2.7   Power Pocket

Comfort and the Application of Effort

"The benefits of a great design will never be realisable if you aren't comfortable and in control."

Control and *power* are essential to the safe management of canoes and kayaks. However, a boat should also be comfortable enough that paddlers can maintain their concentration for as long a period as possible. We're all built differently, so a boat that is comfortable for you might not be for somebody else. This can usually be improved by personally outfitting a canoe or kayak (see Chapter 4). *Feedback* from the boat, and *power transmission* through the boat are essential.

Control Comes From Contact With Your Boat

In sprint and marathon racing and in a recreational kayak, you will have two contact points, the back of your seat and footrest. This enables the kayak to be powered forward, held stable, and turned slowly but effectively in a two dimensional plane.

In a white water, surf or polo kayak you will have three points of contact, your seat, thigh grips and footrest so that you can control the kayak in a three dimensional plane more responsively.

Fittings must:

- Hold you in when you want to be held, but not impede your exit when you want to get out. This is *essential*.

- Not be so padded that they isolate you from the feel of the canoe, or prevent you from transmitting your energy into performance.

- Make you so comfortable that you can concentrate for as long as you might have to sit in your boat. For sprint paddlers that might be five minutes, for play paddlers that might be an hour, but for an expedition sea paddler that might be days.

Seats

Seats should combine grip, with support. Kayaks mostly use bucket seats, with adjustable backrests. A playboat may only be sat in for an hour at a time so the top paddlers go out of their way to fix themselves in rigidly.

A sea kayaker will, however, need to be able to stretch out and will need a much greater support area. An open canoe will need comfortable seats, and the ability to sit on the back edge of a front seat so that it can be paddled solo.

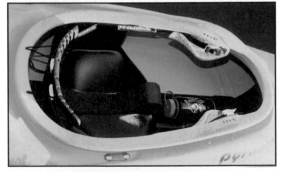

Photo 2.8   'XR' seat and back strap system

Photo 2.9   Polyethylene and wood/webbing canoe seat

Thigh Grips

These are essential for white water competition and recreational kayaks, and are increasingly found on sea kayaks. They should be adjustable for length, and have enough hook to grip your thighs (wherever on your thighs you find it most comfortable), but not so hooked that you can't flatten your legs to bail out *quickly* if necessary.

Footrests

Footrests are essential in most kayaks, and desirable in even the lowest cost recreational kayak. They can be found in several forms, which should all give you the maximum contact area at an angle that is comfortable.

Recreational Footrests

These are simple, low cost units, which are usually an easily adjustable pedal footrest on a runner, on which you place each foot.

A better footrest is found in racing kayaks, which is a broad plate footrest that extends across the full width of the kayak. This enables you to place your

foot in the most comfortable place. They are not as easily adjusted.

For use in advanced white water the footrest must be shock absorbing. A full plate footrest should be able to stop the paddler going over or under (if trimmed properly) in even the most aggressive impact situation. Properly trimmed, they could prevent broken ankles or legs or, in the worst case scenario, save lives.

The Shockbloc

This form of footrest transmits the paddler's effort direct into the end of the kayak, to transmit power into speed, and to stop the distortion of the shell that foam alone would cause. They have been developed because the ends of playboats have got so small that there isn't room for any other system.

Fitted Buoyancy

Buoyancy bags effectively fill the ends of the canoe with air, keeping water out and making the canoe easier to recover.

Buoyancy bags or bulkheads and hatches are essential for beginners and all paddlers in extreme or open water. They save lives.

End Grabs

These must be:

- Comfortable enough to hold the boat when carrying it, or hold onto the craft if swimming.
- Strong enough to be used in a rescue, which in white water may need to be in excess of 500kgs.
- Not easily degraded due to wear, or UV exposure.
- Replaceable.
- Not spin around whilst swimming and be capable of trapping your hand or fingers.

Volume and Buoyancy

A boat needs enough volume or shape buoyancy to:

- Carry a paddler, plus equipment.
- Generate lift to allow the canoe to handle adequately in all anticipated conditions.

Many white water paddlers are consumed by volume statistics. I confess I find them of little use. I've seen a 90kg person trying to squeeze into a kayak designed for a 65kg person. The only way is to test them for yourself.

A number of leading manufacturers have now designed and built various sizes (up to five) for a model of kayak, so that paddlers of different sizes can get the same enjoyment and performance from their kayak.

What counts is your experience and assessment of whether that design feels right and has the features you want. A sea kayak or open canoe will be designed with a displacement assessment, but that is no substitute for your experience, or lack of it, and the storm or testing rapid you may paddle into.

Volume doesn't equate to safety. A safe canoe or kayak doesn't exist. A safe and prepared paddler does.

Dream your dreams and make a decision that is right for your paddling and your aspirations. Don't be a sheep!

Cockpit Shape

Cockpits range in size from the smallest, which are usually found in sea kayaks or white water racers, (at 70cm long x 37cm wide) to recreational touring boats (at110cm long x 50cm wide).

Design considerations are:

- Recreational kayaks should have a large open cockpit for ease of entry and particularly exit.

- Maintaining the rigid structure of the boat.

- Linking the shell to the seat, thigh grips and back strap where appropriate.

Cockpits which might expect to have waves wash over them, need to be covered by a spraycover, and therefore need an effective cockpit rim. They should not be too small for ease of entry and emergency exit, or so large that the spraycover would implode under water pressure. The modern shape is called a 'keyhole' cockpit and is usually about 72.5cm long x 42cm wide. The modern keyhole cockpit has evolved due to the increased severity of water paddled and the improved technical ability of the modern neoprene spraycover. Entry and exit can be made easier by lifting the front of the cockpit, relative to its rear. The paddler should be able to sit on the seat and lift at least one knee out at once.

Setting Your Objectives

A good design must be a marriage of practical and aesthetic values for any aspect of paddlesport.

You must ask yourself many questions before you begin choosing a new or better boat:

Practical

- What do I want to be able to do with this boat, and who else might use it?

- Where will it be used?

- How fast must it be?

- How stable?

- How manoeuvrable?

- How much storage space?

- What safety and other fittings does the boat need?

Aesthetic

- How the canoe should look? "Beauty is in the eye of the beholder."

- What colours to use for safety and to match other equipment?

Words can give you clues, but all canoes and kayaks have different benefits. Try as many as you can with an open mind, and they will educate you, reward you with more fun, and give you the opportunity for more adventures.

A good boat will be the one that fits you and in which you can achieve your objectives. It might never be the best at anything, but it will be comfortable, forgiving, responsive and fun. It will talk to you through its movement, and you will understand instinctively those movements, and it will be an extension of your body. It will be a trusted friend.

The Paddle

A paddle is a more personal choice than a boat, because your use of it has to be *instinctive*. You will change your canoe or kayak more easily than you will change your paddle.

A paddle must:

- Be shaped to allow the paddler control whilst executing many different paddle strokes.

- Be shaped and constructed to transmit the paddler's power smoothly to the water, whilst being as light as possible.

- Communicate what is happening in the water's flow and currents back to the paddler.

A paddle has two important parts, the blade and the shaft, which for an open canoe includes a handle, and it is important that both work in harmony. A light paddle shaft with heavy blades can feel unusable.

Kayak Blade Shape

Flat Blades

These are the most common for complete beginners because they are cheap and the same paddle can be used by right or left handed people.

Curved Blades

These are the most usual blade shape. They are curved along their longitudinal axis, whilst flat (or slightly convex or concave) across the blade face. These are efficient in forward paddling strokes as they 'catch' the stroke better than flat blades. Curved blades are most popular for touring and for white water. They enable the paddler to be able to scull for support, roll and perform other complicated paddle strokes in endless combination. The paddle must therefore be able to move from a power to many other strokes smoothly. This will necessitate a smooth back to the blade so that both faces can be used.

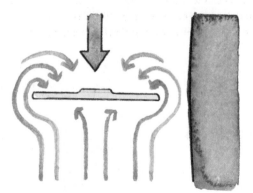

Fig 2.13a   Flat or curved blade and water flow during paddling

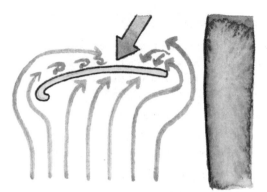

Fig 2.13b   Wing blade with water flow during paddling

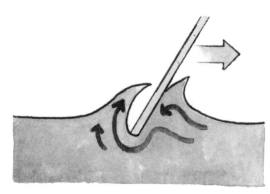

Fig 2.12a   A flat paddle blade allows greater cavitation behind the blade

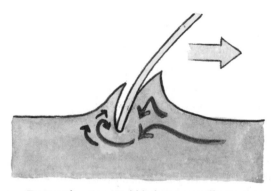

Fig 2.12b   A curved blade is more effective in reducing cavitation and increases propulsion

Wing Paddles

These are designed mostly to power kayaks forwards and are the latest, fastest and most extreme shape for a speed paddle. They are unusual in that they are designed not to be pulled straight back, but back and out from the side of the canoe. This action generates pull and lift, hence its name 'wing'.

The back of a blade is rarely used except to lean on the water's surface for resting; it can therefore be ribbed for strength. It also reduces rear blade turbulance and ensures that more paddling energy is used effectively. (See Fig 2.13b).

End Profile

The end profile of blades can be Symmetric or Asymmetric. The latter is now far more popular for all paddling due to its improved balance in the 'catch' part of the paddling phase.

Blade Size

Kayak blades are usually similar sized for recreational use, but for advanced paddlers they will come in different sizes; a smaller paddler would use a smaller blade shape, whilst a bigger and stronger paddler should use a larger blade.

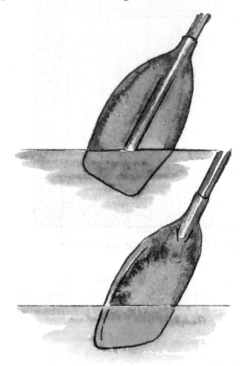

Fig 2.14   End profiles of symmetric (top) and asymmetric (bottom) blades

Feather

Feather refers to the angle at which the blades are offset to each other on a kayak paddle. Traditional Inuit paddles have no feather, and flat paddles are usually offset at 90°, so that both left and right handed paddlers can use them. A 90° feather was introduced for racing; as the top blade slices through the air the bottom one pulls the boat through the water. However, a high degree of feather increases the risk of wrist injury.

Feather is a matter of personal comfort and type of paddling. Most touring and racing paddles have about 70° of feather, and some playboaters have as little as 45°.

Open Canoe Blades

Open canoe paddles are flat, to make all paddle strokes smooth, with a cross-section shape that is smooth for sculling the canoe sideways, 'J' strokes, and other strokes that use both faces of the blade.

With a kayak blade the exit phase of the stroke is least important, but for the canoe this is where the paddler must execute the steering phase, so a curved blade would be less reliable.

Blade shapes vary to allow for paddlers' needs, water conditions and depths.

Material Construction

Injection Moulded 'ABS' or Nylon

These blades are sometimes with glass or carbon-fibre reinforcement for increased rigidity and strength. They have moderate to good performance at low to moderate cost. They are usually very strong and durable, and make great all-round paddles.

Wood

Wooden blades have great feel and are shock absorbing. They are however more fragile to use and require maintenance. They are especially good for touring.

Carbon

Carbon blades transmit energy very well, are very light, very expensive and are hard and unforgiving. These are used by most racing paddlers.

Kevlar

Kevlar can be included with carbon in a blade to improve impact resistance, though edges can't be trimmed neatly so they usually have a furry appearance, best used in white water paddles.

Paddle Shafts

Paddle shafts are as important to consider as the blades. It is the shaft that will transmit your energy, and the water's feel.

Shape & Grip

Paddle shafts can be round or oval in cross section. The oval shaft gives increased strength in the direction of pull, and the paddler a better feel of the paddle.

Some top quality round shafts have a section of plastic bonded to them for a hand grip, to increase the feel of the shaft whilst still allowing for the technology's ability to only make a rounded shaft.

Most shafts are longitudinally straight. Some kayak paddles have cranked handgrips to allow the paddler's hands a better and more comfortable grip.

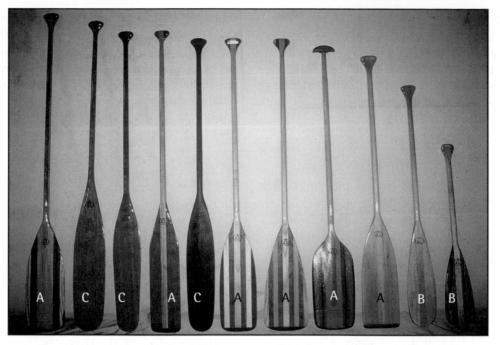

Photo 2.10   A selection of paddles, square tipped (a), beaver tail (b) and otter tail (c)

Some open canoe shafts are bent to give a more efficient 'catch' phase for open canoe racing. They are difficult to steer with, so the paddler has to switch paddling side to compensate.

Photo 2.11   Bent shaft canoe paddle

An open canoe paddle has a grip for the top hand to allow the paddle to be pulled or twisted in manoeuvres.

The grip can be variations of the following shapes:

- 'T' Grip – usually used by racing or white-water paddlers to give the optimum grip.

- Palm Grip – usually used for touring as it is more comfortable and relaxing to use and where the ultimate grip is not required.

Construction

Paddle shafts can be manufactured from:

Wood

The shaft is made from a solid piece or by laminating different woods, that optimise strength, resilience and low weight; ash for compression and tensile strength, and spruce for light weight cores are the most common performance woods.

Alloy

The shaft is anodised to prevent corrosion and covered with PVC handgrips because of its cold feel. These can be extruded or welded tubes.

Glass or Carbon Reinforced Resin

These are usually laminated over a mandrel, giving the lightest weight, highest strength, and highest cost.

Length

Length varies considerably with your height, your boat's width and the performance you want.

A short paddle can accelerate your boat quickly. If it is too short, you won't be able to reach the water.

A long paddle will be slow to accelerate, but will make long distance paddling more comfortable. If it is too long, it will be extremely difficult to use.

As an example of the variations, paddles for kayaks will vary from:

Sprint & marathon	210-225 cms
Slalom	195-208 cms
Surf	190-200 cms
Freestyle	190-200 cms
Canoe polo	198-208 cms
Sea touring	210-330 cms
Inland touring	208-220 cms

Paddles for canoes:

Inland touring	50-63 cms
White water	48-54 cms

You Will Never Feel a Great Paddle!

A paddle which is not great will leave you with nagging doubts that it might suddenly slice the water and tip you in. It might be heavy; its shafts might be too thick or too thin. It will just not feel right, and the money you saved could soon be an expensive mistake. A great paddle will feel so good that you hardly notice that you are using it.

Further Reading

Canoe Design and Construction, Byde A, 1975, Pelham Books, London, 0-7207-0862-1
A good book in the basic principles though out of date now for specialist canoes and kayaks. The construction element of the book covers period GRP technology.
The Shape of the Canoe, John Winters, 1996, self published
Based on a series of articles written in the US Canoesport Journal between 1988 and 1991, a technical look at Canoe Design.
The Bark Canoes and Skin Boats of N.America, Adney, Edwin T and Chappelle H, 1964, Smithsonian Institute, Washington DC, Stock No 047-001-00021-8/Catalogue No S13.3:230
The definitive book on N. American Indian open canoes and Eskimo kayaks.

Graham Mackereth

Graham started canoeing when he was 15 years old with a £12 Granta Kingfisher double. He and his scouting friends started building and racing their own boats, and he designed and built his first boat in the summer holidays of 1967. Before long he was competing at international level in marathon, sprint and wild water racing.

In 1971 he started up Pyranha, and although in 1972 he was a part of the Munich Olympic Team he decided to retire from serious competitive paddling. However, his competitive instinct remained so he took up sailing an International Canoe, an activity where he has had some success and a great deal of enjoyment.

His passion for design has found success and outlet in a number of ways. World Championship winning slalom designs from 1977 to 1985 (mainly in co-operation with Albert Kerr and Richard Fox), expedition designs that started with Mike Jones' 1976 Everest Expedition, and currently pushing the limits with freestyle and advanced white water designs.

The author making his excuses to the BCU Style-police

3 Clothing and Equipment

It was a cool, early spring day, with a chilly offshore breeze holding up the waves and giving fantastic surf conditions. As I carried my kayak back up the beach, I couldn't help but grin as I realised that with my dry top and neoprene deck I was warm, dry, and comfortable. I actually laughed out loud as I remembered the early days... woollen jumpers with holes in the sleeves, a sailing anorak that wouldn't seal at the neck and a leaky nylon spraydeck that really did 'implode' under the force of a big wave. The good old days... you must be joking!

Introduction

It's not what you've got, but how you use it that counts. Skill, knowledge and judgement make paddlesport the exciting creature that it is. If our bodies are overloaded with kit then performance will be affected. It is important to ask the question, 'Do I really need that piece of kit, or is it surplus to the requirements of the paddlesport activity I am doing and, in fact, a hindrance?'

Yvon Chouinard, in his book 'Climbing Ice' (1978) talks of not taking bivouac gear on alpine climbing routes in the Rockies. He never planned or intended to bivvi, therefore bivvi kit was not necessary. In any case he could move more quickly without the bulk and weight, and thus was less likely to need it anyway!

A strong mindset from a strong character – yet Chouinard's message is valid for paddlers. Think about what you use and ask the question, 'Do I really, no I mean really, need it?'

In the following chapter on equipment and clothing remember... you won't need it all!

Considerations

The equipment and clothing we have as paddlers needs to be functional, reliable and as comfortable as possible. Any equipment that does not do the job properly, doesn't always work as it should or is uncomfortable, can be frustrating, possibly unsafe, and does not help us to get the most out of our paddling. We also need to be happy to wear it, in the belief that it meets our needs and is suitable for achieving our expectations.

It is important therefore that we consider:

- Its purpose.
- How it is made and what it is made of.
- Its design and features which aid comfort and usefulness.
- The expectations of the user, i.e. the type of paddling to be undertaken.

Clothing

Needs to:

- Offer protection from a range of weather conditions, be it warm or cool.
- Offer the most unrestricted movement of the body possible.
- Act as a source of protection for our safety.
- Enable us to live on the water in comfort.
- Allow the wearer to swim safely in the water.

The range of available clothing is vast and many combinations and styles of dress are possible, depending on the individual and their preferences. What follows is a broad overview of what is available to the paddler.

Environmental Context

In winter the priority of clothing is usually to keep the paddler warm; in summer this usually changes to keeping the paddler comfortable, possibly cool. Our weather is so variable that we often need to decide what type of clothing we will need just before we go paddling. On hot, sunny days a base layer vest and a peaked hat may be worn as protection from the sun rather than as a way of keeping warm.

Clothing can only trap heat that is created by the body or absorbed from the sun's rays. The higher the intensity of the exercise, the greater the body heat generated. In reasonable weather, racing paddlers often train and race in shorts and a vest. For the limited duration of the race or training session, the amount of heat generated more than compensates for the amount lost to the combination of wind and air temperature.

Male vs. Female

Manufacturers are only just beginning to respond to the fact that males and females require differently cut clothing. Most still go for the 'one (male) size fits all', but clothing and equipment cut for the female form is now becoming available.

Types of Clothing

Paddler clothing generally fits into 3 categories:

- Base layer - worn next to the skin, e.g. thermal underwear.
- Mid layer - often worn over the base layer, this gives extra insulation, e.g. fleece tops.
- Outer layer (shell clothing) - this is the waterproof layer, which is also windproof, e.g. cagoules and overtrousers.

Alternative systems include wetsuit clothing, pertex pile clothing and 'gimpwear' stretchy rubber... Steady!

Base Layer

Base layer clothing is often called the 'wicking layer'. It is not only warm, but dries or 'wicks' very quickly, leaving the paddler feeling drier and subsequently warmer. The material used helps to retain body heat and uses it to transport dampness away from the body side of the material. It is important that such clothing is close fitting, but not so tight as to restrict blood flow, which will tend to leave the paddler feeling cold and uncomfortable. If it is too loose it will not 'wick' and feel cold and clammy.

Base layer clothing can come in the form of long sleeved tops, short sleeved tops, vests, underpants (some versions even have a windproof front section, which can come in handy at times!), shorts, long john trousers, all in one suits, socks and balaclavas. Such clothing can form a light, warm weather clothing system on its own.

Photo 3.1   Base layer clothing

Mid Layer

Mid layer clothing provides extra warmth in colder weather. Not quite as close fitting as the base layer, it is nevertheless slim fitting for thermal efficiency and easy movement of the body. Generally made of quick drying fleece or similar, it comes in a variety of forms such as long and short sleeved tops, trousers, salopettes, socks and hats. Unfortunately, no underwear is known to exist in mid layer fabric outside penguin country!

Photo 3.2   Mid layer clothing

Outer Layer (Shell Clothing)

This is the 'armour plated' layer, which is waterproof, windproof and, depending on the material used, can be breathable. It also can come in literally any colour so that the fashion opportunity for shell clothing can be exploited. The range of fabrics available for this type of layer is considerable.

Photo 3.3   Shell clothing

Non-breathable fabrics such as nylon are cheaper, can be hard wearing, but may be hot and sweaty in warmer weather and create levels of condensation in cold weather. Breathable fabrics on the other hand tend to be more expensive and not always as hardwearing, yet due to their breathability can be more comfortable. It is possible to dry base and mid layers through a breathable shell whilst wearing them. However, when constantly splashed, it can be argued that breathability may be impaired. If pores are blocked with dirt, breathability may be further impaired, thus reducing their effectiveness. Such clothing can come in the form of short and long sleeved cagoules, hooded jackets, salopettes and one piece suits (dry suits/immersion suits).

The seal to the body can be a dry or a wet seal. Dry seals use latex rubber cuffs to grip the wrists, neck or ankles tightly to exclude water penetration. These have revolutionised paddle clothing, as total dryness is possible. However, the tight gripping of wrists with latex seals and subsequent squeezing of the tendons and soft tissue can be painful and in extreme cases lead to tynosynovitis, so be aware. Wet seals consist of Velcro or neoprene rubber cuffs. They tend to be looser fitting and allow some water penetration. A pertex type shell layer can be used as a windproof, shower resistant, highly breathable and lightweight outer layer, ideal in relatively dry but windy conditions.

Pertex/Pile Clothing Systems

Some paddlers, especially open boaters, favour this clothing system, which in some cases can be used as a combined base, mid and outer layer. It consists of an insulating pertex pile layer covered in a windproof and shower resistant layer. The insulating pile layer wicks moisture away from the skin to be evaporated away through the outer shell layer, leaving the garment dry in a short period of time. This type of clothing is very quick drying and it is recommended that it is worn next to the skin without a traditional base layer for best results. To work efficiently it must also fit the wearer well. This tailored fit is crucial and, in part, explains why manufacturers often charge more for this type of clothing. They make a greater number of sizes so that paddlers can achieve an efficient fit. Such garments may be sized 40,42,44,46,48 chest rather than S,M,L.

Photo 3.4   Pertex/pile clothing

Wetsuit Clothing

Neoprene wetsuit material comes in a variety of thicknesses from 3mm to 8mm (much thicker and body movement in a paddlesport context will be hindered). Wetsuit garments need to be close fitting without being so tight as to restrict blood flow (very much like base layer clothing). They work by allowing water in. This 'trapped' water between the paddler and the wetsuit material is warmed by body heat and thus provides warmth for the wearer. Wetsuit clothing is not windproof, however it is very suitable for wet conditions, i.e. where the wearer is going to be in, or frequently covered in water. Surfers use thin all-in-one suits called steamers.

Although less comfortable than other alternatives, wetsuits are also favoured by some white water paddlers, as they offer some protection in the event of a swim in rock infested rivers.

Garments come in long john, short and long sleeved tops, shorts and trouser options. Wetsuit boots/shoes/socks are almost standard wear in recreational paddlesport.

Photo 3.5a-b Wetsuit (left) and steamer (right)

Gimp Wear (Thermal Rubber Wear)

Photo 3.6 'Gimp' wear

This thermal stretch material, which is a type of fleece-lined, inner fabric with the outer as a water-proof breathable membrane, is a relatively recent invention. It needs to be close fitting for thermal efficiency. It can be used as a base layer on its own, or in combination with thermal base layer clothing. In warmer weather it can be used without an outer shell. It is comfortable, warm, and wicks well, leaving the paddler feeling dry. It is affectionately known as 'Gimp' or rubber wear, and by a few other names too!

Other Styles and Combinations

Many other styles and combinations are possible, particularly as advances in technology are made. Many open boaters, for example, are using hill/mountaineering clothing; when carefully chosen it is proving to be ideal, particularly on extended trips.

Headwear

Ultra-thin neoprene wetsuit material or thermal stretch (Gimp) fabrics can be used to make skull type caps. These work well under helmets for cold weather paddling, and when covering the ears, help to prevent the medical condition known as 'swimmer's ear'. This condition particularly affects freestyle and white water paddlers, who are often subjected to sudden injections of cold water into the ear, leading to bony growths and hearing difficulties. Communication can be a problem when wearing a skull type cap, as the ear is covered by the garment.

Photo 3.7   Skull cap

Footwear

Footwear is an essential item of equipment for most paddlers, as it offers protection whilst walking to and from the water. It also provides insulation and protection whilst in the boat, and in the event of a swim will offer protection from cuts, bruises, impacts and such things as broken bottles and jellyfish. Some paddlers such as wave skiers, playboaters, slalom and racing paddlers, choose not to wear footwear, for reasons of performance and the desire to squash feet into tight places!

Various designs and styles are available:

Wetsuit Boots

A wetsuit ankle boot with a fairly thick sole and a side zip to aid entry is very popular. These can be worn next to the skin or for even greater warmth used with a wetsuit sock or woolly sock. They provide foot and ankle protection and a good overlap to fit snugly with overtrousers.

Water Shoes

Recently some American style 'water shoes' have appeared on the market with ultra sticky soles for greater traction on wet rock.

Photo 3.8   Wetsuit boots (left) water shoes (right)

Wetsuit Slippers

These are very popular and due to their slimline style they generally allow the paddler greater ability to fit into tighter kayaks. They tend to be lightweight and very comfortable.

Sports Sandals

These are great in the warmer months. Check that they don't come off if you go for a swim!

Photo 3.9   Slippers (left) sports sandals (right)

Wetsuit Socks

These can be worn to keep your feet warm and enable you to wear your sports sandals even in the colder months.

Sailing 'Wellies'

Preferred by some sea paddlers and open boaters, these slim fitting wellington boots allow wading in shallow water, whilst keeping the feet dry. Due to their slim leg fit and easily collapsible sides, they are designed to fill with only limited water in a swim, so as not to put the wearer at a massive disadvantage during the 100m dash! Normal wellingtons would be almost impossible to swim in.

Tight fitting neoprene 'wellies' from America are now available. These are of good technical specification and are specifically made for paddlesport.

Easy or Hard to Swim In?

Some clothing systems are easy to swim in and absorb little water. Some systems, especially heavier pile clothing, can absorb large amounts of water and inhibit your ability as a swimmer. Test your chosen system in a safe spot.

Equipment

Buoyancy Aids (Personal Floatation Devices)

Let us begin by defining the difference between buoyancy aids and lifejackets. A lifejacket is a device which is usually pulled over the head, has some fitted inherent buoyancy, which can be considerably increased by the wearer inflating it by blowing into a valve. Theoretically, it will keep the wearer independently floating face out of the water, even if unconscious, as the buoyancy is centred around the chest area. However, if the wearer has some other form of buoyancy on them, such as a wetsuit or a dry suit with trapped air in it, this principle can be greatly compromised.

A buoyancy aid can be pulled over the head, or in other designs worn as a short jacket and zipped to fix it securely to the body. It has all-round buoyancy (usually foam) built into it and is ready for use. It will allow you to float in a variety of positions and let you use a normal swimming stroke on your front, back, or side.

Buoyancy aids are the standard personal floatation device for paddlers, because they allow ease of movement in the boat, are comfortable, allow ease of swimming and are easily put on and taken off. They also provide a more all-round armoured body shield for the paddler, as the 'foam' acts as protective padding (which is good if you don't already have some!)

CEN 50N Standard for Buoyancy Aids

The British Canoe Union recommends the CEN 50N Standard as a minimum standard for all paddlesport activity. The CEN 50N Standard is part of the minimum buoyancy that a buoyancy aid may contain as regulated by European Law, which comes under the European Community Directive on Personal Protective Equipment. In simple terms, a 50N buoyancy aid should be able to support a 5.5kg lead weight attached to it in the water; this equates to a person weighing 70kg or more on dry land. Table 1 outlines the sliding scale used to determine the minimum buoyancy needed for a person of a specific weight.

Weight of Paddler	Buoyancy
30 – 40 kg	35N
40 – 50 kg	40N
50 – 60 kg	40N
60 – 70 kg	45N
> 70 kg	50N

Table 3.1   The CEN 50N Standard

What Must a Buoyancy Aid Do?

It should:

- Be CEN 50N Standard minimum.

- Be correctly sized for CEN 50N Standard to operate.

- Be comfortable to wear, so that the body's movement is unaffected.

- Be suitable for the particular paddlesport to be undertaken.

Note:

- A buoyancy aid should be brightly coloured, so that it can easily be seen; its primary function is that of a piece of life-saving equipment.

- A whistle, attached to the buoyancy aid for emergency use, is advisable.

Buoyancy Aid Styles

There are an infinite number of designs; it is possible to categorize them as follows:

a) Children

b) General Slab/Slalom/Rodeo

c) Touring - possibly with a range of pockets

d) White Water – which may include a white water rescue harness

Children's Buoyancy Aids

As the title suggests, children's buoyancy aids are appropriately for children; some come with crutch straps for added security of fixture. It is vital that our younger paddlers have correctly sized equipment for them to make the most of learning and enjoying their paddling. It is important that they feel that they have the proper kit – children know when they are being fobbed off and are actually quite discerning about equipment. They want and deserve the best and should not have to do with poorly fitting kit.

Photo 3.10   Children's buoyancy aid

General Slab/Slalom/Rodeo Style

Photo 3.11   Competition buoyancy aid

These lightweight, excellent fitting buoyancy aids with extensive arm movement available, due to their 'cut away' areas under the armpits, are the popular choice of many paddlers. They vary in features, from shoulder 'cinch' buckles and waist draw-cord ties for providing a snug fit, to chest straps which enhance the body fit and reduce further the possibility of the buoyancy aid being 'sucked' off in more turbulent white water. Their flexible foam also contours somewhat to the body to aid comfort and fit. Some models have small pockets for car keys or a knife.

Touring Buoyancy Aids

Essentially these are General Slab/Slalom/Rodeo style buoyancy aids, but with larger or a greater number of pockets stitched on for ready access to such things as are determined necessary by the paddler, e.g. flares or snacks. A word of caution here: the more kit you carry in your buoyancy aid, the heavier you make it to wear and the harder you make it to roll, swim in, climb back into your boat or to crawl back up the bank! Wisely used for essential items they can be useful. Many designs in this category have waist buckle/webbing fastening systems, for easier waist adjustment, as clothing is likely to vary more according to the activity and season.

Photo 3.12 Touring buoyancy aid

White Water Buoyancy Aids

Photo 3.13 Specialist white water buoyancy aid

A variation of General Slab/Slalom/Rodeo style. These buoyancy aids are generally made of harder wearing cordura or heavyweight nylon and the stitching and construction tends to be more robust. Waist buckle/webbing fastening systems give greater security of fixture to the body. Such features as specialist knife pockets, specific pockets for rescue equipment as well

as a fixed chest harness for white water rescue are common. When the harness is in the buckled up position, it has the advantage of enhancing the security of the buoyancy aid fit to the wearer, and is therefore less likely to be sucked off in turbulent water.

These are specialised pieces of kit and require specific training, such as that provided on a white water safety and rescue course.

Lifejackets

CO_2 inflated lifejackets are sometimes used by paddlers for certain applications. They can be worn over conventional buoyancy aids to provide backup personal floatation for anticipated extended immersion (before rescue), such as in large open sea crossings. These are specialised cases, but nevertheless provide an option.

Photo 3.14 Inflatable lifejacket

Helmets

Helmets are essential protection for the 'brain box', particularly where white water paddling is involved.

Helmets should:

- Be CE approved – CE 1385.
- Be made of strong, lightweight material, e.g. plastic or carbon fibre.
- Cover the head well and provide ample protection to the forehead, temple and back of the head.
- Have enough positive buoyancy to float; too much buoyancy will actually hinder rolling.
- Be a good fit so as not to move, but not be so tight as to be uncomfortable.
- Have an effective strap/buckle, to fix the helmet securely in place.
- Have a good lining to absorb the shock from impacts and to provide a separation distance

between the outside of the helmet and the paddler's head – important if the helmet was to be punctured by a sharp object during use.

This vital piece of safety kit is valuable:

- On the water for protection from objects above the water, e.g. tree branches.

- In the event of a capsize.

- Whilst moving around on a slippery, uneven river bank.

- For personal protection during rescue.

It is therefore important that, once the decision has been taken to wear the helmet, it is securely fixed at all times to the head because you don't know when it will be needed for protection.

Face guards are available to fix onto helmets. Although useful for protection in canoe polo, for general recreational use they are an unnecessary complication. They reduce vision, offer snagging points and look overly macho. For these reasons they are not recommended.

Chin cups are also not recommended on helmet straps. Experience has shown that they do not work effectively (this is born out by similar experience in the motorcycle industry). The strap on a helmet should go under the chin.

Photo 3.15   Paddling helmets

Spraydecks

A spraydeck is essential for keeping the water out of the cockpit of a kayak. There are a vast number of designs available. Rough water paddlers choose 'decks' made out of neoprene rubber (wetsuit material), which are tailored to fit specific cockpit designs and stretch to give a good snug fit around the cockpit coaming. The body tube can also come in a tailored size to give an equally snug fit. The sealing system where the deck joins onto the cockpit is crucial, as this

is where water seepage is most likely to occur. Various 'beefy' rubber band and heavy gauge, stitched elastic cord systems are available, which are very effective.

The 'rip cord' (quick release cord) is important for releasing in an emergency. Some kayaks have an independent back up release system fixed onto the cockpit to compliment the release on the deck.

Decks can also be made of nylon materials. These provide cheaper decks, often with greater adjustability, ideal for use with a range of novice paddlers in the early stages of learning. These decks are popular with centres and youth organisations. They provide an adequate seal and fit, but don't match the performance specification of neoprene decks. They can be reinforced easily at high wear points. Some models have 'belly pockets' on the body tube and shoulder braces.

Nylon decks can also be worn over neoprene decks to protect them from abrasion in rescue situations or carried as a lightweight spare, e.g. sea paddling.

Photo 3.16   Neoprene spraydeck - note quick release strap must be outside the boat when deck is fitted

On days when wind driven spray and rain would fill their boats, racing paddlers also use spraydecks. As with open boat spraydecks, these are fitted to the

Photo 3.17   Racing kayak spraydeck

boat first. The paddler, once in the boat, uses a zip to fasten the body tube in place.

Open boat spraydecks are also available, these monsters are a sight to behold!

Miscellaneous

Knife

A good sharp knife is a handy piece of kit. Where ropes are likely to be encountered they become essential. Folding knifes are ideal; they need securing safely in an accessible pocket. If the knife is to be fastened in by a piece of cord, the cord needs to be very short to reduce tangling. It also needs to have the capability of being unclipped, as it should only be used when not attached to the wearer – for obvious safety reasons. Externally mounted knives in scabbards are not recommended for the following reasons:

- They offer a snagging point.
- They can easily self-release from their own locking systems, leaving a useless empty scabbard.
- Experience has shown that you don't need the knife to be that accessible in any case.
- They can look aggressive and intimidating.
- Certain legal constraints can apply regarding the length of blade and perceived use by the owner.
- Why dress up like a member of the special forces?

Photo 3.18   A selection of safety knives

Lights

On occasions paddlers operate at night and thus may need lighting. 'Cyalume' light sticks, strobes and waterproof headtorches are all useful items. Any sealing of rubber seals is best done with silicone grease, as this not only enhances the waterproofing of torch seals but also does not have an adverse corrosive effect on the rubber seals themselves.

Night vision should not be underestimated. It is surprising just how much can be seen at night without a lighting device.

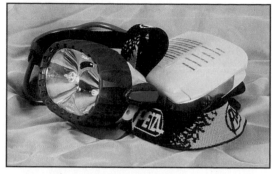

Photo 3.19   Waterproof headtorch

Mobile Phones

Mobile phones definitely do have a use. However, self-reliance and independence should be considered as an essential aspect of paddlesport. To rely on a mobile phone is to reduce decision-making and judgement.

All paddling trips should be planned so that they can be executed without the use of electronic communications. The mobile phone should be kept, like your first aid kit, as an emergency tool.

Personal Flask

A flask is useful, even essential at times, especially amongst the tea drinking fraternity! Drinks can be kept cool or warm, depending on the environmental context of the paddle activity. Rehydration will be necessary at times and hot drinks can also provide psychological comfort. Metal flasks are very popular and come in dinky small sizes which, due to their low bulk, fit easily into kayaks.

Packed Lunch/Emergency Food

On longer trips packed lunch food may be taken. Spare emergency food can also be a consideration in certain situations, e.g. sea paddling or touring. High-energy type foods are ideal here.

Survival Bag

A 2x1 metre plastic survival bag is a useful emergency device for providing shelter or dealing with an injured person, e.g. hypothermia. High visibility orange bags are easily seen.

Group Shelters

These come in many sizes to take various numbers of people and provide excellent shelter from the weather. They also retain the heat given off by the occupants and provide a psychological microclimate of security. Lightweight and strong, they are an invaluable aid to living outside.

Photo 3.20   Group shelter

First Aid Kit

From time to time, first aid may be required during activity. HSE guidelines exist as to the contents of first aid boxes in the work place; our first aid kits will depend on our first aid experience and who the kit is for. Some experienced paddlers on personal trips may take a roll of 'gaffer tape' and improvise with their skill, knowledge and creativity. Others will prefer a more 'standard type' first aid kit. Whatever is used, it must be capable of dealing with the type of injuries to be encountered, and capable of being used appropriately by the person concerned.

British Red Cross, St. John's Ambulance and St. Andrew's Ambulance Association current first aid manuals give details on how to treat all maner of injuries. Better still, consider attending a first aid course.

You can make your own first aid kit or buy a purpose made outdoor first aid kit. Either way, it needs maintaining and expiry dates checking for currency.

Repair Kits

With the advent of plastic boats the form of a repair kit has altered. Generally some means of drying the boat will be required – anything from a dry cloth, lighted meths or a small blow-lamp are commonly used. A roll of 'gaffer' tape will usually suffice in most situations to cover a crack or small hole. The repair during the activity is only a first aid measure. If metal fittings are maintained and checked, a universal hardware shop need not be carried!

Repair kits for glass-fibre boats, which are likely to sustain more damage due to the brittle nature of this material, may require some type of flexible plastic sheet material, e.g. a cut up 'squeezy' bottle, to cover larger holes. This can be fixed in place with 'gaffer' tape.

A wet hole repair material, such as 'Sylglass™', or some other tape used by plumbers for emergency repairs, is always useful for those big expanses of water, where the shore is a long way off and your repair kit is inside your sinking boat!

Repair kits depend on how you actually paddle a boat. If you don't damage it, you won't need to repair it. They also depend on how isolated you are from help, and how resourceful you are. After all, a hole in a boat could be plugged with all kinds of materials!

Waterproof Containers

See Chapter 16.

Don't forget, its more important to be out there paddling than wearing this year's fashion item!

Robert Cunnington

Robert is a BCU Level 5 Coach with some 25 years paddling and coaching experience. He is a qualified teacher with a B.Ed (Hons) degree and an M.Sc in the Sociology of Sport and Sport Management. He also holds a Diploma in Sports Psychology.

He is based in Northumberland, and has coached and paddled in the UK, Europe and the United States. Predominantly from a white water kayak background, he has paddled widely on northern rivers and becks, as well as having extensive alpine guiding experience. He also has a keen interest in white water safety and rescue, open boating, sea kayaking and surfing.

4 Foundation Kayak Skills

When I was 10 years old, I was helping out at the Slalom World Championships in Bala with my brother and father, digging trenches, taking tea to the judges and other such menial tasks. It gave me free entry to the event and meant that I had a pass allowing me to all areas of the course!

I vividly remember being at the start area whilst the competitors were warming up and seeing Richard Fox preparing for his first run. You could feel the electricity coming off him, no one would go near him. The other competitors could feel it and everyone on the bank watching could see it. We could all feel he was going to win! As I watched him paddling around, his technique was so smooth and effortless; his boat glided over the water and he seemed to put just the right amount of power into each stroke to get the most from it, not too much and not too little. Of course he won, it was his first World Championship title with more to follow! I went away from that event inspired to learn impeccable technique and to try and learn to feel and use the water around me just like I had seen Richard do.

Introduction

The foundation kayak skills are the basic skills required for a paddler to become proficient. If a kayaker builds a solid base of skills they will be able to progress and master the art of kayaking in whichever discipline they choose!

Within this chapter I have grouped the foundation skills into the three B's: boat, body and blades.

These reflect the three core elements of kayaking. It is a union of paddle, body, boat, and water with each element working together.

In each of these areas I hope to provide you with the skills to move your kayak wherever you choose, efficiently and effectively, or to provide you with the knowledge needed to teach this to others.

Developing a solid foundation of skills and technique allows you to progress easily with maximum enjoyment and with the minimum risk of injury. They will provide you with a platform upon which you can apply your own individual style, as developing good technique involves developing individuality.

Many paddlers develop their skills by watching others. Use this to your advantage and make sure you watch and copy people with good technique!

Watching yourself on video is also very useful as it helps you realise what you are actually doing as opposed to what you think you are doing!

Many of the foundation kayak skills will enable you to learn the skills of different disciplines as you choose the direction that you wish to take in the sport.

For example, the low brace:

Photos 4.1a-c Low recovery (flat water) - low brace turn (sea) - low brace (white water)

The First Steps

The most important thing about getting on the water in a kayak for the first time is that you have a good time and that you are safe! It is important to ensure that you are in the right type of kayak, with the correct equipment and at a suitable venue. This is usually best done under the guidance of a qualified coach or experienced paddler. They will ensure that you are safe and help you to enjoy your introduction to the sport. It is no longer common practice to perform a capsize drill during your first session, but the correct procedure is usually discussed to ensure you are aware of how to deal with the situation should it arise!

It is worth spending 10-20 minutes during that first session experimenting. Try to figure out how to use the paddles, how to make the kayak move forwards and backwards, how to stop and how to turn. If you perform all your actions fairly slowly at the start you can usually avoid capsizing! Don't worry too much about where you end up, or about whether you are performing the strokes correctly. Most people can develop a basic control without instruction. Free experimentation is really important. Playing games or going on small journeys can help this process. You can then try to learn how to paddle in a straight line.

Learning to Paddle in a Straight Line

Paddling in a straight line is particularly difficult and frustrating in a general-purpose kayak as every stroke you place in the water has a slight turning effect on the boat. As you paddle, the kayak zigzags to the left and right, with the turning point somewhere around your knees. This means that the nose of the boat swings back and forth less than the tail. Watch someone paddle and see if you can see this happening.

If you watch someone who is veering off course you will see that it is the stern of the kayak that is skidding out. In order to stop that skid you need to use a stern sweep (see page 62).

Some people learn to control the skid naturally by adding a slight stern sweep onto the end of a forward stroke. If that's you, you're one of the lucky ones! If you are finding it difficult, getting a feel for how the stern sweep stops the skid will help.

Boats with longer keel lines, 'V' shaped hulls or a skeg on the back skid less, but are also less manoeuvrable. Many beginners will get into this type of boat first so they can paddle the boat straight with little instruction. The time usually comes however, when you wish to get into a boat that is more responsive; you will then need to learn how to control the skid.

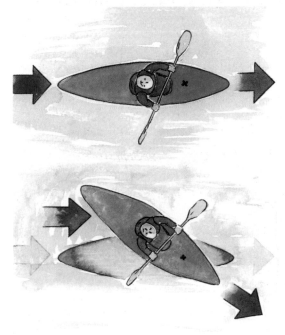

Fig 4.1   Cause of skidding action

Section One – The Boat

One of the main aims of kayaking is to move your boat through the water in a chosen direction. It is therefore important to pay close attention to how your boat travels through the water, and how you can change that to make it go where you want it to!

You can affect how your kayak travels by using your body, your strokes, the boat itself and the water around you.

Characteristics of Different Kayaks

The shape of a kayak's hull will affect how it moves in the water.

For example:

- A longer boat is faster in a straight line than a shorter boat.
- A short boat is more manoeuvrable than a long boat.
- A wide kayak has more stability than a narrow kayak, and is slower.

- A narrow kayak is less stable than a wider kayak, and is faster.
- A light boat is easier to move through the water than a heavier boat.
- The flatter the hull of a kayak, the easier it is to turn.
- The more 'V' shaped the hull, the easier it is to paddle in a straight line.

It is important to understand how the features of your kayak affect its performance. The specific qualities of your kayak can then be utilised in the techniques you use to manoeuvre it. You can also make sure you are using the right type of kayak for the right job!

By trying different kayaks you can learn how easy they are to turn, to paddle in a straight line, and how fast and stable they are. This helps you appreciate the differences and learn how these characteristics can help you. See Chapter 2 for more specifics regarding kayak design.

Changing the Shape of your Kayak

There are occasions when it is necessary to change the shape of your kayak's hull in the water. This can be achieved by edging, leaning and trim.

Edging

Edging is achieved by lifting one side of your kayak up, using the muscles of your hip, torso and legs. (If you lift with your left knee, the kayak will 'sit' on its right edge). The body remains upright with the centre of gravity over the middle of the kayak. Edging is used to assist turning and to create balance within a turn.

Photo 4.2   Edging

The design of the kayak you are paddling will affect how the edge can be used.

When you edge a kayak with a long waterline, 'V' shaped hull and high gunwale, for example a sea kayak or racing kayak, you increase the waterline on the same side as you are edging and this causes the kayak to turn away from that side.

Photo 4.3   Long kayak on 'outside' edge to turn (edge right to turn left)

However, if you edge a kayak with a low gunwale (e.g. a general-purpose kayak) to the outside of the turn, the skidding action over the water will catch the edge and cause instability. When paddling a general-purpose kayak it is necessary to edge the boat to the inside of the turn; this allows the water to pass under the hull creating a more stable turn and will help prevent a capsize.

Photo 4.4   Short kayak on 'inside' edge to turn (edge left to turn left)

Leaning

Leaning the kayak is different to edging in that you lean your body weight over one side of the boat. The resulting position of the kayak is the same as if you edge the boat but your centre of gravity is over one side of the kayak; this can cause a loss of balance. It is important to understand the difference between edging and leaning. Leaning the kayak is not a technique that is used while developing the fundamental kayak skills; it is mainly used during high speed turns, for example when surfing.

Photos 4.5a-b   Edging (top) leaning (bottom)

Trim

You can use your body weight positively to affect the trim of your kayak. This involves leaning forwards or backward to alter which part of the hull is sitting in the water. You can learn much about trim from the open canoeists, as they use it extensively.

Photos 4.6a-b   Back (top) and forward (bottom)

Trim is used by kayakers who are paddling in white water, rough sea conditions or surf as the body weight is used to utilise the effect of the moving water on the kayak. Expedition kayakers and tourers who carry equipment in their kayaks are also interested in this, as how they pack their kayaks will affect the trim of the boat.

It is worth experimenting with the trim of your kayak. For example, try leaning forwards or backwards during a turn and see what happens, can you work out why there is a difference?

Choosing and Outfitting your Kayak

It is important that you choose a boat with the characteristics that meet your needs. If you wish to travel long distances, a boat with good directional stability and forward speed will make your journey more enjoyable. If you are learning to paddle white water, a kayak that is relatively stable and manoeuvrable will make your learning experience more productive.

Your kayak should fit you like a snug pair of running shoes. You create kayak movement by transferring the energy in your body and the water around you into your kayak. You also rely upon feedback from your boat as to how it is moving; a loose fit can reduce this sensation.

In most kayaks you need to ensure that the footrest and seat (plus backrest if applicable) are correctly adjusted, and in rough water designs, that the knees are braced and the hips snug.

Photo 4.7   Backrest

Footrests

Comfort and control are the main aims here. With your legs in the thigh braces you should have the balls of your feet firmly on the footrest. There is no need to have the feet flat on the footrest, as this can be quite uncomfortable.

Backrests

A backrest should provide support to the lower region of the spine and help achieve an upright sitting position.

Thigh Braces

These help keep the knees locked into the side of the kayak and help with edge control. Padding may be added to make these more comfortable or to hold your legs in the desired position.

Photo 4.8   Thigh brace

Hip Pads

These foam pads help 'hold' you in your kayak. They can be handmade from closed cell foam blocks, or can be bought specifically from kayak stores. The pads are glued onto the side of the seat and should hold you in the boat rather than 'squish' you out. This is achieved by having thicker sections at the top of the pad that comes over the hips and a thinner section down the sides of the seat.

Photo 4.9   Hip pad and adjustable seat

If you have your own kayak you can spend the time outfitting it to suit your individual body. However, if you borrow a boat you may only be able to alter the footrest and backrest. It is always worth spending time on the bank to adjust these correctly and then rechecking once you are on the water;

things may feel very different after about 5 minutes paddling around. Allow time to make adjustments if necessary.

Tips for Coaches

Time should always be spent with beginners helping them to make the necessary adjustments and also ensuring the boat fittings are in good working order. A beginner may accept discomfort as they do not know what it should feel like to be sat in a kayak.

Being too tight in your kayak is as much of a hindrance as being too loose. This can cause your legs to go to sleep; you may be pushed off the back of your seat or lose hip control. Good outfitting creates a balance that offers comfort, control and feeling.

Lifting and Carrying

Using the correct techniques to lift and carry your kayak is very important to reduce the risk of injury to your spine. General-purpose plastic kayaks weigh as much as 20kg and are awkward shapes to move around. The risks should be reduced as much as possible and the basic principles of correct lifting and carrying should be applied to each situation, (See Chapter 6).

Getting In and Out of your Kayak

Due to the different situations in which you need to get in and out of your kayak, you need to apply some basic principles that you can use wherever you are.

The problems you are faced with as you get in or out of your kayak are:

1. You cause it to become off balance, and tip in.
2. The boat and bank are pushed apart, with you falling in between!

To learn to get in and out of your kayak you need to ensure neither of these common problems occurs!

The easiest way is to get someone to hold the boat, offering both stability and keeping the boat close to the bank.

If you are on your own however, place the kayak in the water parallel to the bank. Hold onto the bank with one hand and the kayak with the other to stop them from parting. (The hand holding the boat should be in the middle and back of the cockpit rim.)

Step into the middle of the boat with one foot first, then the other (keeping your weight central). Then sit onto the back of the cockpit and wriggle down into your boat.

Getting out is simply the reverse. Come up parallel to the bank, use both hands on the kayak to wriggle out so as to sit on the back deck. Put one hand on the bank and one hand on the back of the cockpit rim. Then, depending on how high the bank is, you can either step out or sit on the bank. Keeping hold of your boat, stand on the bank and take your boat out of the water.

If the river bank is gently sloping, you can get in on the shore and push yourself off. This is by far the easiest method as your boat is mostly on dry land and avoids the two main problems. It can however cause damage to the bank so, depending where you are, it may not be appropriate.

Whatever way you choose, do it slowly, keep the boat in balance and leave your paddle within reach, but out of the way.

Developing Boat Awareness

Time spent learning about your kayak's characteristics and how you can utilise them to your advantage is time well spent. There are many exercises you can use to develop this understanding.

Get on the water and try the following:

Photos 4.10a-d   Getting into your kayak

Exercises

Can you make your kayak go in a perfect straight line?

Can you spin on the spot, with your body as the central turning point?

What happens if you lean forwards or backwards while turning?

Can you turn your kayak around the front of the boat?

Can you turn your kayak around the stern of the boat?

What happens if you are travelling forward and you put the boat on one edge?

What happens if you are paddling forwards and you lean forwards or backwards?

How fast can you make your kayak go forwards, sideways or spin; which is easiest?

What happens when you paddle forwards and then stop paddling?

What happens when you get the boat spinning and then stop paddling?

Can you rock your kayak from side to side? And how far can you comfortably go?

How far over can you put your kayak on edge? And can you hold it there?

Can you paddle your boat forwards while holding it up on one edge?

What happens if you edge to the inside of a turn?

What happens if you edge to the outside of a turn?

Section Two – The Body

This section looks at how you can use your body to help control the kayak.

Bodies

Every body is different, the important point here is to recognise your personal characteristics and ensure you take these into consideration when learning to kayak, or when coaching someone. Here are just a few of our differences:

Strength

Stronger people will often use their strength to manoeuvre their kayak, whereas a weaker person will have to use technique.

Fitness

The fitter you are the longer you will be able to exercise for. This has an impact on how long you can stay on the water for, and how long you can effectively learn new skills. Tailor your session length to ensure you are learning when fresh and not while exhausted. Remember that although you may think you are quite fit, kayaking uses different muscles to most sports and can lead to tiredness earlier than you might expect.

Age

This affects all of the following factors. Younger people usually have less strength, more flexibility and are often smaller in size. However they often have a better strength to weight ratio than adults do, and fitness can go either way. Children also learn in different ways to adults, generally holding back less and learning well through pure experience. Adults on the other hand often have more fear and need to rationalise things in their heads before trying something new. (See Chapter 7).

Size

Small children will often find it difficult to reach over the side of their kayak. This obviously affects stroke technique, as they have to lean over to reach the water. On the other hand, tall or large adults can often be uncomfortable in their kayak and less stable. The key here is to ensure that the boat you are in is suitable for your body size, and to adapt the strokes if necessary.

Gender

Males differ from females, but then we have already said that each person has individual differences. We could say males are stronger, bigger, and less flexible, but don't expect that to be true of everyone. Treat people as individuals rather than as males or females.

Flexibility

Good flexibility is required to perform the foundation skills. Someone with limited flexibility may be hindered. This could be a general lack of flexibility or specific to one part of the body due to injury, past or present. Whichever it is, it is especially important that they warm-up enough to maximise what flexibility they do have.

In the longer term, stretching classes, or if the problem is due to obesity, a diet, may help address the problem.

Clothing

If you are overdressed or hindered by the clothing or equipment that you are wearing you will find it difficult to paddle. Your posture and flexibility can be affected, making it difficult to move as required. During the colder months, if trying to learn the foundation skills, it may be better to do short sessions without too many layers on to allow the freedom of movement necessary. (See Chapter 3).

Warming Up / Down

Whatever level you are at, you must always prepare your body and mind for the activity to follow. You must also let them recover by warming-down. (See Chapter 6.)

Posture

The first time someone sits in a kayak they should be encouraged to adopt a good posture. Correct posture involves the body sitting up and with slight lean forwards. To achieve this position, sit in your boat and push your bottom into the back of the seat. In this position the weight of the body is on the thighs/legs/heels. If you are sitting in the neutral position, you will feel your body weight through your bottom; if you are leaning back, you will feel the pressure on your lower back and bottom.

Correct posture allows:

- Increased stability, as the back edges of the boat are kept out of the water.
- Increased control as your hips are able to work with the boat.
- Greater rotational ability which can be used in stroke work.
- Greater reach, so the strokes can be performed at the front of the boat, where most power is generated from.
- A more aggressive position, where you are ahead and in control of what is happening, rather than reacting.

Using Body Rotation

Most strokes require good body rotation; this allows reach and power to be applied to the stroke. To achieve good rotation you need to sit up with correct posture, the rotation then comes through the whole spine from the base up to the neck. The head is separate, with the eyes either focused on where

the blade is being planted, i.e. when performing the bow sweep or draw stroke, or more often, where the boat is going. Once the body has been wound up it is then unwound throughout the stroke, with the eyes focused on the direction of travel. This unwinding allows power to be generated into the strokes through the torso.

Photo 4.11   Body rotation in action

There are two things you can do to ensure that you are maximising body rotation in your stroke work:

1. Include spinal rotational exercises in your warm-up.
2. Practice your strokes focusing on using good body rotation. Choose a few different strokes and practise each one, winding up and unwinding.

What's Under the Spraydeck?

Just because the boat and spraydeck hide everything below the waist, it doesn't mean that you can forget about them, far from it. Your legs and hips play a crucial part in moving your kayak around.

Legs

Just as you use body rotation to transmit power into your strokes, you can also use your legs, pushing them in the direction you wish to travel. This is particularly effective in the turning strokes.

Hips

These play a crucial role in your balance and control of the boat's stability and edge. You can use your oblique abdominal muscles (at the side of your waist) to lift one buttock and thus raise one edge of the boat. You need to train these muscles to work, just like any other. A good exercise is to try and paddle forwards with the boat on one edge; these muscles then have to work hard to hold the edge up.

Look Where You Are Going!

It sounds simple and obvious, but yet needs to be said! If you are paddling forwards look up and beyond the nose of your boat. If paddling backwards check over one shoulder to see where you are going. If you are doing a turning stroke, lead with your head and look to the new direction of travel.

Photo 4.12   Look!

This simple principle allows two things:

1. You can see where you are going!

2. On turning strokes you aid rotation.

Body Awareness

Spend time learning about your body's characteristics and how you can utilise them to your advantage. Get on the water and try the following:

> ### Exercises
>
> *How far forward can you reach by rotating your body?*
>
> *How far forwards can you reach without rotating your body?*
>
> *How much can you rotate when you lean back, far forwards or slightly forwards?*
>
> *How much edge control do you have when you lean back, far forwards or slightly forwards?*
>
> *What happens during a turn if you lean back, far forwards or slightly forwards?*
>
> *Does your clothing or equipment hinder you?*
>
> *While sitting in a kayak without a paddle:*
>
> *How far forwards can you reach with both hands?*
>
> *How far back can you lean, taking both hands over your head?*
>
> *How far around can you rotate; can you see the back of your boat?*

> *Can you reach underneath your kayak and touch your hands together?*
>
> *What happens during a turn if you look in the direction of travel?*
>
> *What happens during a turn if you look away from the direction of travel?*
>
> *What happens if you wind up and unwind throughout a stroke?*
>
> *What happens if you perform the same stroke with no rotation?*

Section Three – The Blades (Strokes)

Your blades are the means by which you transfer the energy from your body and the water into moving the boat where you want it to go.

Here are some general rules which can be applied to all strokes:

- The whole blade should be presented to the water during each stroke.

- The more vertical your paddle the more directional speed can be generated.

- The flatter the blade, the more stability can be achieved.

- The wider the stroke, the more turning effect the blade has.

- Your arms are never locked straight, but where reach is important, have a slight bend at the elbow. This is a much stronger position and less vulnerable to injury.

- You do not pull the paddle through the water, but pull yourself up to the paddle.

Before trying to master these strokes it is important that you can move the boat roughly where you want, not with great style or finesse but so that you can just about paddle in a straight line and turn around. It is also important to learn good technique early on, so do not delay in learning correct stroke work. Ensure you have read and played with the ideas in the sections on blade, boat and body awareness before trying to master the individual strokes. This will help you to develop an understanding of each stroke rather than perform it word for word. Stroke work is all about moving the boat where you want it to go. The basic strokes are only part of that, and are not the end in themselves.

Which Blades?

The type of paddles you hold in your hands is obviously going to affect what you can do with them! The choice of paddles on the market is huge and decisions must be made as to what are the best blades for you. This is obviously going to be affected by how you want to use them and how much you can afford! (See Chapter 2).

The following factors should all be taken into consideration when choosing a set of blades:

Paddle Length

The longer your paddle, the greater speed you can generate over distance, but this is compromised by having less control over the blades and less acceleration. The opposite is true of shorter paddles. This is why you see freestyle paddlers using short blades and sea paddlers using much longer ones. For a beginner in a general-purpose kayak I recommend a mid-length paddle with between 7 and 14cms between your little finger and the end of the shaft while holding your hands in the correct grip.

Paddle Weight

A light set of paddles are easier to handle and easier to feel the water through the blade. However they are also more fragile! A heavier blade is usually more durable, yet harder to control and less sensitive. The key is to find a balance between the two that you are comfortable with.

Blade Size

If you have a blade that is too big for you, you will find it difficult to pull through the water. If on the other hand your blades are too small, it will feel like you are pulling but nothing is happening! Many manufacturers sell blades in different sizes; youngsters and smaller adults are better suited to the smaller blade sizes, while the mid-range are suitable for most other adults. The large blades are designed for the accomplished powerhouses of our sport!

Blade Shape

Most general-purpose blade shapes are suitable for the beginner; this would normally be an asymmetric or symmetric shape. Specialist paddles (such as polo or racing blades) should be avoided in the early stages as they are designed for specific actions and not as general-purpose paddles.

Shaft Diameter

You should be able to comfortably hold the paddle shaft in each hand, with the thumb overlapping the fingers around the grip. If a shaft is too fat it will be difficult to hold, and the muscles in the forearm may be over-used to maintain grip. Different diameter shafts can be purchased. The control hand should have an oval grip, this enables you to hold the paddle more comfortably.

Shaft Stiffness

The more flexible a paddle shaft, the more forgiving it is on the joints but the more energy is lost through the strokes. Flexible shafts are therefore good for youngsters, beginners and paddlers prone to elbow, wrist or shoulder joint problems. A stiffer shaft is better for sprint paddlers who need the maximum power generation through their paddles.

Paddle Grip

Once you have chosen a suitable pair of blades you then need to make sure you are holding them correctly. By placing the paddles upon your head and moving your hands so that the elbows are at right angles you will find that a comfortable grip is achieved. This position allows a balance between maintaining control of the blades and making effective use of the paddles as levers. Insulating tape can be wrapped around the shaft to mark the correct hand position. Your grip should be relaxed and your hands evenly spaced from the end of the shaft.

Definitions

During this chapter I talk about different blade positions in the water, these are:

Vertically Upright

Photo 4.13a   Vertically Upright

Horizontal

Photo 4.13b   Horizontal

Flat

Photo 4.13c   Flat

Blade Awareness

Get on the water and ask yourself these questions:

- What effect does pulling the blade through the water in different planes have?
- How do you pull on the blade to make you go forwards, backwards or sideways?
- Can you draw shapes in the water with your paddle?
- Can you hold the paddle at one end and draw a circle all the way around the outside of your boat?
- Can you slice the blade through the water?
- What blade position gives you the most support, power, or turning action?
- What happens if you lean on your blade?
- How far away from your boat can you use your blades?
- How fast can you pull your paddle through the water?
- Can you stir the water, like you would a bowl of soup?

Try to learn how the shape of your paddle affects what is happening and how you can alter its shape in the water to have a desired effect. Trying different paddles will help you appreciate the different characteristics.

Power Strokes

With each of these strokes you are aiming to move the boat in a particular direction without turning. To achieve maximum straight-line propulsion from your paddle, it needs to be placed in the water as vertically as possible, and as close to the line of travel as possible. This enables you to pull, or push your boat towards or away from the blade and cause movement in that direction. Try to apply this principle to the following strokes.

Paddling Forwards

Photos 4.14a-b   Paddling forwards

Developing a smooth and efficient forward paddling style is one of the most important steps to becoming a successful paddler. It enables you to move the boat through the water economically, getting where you want with minimum energy expenditure. If the correct technique is learnt early, it will stay with you throughout your paddling career. On the other hand if bad habits are developed they are often very hard to get rid of!

The basic forward stroke involves several important elements: the catch, pull, lift, and push. However, each part of the stroke should flow together with grace and style, moving from one phase to the next seamlessly. Practice paddling smoothly at all times, with rhythm, left-right-left-right.

To make it easier to focus on the stroke rather than steering, practise in a kayak that has good directional stability and does not require too much steering.

The following is intended to act as a solid starting point for anyone learning to paddle, and can be adapted to suit individual and discipline-specific requirements as you progress.

The Catch

The blade should be planted cleanly in the water (with little splash) and as far forward as possible, in a spearing action. The arm is not locked straight but has a slight bend at the elbow. The action is achieved by rotating the body rather than leaning forward. A blade planted up towards the front of the kayak allows you to pull yourself up to your paddle.

As one stroke ends and the next begins, the body starts to unwind; it is therefore important to ensure the blade is planted in the water as quickly as possible, so as not to lose what rotation has been gained. Many people look as though they have a lot of body rotation, but most of it is while their blades are in the air!

Coaching points:

- A piece of tape on the front of the boat can be used as a marker to reach for.

- Imagine you are trying to place your blade by your toes.

- The spearing action can be practised by imagining you are trying to spear fish swimming by your feet.

The Pull

Once the blade is planted in the water, pull yourself up to the blade in a smooth action. This is achieved by unwinding your body, and using the major muscles of the back as well as the smaller muscles of the arms.

The blade moves through the water as close to the boat as possible and as vertically as possible, without hitting the sides of the boat. The blade should be completely covered by water and power should be applied throughout the whole pull phase. However, it is in the first part of the stroke that the most power is generated.

Photo 4.15a   Catch

Photo 4.15b   Pull

Photo 4.15c   Rotation

Body Rotation

This is a key element in the forward stroke. Imagine a pole passing through your head and down your spine. The body should rotate around that pole with your head remaining straight and still throughout the whole stroke. If this is performed correctly the boat will remain flat, with little movement side to side or front to back.

Coaching points:

- If your boat is rocking excessively, try placing a drinks can on the front and try to paddle without letting it fall off.
- The more rotation you can create the better, try to exaggerate it. It is difficult to over-rotate.
- To help increase your body rotation through-out the stroke you can imagine that you have a light shining from your chest, and are trying to shine that light from one side to the other.

The Lift

The pull finishes when the elbow reaches the hip; the blade is then sliced out of the water, away from the boat. The further forward the stroke, the more speed can be generated. There is little need for the blade to continue further back as it will lift water on the exit and is inefficient.

The Push

While the bottom arm is in the pull phase, the top arm pushes forwards with the hand no higher than eye level. If the hand is too high you lose power, if it is too low it becomes more of a sweep. It is not a particularly powerful push, but a controlling move-ment that moves the top hand into position to plant the blade in the water for the next stroke.

The wrist is kept straight throughout the push. A bent wrist is not only less efficient, but it can also lead to injury. The push ends when the arm is just off straight.

The legs can also be used to push. This helps to generate power through the boat and aids rotation. If you are paddling with good body rotation you should feel the pressure change from one foot to the next as you paddle. Some people push with the foot that is on the same side as the pulling hand, and some with the foot that is on the opposite side to the pulling hand; do whatever feels best for you.

Putting it Together

That is a lot to take in, let's remind ourselves of the basic requirements:

- Good forward posture.
- Paddle goes in at the toes, out at the hip.
- Good body rotation.

- Smooth transition between strokes.
- Concentrating on pulling yourself up to the paddle, rather than pulling the paddle through the water.
- An active top arm.

Once this has been achieved you can begin to refine some of the finer points. When your forward paddling becomes automatic it is very difficult to make changes to it. It is therefore important to develop an efficient style early on in your paddling career. If you are a coach, spend time helping begin-ners develop a good style in a fun way... it will stay with them, and make their paddling more enjoyable in the long run.

Paddling Backwards

Many of the same principles apply as with the for-ward power stroke, however it is harder to control the boat when moving backwards and less efficient. Fortunately reverse paddling is usually only needed for short distances.

The first challenge is to make sure you can see where you are going! Looking over one shoulder on every other stroke solves this problem. Looking over both shoulders can cause dizziness!

Photo 4.16a   Plant

The blade should be planted behind the body using good rotation and with the elbow bent and up. Once the blade is planted in the water, you unwind your body and push the blade down into the water, pushing yourself up to the paddle as opposed to pushing the blade through the water. This should be a smooth action. The blade moves through the water as close to the boat as possible and as vertically as possible, without hitting the sides of the boat. Power is applied throughout the whole push. The push finishes when the blade reaches the hip; it is then sliced out of the water, away from the boat. While the bottom arm is in the push phase, the top arm simply moves back towards the shoulder and stays on the same side of the body as the stroke. This arm should be relaxed and moving naturally, with the bottom arm leading the way.

Photo 4.16b   Push

Photo 4.16c   End

The body is in the same posture as when forward paddling and this posture should be maintained throughout the stroke.

As with the forward paddling, the legs can be used to aid rotation, and the boat remains as flat, with as little yawing as possible.

Stopping

Photo 4.17   Putting on the brakes

Putting on the brakes! When you are paddling forwards and wish to stop, you simply need to apply a few short and fast reverse strokes. If you are travelling backwards and wish to stop, you do the opposite and use forward strokes. The strokes are shortened to avoid too much turn being created. The paddle is simply jabbed into the water, level with the hip.

Moving Sideways

There are a number of different strokes that can be used to move the boat sideways. We are going to look at the most basic, the static draw stroke. You usually only need to move the boat sideways for short distances to position yourself against the river bank or alongside a fellow canoeist. One or two strokes are usually enough.

Photo 4.18a   Out to the side, level with hip

Photo 4.18b   In and about to be sliced out

The trunk is rotated towards the side you wish to travel. This enables you to place the blade out from your boat, with the shaft as vertical as possible and the blade completely covered by water. From this position the boat is pulled towards the paddle. The effect of this is that the boat is moving sideways and is in danger of catching up with the vertical paddle, causing you to trip over the blade. The timing of the end of the stroke is therefore very important. At the end of the stroke the blade can be sliced out of the water towards the back of the boat. Better still, it can be rotated through 90 degrees and sliced through the water into position to begin a second stroke; the drive face is facing the back of the boat during the slice.

In order to keep balanced throughout the stroke and to ensure that the boat is moving efficiently over the water, it is important to keep the boat as flat as possible. The tendency is to lean over towards the paddle; to avoid this use the knee closest to the stroke to hold the edge up. Notice how the top arm remains relatively stationary, acting as a pivot to ensure the paddle becomes increasingly vertical as it passes through the water, with the forearm just above the forehead.

Coaching points:

Fig 4.2a   Turning

- As you pull the boat towards the paddle, you can see bubbles appearing on the other side of the kayak. These indicate that you are pulling effectively.

- Try pulling someone who is sitting parallel to you and is holding onto your kayak along with you as you do the draw stroke. This increases the resistance and requires the stroke to be more effective. It can also give you the confidence to really pull on the stroke without the danger of falling in. Make sure both of you are aware of the danger of catching the other with their paddle.

Turning and Correcting

The further your blade is placed away from the boat, the more turning effect it will have. The sweep strokes are perhaps the most effective of turning strokes as they exploit this principle.

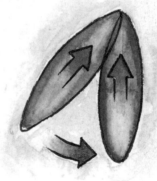

Fig 4.2b   Correcting

ing or correcting strokes can be used depending on the outcome required.

When you wish to turn or correct, always look where you want to go! By leading a turn with your head, you increase your awareness of where you are going and help your body to rotate.

Turning and correcting the boat are two very different concepts:

Turning

Turning the boat requires a stroke placed away from the boat and using your body to pull or push the boat away from the blade, driving one end of the kayak away from the centre line of the kayak.

Correcting

Correcting on the other hand brings the kayak back on course.

If that concept can be understood it will make manoeuvring your kayak much easier, as either turn-

The Bow Sweep

This drives the front of the boat away from the blade and is used to initiate turns. It is achieved by rotating the body and planting the blade by your toes, with the paddle shaft flat and low. The leg on the same side as the stroke and the torso push the boat away from the blade. The stroke finishes when the blade has just passed the body, where it is lifted out of the water. The front arm is fractionally bent and remains so throughout the stroke. The same leg that you are pushing with can be used to hold the edge of the boat up slightly; this will keep the boat flat and stop the edge catching. It is important that the whole blade is submerged in the water. It is not good practice to look at the blade during the stroke; if you watch the blade through the stroke your torso rotation will be in the wrong direction! Once the blade is planted and the body is unwinding from it, the head should be looking in the direction of travel. The top hand begins the stroke near the shoulder and remains at shoulder height throughout the stroke. The stroke creates some forward momentum as well as a turning effect.

Coaching Point

- To help you get a feel for the action of the legs and torso, a coach or another paddler can hold your paddle still while you then push your boat away from or pull it towards the blade.

The Stern Sweep

The stern sweep is a stroke that pulls the back of the boat towards the blade, this is particularly useful to control the boat while it is skidding, or to alter the direction of the boat while moving forwards. The stroke begins out and at about 90 degrees to the boat. The front arm is fractionally bent, the torso twists the stern of the kayak towards the blade, and the legs push the nose of the boat away. The lower arm remains slightly bent and the top arm comes across the body until the boat reaches the blade.

The Reverse Stern Sweep

This is used to push the stern of the kayak away from the blade. It is a very effective way to turn the boat quickly, but it does cause you to lose forward momentum.

As with all the strokes we have discussed so far, your posture remains slightly forward. The blade is planted as far round to the rear of the boat as possible, with the body rotated and the head looking at the blade as it is planted in the water. The blade should be upright in the water, using the back face of the blade as the power face. The shoulders and the paddle shaft can be used as a check to ensure enough rotation has been achieved; they should both be parallel to the centre line of the boat. The arm remains just off straight throughout the stroke and the torso is unwound to push the boat away from the blade. The legs should also be used to aid this movement and to keep the boat flat. The stroke finishes level with the body.

Fig 4.3a   Path of bow sweep

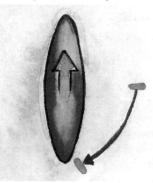

Fig 4.3b   Path of stern sweep

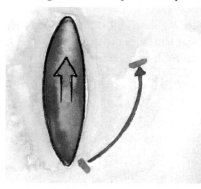

Fig 4.3c   Path of reverse stern sweep

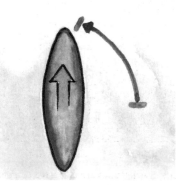

Fig 4.3d   Path of reverse bow sweep

The Reverse Bow Sweep

This is used to control direction when paddling backwards. It begins at about 90 degrees to the boat and the stern is pushed away from the blade.

Full Sweep Strokes

The forward bow and stern sweeps can be combined to create a 'full' forwards sweep stroke, and the reverse bow and stern sweeps can be combined to create a 'full' reverse sweep stroke. These can be used to spin the boat on the spot. This is perhaps the only application of full sweeps.

The Stern Rudder

The stern rudder is a steering stroke that allows fine control of the direction of travel while the boat is on the move, with minimum loss of speed. You begin by first getting the boat moving forwards and then trail your blade horizontally and upright at the stern of the kayak. The shoulders are rotated around to achieve this position, but the head remains facing forwards and the boat flat. Try to keep your hips facing forwards during this stroke as this will help the boat to run straight. Your direction can then be altered by moving the boat either away from, or towards, the paddle. The stern rudder can also be used to maintain a straight run by simply using the stern rudder in a neutral position or with light pressure on the blade, either way.

Photo 4.19   Stern rudder

The stern rudder is more effective at pushing the boat away from the blade than it is at pulling it in.

This will affect your choice of which side you decide to plant the stroke.

Coaching points:

- Remember the stroke only works with forward speed. If the stroke is being performed on flat water it can only be used for as long as the boat has some forward momentum.
- Begin by practising the position while stationary.
- Two kayaks can sit parallel to each other to create a narrow passage for a paddler to steer through.

One difficulty that beginners find with this stroke is that, as they rotate their body to get the blade in position, the boat begins to turn and the rudder becomes inappropriate. It is therefore important that you learn to keep the boat running straight, while getting the blade into position. Something that will help learners is to make the last forward stroke on the same side as the rudder goes in. As more forward control is developed the paddler will be able to control the forward running direction of the boat and this double stroke becomes unnecessary.

The stroke is used in a variety of situations, most of which are fairly advanced. Learning the stroke however does help improve blade awareness and feel, and beginners will find it invaluable when paddling downwind.

Other uses are:

- Controlling direction while wave surfing, either on the sea or a river.
- Steering while making use of forward speed generated by wind or water.
- Steering into a narrow cave or through a narrow gap.

The Bow Draw

This is basically a power stroke that draws the front of the boat towards the blade. The stroke is best performed on the move and with a bow sweep preceding the bow draw. This enables you to capture the energy created from forward momentum and transfer it into the turn.

The blade is planted as shown in Photo 4.20 and the following points must be noted:

- The blade face is 'open', facing towards the front of the boat.

- The top arm is across the forehead, allowing a near vertical paddle.
- The bottom arm is bent at the elbow.
- The body is rotated towards the side of the stroke.
- The head is rotated towards the direction of travel.
- The blade is completely covered by water.
- The boat is edged slightly towards the side of the stroke.

Photo 4.20   Bow draw

Once the blade is planted, the torso, hips and legs are used to squeeze the front of the boat towards the blade. When the 'squeeze' is finished and the boat has caught up with the paddle, the blade can then be either sliced out of the water to perform a stroke on the other side, or it can be continued into a forward power stroke.

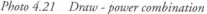

Photo 4.21   Draw - power combination

Safety

Performed incorrectly, the bow draw can put quite a strain on the shoulders. It is important to keep both arms bent at the elbows, with the top arm in front of the head (not above or behind it), as this reduces the strain on your joints. Initiating the turn with a bow sweep also reduces the strain.

Coaching Points

- One of the easiest ways to introduce this stroke is as a follow-on from the draw stroke. The starting position is very similar for both, but in the case of the bow draw the blade's drive face is turned towards the bow.
- Once the blade position has been mastered the stroke can be tried on the move.
- First wind the body up, plant the blade, and then unwind the body!
- Squeeze the boat towards the paddle, not the paddle to the boat.

Bow Rudder

This is very similar in appearance to the bow draw. However, the turn is generated from the movement of water upon the blade, rather than the body doing the work. It requires moving water to be most effective. The water acts on the paddle and the boat to assist the turn. The blade is planted further forward and closer to the boat than for the bow draw, and the boat is put on edge. Be patient and let your boat glide around the turn!

The optimum position of the blade depends on how tight or gentle you want the turn to be. Experiment.

Photo 4.22   Bow rudder

The Low Brace Turn

This is a series of three main actions producing a slow and safe turn:

1. A bow sweep stroke is performed on one side to initiate the turn.

2. The boat is then put on edge to allow it to carve.

3. A low brace is placed on the water to offer support, (low brace is covered on the next page).

The turn is most useful on moving water as the low brace offers support while turning into or out of the current. However, it is best learnt on flat water first.

Photo 4.23   Low brace turn

When the turn has begun to slow down, you can remove the blade from the water, either by slicing it out backwards, or slicing it forwards and moving it into a power stroke.

Providing Support

The blade position from which you can obtain the most support is flat to the water, at 90 degrees to the boat and as far out as possible, like a stabiliser on a bike.

Your body and boat do not allow this to be executed exactly, but each support stroke is trying to maximise this principle.

Before trying to learn any of the support strokes it is first necessary to master how to edge and lean your kayak. This will enable you to control your balance using your hips, torso and legs and also give you a feel for the boat's stability.

Coaching Point

• Rock the boat as violently from side to side as you can or dare, while keeping your paddle out of the way! Once you have mastered that, do the same, but then stop the boat rocking as quickly as you can, upon command.

Low Recovery Stroke

The low recovery stroke is used to quickly bring your kayak back to a stable position before it has gone completely off balance.

The stroke uses the classic 'monkey position' with the elbows up, the paddle extended at 90 degrees to the boat and with the back face of the blade presented to the water as flat as possible. The blade strikes the water and you use your hips, torso and legs to bring the boat back into balance. Keep the elbows up, the shaft as horizontal as possible and do not put too much weight on the blade as this will cause it to sink.

*Photos 4.24a-c   Flat blades - monkey grip
(top), hip flick (middle), slice blade out (bottom)*

Coaching Points

• Practise the paddle position first without going off balance.

• Always practise the full stroke by first putting the boat off balance.

• If you are in a pool get someone to tip you from behind, this helps you learn to react quickly.

- Practise the stroke on the move.

- Practise on both sides.

- Always check the water depth before practising.

The low recovery stroke can be used as a reactive stroke, for example, when knocked off balance by a wave or a very 'twitchy' boat. These situations can arise when sea or river paddling, or when paddling unstable boats like wild water racers or sprint boats, or when playing games such as canoe polo.

It can also be used as a preventative stroke where you get it ready just in case. For example, while waiting on the start line in a racing kayak, the blade is in position ready for the low recovery stroke.

The Low Brace

The low brace is very similar to the low recovery stroke except that it is used as a preventative measure to control the boat's stability.

This stroke has the same basic blade position as the low recovery stroke, but it is used to offer support while the boat is over on one edge. It does not necessarily bring the boat back into an upright position. The stroke achieves this by using water movement and pressure beneath the blade. This water pressure can be created during a turn, or where moving water is pushing against the blade, e.g. when used side-surfing a stopper, the pile is pressing up onto the underside of the blade.

In order to ensure the water passes under, rather than over the blade, the leading edge is lifted slightly.

The low brace is often finished by using the hips, torso and legs to right the boat as you would with a low recovery stroke. (See Photos 4.1b and c).

High Recovery Stroke

The high recovery stroke is similar in principle to the low recovery stroke in that the blade strikes the water perpendicular to the boat, with the blade presented to the water as flat as possible and with the shaft as low as possible. However, the drive face of the blade is used instead of the back face, and your elbows hang underneath the paddle shaft.

This stroke is used in similar situations to the low recovery stroke, however the dynamics of the stroke allow you to recover when the boat has gone much further over. This means that it is very much a reactive stroke. Unlike the low recovery stroke, it can

only be used effectively in kayaks that allow you to brace with your knees.

Photo 4.25a   High recovery stroke, Stage 1

Once the paddle is in position and the boat is off balance, allow the water to come up to the paddle rather than pulling the blade down to the water. Once the blade contacts the water, use your hips, torso and legs to bring the boat back upright. Once the kayak is back in balance, the body and head come back up and your blade is sliced out of the water by rolling the wrist forwards.

Photo 4.25b   High recovery stroke, Stage 2

Most paddlers find the stroke easier on their control hand side, i.e. a right-handed paddler will find it easier to do a high recovery stroke on their right hand side. This is because, when going to the right, their hands are naturally aligned correctly with the blade ready for the stroke. You can see from the photo that this is not true on the left hand side. To overcome this when practising on your off side, first rotate the shaft of your paddle in your hand so that the blade is ready for the high support stroke, and then grip the paddle in that position.

Safety

If performed incorrectly the high recovery stroke can put the shoulders at risk. It is important to keep the elbows bent and underneath the paddle shaft. The elbows then act as a shock absorber and take the pressure off the shoulders.

Photo 4.26   Bad technique!

Coaching points:

- The same coaching points can be applied as for the low recovery stroke.
- Another kayaker can come alongside you and hold onto your kayak to offer support and boost confidence while learning the stroke. Make sure you are both aware of the danger of each other's paddles.

Putting the Strokes Together

Once the basic strokes have been mastered, you can then really begin to learn to kayak! An experienced paddler does not simply perform one basic stroke followed by another. They use a variety of complete and incomplete strokes, parts of strokes linked together (combination strokes) and strokes that are a cross between two strokes (compromise strokes). These strokes are timed to achieve maximum efficiency and effectiveness and are used only when they are needed.

Having said this, it is vital that you master the basic strokes as these form the foundations upon which you will make further developments. It is also true that as you learn these strokes you will begin to make individual adaptations to make the stroke work better for you. For example many beginners learn to put a stern sweep on the end of a forward power stroke to help them travel in a straight line. It is important that they are allowed the freedom while learning to develop feel and individuality, so as not to turn into someone who can perform all the strokes but doesn't react to, or feel the water.

Combination Strokes

These strokes are a series of strokes, or parts of strokes that are combined together to form what appears to be one stroke. The strokes are linked together without removing the blade from the water. For example a bow draw–forward power–stern sweep.

Photos 4.27a-c   Bow draw - power - stern sweep

Many strokes can be combined together depending upon how you wish to manoeuvre your kayak. Another example would be a reverse stern sweep – bow draw.

These strokes require little explanation as they rely upon you developing a feel for what each part of a stroke does and combining those different parts of strokes together to cause a desired effect. I do not wish to be prescriptive here, but would like to encourage you to experiment with how different strokes can be combined.

Compromise Strokes

These strokes are not pure strokes, but a compromise between two. For example where a power stroke is needed with a bit of turn, a slightly wider stroke may be used, i.e. a compromise between a forward power stroke and a bow sweep. Where a bow draw is needed with some support, a compromise between a bow draw and a high support stroke is used.

Compromise strokes can come in any of the following combinations:

- Power strokes can be performed with some element of support or turn.

- Turning strokes can be performed with some element of power or support.

- Support strokes can be performed with some power or turn.

The skill is in using these strokes effectively for the purpose you require. Having a solid base of the foundation skills will help you to make these choices and understand when and where they can be used.

Putting It All Together

We have looked at the boat, the blade and the body and how each of these factors contributes to basic boat control. Each one is linked to the other, and once you have mastered each piece it is time for you to go away and finish the puzzle. Only by spending time in a boat will you begin to put it all together. Try to apply the basic principles, work out the skills as a whole, part, and whole again. And sometimes, don't think at all… just go paddling and have fun!

Further Reading

Canoeing and Kayaking - Technique, Tactics and Training, Bailey M, 1991, The Crowood Press, 1-85223-528-4
Every Crushing Stroke - The Book of Performance Kayaking, Shipley S, 2001, Crab Apple Publishing, 0-9710320-0-9
Kayak, Nealy W, 1993, Menash Ridge Press, 0-89732-050-6
Stretching, Bob Anderson, 1980, Pelham Books, 0-7207-1351-X
Whitewater Paddling - Strokes and Concepts, Jackson E, 1999, Stackpole Books, 0-8117-2997-4

Lara Tipper

Thanks to a PGL holiday and a keen brother, Lara started kayaking when she was 10 years old. She began competing in slalom where she progressed through the divisions, winning the Junior European Championships, gaining a Silver medal at the Junior World Championships and being part of the GB Olympic Squad. A back injury took her away from slalom, but led her to coaching and recreational paddling. She was fortunate enough to work alongside a number of kayaking gurus and, with their guidance, quickly progressed to Level 5 Coach whilst maintaining her slalom coaching with the Great Britain Junior and Welsh Teams.

Lara has taken her kayak all over the world, paddling some of the best white water and achieving a number of first descents. She has also represented GB at the Freestyle World Championships in both 1995 and 2001. She now works for the WCA as National Coach to the Welsh Slalom Team and coaches white water paddling, freestyle and coach education on a freelance basis.

5 Foundation Canoe Skills

No need for torches. No ripples broke the stars mirrored in the surface ahead of us. Automatically I started using the Indian stroke. I lifted the shaft higher so only the fineness of the blade cut through the water. My grip on the paddle was light, the top being spun by fingertips. The only noise to disturb the stillness of the night was the rustle of my jacket. To my right the old burial mound and its yew tree was silhouetted by the starry sky. The water and land were so black that I crashed straight into the shore.

The next day the wind picked up, creating steep waves. Travelling in solo boats, we flew down the lake with wind and waves behind us. Quick strokes would accelerate the canoes for an exhilarating surf. For Linda it was a first solo journey. Her eyes were wide with delight and wonder as we reached the other end. Her only comment: "Again. Again!"

The Versatile Canoe

No other boat has ever been designed and used for such a diverse set of purposes. The same boat can travel up or down white water rivers and negotiate expansive bodies of open water. It can be propelled by paddle, pole or sail, and when all else fails it can be placed on the shoulders and carried.

Our craft and tradition come to us from the birch-bark canoe of North America. Taken up by the two British enterprises, The North Westerners and The Hudson Bay Company, the great trade canoes opened up a country. The 'voyageurs' who paddled these great eight and ten metre boats were almost exclusively made up of Native, French and mixed-race Canadians.

In the USA the way west across the prairies was by foot, horse and wagon. In Canada it was by water and using the birch-bark canoe. The first crossing of the American continent, north of Mexico, was in 1793 by a party of voyageurs employed by the North Westerners and led by Alexander Mackenzie. The North Westerners were eventually absorbed into the Hudson Bay Company. Canada owes its present boundaries to two elements: the beaver and its prized fur and the trade posts and canoe routes of the canoe companies.

What's in a Name

In Britain kayakers and canoeists often have different names for what is basically the same stroke. The prime example is the bow rudder in kayak, or bow cut in canoe. This stroke originated in the canoe which is, after all, the original white water boat. The person who transferred it across to the kayak was Milo Dufek, a fact acknowledged in many North American books in which the stroke is known as a Dufek in both canoe and kayak. I have chosen to use the term bow rudder.

Where an alternative name has been in common usage, by at least some people, I have put this in brackets alongside. Names should point out the similarities within paddlesport and not create barriers.

Definitions

Strokes and manoeuvres can be done *on side* or *off side* or *cross-deck*. The *on side* is where one would naturally paddle. *Off side* is the other side. *Cross-deck* refers to bringing the paddle across the canoe to use on the off side without swapping hand positions.

In many strokes the position of the thumb on top of the paddle is a useful indicator. According to which way the blade is rotated, this thumb can be pointing down or up, inwards or outwards. When learning a stroke this is a useful check, so where relevant I have noted this.

Photos 5.1a-b   Indicator thumb up (left)
Indicator thumb down (right)

I will refer to the drive face and back face of the blade. The drive face is simply the one pulling back against the water on your on side when doing a forward power stroke.

An inside turn is to the on side. An outside turn is towards the off side.

Breaking the Skill Down

It is worth considering breaking any canoe skill or manoeuvre into the following elements: Boat, Body and Blade. I would strongly advise that you look at the first two elements whenever you are either learning a skill or trying to analyse why things are not working. No amount of tinkering with the blade will solve things if the boat or body element is incorrect.

Boat

Here a number of things are worth considering:

- The trim of the canoe from end to end - generally the canoe will be trimmed bow light in any forward running. In learning to paddle backwards the canoe will need to be stern light. If the trim is incorrect the canoe will plough off course. By moving yourself or your kit within the canoe, this trim can be radically altered.

- The balance from side to side – when paddling solo it is often preferable, or easier, to heel the canoe over to the paddling side.

- In white water, the angle of the canoe to eddy lines and the current will be critical to performance.

Body

Note that:

- Experienced paddlers kneel or sit with the hips and body twisted to one side not because they are experienced but because it is easier.

Photo 5.2   Body twisted to one side

- Good paddlers often turn the way their knees point to ease a cross-deck stroke. The way the knees or body are aligned will often greatly help or hinder a stroke or manoeuvre.

Photo 5.3   Knees turned

Blade

The twiddly bits! It is too easy to think that paddling a canoe is about the paddle and blade but unless the first two elements are right, strokes will either not work or be much stiffer and awkward.

The Problem of 'All Those Strokes'

By giving strokes names and a definite description we break up what should be a continuum into separate elements. We end up with a draw stroke followed by a power stroke followed by a steering stroke instead of a continuous whole. By separating with names, if not careful, we separate them in our head and in our practice. Some strokes will be distinct, but during a manoeuvre most will be blended and merge into each other.

It is often easier and sensible to learn a stroke as a distinct entity, but throughout this chapter suggestions will be made on how to put things 'back together'.

Choosing a Paddle

Having a good paddle is critical to both the ease of learning and the sheer enjoyment of moving on water. Wood is more satisfying to use and the warmest of all materials.

There are a number of different grips. The 'T' grip is favoured by competition paddlers and by many white water paddlers. The palm grip is easy to rotate in the hand and is the preferred grip of most recreational paddlers whether on flat or white water.

Length of Paddle

Getting this right is important. The wrong size paddle causes you to lose efficiency.

With a white water paddle a quick and easy check is as follows: stand up straight with the paddle upright in front of you; the top or the handle should be level with your chin.

A better check is shown in Photo 5.4.

Photo 5.4   Judging the length

Kneel on one knee with the upper leg (thigh) on that side vertical. With the body upright the arm is put out horizontally. The hand grasps an upside down vertical paddle just below the point where the shaft widens into the blade. With the grip of the paddle on the floor, the arm should be horizontal or dipping down slightly.

With the exception of a bent shaft paddle, once you have established the correct shaft length it should be the same for all your paddles, regardless of blade size or length.

Bent shaft paddles require a slightly shorter length than that above.

Roles in a Tandem Canoe

When the canoe is travelling forward and straight, it is the stern paddler who does all the correcting. However, it is only small corrections or wider turns that are easily made from the stern. If the canoe goes off course more than a certain amount, the bow paddler should help by pulling or pushing the bow back on line. 'Hanging strokes' are best for this, as they do not kill the forward speed and waste energy. However the bow paddler must not overdo this, but allow the stern paddler to make the fine adjustments.

For most tandem crews the canoe will turn towards the bow paddler's paddling side. This will necessitate a correction stroke at the stern at the end of most power strokes.

Exercising Both Sides

If you are doing more than just 'poottling' about in a canoe, I would strongly urge you to learn most skills on both sides. The solo paddler should learn forward travelling strokes on both sides, and tandem paddlers should regularly swap sides. If you become more and more dependent on one side as you develop your paddling, muscles on that side will become more developed. This can easily lead to an imbalance and the spine beginning to curve to one side.

Nearly all of us will have a preferred side for running rapids, and at times the wind will dictate which side we paddle on, but develop the travelling strokes on both sides and swap regularly. Prevent damage rather than correct it years later.

Learning in the Wind

It is generally easier to learn strokes if there is no wind but too often we have to cope with wind whilst we are doing this.

Exercise

In a gentle breeze try moving from one end of the canoe to the other. Allow the canoe to swing with the wind (like a weather vane). Reasonable with only one in the canoe but can be done two up. It might be a good idea to be within easy swimming distance of the shore!

Some ideas for coping or getting the wind to aid learning:

- If you are learning a new stern steering stroke, go upwind and then trim to run downwind (move the weight sternward). Practise the new stroke going with the wind. Paddle back up with whichever strokes are easiest, and go downwind with the new stroke again.

Photo 5.5   Running downwind

- When learning reverse strokes, go upwind and then trim for wind and reverse travel to practise the new strokes.

In Chapter 17 there are many more ideas for paddling in windy conditions.

Applying the Power

It is far easier to learn efficient forward paddling whilst in the bow seat. With no steering, total attention can be given to the stroke. So for the beginner, the bow paddler can concentrate on producing power and the stern paddler on steering.

The stroke should be made parallel to the centre line of the canoe and not follow the gunwale. This gives the maximum forward travel with no veer. Curiously, if the bow paddler follows the gunwale with the stroke the boat usually veers towards the bow paddle, forcing the stern paddler to compensate. This parallel stroke is often compromised for the stern paddler by the need to steer.

Photos 5.6a-b   Front and side view

Looking from in front of the canoe, the paddles should both be vertical during the power phase. In fact the paddle should be as near vertical as possible throughout the application of power. The top hand should be stacked above the lower and brought back rather than pushed forward. To increase power, the on side shoulder should be rotated forward to lengthen the reach at the start of the stroke and rotated back through the power phase. This way the powerful trunk muscles are brought into play.

The aim for tandem crews should be to synchronise the power strokes in order to give a smooth and joint application of power, however a fair bit of experience with steering strokes is needed before this is possible.

Learning Steering Strokes

Getting the boat started and running straight can be difficult for the novice. Swapping the paddle from side to side will get the canoe running straight in the first instance; then the stern or solo paddler should attempt to use a power stroke followed by a stern rudder on one side only. Learning to use one side only is important.

In learning a new stern stroke, it is often best to get the canoe moving and straight with well practised strokes before swapping into the new one.

Running Straight (or Turning)

Stern Rudder

To correct a turn away from the power stroke or turn the canoe to the paddling side, the blade is pushed away from the stern of the canoe and held against the flow of the water. To keep the canoe running straight, the blade is held parallel to the centreline of the canoe and gently pushed or pulled to make small corrections.

Photo 5.7   Static stern rudder position

Key points:

- The canoe must be moving forward.
- Chest is rotated to paddling side.
- Both hands are out over the gunwale.
- Indicator thumb is up.

- The blade is upright on its edge at the rear of the canoe.
- Don't push the blade out too far from the canoe or it will stall the forward motion and waste energy.
- The stroke can be done on its own or at the end of a power stroke.
- The paddle shaft can be leant on the gunwale to ease the strain or not as need be.

Photo 5.8   Stern rudder being practised whilst pulling canoe forward on a rope

This is the stroke most beginners first learn to steer with. Don't underrate it. It can be used for powerful turns or corrections in advanced situations. You can do this stroke and lean away at the same time which will be useful in certain situations and manoeuvres.

Stern Sweep/Draw

This causes a very powerful turn away from the blade and stops the need to swap sides to steer. It can either be a full stern sweep or incorporate just the last part of the sweep to the stern when it is often referred to as a stern draw.

- Paddle is extended out horizontally at right angles to the stern/solo paddler.
- The blade is swept around in a quarter circle to the stern of the canoe.
- The trunk should be rotated around to the side to create power.
- Both hands should finish outside the gunwale.
- To make it really powerful, the top hand can finish even further out than the bottom hand. Both arms will be bent.

It is the last part of the stroke that is most powerful in turning the canoe. Concentrate on this part.

An Alternative Way

Share paddles! Move into the centre of the canoe and share the paddles. All four hands of the paddlers must be on the paddles but each paddler may not have more than one hand on either paddle. Be inventive!

Photo 5.9　Learning to work together

Draw Strokes – To Go Sideways and Turn

In a tandem boat it is probably best to learn this stroke to turn the canoe, and in a solo canoe to go sideways. It is a powerful way for the bow paddler to turn the front of a tandem canoe or pull it back on course whilst moving.

Photo 5.10　Body strongly turned to stroke side

- The upper body is turned strongly to the side the draw is done on. It helps to swivel the knees and hips to that side.

- The upper hand is pushed out over the side of the canoe and stays there.

- The drive face of the blade is pulled towards the side of the canoe.

The recovery can be done in a number of ways:

- As the blade nears the side, the upper hand drops towards the front of the canoe and the blade 'slashes' out behind the paddler. This works well even when the canoe is moving forward.

- Alternatively, the blade can be 'feathered' back out to the start position. As the blade nears the canoe, it is quickly turned to 90 degrees and is sliced out through the water. The indicator thumb on the top hand will be pointing out.

Exercises

In a tandem canoe there is no need to be both facing forward when learning these sideways/turning strokes. Try facing each other. See what each other is doing. Try turning the canoe by drawing on opposite sides. Try going sideways by putting both paddles on one side (but be gentle or you can pull yourselves in).

In a solo boat, control is achieved in a sideways move by varying the point the blade is pulled to: further forward to bring the bow back into line and further back to bring the stern back into line.

By moving body and paddle radically further forwards and dropping the paddle shaft to a low angle a bow draw is done; a useful turning stroke and far more effective than the bow element of a reverse sweep.

Turning Strokes

Sweep Stroke Solo

A useful turning stroke often used to initiate moves before using other strokes.

- Blade is reached forward towards the bow of the boat.

- Indicator thumb is up.

- The blade is just below the surface throughout.

- The paddle is swept around in an arc so that the blade draws a half circle on the surface from bow to stern.

- By the time the blade reaches the stern, both hands should be out over the water and the chest turned to the on side.

During a manoeuvre it may not be efficient to use the whole stroke and you may need to use only the front (bow sweep) or back (stern sweep) half of the stroke.

Fig 5.1   Arc of sweep for tandem

Reverse Sweep Stroke

Simple, just start at the back and sweep the blade to the bow.

Tandem Sweep Strokes

Things are not quite so simple for the tandem paddlers. One will need to do a forward sweep and the other a reverse sweep on the opposite side.

Now we hit a problem. In solo paddling the pivot point of the canoe is close to the paddler. In a tandem canoe it is between the two paddlers. Try with each doing a full sweep. You should feel that at a certain point you are working against yourself and the turn. Try it with the eyes closed to really feel the effect. A full sweep stroke is ineffective in a tandem canoe.

To be effective the paddle should work in an arc between the end of the canoe and a line drawn at right angles to the paddler. If you start or finish outside of this arc you are working against yourself.

- The bow paddler would start at the bow and sweep to the right angle (bow sweep). The stern paddler would start at the stern and sweep to the right angle (reverse stern sweep).
- To go the other way reverse the above.

Exercises

Try the tandem sweep stroke as described above. Try it with your eyes closed.

Now each paddler tries the manoeuvre with a full 180 degree sweep rather than the 90 degrees. Try it with the eyes closed. You should be able to feel where the stroke begins to work against the turn.

The sweep can be extended with a cross-deck bow draw (an outside pivot turn). This is a very simple extension of the sweep stroke where the solo paddler can end up doing three-quarters of a circle.

- Do a sweep on your on side. Bring the paddle back in front of your chest. Paddle shaft horizontal. Indicator thumb up.
- Keeping the indicator thumb pointing up, swing the blade across the canoe. Considerable body rotation is needed to achieve this.
- Start the sweep back towards the bow on the off side, jump the blade over the bow and back onto the on side.
- Complete the sweep to the stern.
- The indicator thumb should be up and the same blade face used throughout.

Try using this stroke on the move or on eddy lines. It is a satisfying and powerful turn.

In Tandem

The bow paddler can do the same cross-deck bow draw. Remember that once the blade is back on the on side, only half the arc is done.

Using a Bow Draw

A bow draw is far more powerful than doing a reverse sweep.

- A bow draw is done with the drive face of the blade.
- The indicator thumb is down.
- The blade is swept/drawn to the bow.

In a solo canoe it is possible to combine a stern reverse sweep with a bow draw (Inside Pivot Turn).

- Start a reverse sweep. Indicator thumb up.

- At the halfway point in the arc, turn the paddle so that the indicator thumb is pointing down.

- Finish the arc with the indicator thumb pointing down (effectively a bow draw).

This is far more effective than a full reverse sweep.

The Pry

Almost the exact opposite of a sliced draw stroke. It can be used to either turn or move the canoe sideways.

- The upper body is turned strongly to the side the pry is done on. It helps to swivel the knees and hips to the side the stroke is done on.

- The bottom hand rests on the gunwale and holds the paddle shaft against the side throughout. The thumb of the lower hand can be hooked across the gunwale.

- The drive face of the blade is levered away from the side of the canoe.

- The blade is sliced back in at right angles to the canoe, and for maximum efficiency is sliced under the canoe, before being turned and levered back out and away from the canoe.

- The blade should not break the surface during this stroke.

In a solo canoe, the pry can be done a long way forward to execute a powerful turning stroke.

Stern Draw

In reality this is the last part of a sweep stroke but is often used on its own. The real power of the turn is generated close to the stern of the canoe. A high degree of trunk rotation and punching the upper hand outwards make this extremely powerful in correcting or turning the canoe.

Exercises

Try various combinations of strokes to spin the canoe on the spot. Use draws, pries and sweeps to turn the boat. Discover which ones work best. Challenge another pair to a spinning race to test out your theories.

Sculling Draw

Exactly the same body position as the ordinary draw stroke. Instead of pulling the blade in towards the boat, it is run backwards and forwards along a line parallel to the centre line of the canoe for maybe half a metre or more.

- The same blade face is used throughout.

- On each stroke along the canoe, the 'leading' edge of the blade is angled away from the canoe. As you reach the end of the stroke and prepare to move the blade in the opposite direction, the new 'leading' edge is rotated away from the boat.

- A very small angle on the blade gives far more sideways movement than a large angle.

Exercises

Try practising with the eyes closed and try to get an even pressure on the blade. Having the eyes closed will give a real feel for the stroke. It is best to use this as a sideways stroke and not turn the canoe.

Exercises

Try combining strokes in a sequence, say a couple of pries to get the canoe moving one way. Get it going the other way by using draw strokes and then continue with a sculling draw.

Try lots of combinations in tandem to make it go sideways, make it spin, stop a movement.

Try using a draw stroke in the bow whilst the canoe is on the move. Use it to start a turn or to pull the bow back on course.

Photo 5.11   Cross-deck sculling showing body rotation

Cross-deck Sculling

Simply scull on the off side without swapping hands. Rotating the knees and chest to the off side makes this straightforward.

'J' Stroke

This a foundation stroke for a whole group of strokes. Initially it can feel awkward but soon becomes natural. It can be used for straight running or turning.

> ### Note
>
> *With all the following strokes it helps immensely if the trunk is rotated to the paddling side. This is easily achieved by kneeling and having the knees pointed to the paddle side.*

- Do a normal power stroke.
- As the blade comes back towards the hip, the indicator thumb begins to twist down towards the water at the same time as the blade turns out from the canoe. (The path of the paddle describes a 'J' shape as it moves through the water).
- Do this slowly and try to keep pressure on the drive face throughout. The drive face should end up facing away from the canoe.
- Initially try pitching the blade over at an angle of 70-80 degrees. Leave the blade in the water briefly to feel the turn.

Photo 5.12   Notice hand positions in relation to the gunwale plus angle/pitch of blade

Additional Points:

- The lower hand should be outside the gunwale throughout.

- The paddle shaft can be rested on the gunwale to take pressure off the steering. The gunwale would be between the two hands.
- It should be a smooth stroke with pressure on the blade throughout.
- After learning at one 'pitch' try varying the angle. If little steering is needed, the angle drops, (in the end it naturally becomes a knifed 'J'). In some turns on flat water the pitch can go beyond 90 degrees, (this however is done by committing the body over the paddle and so is not of great use on white water).

The Top Hand in the 'J' Stroke

Don't over-grip the handle or 'T' grip. As you reach the last part of the stroke, it is best to relax the grip of fingers and thumb and steer by pressing back with the palm. Over-gripping leads to a very awkward hand position in all 'J' strokes.

> ### Exercises
>
> *On a nice calm day and with plenty of room, use the 'J' stroke to make a gentle turn to the on side. Much easier to learn to use the 'J' in a gentle turn, rather than trying to go straight.*
>
> *If conditions are easy, the bow paddler can face the stern and, once the canoe is moving, stop paddling. This enables the stern paddler to get the feel of the 'J' without any distractions. The bow paddler can even offer advice!*
>
> *On a windy day learn the new stroke whilst going downwind.*

The 'J' Stroke Family

It is sometimes easy to see the differences between strokes, but here the divisions become more and more artificial. Each has the 'J' stroke as a basis or as part of the whole. Often the paddler is swapping between different 'J's to perform a manoeuvre. Each has distinct advantages and disadvantages. Accomplished canoeists will have them all as part of their repertoire. Whether you are doing 'J', 'Knifed J', 'C Stroke' or 'Indian Stroke', they all have this basic 'J' Stroke element.

The 'C' Stroke

This is one of the key strokes. It gives a smooth turn and gets the paddle under the canoe. This is in fact another 'sweep' type stroke with a key difference: in the 'C' stroke the arc starts out from the front of the canoe, sweeps under the canoe and continues out on its arc from the back of the canoe.

In solo canoes it can be used as a means of turning the canoe to the on side, or as a means of starting the canoe in a straight line without yawing.

For solo:

- Start a little way out from the bow.
- Indicator thumb will be down throughout the manoeuvre.
- The drive face will be used throughout.
- Sweep the blade in on an arc that continues under the canoe.
- Keep the arc going and it should reappear at the stern, with the blade still effectively in a very steep long 'J'.
- Power should be kept on the blade throughout.

Photos 5.13a-b   Blade going under canoe and emerging in 'J' position, the smooth combination giving the 'C' Shape

- This is not a stroke with phases; it should be one fluent arc, a clear 'C' shape.

Exercises

Try from stationary to get the solo canoe running in a straight line with a single 'C' stroke before continuing with a 'J'.

Exercises

Again solo, try a whole series of gentle 'C' strokes to keep the canoe running in a gentle turn to the on side.

For tandem:

- Performed by the bow paddler, only the first half of the stroke is done and then it is cut out to the side.

Indian Stroke

A most elegant stroke! Learning this gives a real fluency to your use of the blade. It gives good control at all times and is useful in eddies on the river, pulling the canoe into a turn during gusty weather or enabling you to move in perfect silence across the water. It is worth learning this stroke in two stages.

First Stage:

- Paddle the canoe along slowly and in a straight line.
- Perform a long 'J' with a very steep blade angle. Blade should be up on edge and vertical. Hold this position for a couple of seconds.
- Indicator thumb is down at this stage. Without moving the paddle, swap the top hand around so that the thumb is on top.
- Slash the blade forward to the front of the canoe. Turn the blade in for another power stroke. Do not switch the top hand around.
- Having used one side of the blade for the last power stroke, you should now be using the other face for this power stroke. On each stroke you alternate blade faces.

Second Stage:

- Everything as before except where and how you swap the top hand.
- Hold the 'J' stroke for a second or two and hold the top hand with thumb still down. It is however easiest if the top hand fingers and thumb are released from the paddle, and steering achieved with palm pressure.
- Begin the slash forwards and simultaneously roll the hand, so that the grip is switched on the way forwards, rather than at the back of the canoe. This is known as a palm roll. As before, the new power stroke is done with the alternate blade face.

This stroke can be done powerfully to control the canoe or slowly to achieve a silent stroke. By slashing the blade outwards and forwards on its return, a powerful turning stroke is achieved, but more on that in combining strokes below.

Exercises

If the conditions are easy try this stroke with the eyes closed. Do everything very slowly to get the feel of the stroke. (Either have a spotter to stop you hitting things or only do short distances!) Paddling with the eyes closed increases your dependence on feel and strokes can smooth out quicker.

Knifed 'J'

Another elegant stroke. Many paddlers develop this variant quite naturally after months or years of using the long 'J'.

- The blade is swept back to a very shallow angled 'J' stroke.
- The blade stays in the water at this shallow angle with the leading edge still down.
- The blade is brought forwards with the leading edge still down, so effectively lifting water without breaking the surface. Steering is partially achieved at the back and partially on this move forward.

Photo 5.14   Knifed 'J' with blade knifing back through the water

- The lifting action is achieved by either lifting with the bottom hand or by levering up off the gunwale.
- As soon as enough steering has been achieved, the angle is relaxed and the blade jumps to the surface.

Combinations

We spend so much time splitting strokes up, so here is one of the really satisfying combinations for the solo canoeist. Done well, it is fluent and smooth. The canoe is kept on a turn without stalling.

- Get the canoe up to a good speed in a straight line. Lean the canoe over to the on side.
- Initiate a gentle turn to the on side with a long 'J'.
- Throw in a bow rudder (bow cut). Do not open the blade too far. Do not stall the canoe.
- As power dies on the blade, sweep the blade in and under the canoe in a 'C' stroke.
- As always the blade should come out at the back as a long 'J'. Hold the 'J' for a brief moment. Do not push it out far, as it will stall the boat.
- Palm roll the top hand and slash the blade forwards through the water to the bow rudder position (in reality an Indian stroke).
- Repeat the sequence. Because of the palm roll you have swapped blade faces, and are starting the pull into the 'C' stroke with what was the back face of the blade on the initial stroke.

This manoeuvre gives us a much more holistic approach to strokes. No longer are they distinct entities but each blends smoothly into the next to make a continuous whole.

Cross-deck Forward Paddling

Without swapping hands, the paddle is brought across the canoe and the same drive face is used. The body is leant forward and short quick strokes are done well forward. The stroke terminates before it reaches the hips. By quickly rotating the blade so that it is parallel to the canoe, it can be slashed back to the front to start another cross-deck power stroke. Indicator thumb will be pointing towards the bow during the slash forward. The blade does not exit the water.

Very often this stroke is done to apply power after using a cross-deck bow rudder and it is well worth practising this combination.

Bow Rudders and Pries

Bow Rudder (Bow Cut) in a Tandem Canoe

The bow rudder is easiest learnt in the bow of a tandem canoe, so this is dealt with first. This is a powerful turning stroke done on the move. The canoe needs good forward speed.

The stern paddler initiates a turn towards the bow paddler's on side. As the turn starts, the bow paddler does the following:

- The upper body is turned strongly to the side the bow rudder is done on. It helps if you look in the direction you wish to turn.

- The upper hand is pushed out over the side of the canoe and stays there.

- The drive face of the blade is facing towards the side of the canoe.

- The blade is best placed to slice through the water before being opened (leading edge turned away from the canoe). The amount the blade is opened will depend on the pressure you can withstand and the amount of turn needed.

- The lower arm is kept flexed to give a strong position.

While this is happening up front, the stern paddler can use a brace for support or to turn and slow the canoe.

Bow Rudder in a Solo Canoe

Very much as above but with the turn initiated with a rudder or 'J' stroke. The solo paddler will need to place the blade a little further forward to help the turning effect.

Photo 5.15   Solo bow rudder

Cross-deck Bow Rudder

Very much the same effect as above, but done on the paddler's off side. The turn must be initiated to the solo or bow paddler's off side. The paddle is swung across to the off side with the indicator thumb pointing up. This means that, once across the canoe, the drive face will be towards the boat.

Again it is best if the blade is placed in the water to slice, and then opened away from the canoe to cause a turn towards the blade.

Photo 5.16   Cross-deck bow rudder

As the pressure dies on the blade, it can either be turned into a series of cross-bow draws or pulled in and then power applied in a cross-deck forward paddling sequence.

Hanging Draw in a Solo Canoe

This is a dynamic stroke done on the move to cause a sideways shift while maintaining forward movement.

- The canoe needs forward speed.

- The position is as for the bow rudder but done alongside the paddler. It is very important that the chest is twisted to the paddle side so as to keep the arms in a strong position.

- The blade is sliced and then the leading edge opened away from the canoe.

- A sideways movement should start. If necessary move the blade backwards or forwards to keep the boat running straight.

Photo 5.17   Hanging draw

The same stroke can be done cross-deck, in which case it is very important to move the knees to the off side and rotate the chest to give a strong position.

Bow Jam in a Tandem Canoe

This is a dynamic (and bold) stroke done on the move. It causes a powerful turn away from the bow paddler's on side. The turn should be initiated by the stern paddler towards their own paddle side. Once the turn has started the bow paddler does the following:

- The blade is placed against the side of the canoe, slightly forward of the bow paddler's position but with the tip of the blade still above the water.

- The drive face is against the side of the canoe.

- The blade is slid down the side of the canoe and under the boat.

- Hang on!

Photo 5.18   Bow jam

The turn is so powerful that the stern paddler needs to be low and with a brace on his/her own paddle side to provide stability.

Running Pry Solo

Very similar to the above but used to side-slip a moving canoe away from the paddle. The stroke is done just in front of the body and the paddle is held against the side of the canoe. The paddle is rotated so that the rear edge of the blade is further away from the canoe (the opposite of the hanging draw). If necessary the paddle is adjusted forwards or back to counter any turn.

Exercises

Side-slip a moving tandem canoe.

In many respects it is easier to side-slip a moving tandem canoe than a solo one. The idea is to go from travelling forward in a straight line to travelling forward and sideways. It is satisfying and...

...slick when done well. It depends on stroke combinations, the action of the bow paddler being matched by the stern.

To get you started, one combination would have the bow paddler doing a hanging draw and the stern paddler holding a stern rudder in place while the boat is moving forward.

You should be able to come up with several combinations to side-slip the canoe. It does help if the bow paddler puts his/her stroke in fractionally before the stern does.

Try travelling parallel to a bank or jetty and make a very posey landing by side-slipping the canoe.

Use the side-slip to move around buoys or posts.

Reverse Strokes

When learning these manoeuvres it is far easier if the boat is stern light. With a stern heavy canoe the back will dig in and push off-line, making steering a nightmare. In tandem the stern paddler can move forward to un-weight the stern, and in solo you can move over the mid-point of the canoe.

Tandem crews can remain on their own side of the canoe and in the simplest case, reverse paddle using the back face of the blade. However, like the solo paddler they may need other strokes to steer.

This is easy on the on side.

Solo Using Cross-deck Strokes

Control and speed are obtained by paddling backwards on both sides of the canoe. On the on side things are easy. Simply paddle backwards using the back face of the blade. It is on the cross-deck stroke that things feel strange initially.

- Knees are shifted to point slightly towards the off side allowing the body to rotate more easily.

- The paddle is swung across the canoe, the chest rotated strongly to the off side. It helps to look at the stern at this moment.

- Reach back with the paddle, and at this point the rotation of body and paddle should end with the drive face of the blade facing the bow of the canoe.

- By unwinding the trunk the blade is pulled powerfully towards the bow.

- A 'normal' reverse stroke is then done on the on side.

Photo 5.19 Lots of chest/torso rotation

For the solo paddler this is a very powerful way of slowing or reversing a canoe.

Reverse 'J'

This stroke allows the solo paddler to reverse under control whilst paddling on one side only. The reverse 'J' is also used by the bow paddler in tandems.

- A reverse stroke is made on the on side and then, as the blade passes the body, the indicator thumb turns down.
- As in the 'J' stroke the same face of the blade is used for power and control.
- The shaft is run along the gunwale for the last part of the stroke.
- The outward turn of the blade is achieved by levering off the gunwale. The work is done by the top hand and not by pushing with the bottom one.
- The bottom hand is opened to allow the paddle shaft to be angled further forward.

Photo 5.20 Reverse 'J'

Far Back Stroke

A powerful reverse or slowing stroke, this utilises the powerful trunk rather than arm muscles.

- On the on side rotate the upper body and head to face the stern.
- Reach back with the paddle towards the stern. In doing so the drive face should now face the bow of the canoe.
- Pull the blade back towards bow. The effective part of this stroke is done before it reaches the hip.
- The blade can be rotated and slashed back towards the stern for another 'far back stroke'.

Photo 5.21 Far back stroke

An alternative way of finishing this stroke gives an even more powerful combination (combined back water stroke). After doing the initial part of the stroke, flip the paddle over to continue with a normal on side reverse stroke using the back face of the blade.

Support Strokes and Braces

Exercises

Stand in the water next to an empty canoe. Tip it on to its edge. Let go. Most open canoes automatically fall back upright. The 'kayak' low brace, when used in a canoe leaves the body outside the gunwales. When the boat is steeply on edge, this causes the final capsize. To be effective in a canoe, the low brace support must transfer the weight back between the gunwales.

Whilst kneeling try rocking the canoe by transferring weight from one knee to the other. Try to keep your weight between the gunwales.

The Low Support

To start with you must be 'locked' into the canoe. This may be as simple as to be kneeling with your feet hooked under the seat or using kneeling thwarts and thigh braces.

Tip the canoe. Let the paddle blade hit the water at right angles to the boat. Now for the first critical difference; drop the head right down to the paddle shaft. Like the paddle, the head and shoulders are out at an angle to the canoe, your eyes looking straight down to the bottom of the lake. Don't press down on the paddle but bring the paddle, head and upper body straight back across the canoe. Your nose should just miss the first gunwale and carry on all the way across to the other. It is important that the paddle does come back across at the same time as your body. Once this motion is under way avoid the temptation to press on the blade. At some point your face will be just above the shaft of the paddle on one side of the gunwale and the blade the other side. Pressing the blade down at this moment is not a good idea.

The dropping of the head to the shaft and water, followed by the move back across the gunwales is critical. Keep your head and body low. Only come upright once the canoe has levelled.

Photos 5.22a-b   The low support

The High Support

This has absolutely nothing to do with the kayak high brace! This stroke is used when you are falling away from the paddle. Reach for the water and do a fast draw stroke. This pulls your body back between the gunwales. The weight transfers from the off side knee to the paddle side knee and the canoe hopefully rights itself.

Photo 5.23   The high support

This stroke can be used very effectively as a static stroke whilst people are side-surfing small stoppers. A limit is quickly reached when you can no longer reach the water over the hull of the canoe; it is then swim time.

Towing

In a canoe there is no necessity ever to use a tow system that attaches to the body. Either a separate rope can be used, or better still, a painter (bow line) from the towed canoe.

The rope is brought into the towing canoe and then:

1. The rope is wrapped once or twice around a thwart, and a knee or foot placed on the end of the rope. Release is done by removing the knee or foot.

2. The alternative is to use a releasable knot on the thwart. A clove hitch with a bight of rope pushed through enables a simple pull to release even when under load.

Photo 5.24   Towing using a turn around the thwart, with the knee on the free end

Any tow system must be releasable under tension.

Gunwale Bobbing:

A good wet game to finish with.

- Try standing with both feet on the gunwales towards the back of the canoe. Gently flex the knees and, as the canoe starts bobbing, bob in time with it. Some people can achieve impressive forward speed by this method! (Do make sure there are no obstructions to hit and, if doing it in a group, it may be worth putting a helmet on).

- For the less bold this does work whilst stood on the floor of the canoe.

- Some do it tandem.

Photo 5.25   Gunwale bobbing

Above all, remember this:

"If you're not having fun, you're probably not learning."

Further Reading

History

Company of Adventurers, P. Newman, 1985, Penguin Books Canada, 0-14-010139-X
Caesars of the Wilderness, P. Newman, 1987, Penguin Books Canada, 0-14-008630-7
Building a Birchbark Canoe, D. Gidmark, 1994, USA, Stackpole Books, 0-8117-2504-9

Technique

Path of the Paddle, Bill Mason, 1984, Van Nostrand Reinhold Ltd., Toronto, 0-904405-18-4
Paddle your own Canoe, G. & J. McGuffin, 1999, Boston Mills Press, Ontario, 1-55046-214 8
Canoeing, a Trailside Guide, G. Grant, 1997, W.W. Norton, New York, ISBN: 0-393-31489-8
Canoeing and Kayaking, L. Guillion, 1987, Menasha Ridge Press, Alabama, 0-89732-136-7
Open Canoe Technique, N. Foster, 1996, Fernhurst Books, Arundel, ISBN: 1-898660-26-3

Videos

Path of the Paddle, Solo Basic and Double Basic by Bill Mason
Solo Playboating by Kent Ford (in ww specialist canoes but very useful for stroke technique)

Websites:

www.acanet.org - American Canoe Association
www.crca.ca - Canadian Recreational Canoeing Association
www.wilds.mb.ca/redcanoe/books.html - Bill Mason Books
www.canoemuseum.net - The Canoe Museum
www.civilizations.ca/index.asp - Civilization Museum (Canada)

Ray Goodwin

Ray Goodwin has paddled throughout Europe, North America, and Nepal. His British canoe trips include: the Circumnavigation of Wales, the Irish Sea Crossing, a North to South Crossing of the Scottish Highlands and a trip from the Outer Hebrides to the East Coast of Scotland.

Ray is a BCU Level 5 Coach in Canoe, Inland Kayak and Sea as well as holding a Mountain Instructor's Certificate. He has gained a considerable reputation as a Coach running his own business, Ray Goodwin Coaching.

6 Safety and Leadership

Guidelines are … "for the blind obedience of fools and the guidance of the wise". Below are some simple guidelines which help us stay safe. With experience we will learn when it is safe or even necessary to ignore them. The novice is best advised to stick to them for now.

- *Don't paddle alone.*
- *Wear a buoyancy aid.*
- *If head injuries are a significant risk, wear a helmet.*
- *Let someone know what your plans are.*
- *Check weather forecasts, and if appropriate, water levels or tides.*
- *Stay flexible; be prepared to change your plans.*
- *Be a 'team player,' put the best interest of the group first.*

Introduction

Safety affects all of us. Nobody wants to get injured, but going into the outdoors, paddling and facing dangers (real or apparent) makes it an adventure experience. It is very difficult to take away all of the dangers or hazards. Being exposed to risk is an inherent part of paddlesport; what we have to do is decide what level of risk we are prepared to accept, and then manage it.

Safety is also about the leader and the expectations made of that person. We would expect that person to be reliable, to be someone in whom we

feel confident when they are leading us or managing the risks we face. We must feel sure that they will take the precautions needed to make the paddle safe, but interesting and exciting. The leader must be trustworthy.

Why Do You Participate?

Consider why you paddle. What are you trying to achieve from the experience? Why do you coach or lead others? Are you trying replicate your previous experiences for them? Why sacrifice personal paddling time for other people? Is it money, ego, or have you been drawn into a coaching situation almost by accident.

The point here is that why we do certain things will often define how we do things. Therefore, before we can look at how to take care of ourselves or lead a group safely we must question in our own minds why we paddle or coach.

Exercise

Take a few moments to write down your responses to the half dozen questions I have just raised. This exercise is personal to you, so be honest.

People take part in paddlesport for many different reasons. It could be the physical challenge of the race, pitching our skills against a rapid, or learning new and exciting moves on waves. For others it is the social world that paddlesport takes us into, meeting new friends with 'après canoe' being a very important part of the fun.

Leaders versus Groups

Does your reason for being a paddler and your approach to paddling match that of the people you coach or lead?

As coaches or leaders, we need to appreciate why other people paddle, if we want to service the needs of the people we lead.

- What are the expectations of the people you lead?
- What is it that they want from you?

For the parents of the child, it is to have a reliable, trustworthy person who has the technical knowledge and the experience to be able to make appropriate decisions throughout the day. For the child, it is about trusting you to bring them back unharmed, after giving an exciting, fun-filled day. For a centre manager, the expectations would be to work within guidelines and give the customer value for money. We need to be able to fulfil all of these roles.

How Do Others Perceive Your Role?

Do they look for authoritative leadership, or just someone who knows how to manage the day without being at the front of the group shouting? They may simply see you as a solid paddler who they can rely on to 'sort things out' when they go wrong.

A State of Mind

Being a safe paddler is about managing risks in all the different environments we face. It's about weighing up the risks against the benefits gained from the experience. Do the benefits outweigh the risks? If not, what control measures can we introduce to manage the risk? When we have learnt to do this consistently and we are able to manage risk in a dynamic (continuous) manner, then we will be getting closer to finding the right balance for everyone.

Evaluating Your Performance

How do we know if we are making the right decisions? Are we so safe the session is dull or have we taken our students past their adventure frontier and into misadventure? How do we know when we are right? Training courses can only give you the basics, the techniques and some procedures. From there you will need to train, practise, work alongside other coaches and paddlers. You will need to analyse your performance and learn from your experiences. Making skilful judgements is about using the right technique or system at the right time and in the right place.

Technique + experience + being dynamic = skilful judgements

Environmental Hazards

This section is reproduced from 'White Water Safety and Rescue' with the kind permission of the author and publishers.

Sudden Immersion

In very cold water this can stop a paddler from thinking clearly and reacting. Prevention is simply a case of wearing a foam-lined helmet or a neoprene skullcap under your helmet and suitable protective clothing (see Chapter 3).

Another effect is a form of hyperventilation. The cold causes people to keep trying to breathe in and feeling unable to breathe out. With habituation cold water immersion is less likely to have this effect. Some raft guides brief their clients to counter this by shouting as loud as they can when they surface. This has the effect of expelling air from their lungs as well as attracting the raft guide's attention.

Hypothermia

Hypothermia is a condition brought about by a lowering of the body's core temperature, which can ultimately result in death. It is caused by a person being unable to generate enough heat to counteract the effects of cold due to exhaustion, or, more commonly with boaters, through the rapid lowering of the core temperature caused by immersion in cold water.

... *'even in its mildest form, hypothermia can drastically affect a person's judgment.'*

Being mammals, humans need to maintain the vital organs of the body at a constant 37 degrees Celsius. The critical thing about hypothermia is that even in the early stages, in its mildest form, it can drastically affect a person's judgment. Therefore if you are feeling very cold, you should take remedial action or get off the river before you start making dangerous mistakes.

Prevention

Once again, the emphasis should be very much on prevention.

1. Avoid taking long swims by careful scouting, thorough assessment of the risks involved and skilful paddling.

2. Maintain a suitable level of personal fitness.

3. Eat well before and during a river trip. Complex carbohydrates such as rice, pasta, bread, cereals provide energy in a form that is made available to your body at a steady rate and over several hours.

4. Wear suitable clothing for the conditions and type of paddling.

5. 'Buddy' up and keep an eye on each other for the early signs of hypothermia.

6. Be prepared to shorten or abort a trip if members of the party show signs of getting too cold.

7. If one member of the party is suffering from hypothermia, there is a good chance that the conditions that affected them are affecting everyone else. Therefore action should be taken to protect the team as well as treat the victim.

Signs and Symptoms

The good news about immersion hypothermia is that if someone takes a long swim in glacial melt water it is obvious that we should suspect its onset. Unfortunately exhaustion hypothermia can easily go unnoticed in its early stages. Paddlers can fall prey to either form or a mixture of both. Therefore, whenever we paddle in cold conditions or someone goes for a swim in cold water it is important to look out for the signs and symptoms.

In a hospital, doctors would take a core temperature. This involves the use of a rectal thermometer which is not very practical on the river bank and would probably result in the first aider being assaulted by the victim! The signs and symptoms are what matter. The figures in brackets indicate the core temperature at which they normally occur. Note that a victim may not exhibit all of the signs and the order they appear in may vary slightly. (Normal = 37 degrees C)

Early warning :

- Feeling cold and tired   (35ºC)
- Numbness of hands or feet
- Blue lips
- Intermittent shivering

In an alert group of boaters who work as an effective team, hypothermia would rarely be able to progress beyond this stage unnoticed or untreated.

Serious :

- Continuous shivering
- Unusual, uncharacteristic behaviour   (34ºC)
- Physical and mental lethargy
- Slurring of speech
- Violent outbursts of unexpected energy
- Lack of muscular coordination
- Failure or abnormality of vision

Deep hypothermia :

- Shivering stops, lowered conscious level (33ºC)
- Limbs stiffen up   (32ºC)
- Victim drifts into deep unconsciousness   (31ºC)
- Pulse irregular   (29ºC)
- Unconsciousness, coma, death   (24ºC)

Treatment

In the case of immersion hypothermia, the body hasn't depleted its energy reserves. This means that victims will respond more quickly to treatment and are more likely to make a complete recovery. The field treatment for both types of hypothermia is essentially the same, except that if exhaustion hypothermia is suspected, one should assume that victims are unfit to continue, even if they appear to have made a full recovery. If remoteness means that the easiest way to evacuate them is to continue paddling, they should be made to rest and eat for as long as is practicable before setting off.

Early Stages

- *Prevent further use of energy* - Exercise will draw warm blood away from the core where it is needed and use up energy reserves which the body needs to generate heat for the core.

- *Prevent further heat loss* - Provide shelter from wind and rain. Put extra clothing on victims. Put them in a bivvi-bag, (a two by one metre plastic bag). If available put them in a sleeping bag. Be aware that the insulation in a sleeping bag keeps heat out as effectively as it keeps heat in. Therefore it is best to put a warm-bodied person in with the victim.

- *Slowly reheat victims* - This is best achieved by providing an environment in which they are breathing warm moist air. In this way they are rewarmed from the inside. In a house this can be achieved by sitting them down in a steam filled bathroom heated to 40ºC. In a hut or tent, heat and humidity can be provided by boiling a pot of water on a stove, being careful not to knock it over and burn the victims. On the river bank the most effective way is to get all the members of the party in a 'group shelter', (Photo 3.20). Once inside everybody's body heat and breath soon provides a warm moist environment. This has the added bonus of ensuring nobody else develops hypothermia as well as rewarming the victims.

- *Encourage the victims to eat* - Give them food that will rapidly provide energy with which the body can generate heat; glucose and sugars, (simple carbohydrates).

Serious Hypothermia

As for early stages plus:

- *Seek hospital treatment* - even if the victim appears to make a full recovery.

- *Stretcher evacuation* - unless the victim appears to make a full recovery he should be evacuated on a stretcher and not permitted to use energy by walking or paddling.

Some Don'ts

- Do not rub victims

- Do not place warm objects on the victims' bodies

- Do not give the victims alcohol

The body's natural defence involves shutting off circulation to the limbs and surface blood vessels. This ensures that warm blood is retained in the core where it is needed and cold surface blood isn't allowed to cool the core further. All of the above 'treatments' have the opposite detrimental effect.

Sunshine

It is sometimes hard to believe this is a problem in Britain. Paddlers in sunnier climes are well aware of the potential damage.

Hyperthermia

Hyperthermia is caused by the body overheating and can be divided into two distinct stages.

Heat exhaustion is caused when the body overheats, and having lost too much water and salt through sweating, is struggling to maintain a normal body temperature.

Untreated it can lead to heat stroke. This occurs when the body is no longer able to sweat and the body's temperature rises unchecked. This condition can become life threatening.

Prevention

Prevention is simple, In warm climates drink plenty of water; don't put your wet suit on until just before getting on the water and have rest/lunch breaks in the shade. On white water stretches the constant splashing with cold water keeps paddlers cool. On long flat stretches it may be necessary to splash oneself or roll from time to time.

Heat Exhaustion - Signs and Symptoms

- Feeling unwell, headache, dizziness, nausea, cramps

- Weakness

- Moist skin

Treatment

- Remove to cool area.
- Give fluids.

Beware! Although not in itself a serious condition it will progress to heat stroke if the casualty is not removed from the source of heat.

Heat Stroke – Signs and Symptoms

- Confusion/loss of consciousness
- Skin hot and dry
- High temperature

Treatment

- Reduce temperature by removing to cool area.
- Bathe with tepid water. (Drenching them with very cold water could cause heart failure).
- Fan the casualty.
- Seek urgent medical attention.
- If the casualty is unconscious, place in the recovery position.

Dehydration

Peeling off layers of paddling clothing is very inconvenient. It is therefore tempting to drink as little as possible to avoid having to go to the toilet. This is a great mistake both in terms of the risk of hyper and hypothermia and in terms of reduced performance. Paddlers should drink frequently in hot and cold climates.

Sunburn

British paddlers abroad are particularly prone. They are so used to paddling in the rain at home they don't realise how quickly and badly they can burn.

Prevention

- Avoid the noon day sun and rest in the shade whenever possible.
- Wear long-sleeved garments and sun hats that protect the ears and neck.
- Use waterproof sun block creams on all exposed skin and apply frequently.

Treatment

- Cool affected area by bathing in cool water for 10 minutes.
- Prevent infection by not bursting any blisters and covering any that have burst with a sterile dressing.
- Prevent any further exposure to direct sunlight.
- Ensure that the victim drinks plenty of fluids.
- If the sunburn is severe and covers an extensive surface area, medical attention should be sought.

Eye Damage

Sun reflected off water can cause eye damage in the same way as sunlight reflected off snow. In the short-term this can cause extreme discomfort and in extreme cases temporary blindness. In the long term the accumulated permanent damage can lead to cataracts and other forms of eye damage.

Prevention

- Wear sunglasses and peaked hats.

Signs and Symptoms

- Headaches
- Tears
- Gritty, painful eyes

Treatment

- Rest in a dark room and seek medical treatment.

Aural Osteomata

This is also known as 'swimmer's ear' or 'surfer's ear'. Subjecting one's ears to frequent incursions of cold water causes bony growths to develop, which narrow the ear passage. Eventually this causes frequent ear infections and even deafness.

One method of prevention is to wear ear plugs. Even with the ear plugs in place, one can still hear well enough for normal river communication. It is also a good idea to tape up the ear-holes on your helmet during the colder months.

Some manufacturers now make very thin neoprene or lycra skull caps that fit easily under a helmet to cover one's ears and are designed to prevent surfer's ear.

Polluted Water

On our crowded planet it is a fact of life that many white water rivers or sites are polluted to some degree. Rivers that are heavily polluted with industrial effluent are out of the question, but many less polluted rivers are paddled regularly. In 'developed' countries where sewage is treated, the risk of getting a viral infection is least in the warm summer months when water levels are low. This is because the 'bugs' used in the treatment plants to break down the sewage are at their most efficient in the warm months.

Periods of higher flows are higher risk, summer or winter, because accumulated rubbish is washed out of storm drains and high flows of water can cause the treatment tanks of sewage plants to overflow. This means that untreated or partially treated sewage gets into the river.

In poorer countries, the disposal of rubbish and faeces, and in some places, the bodies of those too poor to afford a funeral pyre, take place on the river bank. This is deliberately done above the normal high water mark. This means that the water is as clean as it can be for most of the year. In the monsoon all this detritus is swept downstream to fertilise the plains. During the early part of the monsoon almost everyone, canoeists and locals, are ill with some form of stomach bug.

Prevention

- Avoid paddling polluted rivers in periods of high flow.

- Remove wet clothing and wash hands and face in clean water, or better still, take a shower before eating or drinking.

When paddling in countries where the water is untreated:

- Treat your drinking water. Either use one of the commercial systems where you pump through a filter that also adds iodine at the required dose or add two drops, (more if the water is heavily polluted), of tincture of iodine, (available from any chemist) and leave to stand for an hour before drinking. (Note that chlorine-based water purifying tablets will not kill the cysts that transmit amoebic dysentery).

- Only eat food that has been thoroughly cooked and is still hot.

- Don't take milk in tea or coffee unless it has been boiled.

- Don't eat locally made ice cream or items such as salads which have probably been washed in polluted water.

Note

Although safe in small quantities, iodine is a poison that builds up in the thyroid gland. Therefore if you are going abroad for an extended period it may not be a suitable solution.

Leptospirosis or Weil's Disease

This is a potentially serious disease that is transmitted when rats' urine is washed into water courses. The main symptoms are very much like those of flu. Weil's Disease is not very common and is usually associated with sewage workers. This means that many doctors in general practice are unlikely to suspect it.

It is just as prevalent among paddlers as sewage workers. Therefore if you suspect you may have it, you may have to insist that they send off a sample of blood for testing urgently. If undiagnosed and untreated, Weil's disease can be fatal.

Drowning

In a water environment we are more likely to have to intervene in a drowning situation. To be technically correct, drowning is what occurs if the victim doesn't survive. If the victim does survive, the medical term for what occurs is 'near drowning'. The reason why many people do survive near drownings is that the human body is capable of a number of remarkable 'reflexes'.

Dry Drowning

The vast majority of both drowning and near drowning victims have little water in their lungs. In a last desperate attempt to survive, the human body will cause muscles in the throat to spasm and block the airway. The victims do not so much drown as suffocate. Blowing air into the victim's lungs, (rescue breathing), will of itself open the casualty's air passage.

Water in the Stomach

Due to the effects of dry drowning most of the water that the victim swallows goes into the stomach. During or after resuscitation, rescuers should not attempt to squeeze or in any other way force the water out. The danger is that this water is accidentally aspirated into the lungs.

Mammalian Diving Reflex (MDR)

This reflex usually occurs in very cold water and mostly affects children and fit young adults. As well as the throat constricting, the victim's heartbeat slows down to an imperceptible one beat a minute or less. The majority of the cardiovascular system is shut down and what little oxygen there is in the bloodstream is diverted to the vital organs, in particular the brain.

The norm is that permanent brain damage occurs to the brain after the casualty has stopped breathing for four minutes. There have been rare instances of people who have been submerged in icy water for three hours, being resuscitated and making a complete recovery. The norm is to assume that a person submerged in cold water has a chance of survival for up to one hour.

Secondary Drowning

Anyone who has been the victim of a near drowning must be admitted to hospital for tests and observation as soon as possible. This is the case even if the victim feels fine and is convinced that he has fully recovered.

The human body deals with any water that does get into the lungs by absorbing it into the bloodstream. This leads to dangerous, often lethal complications, chief amongst which are:

1. Chemical imbalances in the bloodstream which can cause vital organs to malfunction.

2. Water seeping back into the lungs, (usually while the victim is asleep).

3. Swelling and subsequent blocking of the air passages caused by the lung tissue being irritated by water.

4. The possibility of pneumonia developing extremely rapidly, (it can happen in two hours!)

Resuscitation

The information here is a useful reminder of what to do. However there is no substitute for learning and practising resuscitation skills on a first aid course.

Basic Life Support Protocol

As always the first priority is to assess for danger. That done the victim's level of consciousness is assessed. Anyone dealing with an unconscious casualty, whatever the cause, should clear and open the victim's airway, (see Mouth to Mouth ventilation stage 1 and 2), and check for breathing. It is suggested that the first aider should look, listen and

feel for ten seconds before deciding that breathing is absent.

One Rescuer

The protocol is complicated by the fact that there is a different procedure for victims of drowning or trauma than there is for suspected heart attack victims, (anyone who has stopped breathing for reasons other than drowning or traumatic accident). These differences only apply if the first aider is the only person who can go and summon help. The differences are:

Unconscious/Not Breathing - Drowning or Trauma

- Give 2 breaths

- Check for pulse or signs of circulation

Pulse Present:

- 10 breaths of rescue breathing

- Go for help

- Return and reassess

No Pulse:

- Give CPR for 1 minute (see page 92)

- Phone, radio, or go for help

- Return and reassess

Unconscious/Not Breathing - Other

- Phone, radio, or go for help

- Return and reassess

Multiple Rescuers

When there is more than one rescuer involved there is no need for decisions on when one should go for help. The first aider gets on with the resuscitation while someone else goes for help.

Rescue Breathing

When we breathe in and out at a normal rate we only use a small amount of the oxygen in each lung full of air. This leaves more than enough for the casualty's needs during rescue breathing. Breaths should be given at a rate of about ten per minute, (one every six seconds), and the pulse should be checked after every ten breaths.

Mouth to Mouth Ventilation

1. With the casualty lying flat on their back, if possible, look inside and remove any obvious obstructions from the casualty's mouth. Leave

well fitting dentures in place but remove any that are broken or displaced.

2. Open the airway by placing two fingers under the casualty's chin and lifting the jaw, while at the same time putting the fingers of the other hand on their forehead and tilting the head back. Take care to keep the neck in line if there is any reason to suspect injury to the cervical spine.

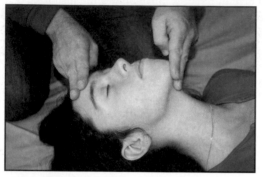

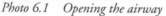
Photo 6.1   Opening the airway

3. Close the casualty's nose by pinching it between your finger and thumb. Take a full breath and place your lips around their mouth, making a good seal.

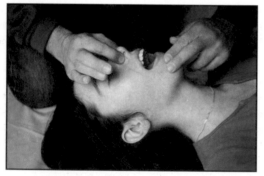

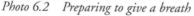
Photo 6.2   Preparing to give a breath

4. Blow slowly and steadily into the casualty's mouth until you see the chest rise. It should take about 2 seconds for a full inflation.

5. Remove your lips and allow the chest to fall fully.

Chest Does Not Rise

If you cannot get breaths into the casualty's lungs, check that:

- The casualty's head is tilted far enough back.
- You have remembered to pinch the casualty's nose.

- You have a firm seal around the casualty's mouth.
- The airway is not obstructed by blood, vomit or a foreign body.

Clearing Obstructions

These measures should only be taken if one is certain that there is an obstruction, because the other possible causes of the chest not rising have been eliminated. Providing the jaw is relaxed, open the casualty's mouth, and looking for the obstruction, carefully sweep a finger around inside the mouth. If this fails because there is a blockage in the throat, turn the victim on their side and slap him or her firmly between the shoulder blades. If after five slaps the obstruction has not shifted, turn the victim back on their back, kneel astride him and give up to five abdominal thrusts.

Put the heel of one hand below the ribcage, cover it with the other hand, then press sharply inwards and upwards. If this fails, alternate five slaps and five thrusts.

Face Shields

These consist of a simple sheet of plastic with a valve, through which the rescuer ventilates the casualty. The shield simply acts as a barrier. Although the risk of infection through contact with saliva is minute, contact with saliva, blood or vomit is far from pleasant. Face shields pack so small that it is feasible to carry one in a pocket.

The risk of infection through performing rescue breathing is negligible and rescuers who do not have a face shield should not hesitate to give help in this way.

Cardio Pulmonary Resuscitation (CPR)

Cardio Pulmonary Resuscitation consists of rescue breathing combined with chest compressions. The casualty is given two breaths of air to oxygenate the blood, followed by fifteen chest compressions to pump the oxygenated blood around the system so that it reaches the vital organs.

Chest Compression

Although more difficult, it is possible to perform rescue breathing with the casualty in a variety of positions. Chest compressions can only be performed effectively if the casualty is lying on their back on a firm surface. It is essential to remove the victim's buoyancy aid or the foam will absorb much of the pressure being exerted by the rescuer. It can also make it difficult to achieve a full release.

1. Kneel beside the casualty and using your index and middle finger find one of the lowest ribs. Slide your fingers along until you find the point where the lower ribs meet. Place your middle finger on this point and your index finger on the breastbone above.

2. Place the heel of your other hand on the casualty's chest and slide it down the breastbone until it reaches your index finger. This is the point at which pressure is applied.

3. Place the heel of your first hand on top of the other hand and interlock the fingers.

4. Lean over the casualty, and with your arms straight press down vertically to depress the breastbone about 4-5 centimetres, (2 inches). Release the pressure without removing your hands but ensuring that you allow the rib cage to fully expand, (this allows the heart to expand, sucking in more blood).

5. Repeat the compressions, aiming at a rate of about 100 compressions a minute.

Full CPR

1. Ventilations and compressions are combined at a ratio of 2 breaths to 15 compressions.

2. Check for breathing and pulse if and when the victim shows any sign of improvement, such as a more normal colour returning.

3. If more than one first aider is present, one should rest and one perform CPR, swapping over frequently. It is possible to work as a pair and work at a ratio of 1 breath to 5 compressions. However, coordination is difficult and it is no more effective.

Unconsciousness

People who are less than 'Alert' are deemed to be unconscious in terms of treatment. The main worry is that they cannot protect their own airway due to the loss of their choking reflex.

They should be placed in the Safe Airway Position. (Photo 6.3). From a medical standpoint, people who are less than completely conscious are in a state of unconsciousness. Forty per cent of unconscious victims who die might have been saved if their air-

ways had been protected. The SAP does this by putting casualties in a position that ensures they cannot swallow their own tongue and that any fluids drain out of their mouths rather than into the back of their throat.

Photo 6.3 Safe Airway Position

Ideally, casualties should be monitored at five minute intervals and the first aider ready to intervene with resuscitation at any time.

Key Points

1. Most victims who survive a near drowning still have a heartbeat.

2. If the throat has constricted, the act of opening the airway by removing any debris, tilting the head back and giving the first breath or two of rescue breathing is the action that is most likely to save the casualty's life.

If you are ever unlucky enough to come across a resuscitation situation, you must be mentally prepared for the fact that the odds are against the victim. This means that the odds are that the victim will die. If he or she does it will not be your fault! Anything you do will give a victim more of a chance than he or she would have otherwise had.

Practice

Like a good deal of first aid, it isn't what you know that saves lives, it's what you do. Rescue breathing and CPR are skills, and skills need to be practised if they are to remain effective. Keep your resuscitation skills up to date and organise 'top up sessions' using the practice mannequins.

'Keep your resuscitation skills up to date'

Risk Management

Risk assessments are an everyday occurrence both in the workplace and in the outdoors.

Their purpose is to identify potential hazards, calculate the risk and try to omit or reduce that risk to an acceptable level.

Generic Risk Assessment

Generic risk assessment is important because it formalises our thinking and gives consistency to the way an organisation works. The disadvantage of a generic risk assessment, written for everyone, is that it can become static and forgotten in practice. It may be read as prescribed by your supervisor but may not be used when you are working during a session.

Such risk assessments are useful for the inexperienced in managing the unexpected. They offer basic core principles, which can then be applied and adapted. They can encourage a more proactive approach to preparation, through training and equipment that might be carried.

Dynamic Risk Management

The ongoing assessments we make throughout the day or the session are referred to as 'the Dynamic Management of Risk'. This is done in addition to generic risk assessment. Dynamic risk assessment is a continuous process of identifying hazards. The risk is assessed and action taken to eliminate or reduce risk. In this way we are continually monitoring and reviewing the rapidly changing circumstances within paddlesport.

Leaders take clients, students or friends into *potentially* hazardous environments and situations. This is because they are prepared to accept reasonable levels of risk in order to provide an adventurous and interesting experience. Leaders must, however, seek to minimise the risk.

The 'Safe Person' Concept

In paddlesport we work and play in an inherently dangerous place. People go there for adventure and it's not always possible or desirable to take all the dangers away from the environment. The alternative is to direct our efforts into making the person (participant, coach, client or student) safe.

This approach is called the 'safe person concept'. It must be clearly understood that all leaders of what-

ever level have the authority, as well as the duty, to take immediate action in the interest of safety. This is a fundamental part of the safe person concept.

The Dynamic Management Process

Dynamic management process is the continuous assessment and control of risks in a rapidly changing environment. Each paddler should take on a degree of responsibility for their own and the rest of the party's well-being. However, the overall responsibility for this lies with the leader. The leader must ensure that safe practices are followed and that, so far as is reasonably practicable, risks are eliminated or reduced to the minimum. It should not be forgotten that leaders are also responsible for their own safety.

As the day progresses, you will need to gather information, evaluate situations and then apply your judgement to decide the most appropriate course of action. Hazards must be identified continually and the risk to all concerned considered. The benefits of proceeding with a task must be weighed carefully against the risks.

The consequences of a wrong decision in the initial stages of an incident may be irreversible.

Start making your decisions before the group arrive; think about the weather, water levels, level of paddler, game plan and the kit needed. What information is available? Has someone already done a generic risk assessment? Is there anyone from whom you could obtain some local knowledge?

Fig 6.1 Weighing the benefits against the risk

Fig 6.2   The domino theory

Although there are always time constraints on decision-making in emergencies, this should not be used as a reason for accepting the unacceptable.

If after implementing all available control measures, the potential cost of proceeding with a task still outweighs the benefits, *do not proceed*, but consider viable alternatives or introduce additional controls such as:

- Use of additional personal protective equipment
- Use of specialist knowledge
- Bank or boat support

Paddlers, and in particular leaders, need to manage safety by constantly monitoring the situation and reviewing the effectiveness of existing control measures. If additional control measures do not reduce the risk, *do not* proceed with the task!

How to Play Dominoes

Much work has been done about what causes accidents and it has been shown that injuries invariably result from a complicated sequence of factors, the last being the injury itself.

This is often referred to as the domino theory. The model above shows a series of factors leading up to the injury itself. These factors can be in any order.

This means that an accident can be prevented if you take action at any one of the stages of the sequence. If you are alert and using the dynamic approach to risk assessment, the odds are stacked in your favour. If you manage each of the factors in its own right and in relation to the other factors for the day, you should be able to break the domino effect.

Decision-making

Stress can adversely affect the quality of decision-making. Do we always recognise the signs of deterioration in the process?

Learning from the Event

Once you have dealt with the situation you should not become complacent; when does your responsibility for your companions, students or clients officially and morally finish? As the urgency of the situation diminishes you should start to record the information and perhaps pass it on to other leaders. If a review is to take place or feedback given, it should be completed as soon as possible after the activity and the situation is over. This could be formal (i.e. a staff meeting), or informal (i.e. comparing experiences over a mug of tea in the café).

Fig 6.3   Stress

Warm-up and Cool-down

Injury Reduction

Preparing the body for physical activity is an important part of your safety strategy. Risk of injury is increased by lack of pre-activity preparation or inappropriate exercises. It is, therefore, very important that you research and plan what you intend to do. Make sure your cardiovascular activities and stretches are based on current practice and that they are demonstrated and then carried out correctly.

The cool-down phase is often neglected or forgotten. This phase of physical activity is just as important as the warm-up as it will prevent post-exercise stiffness by flushing waste products from the circulatory system.

The Coach's Perspective

It is common for people to undertake a warm-up without prompting. If you observe unsupervised warm-ups taking place, you may need to step in and gain some control, as they may be carrying out unsafe practices. If they are injured doing these in your session, it could be argued that you were the person responsible for them at the time and did not give appropriate guidance.

As you assemble your group ready to warm-up, it is an appropriate time to ask them to consider if they have any medical conditions which will affect their participation in the activity. You must be sensitive to their privacy and point out that they may speak to you later and simply avoid any activity which may be harmful to them.

Warm-up / Cool-down summary

Warm-up

Activity:

- *Pulse raise* - Gentle jogging around the car park
- *Mobility* - e.g. Shoulder and arm circles
- *Short stretch* - e.g. Hamstrings, biceps and triceps

Aim:

- Prepare - Joints for work
- Prepare - Cardiovascular system by increasing temperature & blood flow
- Prepare - Neuromuscular response patterns
- Prevent - Muscle soreness and injury

Consider:

- Exercises must increase circulation in all body segments and major muscle groups.
- The exercises must gradually increase in intensity.
- The exercises must be specific and suitable to the individual.
- There must be no time lag between the warm-up and the next component.
- The time allowed must be flexible, taking into consideration temperature, the environment, and the fitness of the individual.
- *Never* stretch a cold body.

Cool-down

Aim:

- Assist circulatory system to remove substances that contribute to stiffness.
- Assist circulatory system to control venous return thereby preventing dizziness.
- Relaxation.

Must include:

- Mild rhythmic activity which gradually decreases.
- Exercises which promote return of blood from extremities to the heart.

Remember:

- The time allowed must be flexible taking consideration of the individual's fitness.
- Never stretch a cold body.

May include:

- If the body is still very warm - developmental stretches to aid suppleness/flexibility.

Performance Optimisation

Performance is optimised by completing a warm-up, whether you are preparing for competition, running a river or taking part in a basic skills session on the canal. This is because your brain and body are prepared for the specific tasks to be undertaken. Bodies are able to respond to the full range of movement that is demanded of the paddler and the brain's neuromuscular responses are prepared for action. To optimise performance, the warm-up must be appropriate to the activity being undertaken. This will lead you to consider if the warm-up should be land or water based.

Land versus Water Based Warm-up

The level of intensity of the warm-up must be sufficiently high to make you slightly out of breath but still be able to hold a conversation. To achieve this in a boat you need a reasonable amount of skill and technique. An easier way (for some people) of achieving the right level in a controllable manner is on the bank.

Experienced competitors or hardened river runners will be able to achieve the appropriate levels of intensity in a boat. However, you will find that many will still carry out a bank based routine. For the more experienced paddlers, the water phase of their warm-up is focused towards the specific activity they are about to undertake.

The level of intensity and time spent on warm-up will depend on the age, fitness level, environment temperature and type of session they are going to undertake.

Land Based Warm-up

For adults and the more serious paddlers, running on the spot or over a short distance in a safe area will work well. Try brisk walking, varying the pace and cadence.

The Coach's Perspective

If adults are embarrassed about bank side exercises try to find somewhere a little more discreet. People who take part in paddlesport are psychologically prepared for something new and different, so they will usually be receptive and enjoy playing some amusing games. This does not, however, give you the right to make fools of your students. Remember their self-esteem and dignity, and participate with them if you want to retain their respect for you during the session.

Water Based Warm-up

In order to achieve a reasonable level of intensity on the water, you or your students will need to be able to paddle fairly hard for a reasonable amount of time.

This type of water based/paddle warm-up can still have variety. Here are a few suggestions:

- Ten minutes paddling upstream, gradually building up the intensity.
- A gentle paddle followed by short sprints of 20 strokes, followed by 30 easy strokes; total time ten minutes.
- Ten minutes paddling with slow, then fast, then medium, then easy and so on, each of 10 strokes (similar to 'fartlek' training).
- Gentle paddle for 5 minutes followed by ten minutes of skill based, technique orientated activities, specific to the discipline (e.g. breaking in/out).

These are only suggestions and must be adapted to suit you and your discipline.

Group Warm-up Activities

These are only a few suggestions, you should expand to suit your needs. Here are a few ideas which are in current use:

Simon Says

- Find a safe flat area on which they can run around, with plenty of space.
- Set a simple course they have to follow you around; start slowly at walking pace and build gradually to jogging and then back down to a walk. Include actions that move the whole body, for example, 'reach for the sky', 'touch the floor', 'swim the rapid'.
- Use your imagination for these but remember this is to prepare for paddlesport, not the 100 metres Olympic final.
- The penalty for doing an activity 'without Simon saying so' could be something like making a silly noise.

Pass the Ball

- Find a safe area where, if the ball gets dropped, you are not going to have students running under a bus.
- Use a medium to large ball, which will make things easier for participation. Have them form a circle and get the circle moving around. Steady pace but gradually getting quicker.
- Use side steps first, get them to throw the ball across the circle to each other, change direction. You can use this as a name learning exercise if you wish, with students shouting their name first, then later the name of the person they are throwing to.
- Try getting them to run forwards in the circle and passing the ball over their head or bounce it on the ground for the one behind.

- Get them to run to the centre, put the ball down then shout the name of the person they want to fetch it. There are a number of variations with this, just use your imagination and be innovative.

Tag

Find a safe area and set the boundaries, warn them of any nearby hazards.

There are many variations on this theme, such as:

- Straight forwards tag - However students can only walk, i.e. have one foot on the ground at all times.

- Chain tag - Where the group starts at one end of the area, and on the whistle have to run past the tag person, to the other end. Once tagged, the two hold hands, they chain across and catch two more and so on. Best on grass.

- Stick in the mud - Once tagged you have to stand with your arms outspread and legs wide open. To be released and made free, you have to have someone who is *not* 'on', crawl through your legs. Game ends when all are 'on' or too tired to run.

Role-play Warm-up Games

For these games you will need to know a set of generic joint mobilising movements that you are familiar with, understand and feel confident to teach safely. You can then introduce each in turn in the form of a role-play exercise.

Shopping

- Find a flat safe area and identify the hazards in the area.

- Have the group form a circle and start them walking round. Tell them they are in their favourite shop (toy shop, supermarket). Issue them each with an imaginary trolley and start your way around the shop. Start off slowly and gradually build up the pace.

- Once warmed up you can introduce your stretches by reaching for items on the imaginary shelf, e.g. reach for the chocolate on the top shelf, the frozen peas which have fallen onto the floor, or turn round and reach the last play station 2 on the shelf behind you.

The Zoo

- As above and visit a zoo. Take the group

Fig 6.4a   Some commonly used land based stretches

around the zoo and meet and imitate all the different animals. This can be enhanced by silly animal noises, and the kids will make up the smells.

The Olympic Games

- As above but introduce as many different sports as you can imagine; e.g. throwing the javelin, swim the 50 metre front crawl final and don't forget the show jumping.

All these games are based around the same principle of gradually warming up joints and muscles and then you can introduce some short simple stretches.

Gentle Stretching

There are two forms of stretching:

1. Gentle stretching designed to prepare you to make full use of your *current* range of movement. This is the form we might use as part of our warm-up.

2. Full on stretching used to *increase* your flexibility. This should only take place when the body is thoroughly warmed up. It usually takes place *after* heavy exercise and in a warm environment. Best initially done under the supervision of an experienced trainer.

There are some very important rules to follow when undertaking any form of stretches. The coach should observe whether the technique is correct, and correct it if necessary.

They are:

- Never stretch a cold body.
- Never bounce into a stretch.
- Never push a stretch to the point where it becomes painful.
- Never throw a limb into a stretch, in a ballistic fashion.
- Only use current, safe stretches.
- Make sure the technique is correct.
- Recognise the difference between stretching and flexibility training.

You must give a great deal of thought to these components and are encouraged to attend a workshop on stretching and flexibility as provided by the BCU or Sports Coach UK. There are also a number of current publications which will be beneficial in furthering your knowledge in this area.

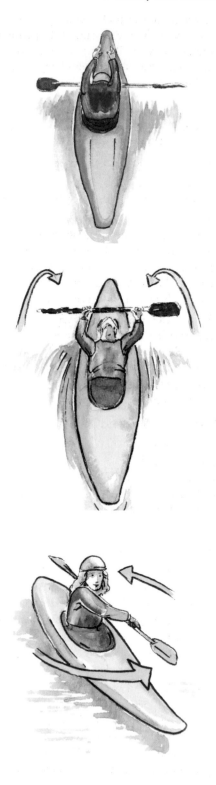

Fig 6.4b   Some commonly used boat based stretches

Manual Handling

As individuals we have an interest in taking care of our own body, preventing injury. Coaches have a moral obligation to their students to ensure they also remain uninjured. If you work as a coach your employers must adhere to the Manual Handling Operations Regulations 1992 (M.H.O. Regs), and take reasonable and practical measures to ensure you avoid manual handling operations that put you at risk from injuries. They must assess the hazardous operations and reduce the risk of injury to as low a level as practical. It is the coach's responsibility to apply those safe systems of work for their students.

Paddlesport is potentially hazardous. We must therefore look first at identifying the hazards and then offer some techniques to assist in reducing the risk of injury.

The Hazards

We encounter hazards long before we get on the water, when we put the boat on the roof of the car or lift it from the rack at the canoe club. We are lifting and carrying heavy weights, often over uneven, unstable, or slippery, wet ground.

Offering assistance to another paddler who has capsized, and performing a rescue of some description involves the possibility of injury especially to the lower back. When we have finished paddling, recovering, lifting and carrying our boat with tired muscles creates more opportunities for injury.

We could identify many scenarios in our everyday paddling which involves the risk of injury. If we have started to carry out an evaluation process we are part way to preventing the injury. A generic risk assessment at a centre may not include all of the possible scenarios. Those of us who paddle at a club or for ourselves will not even have the luxury of having someone identify the hazards for us. It is something we must do for ourselves on a daily basis. If you're not sure where to begin, you should utilise the training on offer through the BCU.

Once you have identified the manual handling hazards you can start to look to incorporate recognised techniques, which will offer some protection and reduce the risk to a reasonable level.

Protecting Your Body

- Carry out a good warm-up prior to lifting and carrying your boat.
- Try to adopt a balanced stance in relation to the object being lifted. Feet at a slight angle to each other, shoulder-width apart and close to the load. Stand so that your centre of gravity is over the load.
- Bend at the knees and use the thigh muscles.
- Get a good grip of the load and if it is low down, keep the arms straight and between the legs.
- Face the direction you will be moving towards. If you have to turn, move the feet first then the body and head.
- Face the load you are about to lift.
- Do not lift when twisted and/or stooping.
- Remember to try and keep the load close to your body.

Here are a few ideas that might help make lifting and shifting a little easier:

- Raise the centre of gravity of the load before lifting, e.g. roll open boats onto their side.
- Get under the load if lifting up to shoulder height, i.e. like a weight lifter uses kinetic energy.
- Use gravity when lowering, e.g. hold boat close to body and slide it down to the floor.
- Avoid asymmetric loads.
- Communicate when working in pairs, plan your intentions and get the timing right.
- Use secondary support, e.g. one hand on a knee when lifting from ground level.
- Use body weight and leg muscles when lifting and pulling.
- Lift and lower in smooth actions.

The BCU Recommends:

- The use of full buoyancy in boats - to ease rescues and reduce the likelihood of injury.

When *possible:*

- Do not carry a boat on your own.
- Do not perform a deep water rescue without assistance.

Capsize Drills

From a capsize point of view there are two types of boat:

- Open canoes and open cockpit kayaks
- Closed cockpit kayaks

Open Canoes and Kayaks

These boats have no deck over the paddler's knees and allow the paddler to fall out. The trick is *not* to hold yourself in by gripping the cockpit or gunwale with your hands.

On capsizing you should:

1. Remain calm.

2. Allow yourself to fall out of the boat.

3. Normally, you will find yourself floating on the surface and to one side of the boat. *If* you find yourself underneath the upturned boat, push yourself under the boat and out to the side where you will float to the surface.

4. In deep water, keep hold of the boat (and if possible the paddle) and make your way to one end of the boat. (In shallow, fast moving water, leave the boat and swim for the side).

5. Either swim your boat to the side or co-operate with any other boaters if they are going to rescue you.

Closed Cockpit Kayaks

These boats are designed to keep water out and the paddler in so that they are able to Eskimo Roll up.

If you haven't learned how or your roll lets you down:

1. Remain calm.

2. Keep yourself in the boat by gripping with your knees until the kayak is completely upside down and lean forward so that your head is touching the front deck. (This will mean that your head is only a few inches under the water and less likely to be bumped along the bottom).

3. Reach forward, and release the spraydeck (if worn) using the quick release strap.

4. Place your hands on the side of the deck, level with your hips, relax your knee grip and feed the boat off your legs (like taking off a pair of trousers).

Fig 6.5   Capsize drill for closed cockpit kayaks

5. In deep water, keep hold of the boat (and if possible the paddle) and make your way to one end of the boat. (In shallow fast moving water, leave the boat and swim for the side).

6. Either swim your boat to the side or co-operate with any other boaters if they are going to rescue you.

Rescues

This section gives an overview of rescue situations and considers some common procedures. It does not prescribe specific methods, as there is no single method of rescue that will suit the many varied designs of boat, water situation or circumstances that exist. You will need to turn to the specific discipline for the methods that best suit the environment and the boats that you use.

Areas given consideration in this section are:

1. The Environment
2. The Boat
3. The People Involved
4. Towing
5. 'X' Rescue
6. Dealing with an Incident

(Considerations regarding throw line rescues are dealt with in Chapter 26 White Water Safety and Rescue.)

The Environment

Deep Water

In deep water where a swimmer may not get to the bank, it is important that they are encouraged to maintain contact with their boat and paddles. Lakes, ponds and open water are often more exposed to windier conditions. In strong winds a kayak or canoe will travel faster across the water than a swimmer can swim, and unless these are retained during the capsize and throughout the rescue the swimmer is left vulnerable and isolated. They need to be given assurance that you are coming to their assistance.

On open water, groups can easily become spread out; get them to come towards the rescue so as to maintain control and assist you if needed.

When you make contact ensure you retain control of the swimmer and their equipment and do not lose control of your own paddle. There are now several options available to you, and many of the rescue options described in the sea kayaking section will assist you here. Once recovered into their boat, they will need to be observed throughout the session, or even consider heading for shore in case they need further assistance.

Shallow Moving Water

Shallow water paddling has its own unique considerations, for example a possible increase in the speed of the flow, rocks and boulders and other underwater debris. Examples of this type of water are: streams, brooks, reefs, becks or flowing water less than a metre deep.

In this type of water, trying to utilise a deep water technique could put yourself and the swimmer in danger. The main priorities are to make sure you don't become a victim yourself and to give support and encouragement to the swimmer. Prior briefing for your group must include a warning that on no account should they attempt to stand up or put their feet down whilst swimming in fast flowing water. Point out the dangers of foot entrapment or entanglement in debris. It is important that they are taught the defensive swimming position and that those going to their aid remind them of this swimming position (see Chapter 26).

Narrow Waterways

Canals, slow moving rivers and small ponds are where many will be introduced to paddlesport. Swimmers are often easier to manage in these waters as the conditions seem less threatening. Your rescue must still be efficient and effective; there are still dangers such as debris and tree roots.

If there is a reasonable landing place and it is not too far away, it may be better to land the swimmer there rather than carry out a deep water rescue.

The Boat

Boats vary greatly both in design and construction. It is important to understand the advantages and disadvantages of different boats during a rescue situation. The vast majority of river running and recreational boats are made from tough plastics. Their recovery in a capsize situation is relatively easy, however, to rescue from one of them is not always so simple. The current fashion is lower volume, shorter boats with flat bottoms and scooped decks.

With the lack of volume some of the deep water rescues are made harder, especially where the boat is being used as a platform for the swimmer to climb on to.

Fig 6.6   Rescues with low volume kayaks

However, getting the upturned boat onto the lower deck is easier. The plastic construction stands up well to the dragging and scraping of one boat over another. In general the tough, shiny plastic and recessed edges help significantly in the slide and glide technique. This is a technique where you initiate movement in the boat you are rescuing, and using the inertia created, slide the boat across the deck of your own. Whilst gliding the boat across, try to keep as symmetrical a shape to your torso during the rescue as possible and minimise the twisting action where possible.

The shorter length of these boats also helps when reaching for the end grab and cockpit, and low volume boats hold less water.

Your choice of boat will depend on the types of groups you are going to be working with.

It must perform well and be practical, not only for the rescues but for its primary use. It must also be safe and not contribute to you becoming a hazard or liability to others.

Specialist Boats

When we look at competition boats from slalom, white water racing, sprint and marathon, we find lighter weight, usually composite construction. Here the hulls are usually stiff but the decks flex and won't stand up to being thrown around in the same manner as a plastic boat. (See discipline-specific chapters).

Your priority is the same irrespective of the type of boat, make sure the paddler is safe and you don't become a victim yourself. If you are unfamiliar with how to rescue a specialist boat, the paddler might be in a position to tell you of the best way of recovering their boat. Listen to them, but remember that you are the one still in your boat, thinking straight, and in a position to do something to assist.

The People Involved

The behaviour patterns of those who capsize and swim will vary immensely. Your basic approach to offering assistance will be the same for all.

Those who are panicking pose a threat to your safety if you approach too soon. Stand off and reassure them. You need to be firm with them, show them you are confident, make it clear in your tone and manner that you will help and that they will be rescued.

Do not make physical contact with a panicking victim. Give them some options to assist themselves, such as holding onto their boat, or lying on their back and kicking their legs. The reason some people panic is because they don't know what to do next. Your job is to open up such avenues for them and guide them verbally and physically to a positive conclusion.

Competition

In a competition, there are rules about your conduct in the event of rescuing a fellow competitor and these must be strictly adhered to. You must know what options you have to rescue someone; speak to coaches and fellow paddlers. The main option is getting them to hold onto your boat and push or pull them to an eddy or the side, encouraging them to retain their boat if possible. Boat recovery can be carried out later if needed, once they are out of the water and safe.

Photo 6.4   Helping a marathon paddler swim his boat to the side

Towing

Towing systems allow us to be independent in our ability to look after each other and get a tired, sick or injured paddler to safety. They are useful on lakes, slow moving rivers, canals and the sea. The principles are the same for all kayaks and are covered in detail in the sea kayaking chapter. The systems used in open canoes are covered in the discipline-specific chapter. Whatever system used, a key safety feature is that they should be instantly releasable in an emergency, even if the towing system is under pressure.

Towing Without a Towline

The boat based push or pull techniques are very simple and require no specialist equipment. They are only suitable for short distances, but they are simple and will offer you close control of the person being towed, giving them a sense of assurance.

Fig 6.7   Supported push to the bank

Avoiding Towing

Proper preparation for your session, and attention to the needs of the group will reduce the amount of towing you have to do. If youngsters are tired, you have taken them too far or you should have allowed more time in the session for them to rest. You should consider carrying spare equipment in case of breakage. In some instances we don't have a choice and to tow is our only option, but be careful that the tow does not become the easy option. Be more effective in your session planning and management.

X Rescues

This is the most common form of boat-to-boat rescue and is usually the first rescue taught to paddlers. It can be used in many types of boat, but caution must be exercised because it relies on dragging one boat over the deck of another. The rescue can be made much easier if the swimmer is able to assist the rescuer. In order for this to be effective, you need to brief your group what their actions should be in the event of a capsize.

Briefing

- The group should watch out for each other. If there is a capsize they should call your attention to it.

- Remind them of the appropriate capsize drill.

- Encourage them to retain the paddle if possible.

- Tell them not to climb on the boat or turn it over.

- Tell them to listen to the instructions of the rescuer.

- If directed to swim to the bank, they should do so on their back with the boat end away from their face.

- The remainder of the group should be prepared to move closer together without getting in the way of the rescue.

- Open boaters need to have a head count and flip the boat over to ensure that no one is trapped under the boat.

As you approach the swimmer, talk to them giving reassurance and purposeful direction. Be firm, as this will help them relax. If they are panicking and do not calm down as you approach, stand off so that they cannot grab your boat and capsize you. Talk to them, tell them what you want to do, and what you want them to do. This should calm them.

When it is safe to approach:

1. Move in and present them with the bow of your boat. Make sure the bow is over their shoulder, away from their face.

2. Take their paddle from them to avoid it drifting away.

3. Take the boat from them, hopefully still upside down and full of air.

4. Bring the end of the boat to your side. Hold their boat at right angles to your boat.

5. Bring their boat up over your deck and rock it until the water is out.

6. Roll the boat back over.

7. Put the boat back in the water and get the swimmer back in the boat.

Safety Considerations

Your body is at risk of injury as you bring the boat up onto your deck. Your spine is twisted and bent sideways. Do not try to use brute force, a water-logged boat can be very difficult to rescue. Here are a few options to consider:

- Use a 'slide and glide' action.

- Get the swimmer to assist you.

- Use tape or a sling on the end grab of the boat to push the boat further away and then pull it back with more momentum.

- Lower the edge of your boat as you drag theirs up. Then hip flick it back as the boat travels across.

- Get another paddler to assist.

- Be conscious of your posture. Do not over-reach or stretch.

- Use a boat with a low deck – providing it is still above water with the weight of a rescued person on it.

- Put airbags in the boats of the group you are taking out.

Getting the person back in the boat also involves some risks, especially if the swimmer is bigger or heavier than you. There is also a risk of injury to the swimmer. Let them know what you want them to do.

Options to consider:

Re-entry from Between Boats

1. Put their boat back in the water with its bow at your stern.

2. Use paddles across the boats, behind you, to add stability.

3. Lean right over their boat, hold the cockpit with both hands and pull tight.

4. Get them to lay back in the water and bring their feet up into the boat first.

5. Hook their feet in the cockpit and lay arms over the top of boats.

6. On an agreed signal they hoist themselves in as you pull the boats together.

Re-entry from Side of Boats

(See Photos 20.20a-c, Chapter 20)

- Put their boat in the water at your side.

Fig 6.8 'X' Rescue sequence

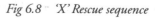

- Put them on the outside of their boat.

- Reach over and pull them up as they kick their legs and hoist themselves up.

- You can use a sling as a stirrup for them to put their foot in and help. This takes time to set up.

Whatever method you use you need to practise it in a safe environment. More importantly, you should be practising with a wide variety of boats with differing quantities of water in them. Practise rescuing boats you are likely to encounter in the groups you paddle with. Practise rescuing from different boats to expand your knowledge. Speak to people who paddle specialist boats, such as competition boats, and ask how they deal with rescue situations.

Open Canoes

Open boaters can use a variation of the 'X' rescue, the only real difference is getting people back in their boat.

1. Get them on the far side of their emptied boat opposite you.

2. As they attempt to climb in, allow the gunwale to be pushed down until it is just clear of the water.

3. As they get their belly onto the gunwale that is now level with the water, push down on your gunwale and 'scoop' them into their boat.

The Curl

An alternative method of emptying the canoe.

Fig 6.9 The Curl

1. Get the swimmer to steady your boat by holding onto your gunwale on the opposite side to the upturned canoe.

2. Turn the swamped boat onto its side with the hull away from you.

3. Holding onto the uppermost gunwale, gently 'curl' the boat onto the gunwale of your boat, taking care to keep bow and stern level.

4. Once all the water is out, quickly flip it so that it lands upright on the water next to your boat.

Dealing with an Incident

Here is a simple routine, generic to all incidents:

R	-	Raise the alarm
E	-	Exercise caution
S	-	Stabilise the situation
C	-	Consider options
U	-	Use support
E	-	Execute the plan
.		
C	-	Continual assessment
O	-	Options post rescue
M	-	Maintain observation of casualty

R = Raise the Alarm

Let everybody know there is someone in the water. Someone may be in a better position to offer support.

E = Exercise Caution

As the test pilot said: 'Never put your body where your brain hasn't been first.' Think about your safety, will you become a victim if you approach? Make it safe, use the features or people around you. Get the swimmer to swim to a safer place.

S = Stabilise the Situation

Give verbal support as you approach; prepare them for the rescue. Give assurance and guidance to the swimmer, they may not be thinking too clearly yet, think for them. Get the rest of the group under control; maintain control of them during the rescue. Prevent the situation getting any worse. No two situations are exactly the same, so be flexible.

C = Consider Your Options

Consider a variety of rescue options. You need to be practised in executing them. Get training from a recognised coach/trainer. Consider pre-planned rescue options in predictable scenarios. Be proactive in your management. Listen to advice and consider its use.

U = Use Support

Use others around you to assist, if it is safe to do so! Don't let the adrenaline take over, use brain not brawn.

E = Execute the Plan

Make sure you have a plan, let others including the swimmer know what you intend to do. Act quickly and efficiently. Communication is essential. Stay focused. Keep control of the whole group throughout.

C = Continual Assessment

Management of the risks involved and the control measures you put in place can change constantly, so observe and analyse the whole picture. Have you reduced the risks involved in the rescue to a level proportional to the benefits of your actions.

O = Options Post Rescue

What are the consequences and repercussions of the rescue on the group and the original session/journey plan? Do you need to shorten the journey or even stop, to prevent the situation worsening?

M = Maintain Observation

After the incident is over, you need to keep observing the group and the individual and watch for changes. It is often possible to predict these, and this is an opportunity to manage the risks in a proactive manner.

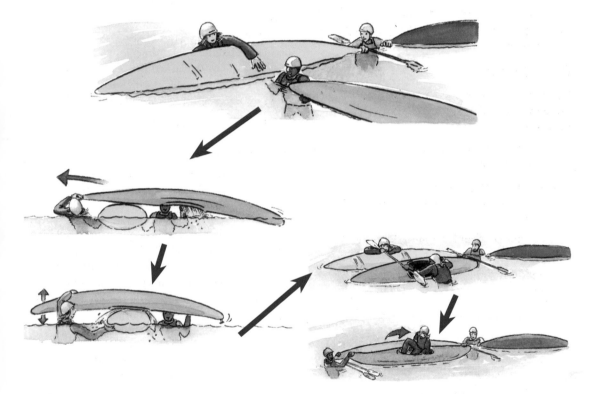

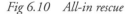

Fig 6.10   All-in rescue

Fig 6.11   Eskimo Rescue (an option for closed cockpit kayaks). Paddle presentation (the best method for sea kayaks) is shown. In short kayaks it is just as easy to present the bow of your boat.

Leadership

This section will help you establish your own set of rules to follow as a leader. It will raise issues which arise on a frequent basis, explore possible solutions and offer guidance if you want to develop as a leader.

Is leadership something that you have always wanted to do or is it a role thrust upon you by external circumstances? Many people find themselves being the leader because of their nature, character or because no one else was prepared to take on the role. In the context of this chapter leadership is not just about leading trips, but also the many other roles we take on as coach, group organiser, longest serving member of the club and in some cases the strongest paddler.

What is Leadership?

Leadership is:

Having a willingness to lead others and having the character to inspire others to follow.

Leadership is about managing people and their needs. When we lead we are invested with a position of authority and trust on behalf of the group. Your role as leader will influence the relationship a person has with the sport.

Informal and Formal Leadership

Leading an informal group (such as friends) is very different from leading a formal group. You could wrongly assume that aims and concerns for the day will be voiced. This only happens if the group know and trust each other really well. You must consider the communication within the group and formalise the decision-making process if necessary.

With a formal group the leader takes on a very different approach, with external factors affecting the session or the day. You will be expected to work within BCU codes of practice and the safe systems of work set by your organisation. You should have familiarised yourself with the analytical risk assessments for your stretch of water, so that agreed and pre-planned working expectations are met. It should be remembered that 'formal groups' are not just commercial groups but can also be from clubs, schools and voluntary agencies. Their expectations of you and their perception of your role will be very similar to those of a paying customer. Your being 'professional' should be consistent, irrespective of the group, paying or otherwise.

Duty of Care

In the UK, all *adults* who participate in adventurous activities and *who are aware of the hazards they may face*, are considered in law to be liable for their own actions. In other words, they can always say "I'm not doing that!" and are unlikely to successfully sue a leader if they are involved in an accident unless criminal negligence can be proved. There is a grey area where people of vastly different experience are involved. In other words if a complete novice decides to paddle a hazardous rapid, a court might deem that he or she lacked the experience to appreciate the real nature of the hazards involved. If a vastly more experienced paddler were present, the court might rightly decide that he or she had a *duty of care* to advise the other paddler not to run the rapid. This would apply whether the more experienced paddler was qualified or unqualified and paid or unpaid. However, formal leaders are deemed to have an enhanced duty of care and this defence does not apply to people under eighteen.

There is a perception that our society is becoming more litigious. As even the cost of defending yourself in court could be considerable, I feel that paddlers should consider taking out personal liability insurance as a safeguard. Other experienced coaches feel that our legal system is pretty sound in this respect and that paddlers who use their common sense, work within the remit of their experience and (where applicable) qualifications, have little to worry about. The choice is yours.

Formal leaders, paid or unpaid, should either have their own insurance or check that the organisation they are working for is covering them.

Leading or Coaching?

There is a strong relationship between coaching and leading. If leading is over-emphasised, it can be to the detriment of coaching. If we only coach, we are in danger of neglecting the safety and welfare of the group.

We must acknowledge our responsibilities for managing the safety and welfare of the group and find the right balance for safety and learning.

The model below shows this need to balance coaching and leading. The coach should aim to work somewhere around the overlap. Our bias will fluctuate as the needs of the session dictate. An inexperienced coach often adopts an autocratic approach to their coaching, because they are unsure how to maintain control. Remember, you do not have to suppress a group to maintain control.

Leading and Coaching Interlinked

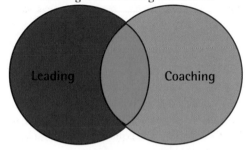

Fig 6.12   Coaching and leading overlap

To maintain the balance we should first:

- Establish the ground rules
- Introduce simple control measures
- Manage the risks in a continuous and dynamic manner

Leading without Coaching

The above model is for those who coach. We should not forget those who mainly lead groups without coaching, for example on river trips. Here, a different model might be useful: Adair's three circled action centred leadership.

This model shows the three main aspects that a leader must bear in mind continually to cope with managing the group through the day or session.

Fig 6.13   Adair's action centred leadership

It is clear that the circles overlap and that concentration in one area will be to the detriment of others. If we concentrate on the needs of one individual, we might neglect the needs of the group as a whole and if we focus only on the needs of the group, the task may be in jeopardy. If the focus is on the task, then the group and individuals within it may lose motivation and concentration. There is then a danger of a reduction of the safety and welfare of the group. An example of this would be pushing on during a river trip when people need a stop for a drink or sandwich.

The ideal is to work between the three areas, paying attention to particular needs at different times as the day progresses and needs change. Consider yourself as a juggler - creating a different pattern or sequence as the needs dictate.

Fig 6.14   Juggler

What Are the Qualities of a Good Leader?

No matter how you see the role, or indeed why you found yourself doing the job, there are generic aspects to the role for all of us. Leaders must:

- Be sensitive to the needs of the group and individuals, including safety and enjoyment.
- Be trustworthy.
- Realise their accountability.
- Plan well.
- Recognise that the group's needs and abilities are different to theirs.

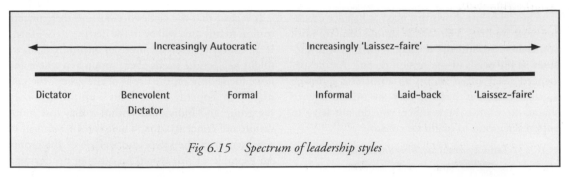

Increasingly Autocratic   Increasingly 'Laissez-faire'

| Dictator | Benevolent Dictator | Formal | Informal | Laid-back | 'Laissez-faire' |

Fig 6.15   Spectrum of leadership styles

How Do I Become a Good Leader?

You must consider how you are leading now and consider developing different aspects of your leadership.

Leadership Styles

People lead in different ways. There has been much written about different leadership styles. One model of leadership styles which might be useful to you is the spectrum which ranges from dictator to laissez-faire. This spectrum is easily compared to the needs of the decision-making process.

Leaders should work predominantly around the middle of the spectrum, moving left and right of centre when necessary. The reason we should move along the spectrum is because the needs of the students are always changing, and different leadership styles are required as the session or day progresses.

For example:

- Lots of time, with a team of friends paddling, then a more laid back approach can be taken.

- In an emergency when a decision has to be made quickly, then an autocratic, authoritative approach is needed.

Another model of leadership styles shows three different approaches. A good leader should be able to change approach and adopt a different stance within the group depending on the changing needs of the group, the individuals and the task.

Having confidence in the leader's ability to make the right decisions is very important. The leader should ultimately strive to give confidence to the group so that they can concentrate on the learning or enjoying the day.

Three Different Approaches

In Fig 6.16a the leader is in the centre of the circle and is the central focus of the group. The decisions are being made by the leader, who is working in an autocratic, authoritarian manner.

Fig 6.16b shows the leader working from the same position as the group. Here decisions are being made with the group through discussion and using a democratic process. Decisions are made through consensus or by majority. This is a less formal style, where time is not such an issue and the views of the students are being taken into account.

Fig 6.16c shows the leader outside of the group, taking a guiding role rather like a shepherd. The group has set the goal or task and the leader offers support.

Fig 6.16   Three different approaches

Relationship Skills

Developing your relationship skills will help you operate effectively. These skills can be listed under three headings:

Communication Skills	Group Skills	Assertion Skills
Listening	Planning	Influencing
Expressing	Organising	Controlling
Informing	Decision-making	Pos. assertion
Questioning	Supervising	Confronting
Clarifying	Monitoring	Resp. to criticism
Facilitating	Mediating	Directing

Planning and Preparation

Planning, formally or informally, should be done as a matter of course with both lesson and journey preparation. Planning and preparation will help relieve some of the pressures when you are out on the water as it encourages you to adopt the principle of:

'Avoidance is better than cure'.

Considerations

It is perhaps worth considering a few of the pressures, which often have far reaching effects on the leader and their decision-making skills.

Time

Time factors will play a key role in the day or the session. It might be to accommodate transport arrangements, to meet tide times, or it could be simply to be off the water before dark. Whatever the reasons, we need to *plan* our time and *allow* for emergencies or alterations. Failure to plan your time properly will at best mean the students, parents or centre lose confidence in your leadership. Ultimately you could jeopardise the safety and well-being of the group.

'Time is not an excuse for accepting the unacceptable.'

Clarify before the start of the paddle what time is available and the circumstances of the group. Find out what the group want from the day or the session and start with some kind of plan in your mind, an outline of the day. You don't have to stick to it rigidly. Being flexible to the group's needs and the environment will allow you to maximise the opportunities as they arise, and thus maximise the experience for all concerned.

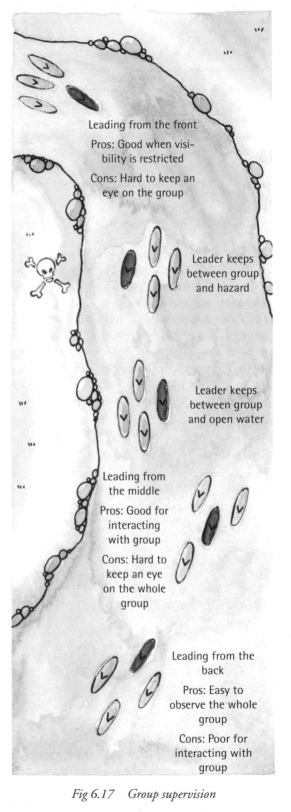

Leading from the front
Pros: Good when visibility is restricted
Cons: Hard to keep an eye on the group

Leader keeps between group and hazard

Leader keeps between group and open water

Leading from the middle
Pros: Good for interacting with group
Cons: Hard to keep an eye on the whole group

Leading from the back
Pros: Easy to observe the whole group
Cons: Poor for interacting with group

Fig 6.17   Group supervision

Ratios

The ratio of paddlers to leader might vary from session to session. If you work for an organisation, centre or club, a prescribed maximum ratio might already exist, e.g. 8:1.

If the circumstances of the group, the water levels or the weather changes, you might need to reduce the ratio to a smaller, more manageable number, e.g. 4:1. This decision will depend on your dynamic risk assessment on the day, your experience as a leader, and any additional control measures you choose to put in place.

You may have heard the rule ' less than three there should never be'. This works well and should be observed wherever possible.

There are, however, instances when paddlers might want to go it alone, for example competition training. Paddlers may argue that they have the skill to stay out of trouble. If you are in a situation when you cannot stop people paddling on their own, you should make sure they are aware of the risks. You should, at the very least, encourage them to wear a buoyancy aid. Get them to tell people where they are going and what time they will be back. Encourage them to work near banks where they can self-rescue.

Equipment

Refer to the chapter on equipment for details on individual items. You will need to remember that whatever you carry must have a purpose and be used effectively. It is not the quantity of equipment that you carry but your ability to use it that counts.

The kit you carry will change from day to day depending upon circumstances.

Crisis Management

When a session starts to encounter problems, the coach needs to make decisions quickly. As in a rescue, we must ask ourselves if we are using a pre-planned strategy or we are flying by the seat of our pants. Our ability to make clear decisions can be seriously affected by pressure and inexperience.

Crisis management is 90% psychological and 10% physical, so save your energy and use your mind.

Always try to draw from previous experiences and the lessons learnt there. Inexperienced leaders are able to learn a great deal from observing others or talking with other leaders about their experiences. They can then pre-plan a strategy for the situations they might find themselves in, for example weather changes and the additional equipment needed to cope with any changes.

Conclusion

The role of managing someone in the outdoors is not one to be taken lightly, but when you get it right with everyone going away happy and fulfilled, that is a good feeling. You are responsible for the atmosphere within the group and the stewardship of these people, and the experience they gain from paddlesport is down to you.

Remember to ask yourself just what you and the students want from the day and try to marry the two together for the benefit of everyone.

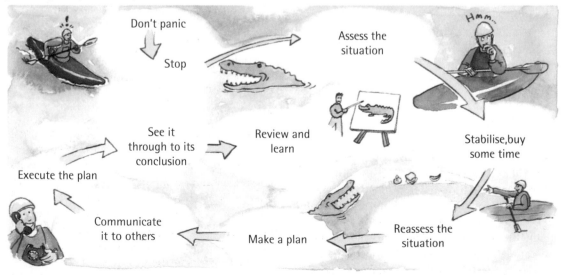

Fig 6.18   Crisis management

Working With Young People

Some experienced coaches may ask, "Is this relevant to me? I've been working with young people for years and never had a problem". Times are changing, and you need to remember your vulnerability and exposure to accusations whilst working in certain situations, whether as a paid worker or as a volunteer.

When working with young people, you usually need to hold a formal qualification or registration to say you have been approved by a recognised body. Most voluntary youth organisations require a minimum of screening with the Criminal Records Bureau.

Issues to Consider

Mixed Gender

If you have a mixed group, good practice would encourage you to have both male and female leaders. Avoid inappropriate situations with students of the opposite sex; for example, physical contact when adjusting close-fitting buoyancy aids or indiscreet changing facilities, by having assistance from someone of the same gender as the student. Young people often need to be able to turn to someone of the same gender to discuss personal matters. This also happens with groups of mixed race or religions where empathy and sensitivity are needed, and having an appropriate assistant can give you that support. It is still very important for you to learn more about other people's needs, beliefs and cultures if you want to show real empathy and gain their trust.

Compromising Situations

Avoid compromising, one-to-one situations. Remain in an open, mixed environment. Where privacy is important, tell someone where you are, who you are with and what you doing. Make sure you have a witness. Being careful can only be of benefit.

Screening

Screening is seen as an important safety protocol. Centres, schools and statutory organisations will have ready access to this facility, but for a club or voluntary organisation it can be difficult to get screening carried out. What do you do then? The Home Office offers guidance to voluntary organisations on this matter but here are some options open to you:

- The Voluntary Organisations Consultancy Service, VOCS can carry out the checks but your club has to be a member of the VOCS.

- You could affiliate to a local voluntary youth group with screening facilities or utilise your local authority's youth service, if they can assist.

- The Department for Health Consultancy Service can give access to information held by previous employers, in circumstances indicating their unsuitability for working with young people.

- It is hoped that in the future the BCU will offer this service to members and affiliated clubs.

Registration

Some youth agencies, for example the National Association of Clubs for Young people (NACYP), are developing a registration scheme for all those who work in close contact with young people. This is to check the suitability of their workers and offers protection to both the leader and the young person. With this scheme the workers are issued with a watermarked identity card and their information is stored on a national database.

What If You Suspect Abuse?

There is a section in the BCU Directory and there are clear guidelines from the BCU in these cases. The NSPCC also has a 24hr phone line, which you could phone if seeking advice.

Remember: It is not your responsibility to decide whether a young person is being abused, but it is your responsibility to act if you have any concerns. It is important to work in partnership with the parents or guardians if there is any concern. Keep a record of your action. Dealing with a situation like this requires sensitivity and care. You should think things through before you act. Always seek advice from experienced people or from a person in authority within your organisation.

Oppression

Always be aware of your language and actions as well as that of the group with regards to being oppressive. You don't always know what personal issues a young person might have, and what you may think of as fun may be deemed as oppressive, and cause unwanted consequences. More importantly, this might affect the young person and be detrimental to their personal development and their self-esteem. Developing their self-esteem is an important part in working with young people, and we should be encouraging and recognising achievement by praise and positive feedback. Try not to speak down to young people but try and treat them as equals.

Areas which are deemed as oppressive are: age, gender, sexuality, race, disability and religion. These all need to be handled with care and sensitivity, so think about the jokes you make, who they are aimed at, and the consequences for those they affect.

Name-calling is common, usually in the form of a nickname, but consider whether that young person really wants to be given a label by their coach. What right do you have to change someone's identity? It is important to treat young people with the same respect you would wish in return. Discuss rather than dictate.

Training

It is important that you receive training in the issues surrounding working with young people. Training is readily available and should run parallel to your paddlesport leadership and coach development. This training can be as simple as workshops with the BCU or the Sports Coach UK, through to an NVQ or full time course in youth work. Training will benefit you, and more importantly, the young people you work with, who are the future of the sport.

Ethical Principles

- Treat young people with respect, value individuals and avoid negative discrimination.

- Respect and promote young people's rights to make their own decisions and choices unless their welfare and safety are threatened.

- Promote and ensure the welfare and safety of young people while permitting them to learn through adventurous, challenging and educational activities.

- Contribute towards the promotion of social justice for young people, encouraging respect for difference and diversity, and challenge discrimination.

Professional Principles

- Recognise the boundaries between personal and professional life and balance a caring and supportive role with appropriate professional distance.

- Recognise the need to be accountable to young people, their parents and others.

- Develop and maintain the required skills and competence to do the job.

- Ensure these principles are discussed, evaluated and upheld.

These principles are based on those laid down by the National Youth Agency for people who wish to work with young people. They have been the basis for good practice for a very long time in youth work.

Further Reading

White Water Safety and Rescue, Ferrero F, 1998, Wales, Pesda Press, 0-9531956-0-0
Leading and Managing Groups in the Outdoors, Ogilvy K
5 Steps to Risk Assessment, IND (G) 163 - Contact HSE Books, PO Box 1999, Sudbury, Suffolk, CO10 6FS,
Tel 01787 881165 - or visit the HSE website at www.open.gov.uk/hse/hsehome.htm

Keith Hampton

Keith has paddled and led groups on rivers in the UK, Europe and the Alps, the United States, Africa and Nepal.

Based at the Leicester Outdoor Pursuit Centre, where he still enjoys paddling and coaching with groups on flat water, Keith is a BCU Level 5 Coach and is involved in coach development in his region.

He has extensive experience in white water safety and rescue, and the coaching process programme. He has been involved in competition both as a competitor and as a coach, and has a background in open canoe, freestyle, sea and surf.

7 Coaching

Back in the late 1980s, living in Nottingham, it was not unusual for me to wander down the length of the artificial slalom course just to watch people paddle. It was late afternoon and there were only a few kayakers training. I sat down on the steps to watch the three or four paddlers who seemed to be working on their breaking in and out.

Standing on the bank with his back to me was someone else watching the action. It only become evident after ten minutes or so that this individual was also involved. Every third or fourth circuit he would speak softly to the paddler who passed in front of him. The odd words I could pick up seemed to be brief and direct; they consisted of: "again", "edge", "think". All simple but understood by the individuals they were directed to, sometimes he just seemed to smile at them. The coaching seemed to have lost direction when the last paddler in the circuit came past, put his hand up and told the coach... 'Yes I know', and then paddled off.

I thought I could learn nothing here so I left.

It was only a number of years later that I realised that the event had all the hallmarks of a productive coaching session. The students were continuously involved; the feedback was simple, understood and particular to each individual. The coach had the perfect position to view all that was happening, and the individual who put his hand up to stop the coach saying something he had realised for himself was fast becoming an independent learner. The coach was Ray Rowe and I had much to learn.

Introduction

This chapter is about the coaching of canoeing and kayaking. Its main aims are to introduce and to provide an overview of the main elements that are involved in successful coaching. Within this overview it will outline the relationships between the ways people learn, and the ways we as coaches can make use of that information in our coaching of paddlesport. It will also suggest that the learning process and the coaching process are one and the same. To be a good coach, a coach first needs to be a good student of the coaching process.

Many of the modern ideas that underpin the coaching process come, not from paddlesport itself, but from the various sports sciences.

The key coaching skills, sometimes referred to as behaviours, are common across most sports and physical activities. I would suggest that there is more that unites the coaching of, say hockey and canoe polo, than separates it. The understanding that students thrive on praise and the coach's support, when learning new skills, is just as valuable in the coaching of hockey as it is in American football. The fact that students like to be kept active and interested when learning a new sport is the same for volleyball as it is for slalom racing.

The next time you watch a hockey coach work, note that the process they use is the same as the one you use. By watching any inventive coach, you can benefit and develop your own coaching skills and therefore the students you work with.

So the Story Goes

In communist East Germany in the 1970s, the government sports bureau decided that, as far as Olympic success went, the efforts that they were putting into field hockey would be better directed to events that could result in a number of individual gold medals, not just a team one.

So they called the national field hockey coaches together, took their hockey sticks away from them with one hand and handed out canoe paddles with the other. They were now canoe coaches.

East Germany went on to be a dominant force in international sprint racing in the late 1970s & throughout the 1980s.

After all coaching is coaching; it's all about people.

The coaching process is the learning process; we are in the business of coaching people to become more effective learners.

Roles and Responsibilities of a Coach

The roles of the coach are manifold, but our main job is to make the time spent on the water or in the classroom the most effective for the students we work with. To be effective means that you have met the aims and goals set for that particular coaching session. A friend of mine had a very simple goal for his first time beginners groups: to get them back on the water the following week. Only then, he would argue, would he have paddlers and something to work with.

Photo 7.1   Take time in the planning process; have you got the right people, in the right place, at the right time?

A number of factors resulting from these roles and responsibilities may have to be considered before the student even arrives to begin the session:

- Selection of the venue for the coaching input
- The choice of equipment, is it suitable for the group?
- Any legal requirements, i.e. parental consent
- Responsibility for the physical and mental well-being of the student(s)
- The coaching undertaken by the learner
- Linkage to the next session

There may be roles and responsibilities other than those listed above. It all depends on the formality of the session and the type of coaching relationship. Some coaches have made a point of making a verbal agreement between the parties. They will do their

A Learning Contract

The students also have responsibilities, e.g. to the safety and enjoyment of other paddlers within the group. It may help if you talk to the whole group about these expectations and roles before getting on the water. Clearly establishing what is expected of the coach and what the coach expects in return can help create a good learning environment.

utmost to coach them to the best of their abilities if they, the students, do their best to be coached. It helps if the learners and coaches are clear on what is to be covered in the session.

One of the key decisions to be made by the coach is the selection of the venue being used for the session. The importance of selecting the right location is difficult to overstate; it needs to be safe, yet challenging and exciting for the student, a difficult balance.

One of the most difficult decisions that a coach has to make is when to stop the coaching session. As with most physical activities, there is a time in any session when the quality of the learning, the students' attention levels, and their bodies' ability to physically perform begins to wane. With beginners or those learning new skills, that productive period when the coaching is really profitable may be shorter than you think. There are no hard and fast rules about when to end the coaching.

"A little taught well is better than a lot taught badly," is a useful maxim.

Some Ideas and Concepts

What makes a successful and effective coach? What can the novice coach do to increase their confidence and develop the range of situations they are happy to coach in? Reading this book is a good place to start, and the coaching toolbox is a useful way of thinking about the ideas and options you have in your coaching. The more coaching you expose yourself to, the bigger your toolbox will become, and in turn the greater number of options will be open to you and those you coach.

Coaching Knowledge

If we watched three different coaches at work at a swimming pool, slalom course or river, we would probably see much the same thing. They may use a demonstration, or set up similar practices. There is very little observable difference between them, but one element that would separate the expert coaches from the others is the range of options that they have to call upon, the *'what if'* factor.

The *"what if"* factor is the thought process that expert coaches use to decide when one practice routine is likely to be more successful than another, and the experience that allows them to understand why

one individual paddler responds in one way and not another.

On the other hand, novice coaches tend to use only the coaching tools that they have been subjected to.

A Coaching Toolbox

I first came across this analogy in a National Coaching Foundation (now renamed Sports Coach UK) workbook a few years ago. Our coaching knowledge is like a toolbox. We can only use the tools we have in our box, but as each student and situation is different, we need a range of tools to work with.

Selecting the right tool for the job is a coaching skill. It produces more effective and quicker results. Students don't get hit with the force of a hammer when they need the precision of a scalpel. More tools (i.e. knowledge) increases the range of situations and students we can help.

So open your box and steal as many tools from other coaches as you can!

Coaching knowledge can be divided into four different forms:

1. Technical knowledge
2. Procedural knowledge
3. Declarative knowledge
4. Interpersonal knowledge

Technical Knowledge

This is the knowledge about the strokes and their application in a particular discipline.

Procedural Knowledge

This is the range and depth of activities and exercises the coach can call upon to deal with a particular aspect of performance.

Declarative Knowledge

This is the knowledge of why things work, the understanding of the learning principles that underpin that choice.

Interpersonal Knowledge

This colours your selection of all the other three. It is the understanding of the student as an individual, which tells you that at that particular time the most productive options for that person are X, Y and Z.

Let's look at an example overleaf:

During the last wild water race Howard, Sue's club coach, notices that she is having problems with her stroke timing and turns. Corrective coaching is required because Sue is using a sweep stroke far too late on the face of the wave to allow the boat to turn while balanced on the apex (technical knowledge). He is aware that she works best away from the squad training sessions and on her own, so they will be working on a one-to-one basis (interpersonal knowledge). The section of water they will use is only 300 metres long, and has a number of wave trains separated by flat glides. This is perfect for Sue to focus on her timing when paddling in the white water, allowing her to think about the next rapid during the easy flat sections. Howard can talk to Sue about his observations and ask her about her perceptions on the short bank walk back up to the top before the next run (procedural knowledge). Howard is also aware that any attempt to change a fundamental aspect of Sue's technical performance is likely to be a long-term issue. He plans a number of coaching sessions supported by goal setting and video usage, so Sue may identify the improvement. In the later session he will introduce a stopwatch and time the practice sections to allow Sue to perform under race conditions, (declarative knowledge).

Who Do We Coach? – The Learner

It may be tempting to treat learners as if they are all the same, with the same difficulties, abilities and aspirations. This in turn suggests that the same broad coaching approach will produce results with all types of learners and in most conditions. The 'one style suits all' philosophy.

However, learners come in all shapes and sizes, with different abilities, talents and skills, and with a range of goals, motives and personal aspirations.

Learning Styles

It has been suggested that learners can be identified will regards to their preferred learning styles.

The Activist

Have you noticed that some people like to learn by doing; they need to experience an action themselves before the key elements of the movement hits home?

Activist

Reflector

Theorist

Pragmatist

Fig 7.1   Learning styles

The Reflector

Others hang back watching, and may ask for a number of demonstrations of the skill before having their first attempt.

The Theorist

Some need you to explain the new movement in a logical order, giving the angles of body, boat and blade. These learners are often helped by the use of abstract theories. They are the ones who often ask for the fine detail of an action before being happy to try it out.

The Pragmatist

For the last group the fact that something works and produces results is all that matters to them.

Within the subject of learning styles, there is debate about how many separate styles there are, and the names that they are given.

There are a number of questionnaires and textbooks which students and coaches can use to identify their own preferred learning style. Individuals will discover that they might not fit into one single box. You might be a mix of a number of styles. You may be a reflecting theorist!

It is important to note there is no best learning style. Those who can learn and coach in a variety of ways are able to choose and value the style that is best suited to the material they are learning. Helping students learn to develop new styles is a fruitful area in which coaches can help their learners to become better learners.

Coaching Styles

We only have to look back at our own experience of learning to remember that different teachers had their own particular approach and style. Once you can understand the application of these differing styles, you are well on the way to being able to match the most effect style to a learner or situation that you are faced with.

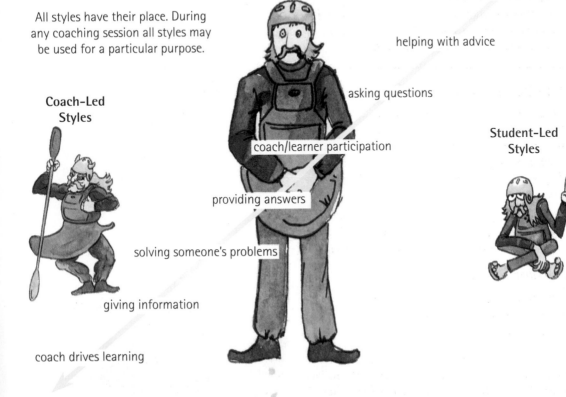

Non-Directive

student drives own learning

helping with advice

asking questions

All styles have their place. During any coaching session all styles may be used for a particular purpose.

Coach-Led Styles

coach/learner participation

Student-Led Styles

providing answers

solving someone's problems

giving information

coach drives learning

Directive

Fig 7.2   The Coaching Spectrum

Styles that fall towards the left of the line are referred to as being coach led or centred. This means that the coach tends to make all the key decisions, such as the selection of venues, content and structure of delivery. This can provide a reassuring framework for those coaching the session, and be comforting for some types of student. Coach-led styles also have the benefits of making good use of the available coaching time and are useful with novices and other situations requiring tight control.

At the other end of the spectrum, the students themselves mould the nature of the learning. The most important aspect to grasp about this range of options is that each style has its correct place. If all your teaching is underpinned by a coach-led approach, then you may stifle many learning opportunities that the student initiates and wishes to explore. So an overly structured approach with a group of mature, competent learners may turn the students off even before the session begins.

On the other hand, student-centred sessions may seem unstructured and take a longer time to produce tangible outcomes.

Most research supports the idea that student-centred learning produces longer-term benefits, and more secure learning. Giving the student more control in the learning process may lead to a more independent learner in the long run.

As well as the type of student you are working with, the selection of coaching style will be dependent on your immediate and long-term goals for that session.

The difference between the leadership and coaching styles you adopt can be indistinguishable in some situations, such as a sea trip. Indeed, in these situations the coach's ultimate responsibility for safety may override their personal commitments to a particular style. For example, letting relative novices make their own decision whether to run a horrible boat-eating weir may not be the best use of a self-discovery approach.

It is all a matter of appropriateness and the coach's judgment.

The Learning Process

The mechanics of how we actually learn is a fascinating and dynamic subject, and we as coaches should all make efforts to keep up to date with new ideas.

There are a number of conflicting theories about the detailed processes that our brain goes through when we are trying to learn any new task or skill.

What follows is a brief description of the major elements in the process of learning.

Performance and Learning

These two terms are often confused. A performance is an observable (often physical) attempt by a learner to achieve something. The quality of that performance will sometimes fluctuate and can be affected by the learner's motivation, arousal levels and degree of fatigue at the time of the performance.

The ability to perform a particular action one week will not automatically result in the paddler being able to perform it the next, i.e. we forget how to do it. Therefore the action had not been learned.

Skill learning is a mental process; it cannot be seen, only inferred by the ability of the learner to reproduce that particular skill at will, and when demanded.

A learned skill should be able to be reproduced (referred to as *retention*) sometime after it was last used. For example, most people never forget how to ride a bike.

A truly learned skill should also be able to be transferred between similar situations (*transferability*).

An inland kayaker decides to try sea paddling for the first time. On the paddle out through the waves he capsizes, but is upright in a flash. The skill of rolling, learned in a different craft on rivers has transferred. The action is a learned skill.

How we get our students to remember what has been covered in each coaching session is the crux of the coaching process. The following section aims to introduce you to some of the main issues.

How Do We Learn?

Types and Nature of Skill

The term 'skill' can be used to describe any number of physical actions and mental thought processes. Here we will look at the few that have a direct relation to coaching and learning:

Motor Skills

Motor skills describe actions that result in a physical outcome. The success of that motor skill is determined by the quality of the end performance. So catching a ball or taking a shot at goal performed by a canoe polo player is an example of a motor skill.

Cognitive Skills

The decision whether to shoot at goal, or to pass to a member of your team is referred to as a *cognitive skill*. Most actions in paddlesport are combinations of both motor skills (the ability to complete the action) and cognitive skills (the ability to decide if, or when, to complete the action). Even the most routine paddle actions will need a degree of cognitive activity to set it in motion.

Our job is to help the student learn, not just the *how* aspects of our sport, but also the *why*; not just how to do a bow rudder but *when* and *why*.

Discrete Skills

Some canoeing actions are *discrete skills* in as much as they have a distinct start and a fixed end. The support strokes are a good example of these discrete skills, often performed in isolation and having a fixed outcome, in this case preventing a capsize.

Serial Skills

Serial skills are those which have a number of discrete skills as their component parts. The Eskimo Roll is a series of individual actions, which must be performed in the right order, with the right element of timing, for the whole action to be deemed successful.

Continuous Skills

Forward paddling is an example of a *continuous skill*, one in which it is difficult to determine any real start or finish. The action is repeated time and time again.

Open Skills

One aspect of coaching paddlesport, which prevents us from having a fixed set of answers to the questions of 'What should we coach and why?', is the unpredictable nature of some of the *open environments* we work in.

The demands made on the paddlers we teach, their skills and the environment that they perform in, are ever changing. We need *open skills*, which we can adapt in different ways and will allow us to fulfill any number of different outcomes. Open skills should have variety in their form to allow us to blend them to new outcomes, even if we don't know what they are yet.

Closed Skills

Having said that, some aspects of canoeing performance take place in a more predictable or *closed envi-*ronment. The length of the 1000 metre kayak sprint is just that, 1000 metres. The paddlers must keep to their lanes, and must paddle a boat that complies with all the rules. Although a performance in this situation is not a closed skill in a purist sense, the event does have major elements of predictability.

The Use of Memory

Our memory is a central player in the learning process. It is suggested that there are three distinguishable types of memory.

Short Term Sensory Store (STSS)

This can hold a vast amount of information but only for a very short period of time. Its main function is to take in environmental and proprioceptive information, which we as humans gather and process all the time. The environment provides information such as the direction of the local wind, water temperature, etc. The proprioceptive information is about what the individual is feeling and sensing throughout their body.

Short Term Memory (STM)

Which chunks of information we hold on to, and transfer to the STM, seems to be determined by the degree of relevance we give it. So while a novice may not pay any attention to the fact that the river is changing colour to a muddy brown, a more experienced paddler may well understand the relevance of this.

Our short-term memory (STM) holds the information, which our brain is attending to at any particular moment of time. It can only deal with limited chunks of information. Research suggests it amounts to only about seven bits of information plus or minus two, depending on the individual. The STM codes this input into groups of similar meaning, such as sounds, movement pattern, and timings. It will only hold on to this information while we attend to it, via practice, or by rehearsing it.

Without the opportunity to do something constructive with this information it fades and could be lost from our memory.

Long Term Memory (LTM)

Where we really remember things is in our long-term memory (LTM). It is here that we can recall information that we may not have used for some time. These memories (based on experiences) when recalled, are the basis on which coaches and paddlers decide what to do next.

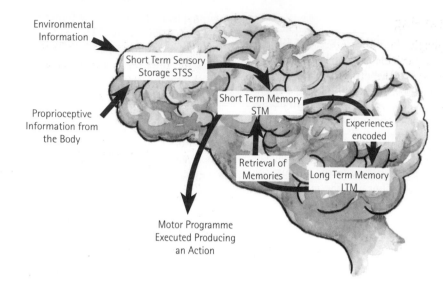

Environmental Information

Short Term Sensory Storage STSS

Proprioceptive Information from the Body

Short Term Memory STM

Experiences encoded

Retrieval of Memories

Long Term Memory LTM

Motor Programme Executed Producing an Action

Fig 7.3   Memory and Learning

Keith and Matt arrive at the top of the section of Grade 2 rapids. For both paddlers it is their first time on this river, but for Keith only the second time on Grade 2 (Matt can start using his LTM, Keith cannot). Matt looks downstream (using STM to receive this information). He notices a number of eddies on either side of the river and, in the middle of the main flow, a rock just covered by an inch or so of water (he remembers what this means from accessing his LTM). Using his own memories gained from past experience (LTM), he leads off, making an eddy turn behind the covered rock and then ferries across the river to the eddy below a tree to wait for Keith.

All Keith can see is a mass of white water (no LTM, and the STM is overloaded with too much information), it is like nothing he has seen before. As he sets off, the boat starts to wobble, a few support strokes keep him upright (all his STM ability is concerned with this action and not planning ahead). As he looks up to see where Matt is waiting, he hits the mid-stream covered rock, sending him spinning around and somehow he ends up next to Matt in the last eddy (completely down to luck).

As coaches we want to ensure that as much of the information made available to our students in their learning finds its way into their long-term memory. That process is not as simple as it sounds, and there are numerous other factors which can either interrupt or help secure this learning process.

Learning New Skills

Your body learns and remembers new sets of canoe sport related movements by building motor performance maps or *schemas* in the nervous system and brain. There is debate on the actual mechanics of this process, but the concept of us producing performance maps during our learning is a useful one. These maps or *schemas* only allow us to reproduce an act that the *schema* is related to, so if we have the *schema* for a sweep stroke it will not necessarily allow us to perform a stern rudder. There will be aspects of transferability between the learned act and the new one, so certain elements of trunk rotation action will transfer between the strokes and give us some advantage. But a new form of performance map will have to be built in order to reproduce a new action successfully time after time.

So we need to build adaptable maps, which give us a better chance to perform in new environments where we didn't originally learn the skill.

It seems that the most effective time to build these maps is when the paddler is both mentally and physically fresh. A safe fear-free environment will also increase the chance of secure learning. The contradiction for us as coaches is that research would support the idea that the most effective place to learn the new skill is in the conditions in which it is to be performed. This provides a number of conflicts for the coach to manage, particularly if the performance setting is a stressful one for the learner.

Stages of Learning

Learners go through a number of stages in their effort to master a particular movement or action. The ability to recognize the stages allows the coach to select the most productive approach for the student, and means that we can choose tasks that are challenging but achievable.

These stages have been given different titles by different writers. One thing unites them, the assumption that as the students make progress, the characteristics of their performance change as well.

Novices

The first stage is referred to as the *cognitive* stage. Any performance at this level takes a lot of mental effort.

Improvers

As we get better, the performance of the skill is more consistent and we enter the so-called *associative* stage. In this stage we are linking new patterns of movement with those already learned; errors still occur, but complex movements begin to emerge.

Experts

Those performers in the final stage, the *autonomous* stage, can produce skills with a high degree of accuracy and in a confident manner. They don't have to consciously think about what they are doing.

One factor to remember is that both coaches and students go through these developments. After all, they are both learning.

Learning and Performance Plateaux

Nothing de-motivates students like a feeling that they are not making progress. These ceilings are not necessarily related to learning but to performance. Students will often measure their own progress with what they can physically do (their performance), and if that seems to have stagnated they may become convinced they are not making progress.

This may not be the case. Students will often increase their understanding of a particular technique, and increase their experience of its application without showing immediate external signs of that improvement. Learning may well have taken place, but may not bear fruit for some time. This is where a coach's support is critical; change the tack of the session or try a new approach to that particular problem. Keep faith with both your coaching and the learner.

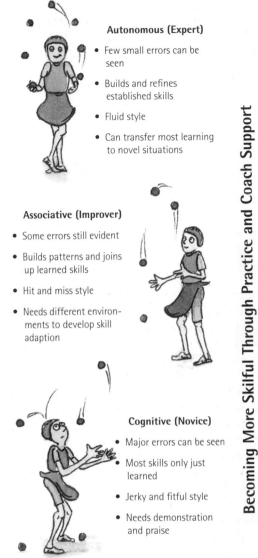

Autonomous (Expert)
- Few small errors can be seen
- Builds and refines established skills
- Fluid style
- Can transfer most learning to novel situations

Associative (Improver)
- Some errors still evident
- Builds patterns and joins up learned skills
- Hit and miss style
- Needs different environments to develop skill adaption

Cognitive (Novice)
- Major errors can be seen
- Most skills only just learned
- Jerky and fitful style
- Needs demonstration and praise

Becoming More Skilful Through Practice and Coach Support

Fig 7.4   Stages of Learning (Fitts and Posner 1967)

Making a Start

Where do you want to go? It will all depend on where you are starting from!

Gaining as much information about the students you are going to coach is one way of making sure the coaching is of benefit to all involved. The reason why this preparation period is so important is that, although your coaching may be inspirational, the venue just perfect and the equipment top notch, without the right start, the lesson could be pitched at an inappropriate level and end up failing all involved.

Holistic Methods

- Work well with novices.

- Take account of the environment.

- Suit certain types of skills (i.e. Gross).

- Can produce quick results.

Deductive Methods

- Help structure the observation.

- Uses structured methods such as Boat/Blade/Body/Brain.

- Can help locate hidden errors.

- Uses questioning to probe deeper.

Using Notation

- Excellent for competitive situations.

- Can involve the reduction of movement to key elements.

- Provides written evidence.

- Useful when observing a team or group of learners.

Using Video

- Excellent for capturing action.

- Can focus attention on fine errors or skills.

- Requires editing by the coach.

- Provides a history of learner's development.

Fig 7.5   Some methods of observation

There are a number of ways of gaining prior knowledge about our learners:

- By getting them to fill in a self assessment form

- Asking the students a number of questions about their wishes and motives

- Structured observation of the students' current performance

We can try and fit all the paddlers into the same predetermined boxes and hope they fit, but it is a lot more beneficial to all concerned if the coaching is tailored to that paddler or group.

Of course the complete beginner or group may have no starting point, so a standard 'come and try' course may be the best option for coach and students. After that first session you will have gained enough information to start moulding the programme to the students and their aspirations.

On the Water Observation

If the situation allows, and after getting people on the water safely, just take some time to sit and watch. This observation time will allow you to gather and assess a mass of useful information.

> *Observation gives the opportunity to establish what sport coaches call 'current reality', i.e. where the individual is, in terms of their performance level and skill base.*
>
> *Paddlers will have their own picture of this position. This is called 'perceived reality'. If this picture is different to current reality, agreement on issues such as feedback and goal setting could be problematic. Students could be undervaluing their own level of performance and end up underachieving, while others overestimate their own abilities and fail to concentrate on fundamental techniques, without which they will fail to progress.*
>
> *The coach's job, if needed, is to bring these two pictures together.*

There are more formal observation approaches that can be used, for example holistic methods can help you quickly pick up major errors, while the deductive ones may allow you to see the fine detail of an advanced paddler.

Key themes in observation:

- Remember that accurate observation takes time to carry out - so don't rush it.

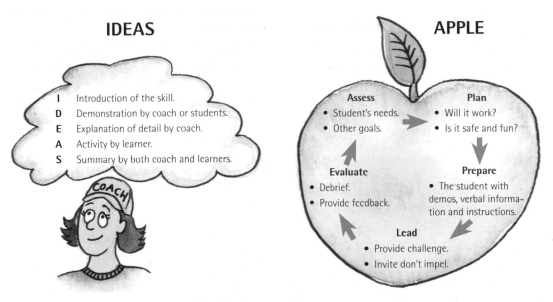

IDEAS

I Introduction of the skill.
D Demonstration by coach or students.
E Explanation of detail by coach.
A Activity by learner.
S Summary by both coach and learners.

APPLE

Assess
• Student's needs.
• Other goals.

Plan
• Will it work?
• Is it safe and fun?

Evaluate
• Debrief.
• Provide feedback.

Prepare
• The student with demos, verbal information and instructions.

Lead
• Provide challenge.
• Invite don't impel.

Fig 7.6   Some coaching structures

• Learners may well alter their performance if they feel they are being watched. Some get better, some get worse. Either way you will not get their true level of performance. Try and provide a relaxed atmosphere.

• Try and view the performer's skills from a number of viewpoints, it will help you gain a fuller picture of the overall performance.

• Ask yourself - is this a normal performance from this individual?

• Write the observations down.

• If you can, consider video taping the performance.

Structuring the Session

This student information gathering process is useful as it provides us with an accurate starting point; it will allow us to check a number of assumptions which are often made by both coaches and learners. Once armed with the picture of where they stand in their paddling progression, we can begin to structure the session around their improvement.

Coaching structures such as IDEAS (see Fig 7.6) can help novice coaches in the planning and running of the lessons they are responsible for. This structured approach gives a method to follow and run a session. As coaches become more experienced in their craft, they often become more reactive in the manner and directions that the session is allowed to take. Many successful coaches have a general aim

for the session they are going to teach, but could not detail the actual method they will use to get there.

Don't be afraid to change direction during a coaching session, if the situation and progress is not as you expected. Sometimes, the environment or individual learners will provide ideal coaching moments. Remember that coaching structures are there to help you, not shackle you.

Length of the Session

With novice paddlers, and in particular children, any aspects of the session where direct coaching is being undertaken should be short and punchy. Learning new skills is a trying business. With these types of groups, interrupt the coaching with a number of games and informal breaks. Research indicates that games are very beneficial to the learning process, even though the students may not be aware of the similarities between what they have just been taught and the movements and strokes the games themselves demand of them.

Try not to focus the session on the learning of any one aspect or individual skill for more than fifteen minutes or so; you can always return to it later. This is a long time for someone's first time in a canoe or kayak. A beginner has a lot of things to think about. Their short-term memory (STM) is jam-packed with all sorts of excitements and fears, which the more experienced paddlers have left behind as they have become more skilful.

More mature learners can handle longer periods of direct coaching, but be aware of the law of diminishing returns.

When teaching someone to roll, they probably only have a certain number of attempts in them, before the quality of the learning experience drops off dramatically. That cut-off time may well be sooner than the learner wishes. They may feel like they can go on, but continuing will lower the performance level and leave them feeling demoralized if they are unsuccessful. It is a hard call (but something a successful coach is capable of) stopping the session before that time arrives.

In any one session you may only be coaching physical motor skills for one quarter of that time. Warming up, setting the scene, explaining the next practice routine, and debriefing the session is all part of what makes up successful coaching behaviours.

Coaching Behaviours and Processes

Coach / Learner Verbal Communication

Cut down to its basic elements, the coaching process is often no more than an exchange of information. That exchange may be used to give verbal instruction, verbal information and in the use of questioning.

Verbal Instruction

This is used when we want the paddler to turn the verbal message given into a physical action.

For example, "Pete, on the next wave, use the trim of the boat to move around".

It will be helped by:

- Planning what you are going to say, before saying it.

- Remembering the type of learner you are talking to, and the stage of learning they are going through. Make the instruction understandable.

- Giving the instruction when the student is in the best physical and mental position to receive it. Wait until they have completely stopped any physical activity.

- Be clear and concise in what you say. Use only 8 or less words in any one set of instructions. Remember, less is more.

- Use language which can conjure up a picture of a movement – such as 'Dig' the blade in.

- Check that the message has been understood; get students to repeat in their own words the instructions given.

Fig 7.7 Linking students' past experiences to new learning

- You must provide opportunities for the instruction to be carried out in a practical application.

- For our learners to turn the words spoken into a required action they must be able to understand, relate to and remember what has been said.

Photo 7.2   Keep verbal instruction clear and concise

Not all verbal communication is used to introduce new movements or concepts. Some verbal input is best used to reassure or keep the individuals on task.

Learners will often turn to the coach when practising a stroke or technique, looking for confirmation that they are on track. A quick 'Yes' or 'Go on then' may be all that is needed.

Verbal Information

Verbal information is what a coach gives to help underpin and support a paddler. Explaining that selecting the right length paddle in the transfer from being a doubles open boat paddler to a solo one is supportive information. The receiver will not turn that input into a particular action but it will help them make decisions later on.

The following points will help your verbal input:

- Don't interrupt the learning.

- Don't turn away students who come to you asking for additional information. These are excellent and potent coaching moments. Take them.

- Try and link the input and new information to a past event or indicate where it may be of use.

Any efforts you can make to individualize the verbal input given to the learners will help build positive relationships. Relating the description of a new activity to a past one will help them associate the action with another learning experience. This action of relating novel action to their past experience is called using 'hooks and hangers'.

A snow boarder, new to modern playboating, will have past experiences which will help them relate to the importance of edge transfer.

Using these help learners build a relationship between different chunks of learning.

Questioning as a Coaching Tool

The use of questioning by coaches can gain and give information that cannot be displayed within a physical action.

Asking students questions about what they are just about to do, or have just performed, gives us an additional indication of the level and depth of understanding the paddler has gained about those movements.

One of the disadvantages in the use of questioning as a coaching tool is that it can take time to get to the end goal. Be careful not to over-play questioning, as it can be frustrating for the student if the type and standard of question are not pitched at the right level.

For example: A coach working with some novice kayakers wishes to develop their understanding of the physics involved in boat movement and the relationships between the boat, body and the blade. After the initial warm-up, the coach asks one of the group to remind the rest of the team what they decided last week about what actually happens during a basic forward stroke. This is done in the form of a question. Having correctly stated that the body is pulled up to the blade, the students are then given the task of practising a variety of sweep strokes and left with the question, "Which parts of the body move during the completion of this stroke?" After five minutes of individual experimentation, the group re-gather with a number of answers and their own set of questions and queries for each other. The coach chairs the discussion, probing deeper and asking each for clarification. The group arrives at their own answer, (i.e. the legs move away from the static blade and upper body).

Questions are also an excellent assessment tool. We often believe that an instruction or briefing given by us is clear and simple to understand, and only when each student disappears in totally different directions and starts doing completely different things do we realize our assumptions were false ones.

The following is a rough guide to the pro's and con's of the major types of question and their uses:

Yes / No Questions

These are to the point but very limited, e.g. "Do you have your 3 Star Award?"

Closed Questions

These still allow only a very limited range of answers and, like yes/no questions, are useful if you are pushed for time and only require very specific information, e.g. "Which Star Award do you hold?"

Open Questions

These are questions that aim to gain a depth of answer from the student, e.g. "What sort of paddling experience have you had?"

Of course when asking such a question, the answer can only be the student's, and we need to remember that the answer may not be the one you expected or wanted.

Leading Questions

These are when the questioner phrases a question in such a way that it is difficult not to give the answer that the questioner wants to hear, e.g. "We don't want to get wet, do we?"

They are often used even when we think we are not using them.

The classic... "Do you all understand?" may seem open, but it takes a fairly confident learner to turn round to the coach and answer, "No, not a single word!"

Reverse Questions

The question in this case is turned around and used to probe the student for his or her own ideas. If the student asks, "Which line should I take on my approach to slalom gate 15?" the coach may respond with, "Do you want a safe or fast line?" or "What options are you considering?"

Other Points

Questions, both written or verbal, may be perceived as being intrusive and threatening. It helps if you already have some form of working relationship with the paddlers and if you, as a coach openly encourage students to ask questions about, and during any coaching delivery.

The main benefit of questioning is to encourage the learners to get away from the false idea that coaches are the sole providers of knowledge, and that effective learning can only take place with them in the coaching relationship. Getting learners to be critical thinkers and take the responsibility for their own progress is a coaching skill; we are there to help students learn, not to provide all the answers. It is important before entering into any verbal interface to ask the central question, "Why am I saying this, and for who's benefit is this being said?"

If you are not convincing in any of the answers you have given yourself, say nothing.

Silence is a hard coaching skill to perfect but a powerful one.

The Effective Use of Demonstrations

Another way of communicating with students is by the use of demonstrations. Much of our early learning as children is achieved through this observational learning, watching others and then reproducing their action. Demonstrations help convey details of a movement that verbal instructions often cannot. They allow students to get a sense of the timing and flow of a movement. These visual pictures are coded by the brain and then turned into a physical representation of what we have just seen.

Demonstrations can also provide goals to aim for as students get to see what their effort should end up looking like. For some learners the visual elements of this type of communication can conjure up a very potent image.

Demonstration can be made more effective by the following:

- Make sure that all of the students can see the demo and any water feature that relates to the timing or position of the action.

- Make sure that the demonstration can be copied by the observer.

Consider the appropriateness of the demonstration at the particular stage of learning. Target it so it is within the abilities of the students. Children and those who may feel insecure with their own learning can feel de-motivated if they believe they cannot achieve what is asked of them.

- Perform the action in silence.

Generally students are fully occupied when taking on this visual information and will only be distracted if you give a verbal commentary over the top of the demo.

Autonomous learners may well be able to distinguish the verbal from the visual, but as a rule, separate them.

- Be wary when showing negative demonstrations.

If we are suggesting that demos are very useful and powerful tools, we need to be careful when showing what went wrong in a performance. It is asking a lot of learners to disregard the last set of visual information given, and then to return to the correct performance.

- Help the learner in the observation.

Point out to the learner the key aspects of the movement that they should focus on. Just saying 'Watch this' can be very confusing for learners.

They may focus on aspects which contribute to the complete action, but are not key elements. So help the learner by giving a short list (no more than three, less if they have no knowledge of the action being shown) of cues for them to keep an eye out for.

- Tell them when the demonstration is starting and finishing.

Frame the demo, giving it a definite start and finish.

- Use others to demonstrate to learners.

Sometimes students may feel that their efforts to copy a coach's demonstration are doomed to failure. They have been paddling eighteen minutes, you eighteen years. Using other members of the class may get over this problem of confidence. Video footage of other paddlers can also produce excellent models.

- Give the student opportunities to practise what they have seen.

Demonstrations help give learners a rough outline of the way a particular stroke or technical movement should be performed. So, for novices with little or no knowledge of the action this is both powerful and appropriate. For those who have the general movement and are picking up additional information, the demonstration may be less potent. What learners do is customize the information gained from these earlier demos.

Each individual student has a whole range of elements that they need to build into their own performance repertoire.

Expert paddlers will have their own style and much of their own improvement is in the development of what they can already perform. The use of video here is useful because it gives them a picture of their paddling actions, which may be different to the image they have of themselves.

Indeed, some elite coaches cannot paddle, and therefore use others to provide demonstrations for them if needed. Their role is more of an observer and provider of information than an introducer of new information.

The Use of Effective Practice

It used to be said that practice makes perfect. We now know it doesn't.

Practice makes permanent. It is clear that paddlers who perform at the highest level still practise a great deal. Top-flight slalom performers still paddle gates even though they have done them a million times before.

Types of Practice

There are different types of practice structures which all have differing results.

Blocked Practice

This is where a particular motor action is performed time and time again. Paddlers practising a particular skill over and over again have an opportunity to *groove* that action. This does allow the paddler opportunities to gain a lot of experience in a short time, but it has the drawback of lacking variety and maybe interest.

Random Practice

Here a number of different tasks are given to the paddler for them to perform. They are reproduced once or twice before going on to something new.

This type of practice has a number of advantages. It allows for a variety of tasks to be performed at the

Random?

The term 'random' can be misleading in this context. A coach may set up a number of practices that are varied enough to be considered 'random' in terms of how our brain 'grooves in' a physical skill, but closely related enough to be retained in memory. This is why some coaches prefer the term 'varied' practice.

For example:

If you ask a student to do 30 break-ins from the same eddy, at the same speed, at the same angle, with the same amount of edge, that would be 'blocked' practice.

You could ask a student to practice break-ins and break-outs (which are similar skills), to do 2 on the left and 2 on the right, 2 at full speed, 2 very slowly, and 2 at cruising speed, 2 at a wide angle of attack, 2 at a narrow angle and 2 in between, 2 with lots of edge, 2 with a middling amount and 2 with very little. You could then get them to repeat all the various variations with different stroke combinations and then move on down the river to repeat the sequence on a different jet of water.

Your student would end up doing a lot more than 30 break-ins but only have done 2 the same way. This would still be termed 'random' practice.

same time, and by a number of learners at different times. The main potency of this type of practice is that it may closely mirror what you might do normally in your paddling.

Pros and Cons

Research suggests that blocked practice may quickly improve the performance of the student, but that improvement may not be long-term and turned into secure learning. However, it does seem to benefit novices who are trying a movement out for the first time, as it allows them to gain a strong picture of something new to them.

Random or *varied* practice may well produce less immediate results, but research suggests that the learning is more secure, allowing greater retention.

Why Should This Random Mixture Work?

It is suggested that because the actions of the learner are broken up, the paddler's brain can relate to the distinctiveness of the individual actions. This separation allows the mind to build a clear picture on what is required to reproduce the particular task. Having other tasks to perform and practise at the same time may help the individual categorize these individual actions. This phenomenon is referred to as *the contextual interference effect*.

The choice of which to use is down to a number of factors. For students who need to see a quick result, blocked practice is probably best, even if they forget it next week, while efforts to produce long-term learning are best served by random practice routines.

For novice learners, practice helps because:

- It allows them to rehearse the demonstration they have just seen.
- It begins to produce a physical element to something, which before may only have been a mental picture.
- It allows them to customize the action to suit their individual bodies and their intended outcomes.
- It provides a memory of a motor action, which can be called upon in future when needed.
- When successfully performed, it provides motivation and reassurance to the learner.

For Associative and Autonomous learners practice helps because:

- It provides opportunities to adapt and mould the action to new environments.
- It builds the experience base of the individual. They will increase the situations in which they can perform such an action.
- It may allow the physical rehearsal of techniques, which if performed in the real environment would be stressful.
- It allows the coach to observe the performance of the student.

Practise Where You Would Paddle

As most paddling environments that we want students to perform in are ever changing, the practice situations we use should reflect this. The most effective environment to practise in is the environment in which the skill is going to be used. The next best thing is to provide as much variety of practice as possible.

The Practice Environment

A classic case of the practice environment not matching the performance environment is in rolling. Most UK paddlers learned their rolling skills in a swimming pool; some of those will go on to be committed canoe polo players, but the majority will spend the rest of their paddling careers in a river, sea or lake environment. However, they learned in a pool, usually rolling without buoyancy aid or other paddling kit on. Then, when they try and transfer the performance to an outside situation they often fail.

I am not suggesting that we should not teach in a pool, but we must use it as a stepping-stone to the environment where the paddler is more likely to need that skill. We need to progress the student in stages towards the target environment.

The practice situation should match the intended performance situation as closely as possible.

Practising on Both Sides

One other element we should build into the practice routine is the use of both sides of the body. Try and select practice areas and routines which have both a two-sided physical and environment element. The idea that we should gain competence on one side before moving on to the other is a false notion.

Encourage your learners to interchange sides as they complete the tasks you have set them.

Some paddlers, particularly beginners, will tend to concentrate on actions which give them confidence and a feeling of success. So don't be surprised to see learners, when given a choice, practise on one side only, and work on something they are already good at.

Research would indicate that the time spent on an individual's weaker side has benefit for both the stronger and weaker sides. So be strict on this dualism.

Using Mental Practice (Imagery)

Paddling skills are a mixture of both physical and mental performance. Before we execute any stroke or technique, we must engage the brain to allow the body to perform the physical element of the task. This mental side to a performance can be practised as well.

The coaching and use of mental practice is a skill, and like many other skills, it takes time to get the

most benefit from its application. The example I give is just one aspect of a diverse and complex area.

Dave and his coach Helen are working at the local weir. Dave is just at the stage where he is beginning to feel comfortable moving along the weir's stopper.

Helen and Dave's aim for the session is to get Dave to a point where he can stop and move forward and backward, to give him greater boat control.

Helen is aware that this type of session can be very tiring, and there is a maximum length of time that Dave can be active before fatigue takes its toll, and the quality of the learning drops.

After a successful practice where Dave is beginning to take the weight off the blade and be more centred over the boat, Helen calls him into a safe eddy and asks him to close his eyes and remember what it felt like to be in balance. Dave talks quietly about his last successful practice. Still with his eyes closed and sitting in the eddy, he imagines making the drawing movements of the paddle as he pulls out of the stopper and into the safe eddy.

Having rested and practised physically and mentally, Dave has benefited from two practice situations whilst only having the stress of one physical practice routine.

Analysing Performance and Giving Feedback

Coaches observe performance and use feedback to support and correct aspects of the movement being undertaken.

In some books this process is called fault correction; this implies a negative approach to the process of feedback. A common fault of coaches is to concentrate on what the student is doing wrong, not supporting them in the reinforcement of the correct performance and what they are doing right. One thing that unites beginners is that they often don't understand or recognize when they are doing something right. Telling the student what is working and why it is, will allow them to continue a practice routine with confidence and focus.

The skill in analysing any paddler's performance is to understand both what the action should look like when performed correctly and if not, why that is the case. The coach also needs to understand the cause of the performance errors they observe.

In novices these errors in performance are often considerable and obvious and are known as *gross motor errors*. In more advanced performers they are referred to as *fine motor errors*. As the names suggest, these aspects of the performance need a keener eye to be identified accurately, and a greater understanding of what is really happening in the execution of the movement.

Photo 7.3   Wait until the student is ready!

Some important considerations:

- Take time in analysing the performance. Some errors are only temporary and the learner will self-correct these after a number of attempts. Make sure that what you see is really consistent.

- Some aspects of a paddler's performance may be very visible but not affecting the quality of the particular task which is being completed. Make sure you can identify and separate a symptom from a root cause.

- Not all causes of error can be seen. Things such as movements below the spray deck, and the degree of psychological arousal, may not be easily noticed.

- If you believe that there is more than meets the eye, you may have to question the performer to complete a fuller analysis of the action.

- After analysing an action, ask yourself if you need to pass comment? Some learners develop their own particular style, it may not suit us, but it is effective for them. Also, do you have the time to address the fault this session, as it might be best left for another day?

After making an analysis and before offering the student feedback, you might wish to question the students about their own paddling performance. Mature learners are quite often aware of their own technical faults and just need you to confirm that what you see is what they feel. If the right analysis and corrections can come from the students themselves, we as coaches are on the road to producing independent learners.

Giving Feedback

Feedback is something about the quality and nature of the performance just seen, performed or experienced. It can also be general in nature, when used to support and praise the learner. "Well done Mike, I could see the effort in your face that time."

If we wish to use it to change or reinforce an action or behaviour, then the feedback given to a student needs to be as specific as possible and related to an action that can be clearly identified.

External Feedback from Coaches

The most common form of external feedback is that which is given to the performer by the coach. This itself can be in the form of verbal input, a thumbs up sign, or an agreeable smile.

Any of these can have the desired effect of encouraging the individual in their efforts and giving reassurance that the performance they are displaying is the correct one.

The process of giving external coach-related feedback could be structured in this way:

- After rehearsing what you want to say in your head, gain the learner's direct attention.

- Wait a few seconds for the learner to finish the practice or activity undertaken.

- When they are ready and only then, give the feedback.

Using this loose structure will help:

Observation - Effect - Change or Repeat

For example:

Observation

" Kerry - On gate number thirteen, you took a wider path before turning downstream."

Effect

"That is why your stern touched the inside pole, and we got a penalty."

Change or Repeat

"So, on the next two runs, turn slightly before the gate, power through and go on to gate fourteen. Are you clear on that? OK, that's good, away you go."

Remember to give feedback on something which can be identified. General comments like, "Well done" are good for showing support for your student but not if you need to change or reinforce their actions.

Sometimes paddlers will not understand when they are getting it right. One of the jobs of a coach is to help confirm to the student that their performance is correct.

So, remember to encourage the fast learners and offer support to those who need additional guidance.

> *Scott is coaching at his local club, which is based alongside a canal. The junior section of the sprint squad are working on their forward stroke. Scott is keen to get the youngsters to develop a more effective swing action in their stroke.*
>
> *He sets them off on a series of 100 metre paddles. He cycles alongside noting the performance of the six squad members. Sally and Glen are performing well, while the others need additional help. Scott calls them over and waves at Sally and Glen to complete another set of sprints. The four are given corrective feedback and later join their friends. Scott lets the team complete two more sets, and supports the four who are picking up the new technique. Sally and Glen feel ignored; they were unaware that they had picked up the new action so well.*
>
> *Scott should have given feedback to the whole group. He could have initially given supportive feedback to reinforce Sally and Glen's performance, and corrective feedback for the rest of the group, followed by supportive feedback to the whole group.*

Other Types of External Feedback

Video

A videotape of the performer is an additional form of external feedback. It is particularly useful for learners who may not take on the feedback given by a coach or outsider. As they say, the camera never lies! The use of video is beyond the scope of this chapter but generally be careful with its usage. Video images of your own performance as a paddler or coach can be very disheartening. We are not always as we see ourselves.

Any video clips used should be previewed by the coach before being shown to the learner and be kept short and sweet. For technical aspects, it also allows the coach and paddlers to sit down and concentrate on those small details, which may only be observable with repeat viewing and the advantage of slow motion.

Photo 7.4   Try and make feedback an individual experience

Peer

Using other students to help coach one another is an excellent method of involving the whole group. Working in teams of two or three helps each individual focus on an aspect of the paddler's action. Beginners will need briefing with this coaching technique, while more advanced learners may already be developing observation skills themselves.

Key pointers in giving feedback:

- Only give one or two points of feedback at a time. Mature learners may be able to deal with three points.

- Check with the paddler that you are both talking about the same event.

- Select aspects that will make the biggest differences first.

- Focus on telling students what they are doing right, use feedback to reinforce correct performance.

- Foster internal feedback within learners (see below).

- Listen to what the learners have to say about their performance – they may highlight things you hadn't noticed.

Internal Feedback

Internal feedback happens all the time. Our bodies pick up a whole range of sense and feeling about the paddling we undertake and the effect of the environment on our bodies.

Internal feedback is like a radio that is on all the time. As a learner, we may not be aware of the numerous messages it continues to send to us while we paddle.

> *Maggie is working on her open canoe solo strokes.*
>
> *She warms up and then goes through her repertoire. With her sweep strokes she feels the pressure on her knees; it seems to transfer from one to the other as the blade is brought around. She feels her lower body twisting around as she completes her forward sweep. Her 'J' stroke is flowing today. She closes her eyes and senses the smooth transfer of weight as she pulls herself up to the anchored blade.*
>
> *The muscles used feel relaxed and fluid as she paddles off. She is listening to her body and its feedback.*

The job of the coach is to get the students to tune in to that radio, turn it up and listen to what is being played. The benefit of the radio is that it plays an individual's own tune. The feedback it gives is not somebody's impression of what happened but our own. The student just has to trust the messages coming from within.

The potency of internal feedback is that it begins to equip students with their own coaching tools. It allows them to seek internal confirmation and to value these unique experiences. Similarly to some aspects of mental self-coaching, not all students find it easy to listen to their own bodies. It may take time, and some patience on behalf of coach and learner for this method to start working. But do persevere, as the benefits are considerable.

Getting Feedback

Sometimes coaches are so concerned with providing or encouraging students to think about feedback, that they forget to ask for it themselves. Students are the central consumers and partners in the coaching process and we should value their views and perceptions of our input. We should make efforts to get their opinions. You may discover that you are better than you think!

Setting Goals in Coaching

Goal setting is a process that helps learners focus on targets for the present and targets for the future. Some paddlers are driven by their desire to learn an individual technique, to complete their first roll, to make that gate, to start slalom racing, to have fun. Others may be focused on the wilderness experience a gentle sea paddle may bring them. Competition paddlers and coaches have long worked with goal setting as part of their normal routine. The act of slalom is a classic example of short-term goal setting - making that gate. Medium-term goal setting - get a top third place in this round of events, and long-term goal setting - in their desire to make the team by their twenty-first birthday.

- Goals improve the quality of practice sessions.
- Goals help clarify expectations of both coach and student.
- Goals help relieve boredom by making training more challenging.
- Goals help coaches and students measure progress.
- Goals increase intrinsic motivation to achieve.
- Goals can be short, medium and long term.
- Goals should be agreed by both parties.

Most coaches will use goal setting to some degree, even if they believe they don't. Very few of us start with no ideas on the direction a session will take.

Effective goal setting, which results in long-term learning, is nearly always a shared activity. The type of goal set may also be subject to the degree of support that you can give the student, and their confidence.

Don't force goals onto your students without their permission. Individuals may feel that they are being manipulated and end up being de-motivated, without any personal investment in the goal setting process.

Having said that, some students, particularly novices have little idea of what is possible, while the coach on the other hand has seen dozens of beginners at their stage of development and learning. Here, the skill of the coach is to convince the paddler of the possibilities that lay before them, to encourage them to push themselves and not underachieve.

It is a difficult balancing game for the coach to get right; you want to involve the student in their learning, but wish them to get the most from the activity.

"Sometimes learners don't know what they don't know yet."

Outcome Goals

Students who are motivated by goals and targets, such as running a particular named fall, or reducing their time for the 1000 metre K1 by five seconds, are said to be focusing on *outcome* goals. They just want to achieve that particular target.

These goals are easily measured and can be determined by a particular event, but they can be problematic. The sprint racer who is striving to knock off five seconds from their personal best time may get injured a month before the end of the season. If that reduction is the sole goal of their season, then it could be argued that they have failed due to the goal set not being met.

The problem with outcome goals is that they fail to acknowledge the improvement process that has taken place in the effort to make the outcome goal, in this case to make that individual faster.

Process Goals

Maybe a better focus is to set process goals which take note of the incremental improvement in technique.

Again, differing individuals will be motivated by differing visions. It is unlikely that an eight year old novice can be driven by a ten-year master plan, but some people can be excited by the opportunities that long-term skill learning may give them. Goals are not obstacles to be got over but bench marks of development. Used purposefully they can help coach and student achieve more than was first thought possible.

Coaching Children

Children are not small adults, nor should they be treated or coached as such.

If we are to coach them effectively we need to understand in which ways they differ. We also tend to clump the under-sixteen age group together, even though a young paddler of ten years of age is mentally and physically very different from a seven year

old. In addition, children can be very conscious of their own age and size, and you may be better off, if selecting groups, to consider the size and physical maturity of the young people rather than just age.

Photo 7.5   Children are not small adults

Most children are introduced to paddling because some adult thought it could be good for them. It is all too easy for the motives of a well-meaning adult or parent to be interpreted as the reasons why the children are there.

Be sensitive to children's own needs, even more so than with adults; children need to be treated like individuals. Learn the name of each child, or the name they would like to be called by. Spend some time listening to what the individual has to say about their wants and wishes. Set realistic expectations for the kids. Remember, not all individuals may take to a new sport, so don't be surprised if there is a high drop-out rate.

Research indicates that for many young people, the excitement of being with their friends, using and trying on different bits of novel equipment is more important than the nature of the activity itself.

The teaching of children and young people requires a set of individual coaching skills in its own right. Not all coaches make good coaches of young people. For some coaches, their only experience of young people is the fact that they once were one.

Children respond to positive reinforcement and are motivated by praise, so make sure that the session involves lots of opportunities for success and that the children are able to recognize that. Most motivation for the child participating comes from the individuals themselves, and it is misplaced to try and convince a child to continue with something they wish to stop. Reverse psychology doesn't work with children.

The coaching of children often produces unexpected results, and the fact that at a young age they are not contained by convention means that sometimes you need to just sit back and watch their imagination at work.

Some top tips and handy hints:

- Learn the reasons why the children are there; don't ask the teacher or parent, ask the kids.

- Remember that children get mentally and physically tired very quickly. Watch for signs of this, and change track, stop the session or have regular refreshment breaks.

- Children will often feel the cold, and will turn from involved individuals to shivering bystanders in a flash.

- Incorporate games into the learning. Young people thrive on involvement and activity.

- Be careful when introducing elements of competition. Not all children enjoy the stigma of perceived failure.

- Be careful when using boats and other items of equipment that are designed for adults. Poor fitting equipment can increase tiredness and put strains on developing bodies.

- Be very clear in your own mind of the moral, ethical and legal requirements of working with minors. If in doubt ask the appropriate authorities (see Chapter 6 Safety and Leadership).

Keeping it Fresh

Being a paddlesport coach is hugely rewarding. It can give feelings of complete joy one moment and considerable frustration the next. The key to reducing those times of frustration to a bare minimum is to keep your coaching fresh. One approach which is worth considering is taking up a new aspect of the sport yourself.

Being a beginner again can remind you of many of the problems and joys that your learners experience. It may help you empathize with the process that they go through with you. It also has the additional benefits that you may get to observe other coaches as they coach you, and you can steal a few of their ideas!

Photo 7.6   The type of paddling may be different, the common element is that we coach people to learn

I would encourage you to work closely with others within coaching, and to listen to all those who have something to offer. Getting someone to coach you on your own coaching delivery is not something we tend to do much of, which is a shame because it can be a very productive process for all concerned.

"You do not have to be ill to get better!"

When you pick up a new coaching tool, remember that like most newly learned skills, we sometimes get its application wrong. If it has not worked that particular time, reassess but don't reject; with a different group on a new day it might just be the tool you need.

Remember, students will always forgive you if you experiment in your coaching, but seldom if you are boring!

Further Reading

The following texts have the Sport Sciences as their knowledge base, and therefore they will have varying degrees of accessibility to those without a basic sport science background. Texts that lend themselves to an easy introduction to the subject area are indicated in red.

Christina R & Corcos D, 1988, Coaches Guide to Teaching Sports Skills, Human Kinetics, 1-800-747-4457

Cross N & Lyle J, 1999 The Coaching Process: Principles and Practice for Sport, Butterworth-Heinemann, 0-7506-4131-2

Gallwey T & Kriegel B, 1977, Inner Skiing - Revised Edition, Random House, 0-679-77827-6

Galvin, B, 1998, A Guide to Mentoring Sports Coaches, NCF, 1-902523-03-2

Kidman L & Hanrahan S, 1997, The Coaching Process: A Practical Guide to Improving Your Effectiveness, Dunmore Press, 0-86469-285-4

Martins R, 1987, Coaches Guide to Sports Psychology, Human Kinetics, 0-87622-022-6

Martins R, 1997, Successful Coaching, Human Kinetics, 0-88011-666-8

Mawer M, 1995 The Effective Teaching of Physical Education, Longman 0-582-095220

Mc Cluggage D, 1986, The Centered Skier, A Bantam New Age book, 0-553-24508-2

Schmidt R & Wrisberg C, Motor Learning and Performance, 2000, Human Kinetics 08801155009

Syer J & Connolly C, 1984, Sporting Body Sporting Mind - An Athlete's Guide to Mental Training, Cambridge University Press, 0-521-26935-0

Wolff R, 2000, Coaching Kids for Dummies, IDG Books world wide, 0-7645-5197-3

Websites:

www.sportscoachuk.org - The site of Sports Coach UK (previously the National Coaching Foundation). A government funded body running coach courses and supplying information on issues such as child protection.

www.brianmac.demon.co.uk - A private site run by a national athletics coach. Lots of information and updated on a regular basis.

www.chre.vt.edu/-/cys - A university based site offering an electronic newsletter for coaches, athletes and parents focusing on youth sports.

www.sports-media.org - A search engine , mainly P.E. based. Has a number of good links.

www.mindtools.com/page11.html - An academic sport psychology site. Lots of information on the mental side of coaching and learning.

www.ais.org.au - Australian Institute of Sports website. Generally considered to be one of the leaders in working with performance based athletes. Has a sports science section and links.

www.peaksports.com - Free psychology newsletter. You can ask the editor questions about coaching situations.

Bill Taylor

Bill is a Londoner by birth and spent most of his early paddling career racing up and down the River Thames in sprint boats. It was only in his early twenties that he widened his interests to include the rest of what paddlesport has to offer. Bill made first descents in Africa, Pakistan and the former Soviet Union, completed a six month solo sea paddle in the South Pacific, and a three month solo canoe paddle along the length of the River Danube. He even managed to represent Britain at white water rafting.

He would now consider himself to be a jack-of-all-trades but a master of none. His current interests are in developing coach education programmes for the BCU. Bill is presently employed by Manchester Metropolitan University, where he teaches Outdoor Education.

8 Use of a Pool

When I was a kid I was repeatedly told, "stop mucking around" and "don't sink the boats". Teaching me to roll seemed to be my instructor's most important objective. Since becoming an instructor myself, I look back and feel that all the playing I did is directly linked to the skill, balance, confidence and boat awareness I have today. Needless to say, it took me a long time to achieve a roll!

Introduction

A pool is a fantastic environment in which to be introduced to kayaking or to learn or refine new skills. Pools are warm; this allows you to get stuck in for as long as you wish without the fear of being uncomfortably cold, any time of year!

A pool is enclosed, has no rocks, trees, moving water or other such natural hazards. It shelters you from the prevailing weather conditions and distracting noises. All of these distractions may be a little daunting for the newcomer, or hard work if you are trying to get to grips with a new skill.

The best thing about a pool is that most people have been in one at some point during their lives (probably to have fun!) This means that they will already be at ease and ready to have even more fun.

This chapter will give some ideas on how the beginner, and even the more experienced can gain confidence and develop balance, co-ordination and reactions through a few exercises, games and challenges.

However, even pools can be hazardous, so we will look at safety first.

Safety

Pools have slippery floors and hard edges. They are full of water and in places they are too deep to touch the floor. Fill them with overexcited people who have boats and paddles and (if it is not managed properly), it becomes an increasingly hazardous environment.

You will have to adhere to the safety rules of the pool you are using. In addition to these, there are safety considerations specific to paddlesport. The BCU produce a leaflet which addresses all of these.

However, here are a few points to consider:

- Is the pool session being supervised by a coach with appropriate qualifications?

- Do the boats or paddles being used have sharp edges which need padding?

- Is the coach to student ratio correct?

- Do you really need paddles? If so, manage the use of them so that people don't get hurt.

Managing a Pool Session Safely

Just by thinking about where you stand as the coach or supervisor, you can lessen the chance of an accident. Wherever possible, someone should be on the side supervising/lifeguarding, with no coaching responsibilities. This means 'the lifeguard' has sight over everyone and everything that is going on. If you are coaching in the pool, stand with your back against the side in one of the corners so you can still help oversee the session.

Photo 8.1   Coach standing with her back to the corner - facing the action

Always know exactly how many people you have in kayaks and how many you have in the water at any one time. By having quick head counts you can rest assured that you know where everyone is.

Do you need to use paddles? If yes, make sure there is enough room, so that no one gets hit. You may have to make activity numbers smaller, and run the session in two or three groups with the others watching from the side.

Make an agreement with the people using the paddle on the amount of attempts they are going to have before giving up and letting the paddle go. For instance, after three attempts the buddy will know it will be safe to go in and help right the kayaker, without getting their toes chopped with the paddle.

Use a command word or a whistle to stop all activity, and brief the group on what this is before the session starts, so that you can have instant control whenever you need it.

Think about the structure of your session. You can easily put someone out of their comfort zone by pitching the session at too high a level. It is better to build people's confidence first, and go through things at a steady pace.

Gaining Confidence

You do not have to be a good swimmer or 'able bodied' to come kayaking because we wear buoyancy aids. We can also wear them in the pool.

Before introducing boats and paddles, have a splash around; get heads wet, play games and be happy. This will get rid of any inhibitions and give you a good warm-up.

Get into the pool, have a swim around. Then, try a forward roll; by getting your head wet and learning to orientate yourself you will build confidence.

Once you've tried a forward roll, try a backward roll, then a sideways roll by getting in a long torpedo shape. To be able to do these rolls, you may have to discover new body movements.

Photo 8.2   Doing a handstand

Trying an underwater handstand or swimming through somebody else's legs will develop your judgement of distance. Underwater objects appear 25% larger and closer, so swimming to the floor, to someone's legs or to the side might seem to take forever.

The direction from which a noise is coming may also be deceiving. Sound travels faster and much further underwater, allowing you to pick up weird and wonderful sounds which may be coming from the other side of the pool. These facts make being underwater a completely new environment, so the more time you can spend in it the more at home you will be.

You can use goggles and a nose-clip if you want. It's not nice having water up your nose when you're upside down in a pool and for some people the water can sting their eyes. Most importantly, being able to see clearly will put you more at ease.

Photo 8.3   Goggles and nose-clip

Your confidence will grow the longer you are in the water. There are plenty of games you can play, like water polo, tag and stuck in the mud.

Polo

For a game of polo you need two teams, a ball and two goals; the goals can be a kayak balanced on its edge. To score you must get the ball into the cockpit.

Photo 8.4   Polo

- With one boat at each end of the pool, the two teams try to score in the opponents' goal.
- You must not touch any of the other team.
- You cannot hold the ball for more than the count of three.
- At the start of the game and after a goal has been scored, the referee throws the ball randomly back into the pool.
- You can play the game with one goal in the shallow end, with both teams shooting at it.

Tag

- One person is 'it' and tries to tag the others. To do this they touch a person's shoulder.

- Once somebody has been tagged they must wait ten seconds before they can go after someone else, allowing everyone to get away.

Stuck in the Mud

Stuck in the mud is similar to tag. However once you have been tagged you must stand with arms and legs wide apart and stay in this position until someone is able to release you.

- The way the others can release someone is by swimming through the tagged person's legs.
- The idea of the game is for the person who is 'it' to tag everyone who is playing.

Sink an Island

Sinking an island is virtually impossible to do but it's good fun trying!

Photo 8.5   Sink an island

- In small groups of 4 or 5, try in whatever fashion imaginable to sink the kayak to the bottom of the pool.

Roll a Boat

Roll a boat is a challenge of wit, speed and strength, and is a good laugh!

Photo 8.6   Roll a boat

- Two people face each other with a boat in the capsized position in front of them.

- The aim of the game is to roll the kayak over towards you, before it sinks!

Introducing the Kayak

Treat the boat for what it is, a piece of plastic which makes a great floating platform. Do not get into it, but get onto it, sitting on the seat, but with legs asplay out of the boat. In this position you are on top of a floating platform and the worst thing that can happen is that you fall off!

Some Challenges

Here are a few challenges whilst you are in this position which will make you think and invent techniques; there is no pressure on coming up with the correct ways of doing them because there aren't any. By exploring what is possible you will develop your own boundaries which you are happy with.

Photo 8.7   Sitting in the boat with legs out

A coach can give these challenges to students to assess degrees of confidence, co-ordination and balance.

- Do not use a paddle and try and make the boat go forwards, backwards and sideways.

- Now try and spin the boat on the spot.

- If you wiggle your bottom, transferring your body weight from one cheek to the other, you can discover the balancing point of your kayak and how far you can push it. Remember, the worst thing that can happen is that you fall off. It's amusing watching somebody else doing this as they counterbalance themselves with arms, head and toe curls.

- Try spinning around through 90 degrees so that you are facing out to the side rather than to the front. This will feel like being in a hammock, try rocking the hammock. In whatever fashion you choose, make the boat go forwards, backwards, sideways and spin it on the spot.

You may invent a technique that has never been seen before. You may have to rotate your body, stretch and explore your sense of balance to get results.

Photo 8.8   The hammock position

Now spin another 90 degrees so that you are facing the back of the boat and go through all of the manoeuvres again, starting with wiggling your bottom.

Moving around the boat, then having to move and turn the boat from these contorted unbalanced positions will develop the fundamentals of paddling:

- Propulsion

- Changing direction

- An awareness of boat balance

- Co-ordination of head, legs and arms and weight distribution

All this just from having fun.

More Challenges

Spin back so that you are facing the front of the boat, ready for the next challenges, which are designed to build confidence.

Photo 8.9   Hopping off and on the boat

- Hop off the boat into the water without the boat flipping over to the capsized position. Then try and hop back onto the boat again without it capsizing, (its a bit like wrestling a crocodile). It's harder if you don't use the floor of the pool.

For the next challenge you must make sure no one is anywhere near you and you are in the centre of the pool, well away from the sides.

- Balance yourself and try standing up with your feet inside the kayak; if you can do that then try and do it on one leg. It's a game of balance!

- To make this easier, get somebody to hold the bow of the kayak first.

Photo 8.10   A game of balance

If the boat does flip, don't empty it just yet.

- Duck under… put your head under the cockpit and breathe in the air pocket that is trapped in the boat. You will look like you have a big Mexican hat on! Whilst the boat is in this position it will not sink, unless you right it or climb on top of it.

Photo 8.11   A Mexican hat

Emptying the Boat

An air pocket is caused by the cockpit forming a seal on the surface of the water. To empty the kayak you must break this seal or it is virtually impossible to lift the kayak, due to the cockpit creating suction

on the water. First tilt the boat slightly on its edge; this will break the seal allowing you to put the bow of the boat on the side of the pool. Once you have done this, bend your knees and with a straight back lift the kayak with your leg muscles. Whenever possible get someone to share the load. The water can then drain out. See-saw the boat up and down to get rid of the excess water.

Rubbing Noses with Your Kayak

Before continuing, try this for a great balance exercise. Get on top of the emptied kayak, back into the original position legs asplay, then get onto your belly and shimmy along to the bow. Once you are right at the edge rub noses with your kayak. Can you get back?

Photo 8.12   Rubbing noses

Capsize Drill

Capsize drill does not have to be done with a tight fitting neoprene spraydeck straight away. You can build up to this through the following progressions and move on when you are happy.

Photo 8.13   Capsize without a spraydeck

1. Start by capsizing the boat but with legs outside the boat, as in the first few exercises.

2. Then try with feet in, but knees out.

3. Finally, with your thighs inside the boat… braced.

Remember that gravity is on your side. If you panic you will still come out but you may bruise your legs by trying to kick out, so you must try and relax.

When the boat has capsized, grab the cockpit rim with both hands by your hips, relax your legs from the thigh braces and push the kayak away from you. (It's like taking off a pair of trousers). You may find that forward rolling out of the kayak helps!

Safety Point

When people are practising capsize drill for the first time, particularly if it is the first time with the spraydeck, they should be closely supervised. Stand next to the kayak, and when they go upside down, watch the boater carefully. Problems are rare but to be on the safe side you are looking for:

- *Signs of panic (undirected, futile movements), or:*
- *Signs of counter panic (no movement), i.e. the paddler freezing.*

If either of these occur you can right the boat by:

- *Leaning over the upturned boat just behind the cockpit*
- *Grabbing hold of the upturned deck of the boat*
- *Leaning back and so rolling the boat upright*

See Photo 9.4 in Chapter 9.

You can then introduce a nylon spraydeck. Put the spraydeck on, but attach the front only, leaving the back off. Before capsizing, shut your eyes, put your hands to the sky and practise reaching for the release tag.

Once you have done this it is time to capsize with the spraydeck on fully. (See Chapter 6 for details of capsize drill).

Photo 8.14   Practising support strokes

Support Strokes and Rolling

Support strokes and rolling are easily taught in a pool because somebody can support the boat and coach from close proximity whilst standing in the pool. This will prevent needless capsizes and give protection from overextended arms, risking injury. Once techniques have been perfected, the person in the water can go around to the back of the boat out of sight. They can then throw the boat off balance to test and develop reactions.

Boat on a Rope

Another way of putting your reactions to the test is to attach both ends of the kayak to some floating line and have two people pulling the kayak up and down the length of the pool.

Photo 8.15   Boat on a rope set up

At first, allow the paddler to watch exactly what's going on. Start off very slowly and let them know when you are going to change direction, so that they are perfecting techniques and not reacting at this stage. The paddler will have to balance the kayak on the appropriate edge and change the edge with the change of direction. You will need to edge the kayak away from the way you are travelling; this is exactly like 'Bongo Sliding' when surfing and is good practice for this skill (see Chapter 21).

When the paddler is happy with the concept of edging and changing the edge, you can go a little faster. By gentle pressure on the paddle blade, you can develop your low and high brace strokes.

Once safe techniques have been developed you can then try it blindfolded. Start off very slowly, shouting out exactly when the direction is going to change. This allows the paddler to feel and develop their skill further kinaesthetically. It also gets them used to the fact that they can't see!

To develop reactions, have a go without someone shouting when the direction changes.

Photo 8.16   High brace

Photo 8.17   Blindfolded

If the inevitable does happen and you capsize, have a go at rolling even if you haven't succeeded before. The boat's momentum makes it very easy to roll; just reaching to the surface and pulling sometimes does the trick. Once again this is similar to how easy it can be to roll up in 'the soup' (the area where the broken waves roll into the beach) when surfing.

Safety Points

- *No one else should be in the pool at the same time.*

- *It is best to have the instructor on one of the lines to be sensible about the speeds at which it is done.*

- *Do not go too near the sides of the pool and allow for further travel through the boat's momentum when changing direction. (Once you've changed direction, the boat will continue to travel in its original direction until the lines go taut again).*

- *Only do this activity with people who are confident to do so. You do not need to go all the way to the blindfold stage.*

Sunken Boats

When I was a lad, one of the things I used to do was sink the boat while I was still in it, because it was a laugh! By doing this you can develop many fundamental kayaking skills. When you are in a boat which is partially sunk, you must control it with your knees and hips or it rolls over. As it is full of water, any slight movement will throw it off balance. You must react to this by counterbalancing with weight transfer, knee movements and hip thrusts. If the boat capsizes you can just swim out, you never need to feel trapped. However, if you keep your weight forwards you can swim the boat around into the upright position again with your arms. This is shown in the photograph with somebody on the side helping. This is a good tool to get you more orientated whilst upside down. It also gives you a sense of achievement, as it may be the first time you have rolled a boat.

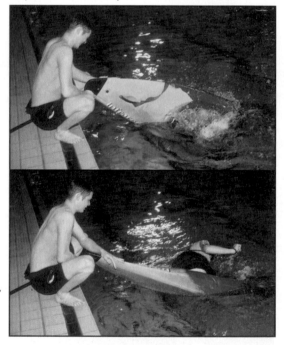

Photos 8.18 a-b   Rolling a half submerged boat

You can also use a paddle and practise support strokes. Doing it this way minimizes the stress on your shoulders and if you fail it is no big deal, you can swim the boat around and try again.

With help from a friend you can front loop the boat. Get them to push the stern over the top of your head. This is good for orientation if you want to learn vertical playboating moves.

Photo 8.19   Practising support strokes

Photo 8.20a   Front loop

Rescues

Using the pool to perfect rescues makes complete sense. It is a pleasant environment to learn or practise new techniques. The more you rehearse these techniques the slicker you become. A pool is a safe place to practise all-in rescues, swimmer carries and tows, or to experiment with ideas which you have not tried before.

However it is very important to make sure you can do these skills outside, and go on to practise them in gradually more testing conditions.

Photo 8.20b   Back loop

Further Reading

The Canoeist and the Swimming Pool - Guidance to Coaches, Clubs and Pool Managers, BCU Coaching Service UK - Tel 0115-982-1100, Fax 0115-982-1797, e mail info@bcu.org.uk
Available for download from website - www.bcu.org.uk

Leo Hoare

Leo started paddling at the age of nine at Proteus Canoe Club in Peterborough.

By the age of fourteen he had reached the Premier Division in slalom and had been selected to race for the British Junior Team. Leo spent six years in the British Team and went on to coach the Welsh Slalom Team for a following two; this was the start of his coaching career.

He presently works for Plas y Brenin, the National Mountain Centre. Leo is a Level Five Coach Inland and Level Four Open Canoe and Sea. Paddling still runs his life, with his efforts being put into expeditioning and just enjoying paddling.

9 Performance Rolling

My first roll in moving water was an inspirational moment; still with me today. The Swellies, North Wales, July 1982; the sun was out, the water challenging but not too scarey. I was with my now good friend and mentor from a local centre.

Wham... My first moving water roll!

The realisation that I could experiment with new ideas, up to and now beyond the limit of my current ability, was a real buzz. The amazing concept that I could look after myself... What might that lead to?

I would like to see that roll now on video. I'm sure it was awful, still that was then...

Introduction

This chapter has two main aims. The first is to explain the mechanics of modern rolling techniques. The second is to show how to transform an understanding of these techniques into the practical skill it must become, given the demanding environments paddlers frequent.

Paddlers need to be able to select and apply the right technique for any given situation in which they find themselves upside down. When learning to roll, we have to think long-term and keep this goal in sight.

The modern performance roll needs to be flexible in terms of its starting point and the blend of tech-

niques used. The blend selected will depend on the paddler's position underwater and how the water around them is behaving.

To fully understand these techniques the chapter will be divided into the following sections:

1. Effective learning

2. Equipment

3. Dynamic seating position

4. Introductory exercises

5. Important principles

6. Hip flick

7. Recovery

8. Different types of roll

A Paddle Roll Defined

A paddle roll is effectively a recovery stroke started from a capsized position. It can be broken down into the following phases:

- Start position
- Hip flick
- Recovery

Start Position

The body's (and hence the roll's) position, once a capsize has occurred, should be the starting point for the skill of rolling. It can be described in one of three basic positions: forward, upright or back. As the paddle can be on either side of the boat, this gives us six broadly based starting positions.

Whatever the body's start position, the aim is to get to a point from which to initiate the hip flick. This involves moving the paddle out to the side, and away from the boat, so as to create some leverage to right the boat. The paddler's body is arched up to the surface, effectively 'wound up' ready for the hip flick.

Photo 9.1   From whatever position you fall in, you need to get to a good position from which to hip flick.

Hip Flick

Using the paddle for support, the hips are used to rotate the boat to an upright position, whilst leaving the head and shoulders in the water.

Recovery

The head and shoulders are kept as low as possible, so that they are supported by the water as long as possible, and then flicked into the centre line of the

boat. The head and shoulders can be brought into the boat over the front, side or rear of the boat. Ideally all three should be encouraged. However, some people may not be flexible enough to come over the bow.

Photo 9.2a   Recovery over the bow

Photo 9.2b   Recovery over the centre

Photo 9.2c   Recovery over the stern

Effective Learning

There is no doubt, when learning any skill, particularly one as complex as rolling, that there exists a perfect set of conditions or environment for any given stage of learning. For a beginner roller and coach alike, a swimming pool with all its comforts and convenience will generally be this environment. It gives the learner a comfort zone that allows thought processes and body movements to be isolated and developed without stress and discomfort.

At this point an understanding of the true complexity of learning a 'performance' roll, rather than a simplified 'pool' roll is needed. The main difference can be summed up in a single word: *variability*.

Variability is the need for any given technique to cope with a variety of different conditions (environmental, physical and mental) and the performer still be successful in the required skill.

This means informed 'practice' in a variety of contexts that represent the real situations in which the skill will ultimately be performed.

It is the missing *variability* within the skill which is the cause of failure when the roll is first used in anger. This is common if the pool environment is used exclusively when learning the skill.

Put practically, if you are required to roll in a Grade 2 rapid it will require a Grade 2 level of skill in the roll for it to be successful, and will contain subtle differences to the roll used on flat water. The core elements are the same or very similar, which is where we begin when learning our roll, but there are also elements that will be adjusted in their position, degree and timing.

With skill and imagination, the pool and almost any canoeing situation can be used to learn different aspects of the skill of performance rolling. It is even possible to develop many aspects of rolling skill on dry land, as much of the body's education can be addressed on a piece of grass or on a sunny beach.

The perfect world is rarely available and compromises are all part of the fun. However, it would be ideal if, after the initial stages of learning, the environment can be adjusted to build 'variability' into the roll.

A possible learning progression a learner would benefit from could be:

- An indoor pool
- A varying depth, clean, sheltered lake
- 1 foot waves or Grade 1/2 water
- Grade 3 water or 2 feet of surf
- Increasingly turbulent water

Equipment

Learning to roll can begin in the pool wearing swimming kit, or the usual equipment used in the outdoor environment. The basic minimum of equipment is a boat! This is followed by a spraydeck and eventually, a paddle.

Boats

A polo/pool boat or similar general-purpose boat is the best learning craft. These boats tend to have a rounder cross-section under the cockpit, allowing the boat to rotate smoothly. The more modern playboats are commonly deep, beamy, hard-edged and flat-bottomed, leading to changes in resistance throughout the roll. This is one of the problems when taking a roll from the pool environment with its roll-friendly pool boats into a specialist boat of any kind. It requires a variation in technique that may not have been practised.

Fittings

More important than the boat, especially at the outset, are the fittings within the boat. These could be any or all of the following:

- Footrest
- Thigh braces
- Seat position
- Back-rest

A snug fit definitely gives the learner a better chance, so it is essential to adjust these to fit the individual. See the section on outfitting in Chapter 4.

Spraydeck

The spraydeck really only needs to fit easily to a variety of body shapes and sizes and thus nylon is probably best, allowing quick fit and cheap replacement when the effects of chlorine or old age mean that it is time to replace it.

Paddles

Paddles need to be pool-friendly, commonly with 'soft' blades so as not to damage the pool fabric. The use of paddles that have an oval in the shaft is a useful tool to the beginner roller, allowing the hand to grip the shaft 'naturally' at the correct angle.

Cheap, round-loomed paddles can be made oval by taping a pencil or sliver of dowel to the shaft. For a more permanent solution, the shaft of a basic paddle can be gently squeezed in a padded vice to produce an oval. These ovals need only be provided on the control hand part of the shaft.

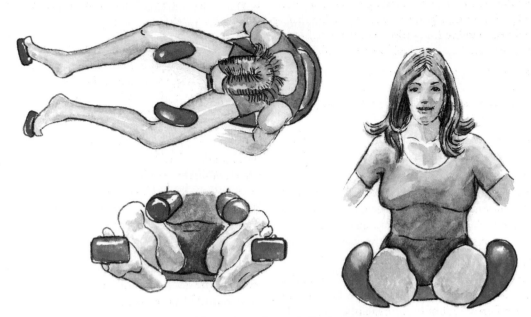

Figure 9.1   Dynamic Seating Position

Other Equipment

Other equipment commonly used include nose clips, diving masks, various size pool floats, arm bands, hand paddles, old table tennis bats, buoyancy aids and all types of balls.

Dynamic Seating Position (DSP)

This is the accurate fit a paddler needs to establish in the cockpit of the boat, by exerting pressure on the feet and knees to 'lock' the lower body into the boat. Although proficient paddlers can achieve the DSP given almost any cockpit design or level of fitting, the learner will be greatly assisted if the footrests etc. are adjusted correctly. This fit is absolutely necessary, not just to roll a boat but for almost all boating skills. (See the section on outfitting in Chapter 4).

Simple exercises for checking the fit can be carried out on dry land, they include:

- Rocking the hips, and therefore the boat, from side to side.

- Turning the boat in a circle using the hands.

- Trimming the boat significantly forward and backwards.

- Gently lifting the paddler under the arms to try to unseat him or her.

When the progressions are being worked through in later stages, it is always worth checking that the DSP is being maintained. One method of checking this is by watching paddlers after their roll, to see if they re-seat after righting themselves, or in a pool, listening for the tell-tale squeak as either knee or foot is forced out of position by the rolling motion.

Once the learner and coach are satisfied that the DSP has been established as far as possible, the next stage is to acquaint the kayaker with the feeling of the rolling motion.

Introductory Exercises

The first stage in developing a roll is to learn to orient oneself when capsized. The next stage is to train the body to harness the forces involved to right the boat.

The 'dynamic seating position' is at the core of this education, along with exercises that allow the paddler to develop an automatic control of their feet and knees, leaving their upper body and hips to do the moving.

These initial stages might include such exercises as:

- Somersaults, handstands and submersion exercises.

- Making a clean exit from the boat.

- Being righted after a capsize by their partner.

- Swimming the boat to the side of the pool.

Dry land exercises such as rolling the boat over on a piece of grass, or on a beach, can assist in this process of understanding the body's link with the boat. (See Chapter 8 for more ideas).

Important Principles

It is vital at this point that some principles are established, to develop a sound technique later.

1. Research tells us that practising on each side when learning a skill will result in a faster route to *complete mastery* of the skill.

This is a difficult issue. Practice on one side only *will* give a faster result, in the form of a weak 'pool' roll. Many coaches opt for this 'quick fix' because it is good for the learner's motivation at this early stage. Unfortunately, if the long-term aim is a 'performance roll', it will do more harm than good.

2. During these early stages, any form of the 'set up position' being established before the capsize should be avoided wherever possible. (See Types of Roll)

Moving into a position to begin the 'hip flick' element of the roll is one of the most important points of the body's education. Proficient rollers will want to start their rolling sequence from any starting position and thus link the position of their body in the capsize to the nearest reference point, i.e. front, side or back.

Novice rollers *will* need to find a reference point (a position from which to start the hip flick) when faced with the disorienting situation of being upside down in their kayak position *underwater*. This is commonly missed out on the surface by coaches '*setting up*' the beginning of the roll for the learner. The result of this basic error is seen in later stages as one of the most common reasons for the failure to roll. It is not that the paddler cannot roll the craft, it is simply that they are not able to reference an accurate position from which to begin the rolling (hip flick) action.

3. Learning that to move backwards, sideways or forwards is '*the way*'.

It is common to see learners being taught only one of these actions, and although this is completely understandable, it is again the beginning of the single solution roll.

4. The rolling action is fundamentally based on *timing*.

The body's education should begin with allowing the learner to feel the subtlety of the timing. This timing can be generally summarised as the 'hip flick'.

Hip Flick

Timing the forces available, from the top of your body through the hinge at the hips into the 'dynamic seating position', is known as the hip flick. Irrespective of the type of roll, this hip flick is the single main component in the skill of rolling.

The hip flick needs some form of lever and a hinging action to begin to right the boat. From whichever starting position you begin with, this movement can be created. For example, if you are sitting back when you capsize, you can move your body forward and up to the surface. This would enable you to reach out and to the side of the boat, and to reach the 'C' position (see Fig 9.3), one of the most powerful positions from which to begin the hip flick. If you are sat upright at the time of capsize then the hinging action will be directly over the side. Beginning to learn this body action, and awareness of what movement to begin the roll with, is possibly the biggest learning stage.

Using A Partially Submerged Boat

Exercises that might be used at this crucial stage include the following:

Photo 9.3   Partially submerged boat

1. Using boats with good buoyancy in the stern, fill the boat with water so as to sink the bow, allowing the paddler to sit in the boat even without a spray deck on and feel how to hand paddle to keep the boat in position. Paddling the boat forwards and backwards with the hands can follow this. These simple exercises reinforce the fit in the boat and allow the learner to appreciate the forces at play when beginning to rotate the boat.

2. Working with a partner stood behind the boat and spinning the boat 360 degrees by using doggy paddle or breaststroke. *This should be done in equal measure in both directions, so that from the outset no favoured side is established. It should also be initiated from a variety of starting positions.*

3. Once the learner is proficient at Exercise 2 and doesn't need the help of their partner to right the boat, torso movement in relation to the starting position can be explored. This allows the roller to learn how to time and distribute the power available through the roll, in sync with the stages in the boat's rotation.

4. The next element to experiment with is to move the torso forwards or backwards to assist the rotation.

When rotating the hull back to an upright position, there are varying amounts of force required at different stages. At the start of the motion, a large amount of force is required to begin the rotation. Once in motion, less effort is required to keep the rotation going. Finally, as the body leaves the water, extra force is required, so as not to stall the rotation before the body is back inboard and the boat is upright and stable. This is even more of an issue when the boat is floating, especially in the modern, flat-bottomed boats mentioned earlier.

With the boat partially submerged, less effort is needed. It is also much easier to feel how much force is required at any given stage, and what part the torso plays in rolling.

Variability

With a little imagination, considerable variation can be introduced into these exercises. By bringing in the paddle and introducing other elements, such as surprise capsizing to simulate different starting points, it is possible to learn almost all the rolling technique. Again, it should be highlighted that wherever possible these exercises should be evenly distributed between both sides. (In coaching theory this process is known as *bilateral transfer*).

Using Floating Boats

The next exercises are already commonly used in the teaching of rolling. There is extra realism in that the boat is fully buoyant, so the forces required to right the boat are different.

Exercises

All of the below should be done on both sides, and use different torso movements so as to start and finish the recovery in all three positions. Once the kayak is fully capsized it can be brought back upright, either by reversing the direction of capsize or by completing a full 360 degree rotation. Both should be practised.

1. The righting of the capsized paddler by their partner to build confidence and reinforce the dynamic seating position.

Photo 9.4a-b   Righting your partner

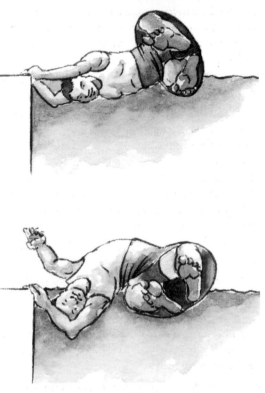

Fig 9.2   Poolside bar work

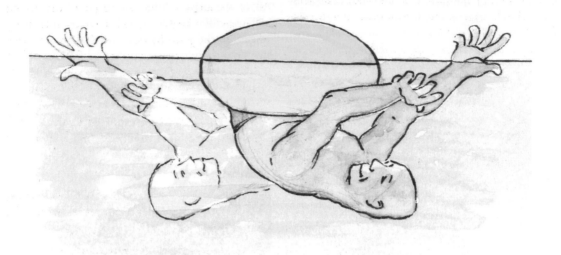

Figure 9.3   'C' to 'C'

2. Using the poolside, progressively tip the kayak further over and right it again (see Fig 9.2).

3. Capsize, and while still in your boat, swim to the poolside and right it.

4. 'C' to 'C' underwater, before being righted by your partner. The paddler reaches up to the surface into the 'C' position as if to start the hip flick. He then changes to the 'C' position on the other side. This rehearses the movements involved in reaching the 'C' position and starting the hip flick.

5. Floating in clear water, tip the kayak until a recovery flick is necessary. Do this slowly and quickly.

6. Use two large floats held together flat to the water and do the same as in Exercise 4.

7. Kiss the water.

Photo 9.5   Kissing the water, forward lean

In a lake or on a shallow beach:

1. Use the bottom to gradually get deeper and deeper.

2. Use a buoyancy aid, rolled up to increase difficulty.

3. Capsize, using a small wave to assist rotation.

It is important at this point to note that we are not necessarily trying to learn to 'hand-roll', but educating the body in its positioning, timing and hip action. This then allows the paddle to be introduced so as to increase the righting force.

There are many more games and exercises which can be used. Some are technically more useful than others, some are just plain fun. By following the introductory principles, and staying within safe and enjoyable learning situations, it is possible to build a hip action that will be:

• Relative to the body's starting position
• Performed on both sides
• Well-timed
• Powerful
• Variable

Introducing the Paddle

It doesn't matter whether the rolls developed from this point involve the paddle moving from front to back, back to front or any other way. If the hip action and its qualities have been established, the introduction of the paddle action becomes a relatively simple stage in the development of a successful rolling skill.

The principles for the introduction of the paddle are:

1. Keep the hands in the normal paddling position.

2. Link the exercises into the previous exercises i.e. sink the bow of the boat and use paddle instead of hands, to rotate boat.

Photo 9.6   Reaching for the paddle - partner makes sure it stays within reach

3. Capsize without paddle and reach for it in a planned position, i.e. between the poolside and the boat hull, lying alongside the boat or resting on the boat hull perpendicular to it.

4. Linking in to other paddle skills such as sculling.

5. Capsizing in a variety of positions, on both sides.

6. Returning to a 'no paddle' exercise regularly to reinforce understanding.

7. Use of slow motion demonstrations by another paddler.

8. Regularly changing focus to avoid overloading the learner.

It is important to stress that an unaided righting of the boat is not the only success that should be used to motivate the roller. By using subtle techniques such as a partner holding the bow or stern to finish the roll off, or pushing down on the top cockpit rim it is possible to give the learner sufficient success to sustain their motivation.

There is no denying however, the powerful boost that the learner receives when they succeed in an unaided roll.

The Recovery

This term refers to the last stages of the rolling action, and the body's immediate reaction to being upright once again. In many of the environments that cause capsizes, righting the craft will need to be followed by an immediate action to get out of trouble. Whether the roll was finished with the torso coming over the front, side or rear of the boat, returning the torso to a good upright position, and controlling the hips to apply an accurate edge or to flatten the hull are the minimums.

Immediate Actions

Actions that can be practised in a sheltered learning environment and performed immediately after the recovery might include:

1. Paddling forward or backwards.

2. Turning the boat to face in the opposite direction.

3. A support stroke on the opposite side.

4. Turning the head to look behind you, followed by a paddle stroke.

5. Vigorous hip wobbling without excessive head movement.

6. A low brace support position.

7. Similar to No. 1 but adding a bow rudder or low brace to create a break-in.

8. As above but sprinting.

All of the above will need the 'dynamic seating position' to be intact throughout the exercise.

In Summary

The roll begins as the paddler upsets the balance of their craft and finishes when they are back upright and in a stable position relative to the environment they are in.

Common Faults and Solutions

Below are some of the common difficulties when establishing a successful rolling action. Possible solutions are detailed in italics.

1. Paddler fails to begin roll.

Return to the stage of establishing a roll from any given starting point. Try working without the paddle and using a float.

2. Paddle movement is inaccurate or goes the wrong way.

More exercises using the paddle as an extension of the hands, control hand work or giving the roller the paddle in a pre-arranged position.

3. Back hand contacts boat.

Use of the technique of 'cuffing'. The coach or partner guides the paddler's hands to encourage them to push the hands clear of the surface. Both hands must come far enough out of the water to ensure that the paddle goes over rather than into the upturned boat.

4. Paddler only manages the rotation but not the recovery.

Too much dependence on the paddle, not sufficiently competent at the hip action. Go back to timing and boat rotation exercises.

5. Roller flops back in water at the end of the roll.

Reinforce hinge at hips and ensure the head comes out of the water last. Ensure full enough boat rotation, mobility exercises.

Rolling In Moving Water

Rolling in moving water is a logical extension of the skill of rolling. Providing the above principles have been followed, the roll developed on flat water should have all the essential components needed for a performance roll. It is now merely a matter of changing the context in which the techniques are performed and plenty of practice. There are a couple of defining points when learning to roll effectively in moving water:

The Head Game

The overwhelming reaction to immediately eject from the boat in moving water (fight or flight) is completely understandable. The pressure that self-preservation will put on a new and fragile skill is usually too great for success in the initial stages. To this end the learner should be helped to prepare mentally to 'want' to roll.

Going With the Flow

The second point is the technical concept and understanding of going with the water, and using whatever forces are available to assist your roll rather than going against it.

Listed below are a few basic exercises to help begin this process:

- Paddle at speed down the pool/lake and capsize suddenly.
- Pull the boat across the surface of the water, using a line to create a moving water environment.
- Once capsized, helpers push, pull and rock the boat from side to side.

Photo 9.7   Simulating moving water by using a rope

These exercises help the paddler learn how to time the roll, in order to 'go with the flow'.

Changing the Environment

Gradually increase the difficulty of the rolling environment. This should be done in a series of achievable steps, e.g.

- Clean, clear, still, cold water
- Clean, dark, still, cold water
- Choppy lake or sea
- Gentle outflow from a simple 'jet'
- Grade1/2 standing wave with deep water wash-out
- Small surf
- Play wave on grade 2/3 river

This phase of learning requires practice in as great a variety of situations as possible. A good moving water roll will need very little paddle force and is closer to a recovery stroke than a flat water roll.

The secret is to get the paddle to wherever the moving water will provide some support, hip flick at the right moment and bring your head out of the water last. A flexible approach is the key.

As this paddler fell in with her paddle near the bow, she slices it up to the surface and starts her roll (in this instance) with the paddle near the bow. We would still call this a Screw Roll, the only difference is that the paddler doesn't move to a 'set up' position to start the roll.

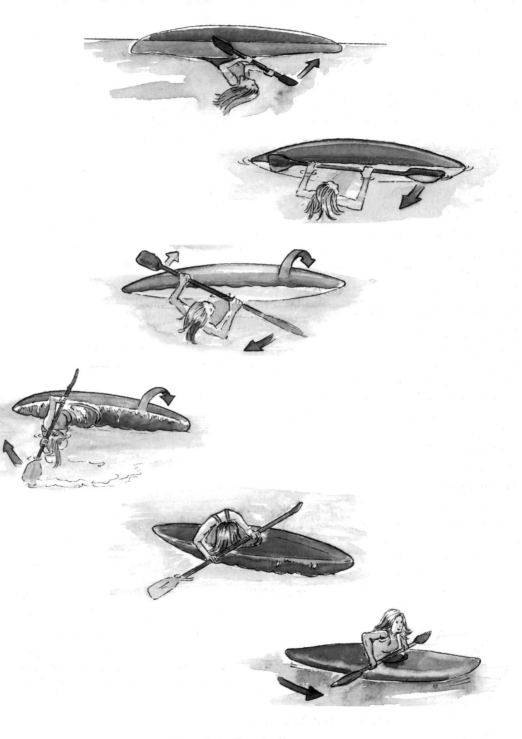

Figure 9.4   'Screw' roll sequence

Roll Types

Traditionally, rolling has been taught assuming that the paddler will start from a predetermined paddle position (the set up). Many coaches have come to the conclusion that this can inhibit a paddler's ability to roll in difficult or turbulent conditions. Therefore, the whole emphasis of the chapter has been to learn from the word go to get the paddle to a position of leverage, ready for the hip flick, from whatever the position the paddle happens to be in.

Paddle rolls were (and still are by many paddlers), classified according to their start position. The following is a summary of the names given to different types of roll. Interestingly, the people who were the most effective rough water rollers were usually the people who could perform the most 'types' of roll, i.e. start from any position!

For the sake of completeness, here are definitions of some of the 'types' of rolls:

- Screw Roll – Paddle starts at the bow.
- Reverse Screw – Paddle starts at the stern.
- Pawlata – Paddle starts at front but is extended by the paddler, shuffling the paddle along until it is held by the paddle blade in one hand, and the shaft in the other. This increases leverage and is usually only taught as a last resort to people who lack the flexibility to perform a screw roll.
- Reverse Pawlata – As for Pawlata except that the paddle starts at the stern.
- Put Across – The paddle is kept at 90 degrees to the boat during the capsize and then fed out at 90 degrees until it is held as for a Pawlata.

The following 'trick' rolls rely on a powerful hip flick and perfect timing, as the paddle is not put in the optimum position to support the hip flick. If you can do these you can probably hand roll!

- Vertical Paddle Roll – Paddle is vertical in the water and support is gained by a form of high speed draw stroke action.
- Storm Roll – Paddler starts in the screw roll position, but starts the hip flick with the paddle still close to the bow.

Further Reading

Bombproof Roll and Beyond, Dulkey, 1991, Cordee
Eskimo Rolling for Survival, Hutchinson D, 1988, Black
Kayak, Nealy W, 1993, Menash Ridge Press, 0-89732-050-6

Ian Coleman

Ian is a senior lecturer in Physical Education at University College Chichester and holds coaching and assessor qualifications in three disciplines. Although originally hooked by sea paddling, the perpetual search for new challenges has led to river and surf paddling. This blend of disciplines has meant travelling to some of the most notable paddling venues around the world, from the notorious Skukamchuck wave in British Columbia to Ireland's classic Inch Reef and from the serene Maidens on Skye to the challenging upper Otz valley.

10 Inclusive Canoeing and Kayaking

I had heard of the slogan 'Sport for All' in the past - it had seemed a worthy concept. As an able-bodied person I had been a fanatical participant in many outdoor activities. These were often physically demanding and frequently took me into wild, remote and spectacular places. An antidote to the trivial things that lifestyles get out of proportion. In hospital, in rehabilitation I had to accept that I would not walk again; it was a fact that was getting out of proportion.

I have been surf paddling on a beach in South Wales and when I have tired and paddled ashore I wave my paddle to get attention. I ask the good Samaritan who responds to my gestures, "Would you bring me that wheelchair?" The response is invariably helpful but also surprised because in my kayak I don't look disabled. I look like a canoeist, not like a paraplegic having a go. In a kayak I can get to the tarmac-free places that cannot be reached in any other way, certainly not by wheelchair.

The rewards of canoeing are varied. They include a bouncy castle of fun of a wave train and the sensation of diving off the high board for the first time that is provided by other rapids on a river. The surroundings at sea and on some rivers provide the satisfaction of the wilderness explorer. These feelings can be very precious to a disabled person. Canoeing allows me to get out of my wheelchair and onto the river to enjoy its rapids, onto the sea to explore a rugged or otherwise inaccessible coastline or play in the surf. I can do this with able-bodied companions that are also sitting down, and also storing up cherished moments in their memories. 'Sport for All' is not only a worthy concept, it is a lifeline. Canoeing is one of the sports that has thrown the line and hit the target because it has allowed me to become a genuine participant again.

- Adrian Disney

Fig 10.1   Who does it involve?

Introduction

Water provides a unique, level playing field for people from all backgrounds. Society now expects that participation and opportunity takes place in a fair and equitable manner. The drive has been, and remains, to remove barriers to make it possible for people to participate on equal terms regardless of disability.

Who is this chapter for

The following chapter is intended for:

- Disabled paddlers - or disabled individuals wishing to expand their understanding of current opportunities in paddlesport.

- People wishing to support the development of inclusive opportunities and practices.

Approach

This chapter looks at participation and access in three areas:

1. Club – based from a clubhouse or boat shed.

2. Touring or Expedition – a brief look at a day trip, which it is hoped will provide the briefest of starting points for those considering larger journeys or expeditions.

3. Event – for those organising races and events or rallies.

Regardless of your chosen discipline, the key is creating opportunities and formats which allow people access to an activity on their own terms.

Key Principles

- Your open-minded, positive attitude as a coach or fellow participant will do as much for the development of possibilities as will enabling equipment or any specialist technique. Work on ability rather than disability.

- Consultation – when offering opportunities for people to perform, ensure that you continue to ask individuals what they want and what they feel that their goals should be.

- Work together on ability, not disability. Start with considering and exploring the possible.

- Never assume – if in doubt ask. Even the obvious common sense question, when asked in a polite manner, will make an individual feel as though you value their opinion. Consider the possibility of one-to-one sessions if you feel that you need to explore issues in confidence or without group pressure.

- Gather and share your information, and check your understanding with the disabled paddler, so that you agree on the objectives and needs. Carers and assistants may often have additional information, however your main working relationship needs to be focused on the performer.

- Don't assume that individuals with a particular need will then automatically have other specific needs. Each individual is different.

- Communication – by keeping it simple, succinct and in a range of formats, you can aid understanding, regardless of whether the individual has a learning disability or sensory impairment. Using visual, verbal or auditory, tactile or kinaesthetic formats can help ensure that you are able to get your message across. Using combinations of different communication techniques can help make your work with multi-disability groups more effective.

Photo 10.1   Education - changing attitudes

Models of Disability

In the past, disabled people were all too often considered to be a problem requiring a medical solution. Individual personalities and achievements were hidden. A person was defined purely by the medical nature of their health state. The social model of disability was developed mainly by disabled people themselves as a reaction to the medical model of disability. The social model describes the life experience of a person as a whole, placing the emphasis on the removal of barriers. In the social model it is the environment which creates the disability, not the individual concerned.

The functional model of disability accepts that barriers to participation are created largely by the structure of society. The aim is to understand the nature of a person's needs in a practical manner, in order to ensure that positive actions can be taken to create opportunities for all. The barriers faced by disabled people wishing to take part in canoeing can largely be overcome by a positive attitude. Organisation and simple physical modifications, when applied with the right approach can achieve more than design modifications alone.

Language and Terminology

Language is the most powerful tool available to those wishing to provide inclusive opportunities. It is important to present people in a positive light as actively participating and most importantly, taking part in a meaningful decision-making process. Presenting a self-determining image is especially important to provide role models that will inspire others. Pay attention to the use of language, whether it is verbal, informal or written.

Don't describe the individual, describe the activity. A person with a spinal cord injury who canoes is a canoeist. If there is a need to be specific the following can be a starting point: a paddler with a spinal cord injury. Even better, use the individual's name.

The exact language which is used is often not as important as the intention; however, it can be useful to define terms to help provide a start point.

Impairment

Impairment can be defined as the functional limitation within the individual caused by physical, mental or sensory impairment.

Disability

Disability can be defined as 'the loss or limitation of opportunities to take part in the normal life of the community on equal level with others due to physical or social barriers'. (Barnes 1992)

These definitions provide a positive starting point, suggesting that 'disability' is more concerned with attitude and society than a deficit or level of dysfunction in the individual paddler.

Disability Groupings

In broad terms, disability can be broken down into the following areas:

- Learning Disability
- Educational and Emotional Disabilities
- Sensory Impairments – Visual Impairment / Blindness, Hearing Impairment / Deafness
- Communication Disabilities
- Physical Impairments

Breaking down the term disability can help in making what can seem a daunting task more manageable.

Barriers to Participation

In broad terms, the barriers faced by disabled people seeking inclusion in society and sport can be considered under the following headings:

- Environmental - physical and sensory access to the urban, rural, or wilderness environments.

- Attitudinal - negative or limited preconceptions
- Legal - increased insurance costs
- Cultural - social attitudes
- Institutional - the attitudes of organisations such as schools and hospitals

Barriers can be considered in a cumulative or cyclic manner. The 'Cycle of Oppression' describes what, if it is not challenged, can be an ongoing negative experience for the individual as well as society as a whole. The need is to challenge the cycle, either through the use of positive language or through pragmatic approaches to encourage participation at a range of levels.

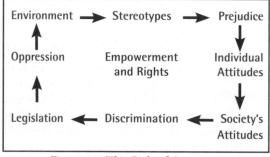

Fig 10.2   The Cycle of Oppression

Access

Access in this context refers to the ability of all people to gain independent, meaningful participation in all the activities associated with a paddlesport. Access involves inclusion, enabling people to be involved at all levels from participation to planning and decision-making. Improving access involves reducing the physical, attitudinal and organisational barriers to taking part, so often faced by an individual wanting to participate in paddling.

Access to a canoe club or canoeing organisation needs to be considered in the widest possible manner if the barriers faced by an individual are to be removed. What follows is an outline of some of the major issues confronting a club or organisation.

Presentation

The way in which you and your club or organisation presents itself is the greatest asset you can bring to bear in making opportunities available. Many potential canoeists may have never been presented with an image they feel is relevant to their self-image. It is essential that you present your aspirations in ways that make it possible for people with sensory and communication difficulties to access your information, as well as get involved in a discussion about what an activity may mean to them.

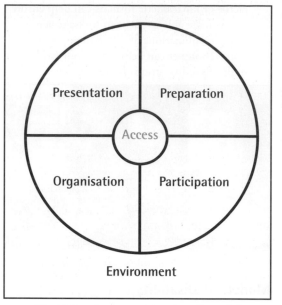

Fig 10.3   Access considerations for a club

Consider the presentation of your image in a holistic way to ensure that what you present is consistent and promotes the ethos that you are working with.

Preparation

Often the first physical activity a potential canoeist will have is their preparation for getting on the water. First impressions last, so it is important that you are able to provide a structure which allows individuals to prepare at their own pace and on their own terms, setting the scene for the session to come. An accessible changing facility is ideal but not essential, considered low key facilities and a flexible approach do more than a hurried or intolerant, ill-prepared session.

Participation

All too often our approach is to provide one-off experiences, but the real challenge remains in providing opportunities which allow access to a range of experiences. This makes it possible for people to choose the way in which they want to participate in paddlesport on their own terms.

People are your greatest asset. You need to ensure that you are able to involve all those concerned, participants, helpers and organisers, to ensure that your solution is both workable and realistic.

Organisation

Working toward an inclusive organisation does not mean re-organisation. The emphasis should be on quality of communication and clarity of club structure to ensure that all paddlers are able to participate in the planning, decision-making and implementation process. Constant, clear communication and dissemination of information is a big job, and needs support, especially if the aim is to present information in a range of formats.

Environmental Considerations

These include the clubhouse or boat shed as well as access to the water; consideration needs to be given to users with both physical and sensory impairments.

The canoeing environment that you work in will contain barriers that need to be identified, and at least acknowledged in the way in which you organise your activities, such as access and egress to the water, banks and launching stages. Think through and discuss the activities that your club undertakes. Consider the journey that a paddler may take from arrival to getting onto the water.

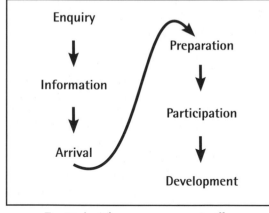

Fig 10.4   The access process as it affects participants

Architectural Access – The Clubhouse

Lack of funds does not equal exclusion. Do not be intimidated by architectural plans and audits. Cheap, simple alterations can make an existing building largely accessible. This may not be ideal, but can be sufficient to provide a start point for access and inclusion. However, undertaking an access audit and informing the club of the results will help generate discussion and raise awareness within the club. A simple plan can then be constructed. Well presented, it will let potential fund providers and supporters know that you are serious, giving them more confidence to support your dream for greater levels of access to your club.

A Tool for Assessing Physical or Sensory Barriers

The aim of the access *audit* is to assess a particular facility, in terms of access and ease of use, by a wide range of potential users, including people with mobility and sensory impairments or learning disabilities. An audit should provide a 'snapshot' of a building at one point in its life. As the starting point of an ongoing access action plan, it can be used to highlight shortcomings and possible areas for improvement.

For access, it can be divided into two stages:

1. Gathering information

2. Agreeing needs and making recommendations

Non-technical people might carry out the first stage, but you may need to bring in an expert such as an architect if you want to go beyond the information-gathering process and propose alterations to a building or centre.

Architectural Factors Contributing to Access

- The building - the most obvious element of a building, which determines its accessibility, is the fabric or shell.

- Fixtures and fittings - no building functions as an empty shell. When the building is fitted out, fixtures and fittings may be critical.

- Arrangement and choice of furniture and equipment - often greater accessibility can be speedily achieved by varying the arrangement and layout of free-standing items of furniture or equipment.

- Use the building wisely - the way a building is used and managed may be important. Accessibility is affected, for example, when untidy working practices obstruct circulation or cause tripping hazards or when over-zealous polishing leads to slippery floors. Continual monitoring by management has a significant role to play. Positive attitudes of employers, employees and users need to be developed.

Carrying Out an Access Audit

Ideally, start with a small, enthusiastic team or an individual appreciative of today's environment, knowledgeable about the club and its access, mind-

Sensory and Intellectual Impairment	Detail
Visual Impairment or Blind Hearing Impairment or Deaf	Colour combination and contrast Tonal ranges Texture Lighting – positioning, shadows and glare Consistency of signage – routes, storage, information Communication format Structure, range and content of information
Physical Impairment	**Detail**
Ambulant Upper Limb Impairments Partially Ambulant Non-Ambulant Independent Manual Wheelchair User Assisted Wheelchair User Independent Electric Wheelchair User Assisted Electric Wheelchair User	Floor surfaces, coverings and gradients Changes in level Doorways and entrance widths Access to work surfaces and storage Consistency of access en route Bathroom fittings Heights of: handles, plugs, sockets and switches

Table 10.1   Summary of specific access considerations

ful of wider responsibilities, and sensitive to the needs of others.

- Checklists (See contacts for Centre for Accessible Environments and FieldfareTrust)

- Plans of the building

- A tape measure (2 metres minimum)

- Knowledge of the building, what it can do, and how it is currently used

- A note book

The key as always is to involve people, to ask and to work in partnership to ensure that real needs are met rather than imagined or perceived ones. Ask a wheelchair user to travel the building with you, or sit yourself in a wheelchair and venture round the site. Walk round with a visually impaired person, or someone with a hearing impairment. Better still, form an active committee with such representation included as essential members. Consider the major activities that take place in the building, look at the major routes that the user groups take. List them in priority; this will help you develop your action plan in a manner which helps you move the world on, one step at a time.

What follows is an overview of some of the functional themes which, if considered during planning and implementation, will help you focus on what can be achieved.

Approaching the Building

- Directions

- Signage

- Setting down/pick up

- Parking - minibus and car

- Public transport

- Lighting around the facility

- Directions and convenience from car park and public transport.

Entering the Building

- Access - bell, security voice/camera, handle/s (height, reach, pressure needed)

- Width (for wheelchair)

- Ramp (provided/needed, angle suitability in wet weather)

- Door pressure needed, swing away from/ towards visitor

- Moving around the building and using this facility

- Signage/directions

- Room to move

- Flooring cover - non-slip, thin carpet which is easy to wheel over

- Height of services - bar/catering/tables/chairs

- Room for wheelchair under table, ability to transfer from wheelchair to easy chair.

- Toilets - one accessible toilet is essential, access for m/f, height of facilities, taps, showers, drying towels/heater/blower.

- Doors - ease of passing through.

- Two way doors need open panel so oncoming 'traffic' may be spotted.

- Corners - negotiation.

- Sounds - consider hearing impaired needs, reduce noise from kitchen and air conditioning.

- Switches - light switches, ease of movement, reach/layout.

- Leaving the building - as a routine.

- Leaving the building - in case of emergency where convenience and speed may have different priorities.

- Building management: cleaning, planning, avoid clutter (the most important factor).

Day Trips, Touring, and Expeditions

The access issues surrounding a day trip or expedition do not change for disabled people, consultation and good organisation remain the key. Use some of the issues that you may have explored in the club house or on your local canoeing area as a start point. However, remember that it can be easy to run out of time, or to place those concerned under time pressure. Balancing the needs of the team with the daily routine will do much to ensure the overall success of the venture.

In broad terms it is possible to take the day and split it into three areas of activity:

- Paddling time

- Leisure time

- Personal care time

Ensure that time is allowed for people to be involved in all three.

Ensure that there is sufficient time in the programme to allow individuals to maintain their independence. It can be tempting to be too helpful, or to forget to explore ways in which a job can be shared to provide a satisfying experience for all concerned, even when darkness threatens and no suitable resting place has been found! Remember that the whole

experience of a day trip or expedition is about being involved rather than being taken along.

Photo 10.2   Mobility? - No worries!

Running an Inclusive Event

Club events provide an ideal opportunity for you to generate interest in your club and gain new members. An inclusive event will ensure that potential canoeists in your community feel that the club is open and positive about involving disabled people in the rest of the year's activities.

Placing the Activities around the Site

When putting your plan together think about the following:

- How far from the car park entrance is the club/boathouse or water's edge? Make sure that orange badge holders can park or be dropped off as close as possible to the action.

- Put your activities in an accessible part of the site.

- Place accessible toilets close to the activities.

- Schedule some stopping points with rest or seating areas, to give some people time to rest before setting off again.

Site Information and Interpretation

- Be prepared to put across site information using a range of different methods. Some people will find one-to-one chats best. Others prefer written information that they can take away and use to get around the site independently.

- Put together an information pack, which all visitors can collect from the reception point when they arrive.

- Consider the design of maps for users with visual impairments.

- Consider the needs of guide dogs.

- Make any written information and interpretation accessible.

- If you are using leaflets and self-guided trails, provide standard text, large print audio-tape and Braille versions.

- Make sure that activities are well sign-posted. Use consistent contrasting colour-coded signs throughout the site so that people know what to look out for. Place these signs at low level so that people can get close up to read them.

Support Services

- Make sure that you have enough staff and volunteers on site to provide information, advice and directions to visitors. They should be able to offer direct support to individuals in particular activities.

- Give all staff name badges and maybe identifying 'T' shirts and caps so that visitors know who to approach.

- Give your staff disability awareness training. This will help give them confidence on the day.

- Where appropriate, consider the use of induction loops in important places, including the reception point, for those with hearing impairments.

- Provide accessible toilets on site. You can hire these for the event. At least one accessible toilet must be able to be used by both sexes.

- Provide portable ramps for the event if needed and familiarise staff with their use.

- Provide tents or shelter around the site to cater for emergency cover and respite care.

- If you are providing catering, make a few tables and chairs available, and also have some strong cutlery, large plates and drinking straws.

- Provide first-aiders, and make sure that you have access to a phone in case of emergencies.

Coaching and Leading on the Water

The aim of this section is to take progressive, modern coaching principles and provide a couple of models to make coaches more comfortable in their ability to cater for a greater range of needs.

Photo 10.3   'Swifty' celebrates his first roll!

Communication

Communication is the key to your success. The way in which you communicate needs to be co-ordinated and positive. By using a combination of verbal and non-verbal techniques, you can accommodate the needs of paddlers with a range of sensory and communication impairments. Communication can be:

- Visual - sign language, gesturing, drawing or using models

- Auditory - clear, simple, spoken language

- Kinaesthetic - patterning or guiding individuals through a movement pattern.

Where communication is challenging, preparation is the key to success. Most sessions or journeys start with the group all in one place. Experiment, and explore the types of communication that work best. Set the goals and ground rules at the beginning of the session, so that you don't have to communicate them whilst fighting against the wind, or to a group which has taken out their hearing aids.

Use colour coding and tactile marking on equipment to make it possible for you to keep your explanations clear and brief.

Be aware of the environment in which you are working. Ensure that your face is appropriately lit, and that your students don't have to struggle to read your lips while your whole face is in silhouette. If there is a chance that you will be finishing in the dark, it will be worth taking a few minutes before last light to discuss plans for getting off the water, in a co-ordinated manner, while people are still able to 'see what you are saying'.

Adaptive Physical Activity - APA

It can be a real challenge to balance the needs of a group with complex and diverse needs. Adaptive Physical Activity can be loosely defined as, 'Changing components of an outdoor activity to include participants based on individual ability whilst maintaining the integrity of the session.' It is possible to break down an activity into the following components, which can be modified or balanced to ensure that your activities are inclusive, meaningful, and address the needs of both the individual and the group:

- Aims and objectives
- Planning and preparation
- Complexity of the task
- Risk assessment
- Environment
- Duration and intensity of the session
- Number of participants in the group
- Ability and skills mix of participants
- The individual/performer
- Grouping and buddying within the group or with additional helpers
- Equipment
- Communication

Health and Safety - Specific Advice

As with any user group, much can be achieved by gaining good information to ensure that preparations are appropriate and effective. Use a proforma to help gather basic information. Leave space for additional information and ensure that information is kept in a confidential manner so as not to compromise any confidence which may have been shared. One key principle is consent. It is important that consent has been given and that the nature of the proposed activity has been understood.

The outdoor industry has become increasingly aware of the need to meet standards and justify the way in which it operates. Operating procedures and codes of practice are now the norm. When considering the needs of disabled paddlers, the technical requirements and procedures are largely the same. How-

ever, it can be difficult to know what to ask in order to make an informed, collaborative decision about what is required.

The following headings can be useful as start points for discussion and co-operative planning between the paddler and the coach:

- Medication and diet.
- Moving and handling or independent transfer on and off the water or into and out of the boat.
- Sensitive areas on the performer's body which may be damaged or which a paddler may not be able to feel.
- The most effective way in which you can communicate on or off the water.

Consider and discuss ways in which the activity session may affect a paddler's daily routine.

As with any group discuss:

- Equipment
- Environment
- Organisation for the session or the journey or event.

> **Note**
>
> *Be careful, at this point, not to concentrate your thoughts on the medical or clinical issues highlighted during the initial information gathering. Remember to work on ability, not disability; information is only of use if it is used in partnership.*

Specific Medical Requirements

One of the commonest misconceptions about 'disability' is that people have a vast array of additional medical requirements, which mean that meaningful participation is restricted. The reality is that most medical situations which may arise can be dealt with using standard first aid procedures. If you are in doubt, ask the individual. The following headings are intended to provide a start point.

Skin Care

Discuss the implications of bumps and bruises, especially to areas in which sensation may be lacking or intermittent.

Personal Hygiene Requirements

Be aware that people may need extra time and privacy to maintain their independence. Be mindful of buoyancy aids, consider posture and transfers to ensure that any catheters or sensitive areas in the groin or pelvis are not compromised - ask.

Dietary Requirements

Continue to be mindful of specific needs; consider the timing and quantities of food required throughout the session or day.

Photo 10.4   Food - a consideration for all members of the party

Medication

Make sure that any medication which an individual may require throughout the day is in a suitable place, so that it is accessible to the individual in the same manner as it would be in their daily life. Use your consent forms as a reference should you need to pass on information to medical personnel in the advent of an emergency. Your aim should be to ensure that, as far as possible, the individual maintains control of their needs in what may be a new and challenging environment.

Warmth

For people with mobility disabilities the need to stay warm can be of even greater importance; consider the timing and duration of outdoor sessions in particular.

Moving, Handling and Independent Transfer

Modern working practices in healthcare and industrial environments have instigated a change in attitude in the way in which we approach moving boats and equipment in paddlesport. Current thinking takes into account the need to reduce the chances of an injury, which may be caused by poor lifting of equipment. The same considerations apply to assisting a disabled paddler. Care must be taken to ensure that the health and safety of all concerned is looked after.

Consider:

- The environment
- The helpers
- The paddler

Two useful mnemonics are:

LITE = *Load - Individual - Task - Environment*

SAFE = *Stop - Assess - Formulate - Execute*

Prepare the environment and try to aim for independent transfer rather than assisted lift. Start with asking or discussing what is easiest for the individual concerned.

Basic Adaptations to Rescue

The basic principles of any rescue do not change when involving disabled people. However, the following are some considerations which you may find useful:

- Time to undertake a rescue can increase involving disabled people.
- The resources required during and following the rescue can be increased.
- The communication barriers faced by those with sensory impairments or a learning disability may be difficult to overcome during a rescue.

Most casualties are likely to suffer from:

- Hypothermia
- Exhaustion
- Hypoglycaemia

Some paddlers with disabilities may be more susceptible to the adverse effects of the environment and can therefore move more rapidly from the chronic to the acute phases of the above conditions.

Practical Issues

The following are some practical considerations, which are aimed to provoke thought and consultation:

- Consider the needs and the strains placed on all those involved in the rescue. Looking at ways to reduce the strain on the rescuer can provide a valuable starting point for exploring adaptive rescue techniques within the team.
- Climate and environmental conditions can have a more dramatic and exacerbating effect on paddlers with disabilities.

- Some paddlers may require additional protection for skin and joints in affected limbs.

- Some paddlers may require additional appropriate support following a capsize. A spare sleeping mat can often be a real help.

- There is a need to ensure that you are able to exchange information and signal in a range of formats at all times to ensure that signals are accessible.

- Some paddlers may have difficulties in dealing with the complex and changing nature of a rescue situation. As with all good communication, there is a need to ensure that communication is clear, precise and effective for all concerned.

- In some situations there will be a need to create a larger, more stable platform for the rescue. Consider how wind or current may affect this.

- On rivers consider the use of 'live bait' rescues (see Chapter 26) in a wider number of instances.

- Regardless of the environment or the team, prepare and consult so that the initial plan provides a start point for common sense and flexible communication.

Equipment

The greatest asset you have is your team and its ability to adapt to the needs of the individuals to provide meaningful activity. However, it is worth considering the way in which equipment affects the nature of an activity or what the performer is able to undertake independently.

Equipment can also have a dramatic effect on practice.

What Makes Up Better Practice?

- The true nature of the skill is represented.

- If the equipment is changing constantly, how do we gain feedback?

- Feedback should be centred around performance not equipment.

- Good equipment makes it possible for the true nature of the skill to be represented.

Why Is Good Equipment Important?

Beginner:

- Access to good advice and feedback

- Technical support

Intermediate:

- Is your time as a coach best spent making adaptations or are you there to facilitate or provide opportunities for gaining experience?

Performer:

- Wants something that will 'go all the way'.

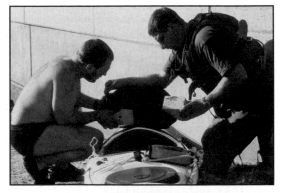

Photo 10.5   Adapting equipment

Making your Equipment Work for You

There is an increasingly diverse range of canoeing and watersports equipment available. Regardless of whether it has been designed for disabled or non-disabled paddlers, the success of it depends on understanding how it works to ensure that you are able to maximise its usefulness.

- Use colour coding of your equipment to help make your communication simpler.

- Create colour differentiation on complex equipment (i.e. colour coded paddle ends) and use this in your descriptions.

- Using colour can help you use non-verbal communication or simple signs.

- Consider the texture of the equipment and make it part of your communication, especially with people with visual impairments or low vision.

- Consider hand function, buckles and straps and the way in which it is possible to get into and out of the equipment, especially tight-fitting cags and waterproofs which may need to be put on in a sitting or lying position.

Some Thoughts on Equipment Design
Boat

- Reach - consider the overall shape of the boat in relation to the ability of the paddler to rotate or place the paddle in the water.

- Weight - for paddlers with limited strength or endurance in the upper body, lightweight paddles can make it possible to concentrate on acquiring the skill, as opposed to the effort required.

- Cockpit design - check that an individual is able to exit the boat as well as fit in extra padding if required.

- Consider the balance between manoeuvrability and directional stability when choosing a boat.

Body - Principles of Posture

Good posture is one of the key attributes to a successful paddling style, regardless of the boat in which you paddle. Good posture makes it possible to transfer force as well as take control of the boat, or simply enable you to see where you are going. A good or attainable paddling posture for one individual may not be the same for another. To some paddlers with limited balance or reduced levels of function in the lower body, posture in a boat may be a challenge which needs to be worked at.

Posture can be:

- Appropriate - to the needs of the individual. Consider the sitting angle (angle between the body and the legs) in which a person is able to maintain their balance.

- Base up - work from the ground up to ensure that a paddler is able to maximise the amount of vision which they are able to gain.

- Comfortable - check comfort levels throughout the session to ensure that a paddler is able to concentrate on the activity, rather than fighting with a growing sense of discomfort. There is also little point in encouraging an individual to use a posture which they are unable to control without the use of their arms to push themselves back up if they fall forward.

- Dynamic - avoid padding and seating solutions which hold the paddler tight into the boat, in a manner which makes it impossible for the paddler to move or adjust position during a session. Ensure that weight is able to be transferred, regardless of whether it is through lower limb control or produced through a process of upper body movements which may help the performer manufacture a more 'paddle-dependant' edge or lean.

Blade

Often the simplest stroke is the most efficient and appropriate. For a beginner, or for a paddler who is having to concentrate on balance, or is having difficulty balancing the strength of each side of the paddling stroke, it can be useful to simplify the issues. By taking the feather out of a kayak blade, or by working in tandem from the front of a canoe, it is possible to concentrate on a simple, controlled power stroke. This removes the need to deal with the complexities of adding in elements of steering or directional control.

Consider:

- Feather
- Weight
- Balance
- Blade size
- Shaft length and symmetry

Specialist Equipment

Adventure Designs

Adventure Designs enjoys a reputation in the outdoor industry as a group concerned with the development of specialist equipment for disabled adventurers.

By including disabled people throughout the design process, from conceptualisation to field testing, Adventure Designs is able to produce innovative well thought-out products. The following equipment has been developed out of these co-operative ventures:

Lite Kite

The *Lite Kite* is a buoyant harness that supports the user in an appropriate position during a swim. The design provides protection and flotation, and can be used to help in an assisted transfer if required.

The Aquabac

Photo 10.6   The Aquabac

A postural support system for people with complementary balance needs or spinal cord injuries for use whilst kayaking, canoeing, sailing, white water rafting, hot dogging or rowing. The *Aquabac* has been developed to provide a versatile, non-captive support system, which can be adjusted as familiarity and skill develop. As used in Perception Kayaks and Mad River Canoes, the *Aquabac* is available through White Water Consultancy International Ltd.

The Fish

The *Fish* is a buoyancy aid which provides an active buoyancy system for individuals with restricted movement or a unique body form.

Features of the *Fish* include textural and colour coding, supported by an 'out of sight, out of mind' one-handed buckle operation system. The *Fish* provides each user with a personal flotation device that is fully adjustable. Available through Peak UK Kayak Co.

Socs and Shoes

During 1997 a team of six individuals successfully completed the Coppermine River Expedition in the North West Territories of Canada. *Socs and Shoes* were developed as part of their preparation for this expedition.

Photo 10.7   White water rescue training for the Coppermine Expedition

The *Socs and Shoes* system provides unique opportunities for people with above, through or just below knee amputations, to one or to both lower limbs. Currently the system has been developed for use in open canoes.

The *Soc* is a carbon fibre, knee length prosthesis that can be used with common prosthetic attachment methods. The Soc provides the individual with a means of protecting their stump whilst being able to apply pressure through the stump to control an open canoe.

The *Shoes* are carbon fibre moulds that are attached to the bottom of an open canoe to provide a place for the user to locate the *Soc*. Together the *Socs and Shoes* make it possible for an individual to be stable in a canoe and to transfer force into the canoe, thus making it easier to steer and paddle independently.

Fist

Fist enables active paddling for people with limited hand function and locates on a range of equipment. The equipment does not involve the hand or wrist in the transmission of power.

Disability Organisations

Many organisations exist which offer support and advice on specific disability or impairment issues. Often it is possible to gain the most up to date information and discuss your concerns with regard to the involvement of an individual in confidence with an advisor or support worker. A list of disability-specific organisations can be obtained from the contacts listed at the end of this chapter.

The BCU

The British Canoe Union promotes 'canoeing for all' and aims: -

- To ensure that all people have a general and equal opportunity to participate in canoeing.
- Not to disadvantage any individual by imposing any conditions or requirements that cannot be justified.

Paddle-Ability

To promote and develop canoeing for disabled people, the British Canoe Union uses the concept and term *Paddle-Ability* to address the issue of participation in paddlesport and recreation.

Paddle-Ability focuses on the individual's ability in canoeing rather than disability. To support this concept, the following activities and opportunities are available:

- A guidance leaflet for event and tour organisers, about how to provide information on the physical access to water to potential participants, 'Guidance Notes - A Different Perspective on Access'.

- Competitive events as part of mainstream programmes, which recognise the needs of disabled competitors. In particular, Paddle-Ability events are available in Sprint, Slalom and Marathon competitions. Information is available from the Paddle-Ability Coordinator (see Useful Contacts and Addresses).

- Paddle-Ability sprint races are held at National Regattas, Nottingham, May to September, (boats, equipment and coaching can be provided). Paddle-Ability Sprint races are also now included in European Sprint Championships.

Check with your Regional Disability Coordinator for local events (see Yearbook).

- A national Paddle-Ability Sprint Squad that receives specific coaching and training plans.

- Disability Awareness Training Courses. The aim of the course is to give awareness of disability issues and demonstrate that disabled people can access all aspects of paddlesport. Information on course availability from the BCU office.

- A policy and process to enable disabled canoeists to achieve personal performance awards and enter the coaching scheme. The BCU has a range of personal performance tests, which are open to disabled canoeists. Where a disability prevents a candidate from completing a particular part of the test, the award will still be given, where it is clear that the candidate has had relevant coaching and can show that they understand the technique and the purpose. Information available from BCU office.

- Improved access to information by the provision of large print copies of leaflets and information on request.

- A text phone is available at the BCU office and the BCU has a Typetalk account.

There are Disability Co-ordinators in each of the regions, who are able to assist and advise individual canoeists, clubs, and event organisers. Each Regional Development Team page in the Yearbook gives details of how to contact the Disability Coordinator for that region. In addition to working on regional and local issues, each Disability Coordinator is a member of the National Disability Committee that formulates policy and develops strategies to address issues facing disabled people.

Useful Addresses and Contacts

BCU Paddle-Ability, Viv Kendrick, 8 Yew Grove, Huddersfield, HD4 5XG. - Tel 01484460154(h) 01484226235(w) - Email viv.kendrick@wynrush.co.uk

English Federation of Disability Sport, Manchester Metropolitan University, Hassall Road, Alsager, ST7 2HL - Tel 0161- 247-5294 - Fax 0161-247-6895

Disability Information Trust, Mary Malbrough Centre, Nuffield Orthopaedic Centre, Headington, Oxford, OX3 7LD - Tel 01865-227592 - Fax 01895-227596

Centre for Accessible Environments, Nutmeg House, 60 Gainsford Street, London, SE1 SE1 2NY Tel 0207-357-8182 - Fax 0207-357-8183 - E mail cae@globalnet.co.uk

Royal Association for Disability and Rehabilitation, 12 City Forum, 250 City Road, London EC1V 8AF - Tel 0207-250-32222 - Fax 0207-250-0212 - www.RADAR.org - E mail radar@radar.org.uk

Fieldfare Trust, 67a The Wicker, Sheffield, S3 8HT - Tel 0114-270-1668 - Fax 0114-276-7900 www.fieldfare.org.uk - E mail fieldfare@btinternet.com

For further information about the Adventure Designs Project or specialist adventure equipment:
The Adventure Designs Project Co-ordinator, Studio 26, Brunel University, Runnymede, Egham, Surrey, TW20 0JZ - Tel 01784 433262 - Fax 01784 470880 - E mail adventure-designs-dfl@brunel.ac.uk

Further Reading

Guidance Notes - A Different Perspective on Access, BCU Paddle-Ability
Access Audit, Centre for Accessible Environments
Access by design (VHS Video tape), Centre for Accessible Environments
Am I making myself clear? Mencap

Basic British Sign Language, The Royal National Institute for Deaf People
BT Countryside for All, British Telecom
Building Sight, The Royal National Institute for the Blind
Buildings and Internal Environments, JMU Access Partnership
Color, Contrast and Perception - Design Guidance for Internal Built Env., Brighton K, Cook G and Harris J
Communicating with Deaf People Who Lip-Read (fact sheet), The Royal National Institute for Deaf People
Deaf and hard of hearing people, The Royal National Institute for Deaf People
Open up your business, The Royal National Institute for Deaf People
Publications Catalogue, The Royal National Institute for Deaf People
RNIB React, The Royal National Institute for the Blind
See It Right - Clear Print Guidelines, January 1998, The Royal National Institute for the Blind
Sea Legs - Access to Coastal Sailing for People with Disabilities, RYA Salability & Fieldfare Trust
Solutions, The Royal National Institute for Deaf People
The Informability Manual, Gregory W
Welcoming Customers with Learning Disabilities (training pack), Mencap
Adapted Physical Activity and Sport (Second Edition),1995, Winnick JP, Human Kinetics, 0-87322-579-1
Canoeing for Disabled People, Smedley G, 1995, British Canoe Union, 0-900082-08-9
Leisure Activities - Safety Guidelines, Howard Bailey, 1994, SCOPE, 0 04682835 0
Safe and Responsible Youth Expeditions, Roger Putnam, 1994, Young Explorers Trust, 0 905965 04 3
Expedition Planners Handbook and Directory, 1992, Expedition Advisory Center, 0-907649-54-8
Signs for Canoeists, Ripley K and Scandrett S, Avon Deaf Children's Society, Enquiries to 8 Fairlawn Road, Montpellier, Bristol, BSA6 5JR
Coaching Athletes with Disabilities, Goodman S, 1995, Australian Sports Commission, 0-642-188203
Coaching Athletes with Vision Impairments, Hokey K and Goodman S, 1992, A.S.C., 0-642-17005-3
Coaching Deaf Athletes, Anne Bremner, 1992, Australian Sports Commission, 0-642-17018-5
Coaching Athletes with Cerebral Palsy, Scott Goodman, 1998, Australian Sports Commission, 0-642 263442
Coaching Wheelchair Athletes, Goodman S, 1996, Australian Sports Commission, 0-642-175-0
Coaching Amputee and Les Autres Athletes, C J Nunn, 1994, Australian Sports Commission, 0-642--16890-3
Canoeing Expeditions for People with Disabilities, Smedley G, 1997, British Canoe Union
Canoeing and Kayaking for Persons with Physical Disabilities, Wortham A and Zeller J, 1990, American Canoe Association, 0-943117-02-X

Suresh Paul

Suresh is the founder of the not-for-profit Adventure Designs project based at Brunel University Design for Life Centre. The project designs and develops a range of equipment for disabled outdoor athletes to remove the practical barriers to participation.

Suresh has been interested in the outdoors and expeditions since his youth, and graduated from climbing bus shelters and brick walls in North London to participating in a range of youth expedition projects. These form the foundation for his involvement in a wide range of inclusive and professional expedition research projects. He is a keen outdoor performer and coach with a strong interest in paddlesport, rescue and mountaineering. He is the founder of the Inclusive Expedition project at the Royal Geographical Society Expedition Advisory Centre.

He formerly trained in Industrial Design and has two Millenium Design Awards from the British Design Council for his pioneering work at Brunel University.

(speech bubble) Is it true that you only paddled the Atlantic because there were no access problems?

11 Access to Water

Richard's first experience of 'the access problem' was at the tender age of 12, when a group of local anglers threatened to do unmentionable things to him if he paddled the river he was standing next to. He was accompanied on that trip by the local access officer who knew that they were well within their rights to paddle, and just happened to be 6 feet 4 inches tall and built like a tank. When 'Big Al' arrived to see what all the fuss was about, the anglers mysteriously disappeared. They did not have any problems on the water that day. Richard's daily work often reminds him of this incident, and he firmly believes that canoeists need the assistance and protection of major figures to ensure that the access problem is resolved.

What is Access?

If canoeing is a bicycle then access is the wheels. Coaching, funding, and participation provide the handlebars, the frame and the power to move the sport forward, but without the wheels you can't go anywhere. If you have no access to suitable water to paddle, you have no sport.

Access includes not only entry on to and along linear waterways but also admission to specific water sites and supporting facilities. Although not an exhaustive list, access can and does include such areas as:

- Paddling along a river, lake or canal, commonly referred to as 'Linear Access' or ' Navigation'.

- The utilisation of sites in isolation such as playspots or slalom courses, referred to as 'Occupation.

- The ability to get from the public highway to the water and vice versa.

- The provision of launching and landing sites, and the ability to utilise lay-by areas for unloading or loading.

- The provision of parking or other facilities such as changing and WCs.

- The arrangements for spectators at events or training sessions.

- The provision of portage and inspection routes along land at or near to rapids.

172

Associated with access is the ability to do all the above without receiving aggravation or coming into conflict with other water users.

Why is Access Neglected and Loathed?

It's your weekend off and the water levels are perfect for paddling. The water is calling you to join it. Your very essence is telling you that you are invincible, that you can go where you want to paddle, and what is more, you'll do it when you like!

If only you could. Provision of access to water in the UK is poor, and there are numerous factors that place restrictions on the ability to use and enjoy water for recreational purposes in the UK.

Broadly speaking, you do not have a right to paddle where you would like. It seems that the answer to the question, "Why is access probably the most neglected, loathed or even feared side of our superb sport?" is that a lot of paddlers, although aggrieved, believe that they can do nothing about the access situation.

Granted the progress and acquisition of greater amounts of access to water is a slow and often painful process. However, if all you get from reading this chapter is the knowledge that every paddler can do something to help improve the access position within the UK, then I feel that it has done its job.

Where Can You Go Paddling?

The basic answer to this question is that you can paddle where you have a right of passage or where you have formal or implied permission to paddle.

Scotland

The access situation in Scotland is different to that of the rest of the UK. Both legally and traditionally, while people have no 'right' in law to be on land or water, they are equally not committing an offence simply by being there. Most access is taken by 'implied consent'. For example, the path down to a river may be over private land but it has been in use without objection for many years - access by tradition if you like. If a landowner objects to a person's presence, he or she can seek an interdict against the individual to prevent them from coming back. Damages can only be awarded if damage or harm has resulted. In practice, interdicts have been extremely rarely deployed against the recreational user of the countryside.

A Public Right of Navigation may be exercised below the high water mark on tidal rivers and estuaries, and on the sea. Where a public right of navigation exists it is superior to all other rights on the water. However, this right to navigate must be exercised with due consideration for other water users. In Scotland, a public right of navigation only exists on the rivers Spey and Leven. Notwithstanding this, the Scottish Canoe Association maintains that there is a basic human right to paddle inland lochs and rivers, based on the "traditional" right to roam in Scotland. The SCA believes this includes passage over water, as well as access to it on foot to embark and disembark, but that it does not include use of a motorised vehicle.

Canoeing is a lawful activity; be confident about your right to be on the water, but do not let this blind you to the need to act responsibly and to take account of other users and operations that may be going on. For details of river advisers and the SCA Code of Conduct refer to www.scot-canoe.org or get a copy of the 'SCA Guide to Scottish Whitewater', available from the SCA office.

New Legislation in Scotland

The draft Land Reform Bill and Scottish Outdoor Access Code underwent a three-month public consultation that ended in June 2001. The intention of the Bill is to improve access to the countryside by introducing a right of access to land and inland water for recreation and passage. The Bill will provide safeguards for privacy, land management, and conservation. It will be accompanied by the Scottish Outdoor Access Code, which gives further guidance on reasonable behaviour.

The new Scottish Bill was intended to reflect and enshrine the liberal traditions of current practice. However, concerns have been raised that the proposed legislation will reduce access opportunities by giving landowners new powers to suspend access rights, and to exclude access rights to land developed for a particular purpose (which could be shooting or angling). It also introduces a new criminal dimension to the act of trespass. The Bill looks set to go onto the Statute Books in 2002, and you are advised to consult the SCA Access Team about its progress and what you can do to ensure the legislation does not reduce the ability to paddle.

A special thanks to Fran Pothecary, the SCA Access Officer for contibuting the Scottish perspective.

The Rest of the UK

Why do you need permission?

All land, including the bed of a river, belongs to someone. The law operates to protect owners of 'Property Rights' from unwanted intrusion or disturbance of those rights.

Photo 11.1   The downside

Property Rights include the Freehold of the land in question, and any interests or rights that were part of the original freehold which have become separated from it due to sale or lease to others.

For example:

- Sporting rights

- Fishing rights

- Navigation rights belonging to particular persons.

Owners can range from the Crown, private individuals, local councils, companies and fishing clubs. All these rights may be exclusive to the owner or shared with other owners.

Riparian Owners & Fishing Rights

'Riparian owner' is the term given to the owner of a river bank. They enjoy property rights over the land covered by the water, although they do not own the water itself. Riparian owners have the right to take fish from the water. It is not uncommon for fishing rights to be leased or sold off to fishing interests and angling associations, giving them a degree of riparian ownership.

On non-tidal waters, fishing rights are privately owned property rights. These rights are protected by the law from interference (e.g. by the public or boats), unless there is a public right to navigate. A right to take fish does not carry with it the right to use the river bank in order so to do. The use of the river bank has to be negotiated with the relevant landowner separately.

How do you get permission?

Permission can come from a riparian owner, or from a right conferred to the public to navigate on a specific waterway.

Public Rights of Passage by Boat

There is a distinction between the law that covers the sea and tidal waters, and that of non-tidal waters.

The Sea and Tidal Waters

On the sea and tidal waters up to the high water mark, the land covered by water is regarded as belonging to the Crown. The high water mark usually refers to the operation of ordinary spring tides, and is marked on Ordnance Survey maps. The Crown permits the public to navigate this water (and fish it) up to the high water mark, so far as the physical conditions allow.

The banks may well be in private ownership. Owners of land adjoining and abutting the coast and tidal waters are not obliged to permit access to the water across their land. The position will be different if there is a public right of way across this land. In some circumstances the bed of a tidal waterway may have been conveyed to an owner other than the Crown. In such circumstances the right of navigation may well have been extinguished.

Non-tidal Waters

There is no automatic right to navigate as in tidal waters above. This is because the law regards the Crown as having transferred the ownership of the bed of waterways to the owners of the adjoining banks. There are some non-tidal waters that have a public right of navigation on them, e.g. the Thames and the River Severn. (Consult the BCU Development Department for a fuller list.)

Public rights of passage on non-tidal water can arise in a number of ways, and the law on this topic is highly convoluted. Interested readers are advised to refer to Halsbury's Laws of England for a detailed explanation.

Regardless of how navigation rights are established there are a few key points to remember.

- Only the channel that is covered by the water at the time of passage is considered to be part of the navigation.

- There is no public right to access across private land to reach navigation. It is necessary to reach agreement with landowners or use public launching points.

- The public right is that of passage. There is no right to occupy a stretch of water for an event or practice.

- Some Public Navigations are only available after taking out a licence or paying a fee, e.g. the Thames or the Severn.

- Rights to navigate are not always public rights. In some cases private rights of passage by boat exist that have been conferred on a limited class of people or craft. A private right may be subject to conditions that avoid interference with other rights, e.g. fishing rights.

- A public right to navigate takes precedence over 'private rights'. However, where you have a legal right to pass down or be on a section of water, the law will require you to exercise that right reasonably and with due consideration to others.

- Certain authorities have powers under statute to make bylaws, which can regulate or even prohibit boating on public rights of navigation.

Permission from a Riparian Owner

The sad fact is that there is not a great deal of water that is covered by rights to navigate, and in their absence you need to obtain permission to paddle from the landowner.

The majority of waterways are in private ownership. Riparian owners and interests are usually unwilling to give permission for canoeing on their waters. Canoeists have access to 3% of the potential paddleable water in England and Wales that is in this category.

Trespass

The BCU advises its members to act in a lawful manner and recommends that all paddlers do so at all times. If you are canoeing on privately owned water without permission then technically you are trespassing.

The law protects the owner's interest in the peaceful enjoyment of his property. Trespass in its basic form is a Civil Wrong (a Tort), not a Criminal Offence. In layman's terms Trespass is an invasion of or interference with another's property rights without consent.

Trespass is actionable per se, and therefore it does not matter whether the owner actually suffered any damage; it is sufficient that the trespasser is there. Entry on to another's land without permission is a trespass, whether or not the entrant knows he is trespassing.

What Can a Landowner Do?

An owner is entitled to ask the trespasser to leave his land. He may use reasonable force to eject them or to deny them entry on to his land. Once on the land, the owner can ask the trespasser to leave via the shortest or an agreed route to the highway. In doing so he can't insist that you take a route over other private property.

A bailiff acting on behalf of the owner can do similar, under the powers given to him by the owners. An Environment Agency Bailiff has the powers of a constable for the enforcement of Salmon and Freshwater Fishery Act related offences, in relation to poaching or damage to spawning beds.

Damages or a fine may be awarded against the trespasser. An injunction may be granted to prevent repetition of trespass, or even to restrain threatened trespass. Failure to adhere to, or ignoring the terms of an injunction would be in contempt of court. This could lead to fining or imprisonment. For damages to be awarded or for an injunction to be ordered, that case will have to go to court.

What to Do if You Are Confronted or Accused of Trespass?

First and foremost, it will be necessary to remain calm and civil toward the other party.

Remember:

- You are an ambassador for the sport of canoeing, and its future.

- Trespass does not attract police involvement, unless a criminal act such as a breach of the peace or wilful damage occurs. Additionally, the police would become involved if the situation were one of Aggravated Trespass. (See below.)

It is futile to claim that the only reason for entry was that you were lost, or even that you genuinely but erroneously believed that you had a right to be there, as it does not constitute a defence to a trespass action. However, if intrusion onto the land is accidental and all reasonable steps were taken to avoid trespass, then there is a possibility that a court will view the incident as an inevitable accident.

In practice, it is rarely worth the trouble and expense of taking a trespasser to court. If you are polite, and agree to leave promptly by an agreed route, that is usually the end of the matter.

If you genuinely believe that you are exercising a public right of navigation or are adhering to terms of an access agreement, then state the case and under no circumstances admit trespass. An act cannot be a trespass if it is legally justified, (using a public right of way over land, or paddling under an agreement). There is no case if you can prove that you are within your rights or have permission.

You must be aware that a person who is legally entitled to enter land can become a trespasser if he or she exceeds or abuses that right or permission. This has obvious references to the terms of access agreements. If your licence or permission to be on the property is revoked, then any further intrusion is a trespass.

Aggravated Trespass

The Criminal Justice (Public Order Act) 1994 introduced the criminal offence of aggravated trespass.

To commit aggravated trespass you must:

a) Be trespassing.

b) Have the intention of obstructing or disrupting a lawful activity, or intimidating those engaged in such lawful activities.

c) Lawful activities include field sports such as hunting, shooting and fishing. The offence was originally drafted to deal with hunt saboteurs, but by its very nature it does have an all-encapsulating effect that will concern paddlers. Canoeists should not fall foul of this law if they canoe in a peaceful and considerate manner.

What the BCU is Doing About Access

Lobbying to Change the Law

The BCU's aim is to secure changes in legislation to improve the legal rights for canoeists to access water for their sport. The reason for this is that other methods of securing access, such as the provision of access via voluntary means, have not proved to be a successful approach. For example, only 605 of the 10,411 miles of smaller rivers suitable for paddling in England and Wales are covered by access agreements.

Additionally, in the absence of an agreement, canoeists either do not paddle, or have to rely on the tolerance of riparian owners who choose not to exercise their rights or not take action for tres-

pass. In accordance with government objectives, the BCU has maintained a dialogue with the landowner and angling interests to seek voluntary agreements through the Angling and Canoeing Liaison Group, which is a forum brokered by the Environment Agency. A process to achieve access agreements and proof of the success of this arrangement is awaited. Additionally the BCU is affiliated to sporting bodies such as the CCPR, the Sports Councils and, in conjunction with the Environment Agency, British Waterways and water users' forums, to promote access for canoeing.

A change in the law is a long-term objective, and it may take a very long period of time before anything positive occurs. Canoeists can't sit back and wait for a change to happen, or be apathetic about the situation. A vast amount of lobbying and groundwork towards a change in the law that will benefit canoeists has to be undertaken before the wheels start to move. The BCU is providing the lead in this lobby. However, to be successful it needs to be able to rely on the support of all paddlers in its campaigns, so that there is sufficient pressure to get the desired results.

Securing Access by Voluntary Means

In the short-term and in the absence of legislation, the BCU will look toward providing increased access via voluntary means. There is no legal requirement for riparian owners to enter into negotiations with canoeists over access to water, let alone to grant them permission. Therefore access to water in private ownership has to be secured by voluntary means. Securing access via voluntary means has been the preferred approach by successive Governments for a number of years.

Securing voluntary access is a complicated process. We need permission to:

- Get to the water from the highway.

- Pass along the water from start to finish.

- Have permission to egress over land and return to the highway.

The complications arise when you consider that a stretch of water, however long, could have numerous riparian interests and landowners along its length, and that permission has to be obtained individually from each owner. It is a hard task just to map out and track down the owners, and it must be remembered that refusal of one owner could put the brakes on obtaining permission for an entire section.

Access Agreements

There are many riparian owners, and numerous objections raised by riparian and angling interests to canoeing and all kinds of other sporting activities associated with, on or around water. These objections range from the truly absurd to the understandable concern. This text does not seek to analyse these objections, but only to state that all objections can be addressed and resolved by providing sensible access agreements.

Photo 11.2   The up-side, access on the Cardiff Bay Development

An access agreement is the main tool to gain access to water via voluntary means. It is used as a control mechanism for canoeing and provides terms under which paddling can take place. More importantly, it can be used to ensure that the concerns of riparian interests can be met or protected, and ensures that harmonious relationships between differing users are cultured.

Riparian and angling interests need to realise that it is far better to permit canoeing under the terms of an access agreement than it is to blindly say "no" to paddling. Saying "no" only encourages acts of trespass and stealth paddling, and increases the utilisation of the limited number of areas paddlers can use, which in turn produces more conflict. An agreement will provide riparian interests with the control they seek, and most importantly, gain them and their interests the respect and consideration of their rights, that they require from paddlers.

Access agreements are hard to achieve and maintain. Canoeists are urged to abide by their terms to ensure their future. Before you set out it is imperative you contact the local access officer about the water you want to paddle, and stay within the terms of the agreement.

The BCU will seek to gain greater access via voluntary means by addressing the concerns of riparian interests and producing sensible access agreements for its members. In doing so, the BCU will ensure that the provision of agreements is a basis that does not prejudice any future ability to prove navigation on the water in question. Additionally, the BCU will strive to ensure that any payments made to landowners are not for simple access to water, but are made in return for tangible facilities that enhance the opportunities or ability to paddle. Such facilities are classed as parking, launching and landing sites, toilets and changing facilities.

Environment

For a detailed discussion of this topic, please refer to the Environment chapter of this handbook. Preservation of wildlife and improvement of the countryside is important to canoeists. The canoe itself causes no erosion, noise or pollution, and leaves no trace of its passing. For this reason canoeing can not be perceived as a threat to environmental conservation. Sensible access agreements can be used to address environmental concerns, as well as promote considerate and environmentally friendly enjoyment of countryside for all types of recreation.

Access Officers

The national organisations forming the BCU have a team of voluntary access officers who donate their own time, skill and patience into improving access for canoeing. Besides maintaining goodwill to ensure that access agreements are kept alive, and working toward the production of greater access to water, access officers are the primary resources for people wanting information on where to paddle.

Access officers provide information and advice on the access situation that is currently in force on their river. The Access Team is usually divided into regions, with rivers within that region having a specific local access officer. It is essential that you contact the access officer for the river well in advance of your trip. By doing so you may avoid conflict, preserve the terms of an agreement, and even gain knowledge of the best places to eat and drink in the local area after your trip. Please adhere to the advice that you are given. Details of whom and how to contact the correct person are listed in the BCU Yearbook or are available from your national governing body.

The work of access officers is varied and interesting. It can involve researching the historical use of a river, preparing and disseminating information about the access situation and physical characteristic of the river, getting to know local riparian interests to keep alive goodwill, and solve problems at a local stage. If you are interested in becoming an access officer, please get in touch with your regional access officer or development head office for more information.

The Future

Despite continual lobbying, access to water was specifically left out of the Countryside and Rights of Way Act 2000. However, the continual lobbying of Parliament and Ministers has proved useful, as the Government has finally accepted that there is a problem. The Government has commissioned a study into the scope of access to inland water for recreational purposes. The BCU has been working closely with the research team, and it is hoped that the study will reveal that positive intervention is needed from Government to address the real issues and provide greater access to water for canoeists.

The BCU continues to work toward the production of further access agreements. In doing so, it seeks to break down the barriers and perceived difficulties of riparian and angling interests to improved access. The research paper into 'The Effects of Canoeing on Fish Stocks and Angling', published in 2000 and produced by the Environment Agency on behalf of the Angling and Canoeing Liaison Group, found that there was no empirical evidence linking canoeing with damage of spawning grounds and stocks. The report also stated that in the light of the representations received in its production, many of the objections to allowing shared access on the basis that canoeing causes damage to fish stock are untenable. It is hoped that partners such as the Environment Agency and the various Sports Councils will assist the BCU to build on the credibility that this report offers canoeing, and act as honest brokers to produce sensible agreements.

The BCU is also continuing to lobby Parliament for a change in the law, and continues its daily activity of responding to new draft legislation and European Directives to ensure that the canoeists' point of view is heard and that measures that could restrict access are not imposed.

What can You Do to Help?

For our sport to develop, we need to convince the Government that there is a need to introduce legislation that would allow canoeing journeys to take place as of right. This can only be done if paddlers actively help the BCU by answering its calls to lobby Parliament, and helping it with its campaigns for greater access. Your help and support provide the numbers that show that BCU lobbying activity has credibility, and that there are enough people who want to see change.

As far as generating access agreements are concerned, it is clear that we will not get far if we breach the terms of the existing ones and lose the goodwill of those who are willing to listen. Please keep abreast with access issues. Contact your local access officer before paddling for up to date information, even if it is just to ensure there is enough water in the river. Keep the access officers informed of any problems that you have encountered, be they confrontations with other users, or physical blockages in the channel such as dangerous trees.

Getting to the negotiation stage with riparian owners depends on the development of goodwill. Every time you paddle you are an ambassador for the sport who can lay the foundations for future developments.

- Drive with care and with consideration to the locality.
- Park vehicles in particular designated places if available. Park sensibly so not to cause obstruction.
- Obtain permission before entering private property.
- Get changed discretely, rather than in public view.
- Be as quiet as possible.
- Unload and load kit in a tidy fashion.
- Do not leave boats unattended or in places where they could cause obstruction.
- Do not leave valuables in the car, or if necessary stow them out of sight.

On the Water

- Observe the Country Code.
- Avoid wildlife damage and damage to the environment.

- Be considerate to other water users.
- Use discretion and approved routes when portaging.

After:

- Change quickly and discreetly.
- Use local pubs, cafes, restaurants and shops.
- Be polite to local residents.
- Avoid being an intrusion to local life.
- Take all litter home with you and leave not trace of your presence.

Final Thought

The following comments about 'tourism' from Peter Bandtock, are taken from Peter Knowles' book 'White Water Europe' – Book 2. The comments are made with reference to the fact that the alpine rivers are often lost to damming. His comments are equally applicable to the context of access, and paddlers' responsibility to promote the sport at all times to gain the all-important support of local communities.

"It's simple things that will make a difference. If paddlers use a campsite, rather than dossing in a lay-by, then they are pumping money into the local economy. If we eat and drink in local pubs and cafes, if we buy our food from local shops rather than city supermarkets - then the same thing is true. If we change discreetly then we become tourists that are welcomed rather than unwelcome parasites who are barely tolerated."

We can all do something!

Further Information

BCU Yearbook - Contact details of Local and Regional Access Officers
CANI Yearbook - Contact details of Local and Regional Access Officers
SCA Yearbook - Contact details of Local and Regional Access Officers
WCA Yearbook - Contact details of Local and Regional Access Officers

Websites

British Canoe Union - www.bcu.org.uk
Canoe Association of Northern Ireland - www.cani@clara.net/cani
Scottish Canoe Association - www.scot-canoe.org
Welsh Canoe Association - www.welsh-canoeing.org.uk

Information Phone Lines

Canolfan Tryweryn 24 hour Water Information Line - 01678-520826
Canoe Access Line Wales, access information and river levels - 0906-4777779

Richard Harvey

Richard Harvey is the National Access Development Officer of the WCA, and has been in this post since March 2000.

Richard grew up in the Brecon area, and spent most of his early paddling days on the rivers Usk and Wye. He started paddling in 1980 at the age of eight when the kayaking bug bit his father, who subsequently spent a lot of money on petrol taking his young boating addict on trips.

All his spare time is spent boating, and he can regularly be found surfing around the Gower area, playboating at Canolfan Tryweryn, running one of the numerous rivers of South Wales, or coaching at Pontypridd Canoe Club.

Scottish information contributed by Fran Pothecary.

12 Paddlers and the Environment

It was a hard portage up through the woods and then back down to the river. The sun was high and the air felt too hot even to breathe. Having taken the canoes on the first trip, we were ambling back along the path, looking about and taking pleasure in walking without the weight of the boats and packs on our backs. It was Keith who drew our attention to a movement alongside the path, and we peered into the grass to see the glassy stare of a slow worm basking in the sun. We watched it for a few minutes and then decided to get just that little closer for a photograph, but sensing our presence it moved off into the undergrowth.

The two families had stopped for a break, and with the boats nestled in the reeds everyone had time to relax. There was a sound of a plop in the water and from across the other side of the canal came a water vole, heading straight for the canoes. When it was within three metres of the boats it veered, and we watched as the vole climbed out onto the bank, shook itself and then started to walk alongside the canoes. As the vole approached, Steve lowered his paddle and the vole just climbed onto the blade and sat down to clean itself. Slowly Steve brought the paddle closer to the children, and they had a few minutes to watch the vole complete its wash before it decided enough was enough, and it was off.

Introduction

As canoeists we are very fortunate to be the only people who have the skills that will enable us to navigate a river from its source to the sea and beyond. We can travel slowly and quietly, leaving no evidence of our journey, and pass through many varied habitats, which provide us with the opportunity to become intimate with the wildlife and environment along the way.

Inland Waters

Rivers and canals vary in character as they pass through different landscapes and drain different kinds of substrate, with sections offering niche habitats for different plants and animals. They can change from one type of habitat to another and then back again, depending on factors such as altitude, rate of water flow, nutrient status, gradient, season and the effect of man.

Photo 12.1   Winter scene

Much of the industrial revolution was linked with rivers and canals and there are still numerous historic sites and buildings that can be seen from canoes and kayaks. These unique areas can provide us with glimpses into the past at what was the cutting edge technology of the day.

Upland Streams and Becks

Here the waterway is in its exuberant infancy, where the plants and animals have to contend with the turbulent, plunging flow of water, which can vary from low flow in summer to high rates in winter. The productive zone is therefore on the river bed. There is shelter and an anchorage available but the fast water flow brings fresh supplies of nutrients and food, and removes waste products.

Some of the classic upland plants such as sphagnum, sedges, bog bean, butterwort and cotton grass will be seen, while in the river the nymphs of mayflies, caddis-flies and stone-flies will be the prey of salmon and trout. Deer, grouse and migratory waterfowl may be glimpsed, but the skylark will be heard well before it is seen in the sky. If you are lucky, otter, mink and various birds of prey might make a chance encounter, but it is the dipper that is the true indicator of an upland waterway.

Chestnut brown with a white chest, the dipper likes water with plenty of boulders on which to perch and fast, clear water in which to hunt for food. Dippers feed on invertebrates by walking upstream under the water on the river bed, turning over stones with their beak. They maintain themselves on the river bed by angling their wings to the flow of the water which presses them down. When they want to return to the surface, they simply change the wing angle, release the pressure and bob to the surface. Each pair has a territory, and the number of territories directly reflect the amount of food available and therefore the productivity of the river.

The Lowland River

The lowland river knows where it is going; the speed of the current decreases and only in times of flood is it really eager to get there. Along with the main river there are meanders, oxbows and backwaters, all providing habitats for wildlife and the canoeist to explore. There is a high nutrient content from organic matter and fertiliser run off, which allows the growth of large quantities of phytoplankton and zooplankton. These are food for larger animals.

In the summer lacewings, dragonflies, damselflies, midges and butterflies abound in the air, while water beetles, whirligig beetles, pond skaters and water boatmen can be sighted on or under the water. Mallard try to hide their youngsters in the trees as paddlers pass; mute swans, aggressive when they are brooding, swim serenely by.

Sitting in the reeds watching little grebe, coot, and moorhen feeding in the shallows while swifts, swallows and martins wheel in the air catching insects, is a must for any sunny summer's day; and it is well worth taking along an apple to tempt a water vole over to feed.

Canals

Throughout the country, most of the population are in easy reach of a canal to paddle on. These waterways offer a year-round highway, bringing wildlife into towns and cities and allowing paddlers to move out into the countryside. During the building and industrial use of the canals, towns and cities were moulded by the canal's presence. There were numerous technological innovations designed and built to aid the movement of cargo in canal boats. Many of these wonders of the waterways, such as the Anderton Swing Bridge, the Foxton Inclined Plane and the Caen Hill Flight of locks, can still be seen. The British canal system is a haven for wildlife, a treasure trove of industrial archaeology and a national gem that we should be justly proud of.

Photo 12.2   Mute swans and cygnets

Lakes

From the man-made gravel pits and reservoirs to the natural lakes in the Lake District and Scotland, there is a wide range of wildlife habitats. Most of the wildlife interest will be around the edges of the lakes and on the islands of larger bodies of water. Nonetheless, the open water will provide areas for waterfowl to congregate, to feed, and if you are lucky, in which to see an osprey dive.

By their nature lakes are areas of deposition; the slow but constant transition from open water to land can be observed. The first plants such as water lilies start to grow in the shallows; these plants slow water movement, increasing deposition and adding to it by their annual die-back. Reeds, reedmace and sedges will become established as the depth of water decreases, and these all increase the amount of solid ground to allow alder, willow and birch to take hold. Finally, if left to its own devices, and after many years, the lake will shrink, with a succession of plants from those free floating at the borders of the lake to mature woodland. Eventually the lake will become filled and lost to the power of plants. Canoeists pottering along the shores of many of our lakes can see all aspects of the evidence of this process in progress.

The Coast

The British coast is very beautiful and varied. We are also extremely fortunate in that none of us lives more than 90 miles from the coast.

Estuaries

Estuaries are where the two forces of river and tidal flow are in relative equilibrium, and there is a rough balance between the deposition of sand and mud from the river and its removal by the sea. The mud is rich in nutrients and can therefore produce a diverse food chain, providing fine pickings for birds such as the shelduck and huge populations of waders. Different species of waders have been forced to evolve to avoid direct competition. A subtle difference in leg or bill length will allow exploitation of the food filled mud to different depths, picking out the animals that have evolved to live at varying levels.

Salt Marshes

These are areas where there is more deposition than removal, and the estuary silts up to provide a different habitat, a mixture of the maritime and terrestrial zones. It is a harsh environment where plants have to cope with total or partial immersion in salt water at least twice a day. Many of the plants are unique to this area and are not unlike desert species with thick, fleshy leaves, concentrated cell sap and hairy, silvery skins.

Sand Dunes

Sand dunes are susceptible to movement by the wind, especially where the protective vegetation has been damaged. Marram grass is superbly adapted to grow in this environment, as it has the ability to grow up through successive coverings of sand, until eventually the wind speed and the angle are such that the sand will no longer accumulate. It also has leaves that roll inwards to prevent water loss and, as anyone will know who has walked through dunes in shorts, serrated leaf edges to prevent grazing. Dunes however, are still mobile; periodic 'blow-outs' can still be caused by heavy storms or freak tides.

Photo 12.3   Guillemots on cliff ledge

Rocky Shores

Rocky shores are fantastic places to see the destructive action of waves pounding the rock strata and eroding it through both physical and chemical means. Rock pools along the shore are worlds in themselves. Even in a small area of shoreline they can be very varied, containing different amounts and species of seaweed, anemones, shellfish and animal life. Many rocks are covered with different shells such as barnacles and mussels. The barnacles are related to crabs, and when covered by sea water, their protective plates slide open to allow their 'legs' to emerge to catch food. Mussels are chemically attracted to attach to rocks where other mussels are present. When moving rocks to search for animals, remember to place the rock back in the same position so that the animals living under or on the rock are not exposed too long to an adverse environment.

Zonation

Distinct distributions of plants and animals can be seen. This is mainly due to the movement of the tides as the tidal zone is covered and uncovered by the sea every 12 hours. The higher points on the shore might be only covered for a few hours on a few days each month, during spring tides.

Photo 12.4   Sea urchin grazing

Whether pottering in rock pools, camping in the dunes, seeing large mammals such as seals or dolphins, birds like the marsh harrier or flocks of waders wheeling in the air on a winter's day, the British coast has a lot of variety to offer the canoeist.

Environmental Awareness

Be proactive:

- Paddlers travel through many areas, some of which are inaccessible to any other form of transport. We can be in the front line against pollution and environmental damage. If paddlers see any change such as dead fish, large cans or canisters, discharges or a change in the colour or smell in the water, they should note the area, possibly take photographs and contact the Environmental Agency.

- Tidy up snagged lines left by fishermen. This will stop birds, animals and paddlers becoming caught in the line.

- If you are organising an event or just regularly paddle in an area, produce an environmental audit of the effect the group is having on the area.

- Groups can work on tree planting, nest box and bat box provision and clean-up campaigns.

- Practise low impact paddling and camping; share transport, make kit last, recycle and learn how to camp correctly.

- Contact wildlife groups such as local RSPB, bat and botanical associations. They can provide specialised information and help with joint ventures. Bat groups will have instrumentation that will enable a group to hear and identify different bat calls.

- Map your area, plot the position of trees, interesting plants, fungi, insects, animals, nests, historical locations. Note changes throughout the seasons, produce canoe trails and routes that can use these places of interest.

- Run awareness days/weekends.

- On trips get participants to find an attractive pebble, leaf or flower. (Don't pick wild flowers, leave them as you found them).

- Get to know common plants and animals. You don't have to get bogged down with learning names!

- There is a wealth of books and magazines that can assist people with observation and identification of wildlife.

- Compile a wildlife diary, either as an individual or as a club or group.

- Learn some environmental games; adapt existing games to illustrate an environmental theme and produce new ones.

- On a paddle just take some time out to sit in the reeds, eddy or bank to chill out, relax and observe what is going on about you.

- Have fun!

Conclusions

The beauty of paddling along any waterway is that there is always something new around every corner. Although you might have paddled the same stretch yesterday or an hour ago, there will be a change in what you see.

It is important for leaders and coaches to pass on information to paddlers they are working with. A study and appreciation of nature can teach self-worth, co-ordination and teamwork. People who enjoy the benefits of wildlife learn to safeguard and sustain their environment.

Photo 12.5   Young Atlantic Grey Seal

Further Reading

Animals of Britain and Europe, Country Life, 0-600-352282
Collins Guide to Insects, Collins, 0-00-219137-2
Complete British Wildlife, Collins, 0-583-33638-8
Hamlyn Guide to Birds of Britain, Hamlyn, 0-601-07065-8
Hamlyn Guide to the Seashore and Shallow Seas of Britain and Europe, Hamlyn, 0-600-34396-0
There are also numerous excellent specialised publications available from organisations such as the RSPB.

Website

www.rspb.org.uk - RSPB website

David Halsall

Dave Halsall lives and works in the Yorkshire Dales and is an active member of the coaching scheme. He had his first taste of canoeing while at school in the 70's, but became a born-again paddler in the late 80's while looking for a method to maintain fitness after sustaining a serious footballing injury. Along with a group from the local canoe club he took part in marathon races, competing in many of the classics such as the Hasler Final, the DW, Liffey Descent and the Avon Stage. He also paddled in a dragon boat team, the Soar Bottoms who represented GB in Malmo, Sweden. He worked with the BCU Environmental Panel and then produced a regular monthly article on the environment in the magazine Canoeist. He continued his writing and penned many articles for Canoe Focus, Canoeist, Paddles and Canoe & Kayak UK. He has journeyed by canoe and kayak throughout the UK, Europe, Scandinavia and Canada.

13 Placid Water

"Believe me, my young friend, there is nothing -
absolutely nothing -
half so much worth doing as simply messing about in boats.
Simply messing," he went on dreamily, "messing - about - in - boats."

Ratty - (From 'The Wind in the Willows' by Kenneth Graham)

Introduction

This chapter is intended to enthuse you to go out, discover and fully exploit the potential of this country's abundant placid water, the true aquatic resource for all.

Features and Benefits of Placid Water

Introducing Beginners

Calm, sheltered water is probably where most of you learnt to canoe; even if not in the cosseted confines of a pool, it was likely to have been easy to perceive the water as safe. I remember introducing one of our raft guides to kayaking on the Colorado, halfway down the Grand Canyon; it made for a steep learning curve, but I'm not sure he's paddled since. So utilising the main feature of placid water, its non-threatening nature, allows you to persuade even the most timid of water-fearing creatures to extend their comfort zones and experience our great sport.

Exploration

An open boat or straight running kayak will quickly allow someone to explore their environment from a totally different angle than before. My teenage years were spent on the polluted canals and slow moving rivers of a Yorkshire mill town. As a result, my knowledge of local history improved just as fast as my paddling by being able to explore places it was impossible to reach on foot. In addition, bearing in mind what unknown murky depths you could fall into, there was always an increased incentive to master your support strokes! The water is much cleaner now and there are thousands of miles of placid waterways that allow us to explore both rural and urban Britain.

Try a Boat

Many clubs up and down the country have for years successfully marketed their placid water haunts, not only as a place for beginners to learn, but for everyone, irrespective of gender, physical strength or disability, to grow into confident paddlers in a range of craft and disciplines. For example the Bell Boat was designed and made specifically with placid water in mind. In the safe confines of placid water, familiarity can be gained with any boat or paddle design, no matter how specialist; indeed there is no better place to develop the delicate art of balancing a racing canoe! Most of my slalom training as a student was done on a canal in the West Midlands, including sprint and gate work, practice which proved invaluable in competition.

Getting Away From it All

In the United Kingdom, placid water paddlers are very lucky in that they are never very far away from some form of access, which is a constraint that often restricts the development of other disciplines of the sport, for example, surfing and rodeo. No matter whether this access be in an urban or a rural area, the simple fact that you are afloat stands you apart from the rest of the population and is an escape in itself. There are few experiences to match the relaxation to be gained from an early morning paddle on placid water as the mist evaporates and the birds skim silently over the surface. Go on, take your friends, your white water playmates, even your granny; it's a wonderful, safe and stimulating environment for all.

Photo 13.1   Children racing Bell Boats

Definition and Types of Placid Water

Categorising Water

Various bodies over the years have categorised canoeing water that is not covered by the river grading system. Although the term 'placid water' conjures up a picture of mirror calmness, 'no wave' conditions can occur on more exposed water, and when the weather is very settled even the largest lakes can be described as placid.

BCU Definitions

The BCU describes *very sheltered water* as, "quiet canals with easy bank side access and egress, small lakes which are not large enough, and do not have difficult landing areas for problems to occur if there is a sudden change in conditions, and specified sites on gentle, slow moving rivers". This is therefore your ideal placid water starting point, however when you feel ready to really 'push the boat out', *sheltered water* is described as "flat water rivers, faster flowing but not involving the shooting of, or playing on weirs or running rapids".

Regarding other open water, the BCU says, "suitable lagoons, or sections of sheltered bays, or large lakes can sometimes be designated sheltered or even very sheltered water by careful and sensible selection". It goes on to warn of the serious undertaking of operating more than 200 metres from the shore, together with the dangers of offshore breezes and low water temperatures, and categorises very large lakes as advanced inland water.

AALA Definitions

The Adventure Activities Licensing Authority on the other hand takes a more pragmatic view in its 'collective interpretation' of what it describes as sheltered water. In its opinion, which is not legally definitive, sheltered water includes all water unless:

a) an adversely strong wind is blowing or is forecast.

b) any tide or current is moving significantly.

c) it is conceivable to be blown or swept into a hazardous or inescapable area.

'Adversely strong' and 'significant' in this context is in relation to the ability of the group as a whole to make reliable progress against it.

Photo 13.2   Urban placid water

To all intents and purposes, the following four categories of water can, when weather conditions allow, all provide placid water opportunities:

Lakes

Lakes range from the very small and sheltered, such as man-made gravel pits, flooded quarries and small tarns, right through to large exposed glacial lochs. The daunting statistics of some of the larger lakes within the United Kingdom are as follows:

Loch Awe in Strathclyde is the longest at over 25 miles. On Lough Neagh in Northern Ireland it is possible to be over 5 miles from shore, whilst Loch Morar in Highland can provide over 1000 feet of water beneath your hull.

Rivers

Rivers are slow moving due to either their natural geography or because their flow is stemmed by a weir or other similar barrage, though the latter requires more care. There are many examples of mature rivers providing calm water on which to paddle. These include: the Severn, Thames, Trent, Humber, Aire, Ouse, Wye, Tay, Nene, Clyde, Spey, Tweed, Dee, Avon, Don, Tees, Bann, Neagh, Tyne, Eden, Usk, Wear, Wharfe and Forth. These are some of the many British rivers which are over 60 miles in length.

Photo 13.3   Exploring the canals

Canals

The UK has a fascinating infrastructure of navigable inland waterways, many of them easily accessible from inner city locations. One main advantage of canals over other placid water venues is that they remain calm even in very windy conditions. BCU membership includes a British Waterways Board licence for most of their canals, giving free, local access for all.

Tidal Waters

If carefully selected, many harbours and estuaries up and down the country provide unique placid water to explore, with the major advantage of very few access concerns. They can provide the opportunity to play safely in a Victorian dock, view wildlife close up in a sheltered haven or explore around a quiet fishing port.

Photo 13.4   Session in a harbour

Placid Water Hazards

Complacency

The most common hazard facing anyone venturing onto placid water is not hypothermia or drowning, it is complacency. Remember, contrary to popular belief, more people die annually in fresh water accidents than in the sea. Both for the paddler and the coach, there is a real danger in underestimating the potential for catastrophe on placid water, simply because its nature by definition encourages a more relaxed attitude and approach to safety, for example by not wearing a buoyancy aid. This error in judgement, especially in those paddlers used to more extreme forms of canoeing can be minimised by recognising and managing the hazards which are unique to placid water, as well as those found across all forms of the sport.

Other Craft

For example, the hazard with the potential to cause the greatest harm on placid water is often other craft, from canal boats to pleasure steamers, from ferries to 'gin palaces'. Worst of all are self-drive hire craft rowed or driven by incompetent and even intoxicated holiday makers, often with no idea of the rules of the road.

Rivers and Harbours

Those hazards familiar to river paddlers, such as sudden changes in level, together with the dangers associated with weirs and pollution can equally affect placid water paddlers on the lower mature stretches. Weirs can create dangerous, 'deep recirculating' stoppers which are in effect drowning machines; so if you are not sure whether it can be safely run or not, portage! (See Chapter 22 Reading White Water).

The use of harbours and estuaries requires consideration of tidal movements, avoiding moored craft during the flood or ebb and fishing lines from piers and quays. (See chapters on Sea and White Water).

Photo 13.5   Paddling on busy waters

Canals and Lakes

Hazards that are more related to placid water include canal locks and their gates and sluices, as well as banks which are often very difficult to climb out onto from a canoe and almost impossible from the water. Submerged objects, often just below the surface, cannot be seen owing to the murky waters which can also harbour algae and bacteria including leptospirosis, which although serious if contracted, is very rare. Advice on this illness, and its deterioration into Weil's Disease can be found in Chapter 6 and the BCU Yearbook. Anyone who has disturbed a swan or goose during the nesting season will recognise the obvious hazards from wildlife, which are of course, for their own interest, best left alone.

Temperature Gradient

Finally, the temperature gradient of still water, that is the rate at which the temperature changes with depth, is far steeper than that of flowing water, so placid water will often have a top boundary layer of warm water concealing much colder conditions below. This warm layer can suddenly be disturbed by wind or rainfall increasing the turbulence on or

under the surface. Therefore, what can be a warm lake on one day can be very cold the next.

Journeying on Placid Water

Range of Opportunities

As mentioned in the introduction, one of the advantages of placid water is its potential to market the wealth and depth of canoeing to all. One of the best ways of doing this is by providing the opportunity for a memorable journey, whether that be a couple of miles up a canal with the local school, or an escapism expedition to one of the more remote Scottish lochs. The opportunities to journey on placid water within the UK are endless, often starting with a short family trip organised by a local coach or club across a harbour, reservoir or down a placid river.

Journeying Organisations

Organisations such as the Duke of Edinburgh Awards Scheme recognise the development opportunities for young people in planning and organising their own journey, a concept used also by the Scout and Guide Associations. The BCU Touring and Recreation committee publish an annual calendar of trips, some of which are on placid water, and organisations such as the YHA advertise canoe journeying holidays on lakes, slow moving rivers and canals.

Photo 13.6   Birdwatching from an open canoe

Related Hobbies

Owing to the relaxed nature of placid water paddling, many other hobbies are compatible and indeed enhance the sport. Bird and other wildlife watching, photography, industrial archaeology, even fishing (often perceived to be at loggerheads with the sport) can enhance a placid water experience.

Journeying Safely

Safety considerations for journeying are no different from other forms of the sport and interestingly, it is the sea kayaking skills and knowledge that often transfer the best. Knowledge such as the importance of fetch across a lake (the distance the wind has to travel to build up waves), or skills such as towing downwind (using a longer than normal line), can be learnt by attending a sea training course.

Placid Water Coaching

BCU Star Awards

Placid water is the ideal location to be given an inspiring introduction to the sport, whilst on the same water be trained and assessed for One, Two and Three Star Awards in all disciplines. This tried and tested progression has formed the backbone of the BCU's tests and awards system for many years now and still provides an excellent framework around which to structure the paddler's learning. (For details of tests and awards see the BCU Coaching Directory.)

The Placid Water Scheme

The BCU's Placid Water Scheme itself was established to encourage the development of a progression of canoe and kayak strokes and techniques to support placid water touring and competition. This introduces the use of fast touring kayaks and canoes, rudders, and asymmetric paddles as well as specialised techniques, such as wash hanging, all before the Three Star assessment. The scheme then goes on to prepare paddlers for sprint regattas, marathons and touring trials on exposed or moving water, including weir shoots.

BCU Coach Terms of Reference

The terms of reference of a Level 1 Coach are to control groups on very sheltered water, and of a Level 2 Coach to supervise groups on sheltered inland and tidal water, though not the open sea. They also cover leading short, simple journeys, although it is not an expedition leadership award. This progression continues until for very large lakes or lochs, the Level 4 Kayak or Canoe Coach is the appropriate qualification.

BCU Youth Programme

The BCU Youth Programme organises and promotes events for young people. It encourages clubs, centres, youth groups and other organisations to work together to translate taster activity into regular paddling in order to provide more opportunities for young talent to improve. This involves the development of the Paddlepower scheme, giving structured progression through a series of challenges, and the Cadet Leader award aimed at 13 to 16 year olds.

Photo 13.7   Training session in racing craft

Paddlesport development officers are also responsible at a local level for providing information on junior clubs, the involvement of canoeing in the National Curriculum and National Bell Boat Regatta events.

Having Fun on Placid Water

Competitive Events

Over the years, many paddlers have used placid water to exercise their competitive spirit for both training and for the events themselves. Probably the most famous of these is the 125 mile Devizes to Westminster marathon race, but many other venues exist up and down the country, notably the sprint regatta courses at Holme Pierrepont and Strathclyde Country Park. Wherever there are rowers, you will see paddlers, utilising large expanses of placid water to reach peak performance.

Aquatic Gym

The use of placid water as an aquatic gym is only limited by your imagination. Slalom training on a canal has already been mentioned, and I know of no better place to perfect your re-entry and roll before trying it out for real in rough water.

Touring Awards

For those interested in recognising their long distance paddling, the Annual Strand Touring Awards are available for completing 100, 250 and 500 miles in any one year and BCU Touring Awards for completing 1,000, 2,500 and 5,000 miles over any period.

Placid Water Challenges

As well as competitions, many challenges also exist on placid water. One of the more recent is the

3L's, which involves paddling the length of the largest natural Scottish loch, (Lomond), English lake, (Windermere) and Welsh llyn, (Tegid), all within 24 hours.

Canoe Games

Any paddlesport introductory session worth its salt should, as Ratty so eloquently said, include the art of messing around in boats. There's more to paddling than practising techniques and going from A to B.

It is important to realise that water confidence can be enhanced more through playing games than through any formal teaching. Even in the cold water months, this is an essential part of keeping the learner's interest levels up. Their importance in placid water paddling cannot be overestimated. From polo to pirates, from swopping places to swamping, each game has its own place in a session and one excellent book in particular exists to give you more ideas, (details at the end of this chapter). After a long paddle into the wind, both adults and children enjoy nothing more than an improvised sail home with whatever is available, be it a bivvy bag or something more sophisticated. This type of creative placid water session transforms the perception of the canoe or kayak into something far more versatile, and that of placid water itself into an aquatic adventure playground.

Further Reading

Canoe Games, 3rd Ed, Ruse D, 2000, UK, Rivers Publishing, ISBN: 0951941348

Websites:

Local tourist association sites are found at www.tourist-boards.com
English tourist boards www. travelengland.org.uk
Northern Irish Tourist Board www.discovernorthernireland.com
Scottish tourist boards www.visitscotland.com
Welsh Tourist Board www.visitwales.com
The Association of National Park Authorities www.anpa.gov.uk
British Waterways Board www.britishwaterways.co.uk
The Royal Society for the Protection of Birds www.rspb.org.uk
The Scout Association www.scoutbase.org.uk
The Guide Association www.guides.org.uk
The Duke of Edinburgh Award Scheme www.theaward.org

David Taylor

The summer of 1975 spent fishing from a home-made slalom kayak along the Pembrokeshire coastline was David's introduction to paddlesport. Within 10 years, he was an advanced sea and inland paddler and had completed the first circumnavigation of the Faeroe Islands. During the next decade, he paddled in the Alps, Scandinavia and the United States and continued his active involvement in the BCU Coaching Service as Chairman of the Northern Region. In liaison with the National Centres, he was responsible for re-designing and implementing the Level 5 Coach Development Programme.

He now lives in the Lake District where he works as a director of a management development company and part-time inspector for the Adventure Activities Licensing Authority.

14 Flat Water Racing

Turning up at Scout 'canoeing night' a few minutes late, as is my way, I found that all the boats, bar one were already occupied and on the water. The remaining two boats were dusty 'Espadas' which, unbeknown to me, was the national 'one design' junior racing kayak. It was handicap race night and I was told they were fast so I took one out. To the delight of my friends (those in the know) I stepped into the boat and fell straight out. That night I fell out a number of times, but I like a challenge and I'd experienced enough of the boat's speed to stick with it. I finished last that night! The handicapping worked in my favour over the coming weeks and I made rapid progress, so much so that by the end of the summer I won the series and was hooked.

Many years and thousands of miles later in my paddling and coaching career, there are I find much easier ways to learn! Thank goodness, I say, because the exciting disciplines of Sprint and Marathon racing are challenging enough in their own right...

Introduction

Racing: "A test of speed" - Oxford English Dictionary.

The test of an athlete's speed in any sporting discipline is a base instinct. Put a group of paddlers together and someone will want to know if they are the fastest! The competitive disciplines of sprint and marathon formally provide that test on flat water for canoes and kayaks. Both disciplines have certainly been around for many years in one guise or another. Indeed the original Royal CC (1865ish)

constitution identified "racing and chasing..." as part of the club's activity, (surely sprint and marathon by another name!) and they still run the oldest sprint race in the world in the form of 'The Paddling Challenge'.

The two disciplines cover a massive range of distances, formats and environments. Indeed in formally recognised events, the range of distances raced go from 200 metres up to 360 miles, (although most domestic and international marathons are over considerably less). Formats involve paddlers competing in time trials, knockout events, team races, and mass start events, in singles and crew boats. Race environments include almost any inland water, from purpose-built regatta lakes, canals and lowland rivers to estuaries and the sea.

Sprint and marathon would, in most sports, be at opposite ends of the competitive range, but in Britain the two disciplines share the same club base. They also share the same basic boat designs and in many cases the same people, complementing each other to provide an excellent sport and recreation for a large number of people with a wide range of paddler physiology and psyche.

Sprint

From a stationary start, in lanes, athletes race over a measured course (see Table 1), head to head in the fastest time they are able. The combination of power and technical skill at its best makes for an awesome display – almost graceful in its execution. In essence sprint provides a true test of kayak or canoe speed.

Racing takes place in both kayaks (K) and canoes (C). It also takes place in singles (K1 or C1), doubles (K2 or C2) and fours (K4 or C4).

Class	500m	1000m
K1 men	1:38	3:38
K2 men	1:30	3:18
K4 men	-	3:00
K1 women	1:48	3:57
K2 women	1:42	-
K4 women	1:36	-
C1 men	1:50	3:54
C2 men	1:39	3:30

Table 14.1   Olympic distances and target times

Sprint racing, the oldest Olympic paddlesport discipline, is very much an international event, with 57 countries represented in the 2001 World Championships. Indeed the desire to send a national team to the Berlin Olympics in 1936 proved to be the catalyst to form the BCU as an organisation. Certainly the Olympic connection has helped to make sprint racing so successful, in that it has attracted many athletes and nations to strive to be the best.

The Champions

Since the mid 1950s, the most successful nations in sprint have come from the Eastern European countries, most notably Hungary, East Germany, Russia and Bulgaria. More recently the number of nations succeeding at World Championships and Olympics has increased. The discipline has also brought forward some amazing athletes; Gert Friedrickson of Denmark raced in 6 Olympic Games between 1948 and 1969. Bridget Fischer of the former East Germany won 27 World and Olympic titles in a career also spanning 6 Olympic Games.

Photo 14.1   Tim Brabants (lane 2)

Britain's first World Championship medals came in the 10km event at Holme Pierrepont, Nottingham in 1981 with a Bronze in the K4, followed by Alan Williams and Steve Jackson who won our first World Championship Gold medal in the K2 10km in Tampere, Finland (1983). Over the Olympic distances, Jeremy West was the first Briton to win a medal at the World Championships (Montreal 1986), where he won double Gold in the men's K1 at 1000m and 500m.

Photo 14.2   Steve and Andy Train

An eleven year gap followed before Britain won another World Championship medal at an Olympic distance when Steven and Andrew Train took

Boat	Olympic Distances	World Championships	National Championships
K1, K2, K4* Men	500m, 1000m	200m, 500m, 1000m	200m, 500m, 1000m, 6km
K1, K2, K4 Women	500m	200m, 500m, 1000m	200m, 500m, 1000m, 6km
C1, C2, C4* Men	500, 1000m	200m, 500m, 1000m	200m, 500m, 1000m, 6km
* There are no K4 500m or C4 events in the Olympic Programme.			

Table 14.2   Race distances

the Bronze in C2 1000m, this time in Dartmouth (1997). Britain's first ever Olympic medal came in Sydney in 2001 where Tim Brabants, in a memorable race, took Bronze in the Men's K1 1000m.

In 1996 the 10,000m events were dropped from International Sprint Racing in favour of 200m racing. There is no doubt that this change has cost Britain medal success.

Paddle–Ability

The sport of sprint racing at a domestic level is integrated, in that a paddler's ranking is governed by their speed – this determines their ability. To improve the accessibility of sprint racing to all, new classes have been introduced at the national regattas in recent years to offer the sport to paddlers with a disability. The recent inclusion of 'Paddle-Ability' events within the European Sprint Championships (2001) has also provided an international programme.

Photo 14.3   Paddle-Ability

Domestic Sprint Racing

The domestic racing calendar hinges around five major national level regattas based at the National Watersports Centre in Nottingham. The Nottingham regattas run one per month, starting in April, and include National Championships (traditionally in July) and the Inter-Clubs Regatta in September. Each regatta provides a full two-day programme of events and normally includes over 400 separate

races! They are a remarkable feat of organisation. The race categories, with the exception of Junior National Championships, are based on ability. This ensures that paddlers get a good race with paddlers at their own level. The chance to race as part of a crew in K2, K4, C2 and C4 adds another dimension to sprint racing.

There are also a number of regional and local events around the country, although these events are small in number when compared to the number of marathon events.

The introduction of the SRC-Cups, a regional competition, is hoped to develop the number of events taking place. Certainly the flexible format is designed to make sprint racing accessible to many more people.

Marathon

If sprint racing can be likened to 'track' athletics, then marathon is quite definitely 'cross-country'. Marathon, in its many guises is the test of endurance canoeing and kayaking and a whole lot more.

Race tactics demand that contestants are able to adapt to the conditions and the tactics used by their fellow racers as the race unfolds. Locks, or other obstructions are portaged and are all part of the race as the paddlers carry boat and paddle round to the next get in.

Photo 14.4   Portage

Covering the distance can be made easier if the work is shared. Racers are able to 'wash hang', literally surf the bow wave of the lead boat. Advantage can be gained to the side and directly behind. The benefit to be had depends on the skill of the paddlers and them having a similar cruising speed. International events will often have sections of the race where large groups of paddlers will bunch up in wash hanging formation as the paddlers work together to cover the distance.

Photo 14.5   Wash hanging

There are over 120 races per year advertised nationally, mostly between March and October, but there are not many weekends without a race somewhere! There are a number of different categories of racing, each with their own unique flavour and challenge.

Divisional Racing

The vast majority of races are run according to the National Divisional System. There are nine divisions where ability is the determining factor on a paddler's ranking. Men, Women, Boys, Girls, Kayak and Canoe all race together. Paddlers gain promotion as they improve; the divisions provide a progressive system to offer a level of competition and distance to suit the ability of each paddler.

K2 Div.	K1 Div.	Course difficulty
7/8, 9	9, 8, 7	4 miles, with minimum practical hazards (no portages)
5/6	6, 5, 4	8 miles, may include portages/weir shoots
1/2, 3/4	3, 2, 1	12 miles with any degree of severity

Table 14.3 Racecourse distance

Another great benefit of divisional racing is that the whole club can attend the same race, so raw novices can rub shoulders with international athletes on and off the water.

The Hasler Series

One of the main competitions run annually is the Hasler competition culminating in the Hasler Final. Regions run their own series of events (which are linked to divisional events so as to allow all club members to compete), where points are awarded to each paddler on the basis of the position they achieve in their race. The scores from the best 12 scoring paddlers (6 K1 & 3 K2's) are added up and the club with the most points wins the event. The best clubs from each region meet to race off at the Hasler Final usually in September. The Hasler Final is one of the big marathon events on the domestic calendar with over 600 competitors taking part.

The National Championships

The other big mainstream race is the National Championships, an annual event run on age group categories. This allows a national age group champion to be crowned each year. In order to allow the whole club to attend there is also a divisional event attached to the main event.

Non-divisional Events

There are also a number of marathon events which, because of the course distance or severity, fall outside the scope of the divisional system.

The Devizes to Westminster (D–W)

The Devizes to Westminster is one such event. Covering the 125 miles (including 76 portages) the race runs from Devizes in Wiltshire to Westminster Bridge in London. Run annually on Easter Weekend, doubles crews have four days to finish the course, but the faster crews race straight through, planning their race carefully to arrive on the tidal Thames in time to catch the outgoing tide. The race record time is one of the few canoeing records listed in the 'Guinness Book of Records'.

There are also a number of other events in Britain similar in nature, all inspired by the DW.

Descent (& Ascent) Racing

On a par with the Hasler Final is the Exe Descent (in terms of numbers taking part). The Exe is an annual event but the challenge could not be more different! 19 miles of the River Exe including 9 major weirs and countless rapids in mid-November provides the opposition (as well as the other 600+ competitors). The event was inspired by the Liffey Descent in Ireland which is one of the world's biggest marathons attracting over 1000 entrants from all over the world. Another notable event in this category, this time an ascent race, is the Bath to Bradford Race on the River Avon in Wiltshire. One of the original 12 Hasler races, it is a 12 mile race upstream which includes a number of tricky portages up weirs!

Lightning Events

Lightnings are junior, polyethylene, racing kayaks which were first introduced in Britain in 1998. The Lightnings are designed to provide an introduction to the sport for the 8-12 age range. The event form adopted has been developed to involve a combination of races into the one event. They include a 2km race, one or more team skill-based relays and a sprint event. The flexible format has been devised to encapsulate many of the necessary foundation skills of marathon and sprint racing. Most of the events are either run locally in their own right, or are attached to regional BCU marathon and sprint events. There are also a number of bigger festivals attached to existing national level events such as the National Marathon Championships.

International Marathon

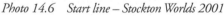

Photo 14.6   Start line – Stockton Worlds 2001

Britain has long been at the forefront of International Marathon and as a nation we have had plenty of success. Originally the big international events were races like the Liffey Descent, the Sella Descent in Spain and the Tour de Gudena in Denmark. They are all still major events in their own right, but to develop the sport and attract new nations the

World Cup and World Championships courses have become more uniform these days. The race duration for seniors is 2 hours 30 minutes to 3 hours, and 1 hour 30 minutes to 2 hours for juniors. In distance this equated to a senior course of 35.8km (4 portages) and a junior course of 22km (3 portages) at the 2001 Stockton World Championships.

The first World Championships was held in Nottingham in 1988, and since then the event has been held in 7 different countries on four separate continents, and only once between 1988 and 2001 has the British Team failed to win medals. As with sprint, the discipline has its exceptional talents. Ivan Lawler (see Title Photo), with six World titles to his name in K2 and K1, Suzanne Gunnarson of Sweden and Anna Hemmings of Great Britain have both won the K1 and the K2 event on consecutive days. Anna achieved the feat in Stockton, partnered by team and club mate Helen Gilby in K2. In canoe the events have been dominated by three nations: Denmark, Hungary and Great Britain, Steven and Andrew Train (Photo 14.2) winning many World Championship medals between 1988 and 1999.

Photo 14.7   Anna Hemmings

Forward Paddling Technique

Common to both disciplines is the need to paddle efficiently. In either canoe or kayak, greatest efficiency is gained when the craft runs smoothly through the water. To gain maximum speed for both canoe and kayak, paddling is a whole body exercise! Whilst the general pattern of movement is common to both Sprint and Marathon, the demands of the sport, the speed of the boat and the rate (and rhythm) of the stroke vary significantly at the top level.

Training (Sprint & Marathon)

Kayak and canoe paddling is a very healthy way to exercise. With body weight supported and a high degree of technical skill required, paddling in racing or fast touring boats provides an excellent way to keep fit. Many people who take part in marathon and sprint do so to keep in shape, as well as the social aspects.

To maximize performance the importance of technical ability cannot be overstated, however it has to be matched by power and endurance to overcome the resistance of the water… and that means training! For an elite performer that means high volume and intensity of training are needed both on and off the water.

Equipment

The kayaks and canoes have undergone many changes in design and construction over the years. The most recent change in ICF rules has been the removal of the minimum width restriction. No longer do the boats have a wing behind the back cockpit. This has radically altered the look of racing boats since the Sydney Olympics, a move that is especially likely to improve the lot of the canoe paddlers.

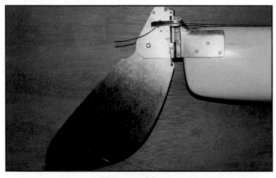

Photo 14.8   Rudder (over-stern)

Photo 14.9   Rudder (under-stern)

By comparison with modern day white water recreation kayaks and canoes, their racing counterpart are long and fine. This in itself poses the problems of steerage. Kayaks have rudders to assist with steering, a tiller bar between the paddler's feet (through cables

to the stern of the boat) provides the controls for the rudder whereas the canoes have no such luxury; direction is governed entirely by the paddle.

In a kayak, contact with the boat is through the seat and the footrest. The intense pressure placed on the footrest through the stroke has led to many paddlers using a foot strap or bar to help fix them in the boat. Seats and footrests are usually fully adjustable to allow paddlers to tailor the set up to get the best trim and paddling position. Racing canoes are open and usually have wooden runners running along the inside to fix the paddler's knee-block into position.

Photo 14.10   Knee-block

The knee-block takes on great significance for the canoe paddler as the load bearer and the main means to glide the boat past the paddle. In that respect its position in relation to the water affects the trim of the boat and the paddler's ability to perform efficiently. The block and board can be seen in the picture above; they are usually made to suit the individual to ensure that the paddler's weight is placed on the kneecap and shin.

Boat	Max length	Min weight (Marathon)	Min weight (Sprint)
K1	520 cm	12kg	8kg
K2	650 cm	18kg	12kg
K4	1100 cm	30 kg	–
C1	520 cm	16kg	10kg
C2	650 cm	20kg	14kg
C4	900 cm	30kg	–

Table 14.4   Hull length and weight restrictions

While the shape of canoe paddles have remained largely unchanged, kayak paddles have radically changed with the advent of the 'Wing' paddles in the mid 1980s. Since then all international paddlers use wings of one type or another and most domestic paddlers. Indeed their usage has spilled over into other disciplines, sea paddling, wild water racing and touring to name a few. (See Chapter 2).

Getting Started

The sports of sprint and marathon are very much club based in Britain, and it is through clubs that most people are introduced to the sport. Many racing clubs have a range of suitable, open cockpit introductory boats to encourage new paddlers and run introductory sessions to get them started. A series of increasingly more specialist boats are used in both canoe and kayak to provide a progression for new paddlers to move into the specialist racing craft. The BCU Placid Water Progression devised by David Train, based on his experience in setting up Fladbury Paddle Club, was adopted by the BCU in 1983 to support racing and fast touring.

Once paddlers have undertaken some introductory sessions and training the next step is to race. For many racing clubs their activity is based around their race programme and, most importantly, their own Club Time Trial or Handicap Race. The Handicap Race, usually over an out and back or loop course, is often the one time when the whole club meet and paddle together. They can also produce spectacular finishes if the handicapper gets it right. However most importantly, this type of race gives anyone in the event the chance to succeed, the first paddler across the line is the one that has improved the most. The best times are recorded and kept on the club notice board. They provide a target for each individual to work on, and for up and coming paddlers a means to compare with others, past and present. At some of the bigger, well-established clubs, such as Nottingham, Reading and Elmbridge, the weekly handicap race regularly attracts 30-40 paddlers.

In recent years the introduction of the Bell Boat, a stable catamaran paddled by 8 – 10 paddlers of all ages and the Lightning, a stable, mini racing single for 8-12 year olds has opened up racing to a whole new group of people. These new innovations, allied to the BCU Youth Programme offer exciting and challenging events, like the National Bell Boat Championships, to encourage children into regular paddlesport participation.

Further Reading

Racing Canoeing, Szantos, published by ICF
Canoeing the Fladbury Way – Getting Started, Train D

Websites:

www.bcu.org.uk - The marathon and sprint pages
www.reading-canoe.co.uk

Richard Ward

Richard Ward started paddling in 1973; much of his early paddling career was with Adlington Scouts in a variety of paddling disciplines. As a junior he went to the Junior European Championships in 1981 in K4 and K2. As a senior he raced in England, Europe and Australia whilst working as a boat builder for Kirton Kayaks. In the early 90's he was appointed National Development Coach for Sprint & Marathon, and National Coach for Placid Water. He developed the BCU Placid Water and Racing Coach awards and travelled in support of the National Team at many internationals and World Championships. During the 90's he was also the Exeter CC coach where he coached a number of juniors to National Team & Squad level. He was also involved in introducing the Lightning K1 for under 13's in racing, and the writing of the World Class Programmes, also for Racing. Finally in 2000 Richard was put out to pasture when he was appointed BCU English Coaching Development Manager.

15 Canoe Polo

Thinking back, it must have been the summer of 1992 when I really got hooked on Canoe Polo. I was at Mechelen, Belgium's National Watersports Centre, with the Great Britain Squad that was taking part in the Flanders Cup, an international competition in which each participating country could enter Men's, Women's and Junior (under 18s) teams. Their combined results determined the overall winners of the competition. At that time, and even to this day, Great Britain didn't have a National Under-18 Team. However, Friends of Allonby Canoe Club's Youth Team, that had recently become National Champions for the second year running, had been invited to join the Squad to play as 'Great Britain Juniors', and my 16 year old son Greg was Team Captain.

Great Britain won the competition by a handsome margin and Greg ended up holding the trophy on the front row for the Squad photograph, kitted out in a tracksuit top borrowed from one of the GB Ladies. A very proud moment for him, and even more so for me.

Introduction

There are not many sports in which this country is pre-eminent. However, with our Men's Team the current World Champions and European Silver Medallists, and our Women's Team the current European Champions and World Silver Medallists, few people would dispute that Great Britain is the world's dominant nation in canoe polo.

Canoe polo is the fastest growing competitive canoeing discipline, not only in the UK but world-wide, with over 60 countries now playing the game. Fabulous to play, and full of spectator interest, canoe polo is a really spectacular, skilful, fast and exciting ball game played by two opposing teams of up to eight canoeists, five of whom may be on the pitch at any one time. Teams compete to score by throwing or paddle-flicking the football-sized ball into their opponent's goal. The goal is a netted frame, one metre high and one and a half metres wide, suspended above the water at each end of a pitch (ideally sized 35 x 23 metres) which can be in a swimming pool or outdoor venue.

Demanding the ball-handling skills of basketball and the tactical awareness of five-a-side soccer, the physical aggression and effort involved draw comparisons with American football. Players are obliged to wear helmets with face guards and padded buoyancy vests to provide head and body protection, whilst their short polo boats must be heavily padded at both ends to prevent serious injury to opponents.

Photo 15.1   Ball handling skills!

In addition to their individual ball-handling skills and team positional play, polo players need to possess a very high level of technical canoeing, including speed, stamina, balance, and the ability to turn and manoeuvre their boats in a very confined area.

How Did It Start?

The origins of canoe polo are a little obscure but it is generally accepted that the game first started in Europe, possibly in the 1930s, when canoeists began throwing a ball to each other for enjoyment.

In the UK, polo seems to have evolved as a way of keeping slalomists fit during the winter closed season, and providing them with the opportunity to hone their paddling and turning skills in a competitive indoor environment. In the early days of the sport, players used to score goals by flicking the ball with their paddles to hit a board suspended above the water. The board was replaced by a suspended, netted goal and players were allowed to score by throwing the ball into the goal as well as flicking it with their paddles.

Who Plays Polo?

The game caters for players of all ages and ability levels with many youngsters taking it up in their early teens. At the other end of the age spectrum, senior players in their 50s and 60s are still enjoying their polo.

The game is played by canoe clubs, youth and Scout groups, schools and universities which compete throughout the year in local, regional and national leagues, and other open tournaments. During the summer months, many UK based teams also compete in international tournaments held in other European countries, which makes a very interesting and enjoyable holiday break. Being a team game, polo has an in-built 'camaraderie factor' which is probably unique within other competitive canoeing disciplines. Teams are easily distinguishable by the colours of their boats, buoyancy vests and helmets, as in many other team ball games such as football, and this all adds to the 'community feel' which is present throughout the polo fraternity. This is particularly evident at large open tournaments where youngsters and novice adult players, who have recently taken up the sport, can freely mix with World, European and National Champions.

In some countries, but not yet in the UK, there are veteran leagues which typically cater for players aged 35 and above who wish to continue to play polo competitively, but not necessarily within the established national league structure.

Organization

BCU Canoe Polo Committee

In the UK, the BCU Canoe Polo Committee has traditionally been responsible for all aspects of canoe polo played at national level, including organisation and administration of the National Open, Women's and Youth leagues, and the National Championships. However, separate polo leagues have always existed in Scotland, Wales and Northern Ireland, respectively organised by SCA, WCA and CANI, although several Scottish and Welsh teams also take part in the BCU national leagues.

In addition, the Polo Committee has been responsible for those aspects of the game deemed to be 'British' which effectively means the Great Britain Squads, education and standardisation of refereeing, and development of training programmes for polo coaches.

When full federalisation is implemented, the BCU Canoe Polo Committee will still be responsible for all wholly 'British' polo activities including the

Great Britain Squads and the National Championships. The current National leagues are likely to become English (ECA) leagues to properly differentiate them from the existing leagues in Scotland and Wales.

The BCU Canoe Polo Committee's website contains a wealth of information on all aspects of the game and can be found at www.canoepolo.org.uk.

Specific information about canoe polo in Scotland, Wales and Northern Ireland can be obtained directly from the SCA, WCA and CANI.

ICF Canoe Polo Committee

In 1986 the International Canoe Federation (ICF) created a Canoe Polo Committee mandated to introduce agreed rules for all member nations. In the main this was very successful, but minor differences in interpretation existed in several countries (including the UK) that had been playing the game for some years. In 2000 the ICF published a totally revised set of rules which were universally adopted by all member countries during 2001.

In addition, the ICF Canoe Polo Committee is responsible for promoting and developing the sport worldwide and in recent years the number of participating countries has grown dramatically. Canoe polo already has well established European and World Championships, and the ICF is now actively promoting canoe polo championships on every continent along the lines of the very successful European Championships. The ICF is also actively sponsoring a World Championship for Juniors, the first of which will be held in Japan during 2004.

Although polo is not yet an Olympic discipline, the ICF has successfully lobbied for it to be included in future World Games competitions. There is a growing body of opinion that canoe polo will be included in the Olympic Games in the not too distant future in view of its massive worldwide growth and huge spectator appeal as a very skilful and competitive water sport.

Competition

European and World Championships

The first European Canoe Polo Championships were hosted by the British Canoe Union at Sheffield in 1993. The following year Sheffield was again the venue for the first World Championships. Both championships are now held on a biennial basis in alternate years.

Great Britain's men were European Champions in 1995, and European Silver Medallists in 1993, 1997, 1999 and 2001. Great Britain's Women have an even better record in Europe as they were Champions in 1997 and 2001, and Silver Medallists in 1993, 1995 and 1999.

Photo 15.2   Speed!

In the World Championships, Great Britain's Men were Bronze Medallists in 1994, Silver Medallists in 1998 and World Champions in 2000. Great Britain's Women were World Champions in 1996 and Silver Medallists in 1994, 1998 and 2000.

European Under 21 Championships

In 1999 the first European Under 21 Championships were held alongside the senior championships. Great Britain's Men became European Champions and our Women's Team were Silver Medallists. In 2001 Great Britain's Women's Team took the Bronze Medal whilst our Men's Team were just out of the medals in fourth place.

Photo 15.3   Physical aggression!

BCU National Leagues

There is a flourishing BCU national league structure covering open, women's and youth teams drawn predominantly from clubs based in England but with a good sprinkling of Scottish and Welsh teams as well. These open leagues are 'open' to men, women and youth players alike.

In the open leagues there are four divisions. Divisions One and Two are made up of ten teams drawn from the country as a whole. Division Three is split North and South with ten teams in each geographical grouping, whilst Division Four is quite complicated and currently contains five separate geographically based leagues: North (A), North (B), Central, South East and South West.

There are currently three National women's leagues: Divisions One and Two are made up of teams throughout the country, whilst Division Three is split North and South in a similar manner to Division Three in the open leagues.

Photo 15.4   Referee!

At youth level (under 18) there are two national divisions. Division One teams are drawn from the country as a whole, whilst Division Two is split North and South to limit the amount of travelling involved in attending tournaments.

The national leagues typically run from October to April, each season closely allied to the academic year. All tournaments are held in swimming pools, usually on Saturday evenings, and teams normally play each other twice during the course of the season. At the end of each season there are demotions and promotions between divisions, based on the final positions attained by the teams, rather like in football leagues.

A full listing of National League Champions can be seen at the BCU Canoe Polo Committee's website.

BCU National Championships

Each year the BCU Canoe Polo Committee holds its National Championships which is a competition open to all national league and non-league teams, rather like the FA Cup in football. In recent years the National Championships have been held at an outdoor venue over the three-day Spring Bank Holiday. All teams entering the competition have a theoretical opportunity of becoming National Champions in the appropriate Open, Women's or Youth competition. Rather than run the Championships on an immediate 'knock out' basis, teams initially play in 'mini-leagues' with other teams of similar standard, and those finishing highest in these leagues then progress to the next round of the tournament where they face more formidable competition.

Over the course of the three-day tournament, teams are progressively knocked out of the competition, to leave two teams in each category to battle out in their respective finals for the honour of becoming National Champions.

The 2001 National Championships were held for the first time at Hatfield Water Park near Doncaster, and this central location close to the motorway network is likely to be the venue for 2002 and subsequent years.

A full listing of National Championship Results can be seen at the BCU Canoe Polo Committee's website.

Regional and Local Leagues

Most of the BCU regions have a volunteer Regional Polo Organiser who promotes the game within their region and is able to arrange Coaching and/or Refereeing Courses as required, and act as a point of liaison between aspiring players and clubs in their area. In addition, many of the full and part-time BCU Paddlesport Officers are becoming increasingly interested in polo, as a means towards maintaining the interest of young paddlers who seem to love the heady mixture of a competitive team game involving a ball and canoes.

There are thriving canoe polo leagues in many of the BCU regions catering for players in open, women's and youth categories that mirror the national leagues. In addition, a large number of Scout groups play polo around the country. In Greater Manchester, for example, there are three separate Scout leagues catering for different age groups.

Universities

Polo is played at many universities within the UK and, despite the annual turnover of students completing their studies, a number of university teams still manage to compete within the national and regional polo leagues. The British Universities Sports Association (BUSA) organises a weekend Polo Championships in May each year which usually attracts over 60 university teams.

Get Involved

Canoe polo is a really fabulous sport for any age group whether you are male or female, so why not get involved? The British Canoe Union Yearbook lists all canoe clubs within the UK that have an interest in polo, and provides contact telephone numbers / postal and e-mail addresses for Regional Polo Organisers who will be able to offer advice about how to get into polo.

The sport caters for all levels of players, from those who are interested purely in playing for fun right through the spectrum to others with a burning ambition to become a European and/or World Champion. Whatever your hopes or expectations, they can be realised in full within canoe polo.

Photo 15.5   Goal action

Websites:

www.canoepolo.org.uk - The BCU Canoe Polo website provides a wealth of information on the sport.
www.canoeicf/canoepolo - The ICF Canoe Polo website

Gerry McCusker

Currently Chairman of the BCU Canoe Polo Committee, Gerry is a member of Friends of Allonby Canoe Club on Merseyside where he was Chairman for 10 years until 1999 and his wife, Hazel, was Secretary for 11 years. He got into canoeing in his early forties shortly after his two children started attending novice coaching sessions run by the club at a local swimming pool. The family's initial interest was river tripping and white water, which subsequently broadened into competitive disciplines when his children took up slalom and then polo.

In 1991 Gerry and Mike Moffitt (currently one of the GB Men's Squad Coaches) organised the first Merseyside Canoe Polo International in Liverpool's Dukes Docks which has been an annual event ever since. In 1993 Gerry became League Secretary for Open Division 2, joined the BCU Canoe Polo Committee as Vice Chairman in 1994, and took on the additional role of Secretary in 1998. He was a member of the four man jury at the 2000 World Canoe Polo Championships in Brazil. He established, and still organises, the North West under 16 and under 18 canoe polo youth leagues.

16 Travelling and Living Outdoors

A friend and I were up in the Fort William area, looking for something 'different' to do with an open boat we had managed to borrow. At the time the Scottish river guide was a bit thin, so we turned to a road atlas for inspiration! We spotted a potential link from Corrour station back down to Loch Laggan via lochs and rivers. I went in search of OS maps while Jon persuaded the man at the ticket office that we could get a five metre boat on the train that evening.

Our plan for portaging the boat from the station down to Loch Ossian was a bit vague, but it began snowing heavily which offered us the simple solution of sliding it down the hillside. Arriving at the loch earlier than we had anticipated, we were keen to get a few miles of paddling done that night.

The wind and snow were pretty wild, but we set off carefully hugging the shoreline. This proved difficult, as the loch's edge was strewn with boulders, which were tricky to spot until the last few seconds before impact! After a few near misses we pulled into the shore to re-consider the plan. The only way we were going to make progress was to get out into the deeper water. Deciding the weather looked like getting better rather than worse, we headed out. We had an exhilarating ride, surfing dark, rolling waves out into the middle of the loch.

True to our predictions, the wind eased. As the sky cleared the moon lit up the shapes of the snow-covered mountains surrounding us. We stopped paddling for a while to gaze at the stars, and could clearly see a comet burning above the mountains. We watched it until the sky clouded over again, then headed for the shore and somewhere to bivvy.

Introduction

The modern sea kayaks and open canoes paddled in the UK today are derived from boats that were built for journeying, either for trading, hunting or exploration. These craft are good load carriers and enable us to journey in relative comfort. The ultimate tool for white water exploration on anything above Grade 3 is the white water kayak. Given an alpine style (travel light/move fast) approach, the kayak allows you to cover large distances of technical white water efficiently and safely. It's not luxurious, but it is effective. Journeying extends the scope of our paddling, allowing us to explore further afield and travel into remoter areas, perhaps taking us to places that are not easily accessed by other modes of transport. It allows us to escape, however temporarily, from the pace and demands of everyday life; and presents new challenges which demand and develop self-reliance and a greater understanding of the environment through which we travel.

Choice of Boat

It is possible to undertake a journey in any canoe or kayak as long as it is in a sea (or river) worthy condition. The design of the boat may impose a limit on what equipment you can carry with you and the nature of the water you can safely journey on.

The chapter on Boat Design will explain why there is no ideal boat for journeying. Each design is a compromise, for example sacrificing speed for stability and manoeuvrability, or lightness for durability. When choosing an expedition white water kayak, you should ensure that you do not sacrifice river running performance in favour of load carrying capacity. Cost is also a factor, as 'top of the range' boats are not cheap. It is well worth looking at the second-hand market for a boat to get you started. As you build up experience you will get a clear idea of what you want from a boat.

In practice, we rarely have the luxury of choosing a boat for a specific journey. It is much more likely that we plan the journey around the boat we own or have access to. Therefore it is important to understand both the strengths and the limitations of your boat's design.

Outfitting and Customising Boats

It is unlikely that a boat 'off the shelf' will be set up for journeying without the need for some addi-

tional outfitting. An important area to consider is making the boat as comfortable as possible. You may be spending long periods of time in your boat over consecutive days. Any 'niggles' on a day trip will become major issues on a longer journey!

The chapters on sea kayaking and open canoeing consider the importance and practicalities of being correctly and comfortably seated or knelt in the boat.

Check that any fittings such as tow systems, decklines, and end grabs are strong enough to use when boats are loaded. Satisfy yourself that there are sufficient points to secure all of the kit you will be carrying, especially items that you may want to keep accessible whilst on the water such as spare paddles.

There are many other refinements and additions that you may wish to make to your boat to enhance its journeying ability, such as deck-mounted compasses in sea kayaks or improvised sailing rigs on canoes. My advice is to add these over time, as it becomes clear what else would be useful to you. Events and symposiums are good opportunities to look over other peoples' boats and swap ideas.

White Water Kayaks

Outfit your boat with comfort and then control in mind. There will be times to run white water and times to paddle the flat water between rapids (these will take longer). Fittings to the deck of the kayak should be kept to a minimum, and those that are essential should be 'beefed up' to deal with the rigours of trip use.

Many boats are set up with the seat too far back; once you start loading the boat the situation only becomes worse! The thing to do (in most boats) is to move the seat forwards, for trips move it forwards even more. When you paddle unloaded, the boat should dive if you are not sitting back on your seat. Your loading of the boat will, inevitably, trim it stern heavy, and compensate for this effect. Once loaded with equipment and paddler, and afloat on flat water, the boat should be evenly balanced and trimmed.

Loading Boats

Adding weight into a boat will alter its handling. Whether loading kit into a canoe or a kayak there are two basic principles to keep in mind.

Firstly the load can alter the trim of the boat. An incorrectly trimmed boat can be difficult and frustrating to paddle! When loading a boat you need to take care not to inadvertently alter the trim by putting too much weight in one end of the boat. With experience you may choose to deliberately alter the trim of the boat when you load it to make it perform better in the prevailing conditions. For example, if you know you will be paddling into a headwind for much of the day, you might decide to pack the boat slightly bow heavy. In an open canoe it is not difficult to alter the trim on the water, but in a sea kayak you may be unable to alter things once you have set off, so experiment with this idea before trying it on a committing crossing!

The second consideration is how the weight will affect the boat's turning ability; adding any load to the boat is going to make it require a greater force (from your paddle) to turn. If the additional load is kept close to the centre of the boat then this effect is minimized; the further from the centre you put the load, the greater the force required to get the boat to turn.

Boats have a large kit carrying capability, and it is tempting to find enough kit to fill them. Whilst it is good to be able to slip in the odd 'luxury' item, do remember that from time to time you need to carry all of your kit, even if just from the camping site to the water's edge. Keeping kit to a minimum will mean less time is spent packing boats, leaving more for your journey - or for sunbathing!

Loading Open Canoes

My preference in an open canoe is to have one large pack and a small day bag. The small bag contains anything I may want to get to quickly and easily during the paddle. It is clipped in with a short length of rope, so that I can move it to be within reach from anywhere in the boat and can quickly remove it when needed. The large pack is tied securely in place towards the centre of the boat, where it has least effect on trim or turning ability, and in such a way that it will displace water in the event of the boat swamping, so acting as additional buoyancy.

Make sure that kit is really secure in the boat, and do not rely on 'fastex' buckles or on jamming things under a seat. The forces involved when laden boats swamp are considerable, and kit will break free if it can.

So long as the big pack has a comfortable carrying strap, your kit is easy to manage in a single load if you need to portage.

Photo 16.1   A loaded open canoe

Loading Sea Kayaks

The same two principles govern how to load a sea kayak. However, things are complicated by the need to fit things in through hatches. Kayaks fitted with the small round hatches in particular need careful thought… and patience!

My approach here is to pack my kit into lots of smaller bags. These will easily go through hatches and pack into any available spaces. It is well worth also carrying a large lightweight kit bag for ease of carrying all the small bags up the beach to the campsite.

The stern bulkhead is usually just behind the seat, but the bow one is relatively far forward in front of your feet, so it is easy to unintentionally put more weight in the stern than the bow. Putting some lighter, bulky items (like a sleeping bag, or spare clothes) in the stern makes use of the space but keeps the trim level. If there is room between your footrest and the forward bulkhead, putting some of your heavier kit there will help. I put my tent there. Beware of putting heavier items in the very ends of the boat and so reducing its turning ability.

Keep things that you may want during the day to hand; behind the seat is a good place if there is room. Apart from essential items such as split paddles, towline, flares, map and compass I like to pack everything else inside the boat. Decks cluttered with kit are more awkward during rescues, and more difficult to handle in wind or surf.

Loading White Water Kayaks

An 'alpine' approach is necessary for white water kayak trips. Travel light and move fast. As a rule your fully loaded boat should be light enough to allow you to run for a bus with it on your shoulder; this includes your paddles (so splits are best). As 'glib' as it sounds, the advantages of being able to move independently with your boat far outweighs the difficulties of having to leave kit in places or organise logistics.

When you explore by white water kayak, identify the minimum equipment you need, and divide it (by weight), into thirds. Load your kayak, a heavy/compact third at the bow, and two thirds divided either side of the internal buoyancy in the stern; this should be loaded with the heaviest items close to the seat. The lighter items can be loaded first in separate dry bags attached to retrieval lines. Once the full kit is loaded, the lighter kit can be pulled closer to the seat and tied in place. The airbags are then re-inflated.

Photo 16.2   Loading a white water kayak

Consider the structure of the boat. Bulkhead footrests can often be modified to carry kit. The foam walls of some boats can be cut to allow some kit to be stowed within the foam; (you will need to give this some thought so as to do it in a way that will not weaken the boat).

Photo 16.3   Adapting your boat

Where to Camp

When planning a journey on UK water, it is necessary to consider not only the access to the water, but also to the land on which you plan to camp.

Some rivers or coasts may have public campsites close enough to the water to be of use. These will make a charge for use, but will in return provide some basic facilities. They can be busy, particularly in the summer months, but can provide a useful place to introduce and practise camping skills. Details of these can be obtained from Tourist Information offices, and locations may well be marked on OS maps.

Whilst many paddlers will choose not to use these sites, we do not have the freedom to camp wherever we please. Some of the most popular touring rivers flow through farmland or other managed areas. Often along these there will be small camping fields provided by an individual landowner. These are cheaper, and the facilities often little more than a tap. Details of these may be found in river guides.

In remoter areas of the UK and around much of the coast it is possible to wild camp, but we still need to remember that all land is owned by someone, and seek permission to camp whenever possible.

It is important that wherever we camp, we are careful to cause no damage to the environment and leave the site as we found it (or better!). Without this approach, the areas where we can camp will be spoilt for future paddlers, and we may lose access to them.

Handling Loaded Boats Safely

A boat loaded for a journey needs to be handled carefully if it is not going to cause damage or injury.

On Land

Whenever possible, move the load separately to the boat. If you need to move the boat loaded, use teamwork. This might need some co-ordination! Try to hold the boat rather than a fitting, which might pull off.

If you need to move the boat some distance on land, consider carrying a folding portage trolley. These are available for kayaks or canoes and several companies are now manufacturing their own designs. Look for a sturdy model, but remember that they will struggle in soft sand or over boggy ground.

Photo 16.4   Portage trolley

On Water

When you are trying to move a heavier boat over a greater distance, it is more important to have an efficient and effective technique. Use day trips to develop and practise techniques, but use a journey to prove them!

Give some thought to your choice of paddle. Paddles designed for short periods of intense activity are not suited to journeying. A longer paddle with smaller blade area allows you to paddle 'in a lower gear' and will reduce the strain on your body.

Rescues

With heavy boats you will need to adapt your rescue techniques to avoid lifting a boat by yourself.

Sea Kayaks

With sea kayaks, carrying a portable pump gives you the option of simply righting the boat and steadying it while the swimmer climbs back in and it is pumped out. This is time-consuming, but with teamwork the victim can be supported by one boat and towed clear of any hazards by others whilst pumping out.

Open Canoes

With open canoes on open water, my preferred method is to retrieve the swimmer into my boat, and get them to help me X-rescue theirs. On rivers it is futile attempting to 'nudge' a swamped or capsized open canoe into an eddy. Get the free end of a rescue line to the shore, either by the victim swimming it there or by another boat. One person alone is unlikely to be able to hold it once the load comes on; they will need assistance. Taking a few seconds to right the boat before heading for shore with the line does reduce the load and helps the boat to swing into the side more easily.

White Water Kayaks

A runaway kayak is a problem on continuous white water where the paddler and boat will become separated. Don't ignore the boat; it contains group food, group kit and the paddler's kit. If it's lost, you will all suffer.

If possible have two chase boaters go after the boat, one to try and get past and downstream of the kayak, the other to do the actual recovery. The downstream paddler can find a good spot from which to recover the boat and be ready to assist in the recovery. The rescuing paddler has time to manoeuvre the runaway boat, and try to push it towards the recovery point where the second paddler can assist.

The best option is to be conservative in your approach; only run what you know you can run. If you have to stop and inspect and think about a line more than twice, perhaps it is time to portage.

Clothing and Paddling Equipment

Canoeing and kayaking clothing and equipment is covered in Chapter 3. From a journeying perspective, the important thing is to have a 'dry' set and a 'wet' set.

It is essential to have a 'dry' set of clothes that are quite distinct from paddling clothes. These are packed securely away in the boat during the day, and only worn off the water. Resist that morning temptation to leave your warm and dry thermal on. No matter how careful you are, kit you paddle in gets damp! Pack the dry kit away and look forward to putting it on again in the evening.

The wet set includes anything that is worn whilst paddling. In wet weather this set should be kept on while pitching tents and put back on in the morning, even if it has not completely dried out overnight. This is because your dry set is very precious and must be kept dry.

A minimalist approach to clothing equipment means that you have a light boat and spend less time packing and unpacking it, and more time relaxing and admiring the scenery. The next time you return from a trip, divide your kit into three sets:

1. Items you used every day

2. Items you used occasionally

3. Items you never used

With the exception of emergency items such as the first aid and repair kit, leave everything in set 2 and 3 behind next time.

Shelter

Tents

There are a huge variety of tents on the market, and an equally wide range of price tags.

Top of the range tents are extremely technical and robust, but are designed for winter mountaineering expeditions rather than camping on river banks and along the coast. This means you may be paying for more than you actually need by going for one of these.

My advice is to look at the mid-range tents, designed for 'back packing'. Most modern back packing tents have flexible poles constructed from either fibreglass or an aluminium alloy. From a paddler's perspective I categorize these tents into two types:

1. Those which are self-supporting, i.e. which pretty much stand up once all the poles are in place. These are usually dome or geodesic designs.

Photo 16.5   Self-supporting dome tent

2. Those which rely on tension from guy lines or similar to keep them up. These are usually tunnel tents, or single pole designs.

Photo 16.6   Tent requiring guy lines and pegs

The big advantage of the first type is that you can pitch them on any piece of level ground, such as on soft sand and shingle, or on ground that is too hard to get pegs in. The second type can limit your options when looking for a campsite.

Manufacturers are usually being optimistic when they state how many persons a tent will accommodate. Unless your planned trip involves a good deal of portaging, there is no need to be a minimalist when it comes to tent size. Some designs of tent have porches at one or both exits, which are invaluable for storing damp kit and cooking equipment.

Tarps

Photo 16.7   Tarp in use

If you are making your journey as a group, tents can be very insular, especially in poor weather; folk retreat to their tents and don't meet up together again until the next morning. A good (and cheaper) alternative is a tarp. This is simply a length of weatherproof fabric with a selection of eyelets around the edges. 'De luxe' versions have corner and central pockets that will allow canoe poles to be attached. Aim to pitch the tarp with the back edge low and into the wind, and the front edge high, attached to trees and propped up with poles or paddles if necessary. Draughts coming from the back and sides can be reduced, by forming a windbreak with the empty canoes.

The sheltered area inside provides space for the whole group to gather in, and to cook and eat together. Stoves or an open fire just outside provide a surprising amount of warmth, and the better circulation of air compared to a tent means that wet kit can be dried more effectively. To sleep under a tarp you will need to put your sleeping bag in a bivouac bag, as it is not as weatherproof as a tent.

A good tarp-site has plenty of trees, which limits its usefulness on a coastal trip. Tarps are sociable, but may not stand up to high winds; tents are very robust but insular. Unless you can be sure of the weather conditions and the environment it is difficult to plan which to use. My tip is to take both. If it gets too windy for camping under the tarp, you can have some excitement improvising a sail with it by day, and then sleep in your tent.

Sleeping Bags and Sleeping Mats

Sleeping Bags

Sleeping bags are rated by 'seasons', but this is an inexact science based on how the 'average' person would feel.

As a rough guide to the ratings:

1 Season	British summer	5 to 15 deg C
2 Season	British spring	0 to 10 deg C
3 Season	British autumn	-5 to 5 deg C
4 Season	British winter	-15 to 0 deg C
4+ Season	Mountain use	-20 to -5 deg C

These figures are based on the bag being used in a tent, and with a sleeping mat.

The main choice when buying a sleeping bag is whether to get one with a natural (down) or a synthetic filling. In terms of insulating properties, down has to be the best. A down sleeping bag will be lighter and pack significantly smaller than a synthetic bag with a similar rating. However, down bags are more expensive, and are difficult to clean, (most synthetic bags are machine washable). If it gets wet, a down bag's efficiency can be reduced by as much as 90%. A wet synthetic bag may not be too inviting, but will still keep you warm. If you opt for down, you need to be 100% confident in your ability to keep your kit dry whatever happens!

Sleeping Mats

Whatever your choice of sleeping bag, it is well worth having a sleeping mat to use with it. For relatively little extra expense, you will get a much better night's sleep! The sleeping mat's main function is to provide insulation against heat loss into the ground. A secondary benefit is that it provides a cushioned surface to lie on.

The most basic are simply rolls of closed cell foam. These are cheap and indestructable, but bulkier than other types. You can also trim bits off it if your boat padding proves inadequate as the trip progresses!

At the more expensive end of the range are mats that are part foam and part self-inflating. These have greater insulating properties and a smaller pack size.

Stoves and Open Fires

When choosing a stove, there are several things to consider apart from the initial cost: the costs of running the stove, the availability of fuel, ease of use and reliability. There are three types of stove that lend themselves to journeying.

Meths Stoves

The best known and most widely used meths (methylated spirits) stove is the Trangia. It is a simple design, which is relatively safe and easy to use. Meths is poured into a burner, which is placed in a housing unit and lit. There are no moving parts and the stove requires little or no maintenance.

Photo 16.8 'Trangia' meths stove

The drawbacks are that the flame is not easy to adjust, it is either on or off. The flame is not as hot as other stoves, so meths stoves are relatively slow to cook with. They use a fair amount of fuel, which isn't particularly cheap, nor is it easily available in remoter areas.

Pressurized Stoves

These burn fuels such as unleaded petrol, diesel, Coleman fuel and paraffin. (Abroad, paraffin is often known by its American name, 'kerosene'. It is widely available but varies in quality.) The fuel is pressurized via a pump incorporated in the fuel bottle, then pre-heated so that it is burnt as a vapour. This results in a much hotter flame so the stove is very efficient, using less fuel and heating food quickly. The flame size is easy to control.

These stoves are not as straightforward to operate as other types, and can seem intimidating until you are familiar with them. They need to be primed to pre-heat the fuel, and can flare up if this isn't done sufficiently. They can get very sooty, especially when primed and run with petrol, and do need regular cleaning and maintenance to keep them running efficiently.

Photo 16.9   Pressurised fuel stove

Gas Stoves

Modern gas stoves run off self-sealing cartridges, which means the burner can be removed from part-used cartridges for packing, without fear of leaks. Gas stoves are clean and easy to use. The flame is very controlled, but they are not the cheapest stoves to run. New cylinders may be hard to get hold of during a trip, and you can never be sure how much gas is left in a cylinder. On the other hand, the stove unit is very light and compact, and the fuel is becoming increasingly available (even in Katamandu!)

Photo 16.10   Gas stove

Open Fires

Cooking on an open fire requires practice and a set of pans with lids. The biggest consideration is the environmental and social impact of having a fire simply for 'fun'. In some parts of the world people cook over fires, and a group of paddlers having a bonfire for a sing-along can use up a village's wood supply. Before you cook over a fire consider the local situation.

Photo 16.11   A 'Star' fire as used by the locals in Nepal - minimum fuel, maximum heat

Safety

Modern tents can catch fire incredibly easily and most camping-related incidents involve being scalded by boiling water. When using a stove, use it away from the tent if possible.

If you must cook in the shelter of a tent:

- Cook in the entrance to the tent, never in the 'inner' part.

- Use one entrance for cooking and the other for getting in and out of the tent.

- If the tent only has one entrance, nobody moves in or out of the tent whilst the stove is in use.

- Ensure that the entrance is kept open and the tent 'flaps' are tied back.

- Never leave a lit stove unattended.

Food

Do not under-estimate the importance of good food, especially on longer trips.

There is a variety of back-packing meals available from outdoor shops. Freeze-dried and dehydrated meals are mixed with boiling water and either left to stand or simmered for anything up to twenty minutes. Meals in foil pouches are dropped into a pan of boiling water and simmered until heated through. They are considerably more expensive than catering from supermarket ingredients, and I have yet to find one that tastes (or looks) like the meal that it claims to be. The advantages of using these meals are that they are designed to be stored for a length of time in a range of temperatures, and to be cooked in one pan. If you cook with 'real ingredients' you do need to think about both of these issues.

Before packing your food for the trip, remove any excess packaging, (but remember to keep the cooking instructions!) You end up with less rubbish to dispose of. Make sure each item is waterproof, zip lock sandwich bags are excellent for this as they are re-sealable and you can see what is in them.

Photo 16.12   Food kept clean

Remember that you will probably be expending more energy than usual, and will need to eat more. Carry food for a couple of meals more than you plan to need, so that if you are delayed (e.g. by bad weather, injury or illness), you can still eat well.

Hygiene

Hygiene issues are important. Do not be tempted to cut corners here; there is nothing more likely to spoil your trip than food poisoning or ill health.

Do not forget the basics of personal hygiene and the fundamentals of safe sanitation:

- Wash your hands prior to preparing food or touching any food preparation items.
- Mark all cutlery, plates, cups and water bottle with an individual's name so that only that person can use them.
- Clean all utensils well after each meal.
- Have a designated toilet area, well away from water collection areas.
- Keep soap with the toilet paper.
- Wash regularly.
- Brush your teeth.
- Drink plenty of clean water.

Lighting

On any overnight trip each paddler needs his or her own torch. Even if you are not planning to undertake any sort of activity after nightfall, just moving around the campsite in the dark is potentially a hazardous activity.

The usual and most useful choice of torch is a headtorch, which leaves both your hands free. There is a range of models, the more expensive of which are waterproof. Less expensive, mid range, 'weatherproof' models are adequate for both night paddling and camping. My preference is for smaller models, which I find give sufficient light without being too bulky and heavy to wear. They are also small enough to keep in a buoyancy aid pocket until required.

Using a halogen bulb will greatly increase the brightness, but will use up batteries more quickly. Whatever model you opt for, keep spare batteries and a bulb handy, where you can find them when your torch has gone out unexpectedly.

Another useful item for campsite use is a lantern. This can be used to give general lighting to the cooking or communal area, and save on torch batteries. It also avoids dazzling other people with your headtorch when you talk to them!

Lanterns powered by a wide range of fuels including gas and unleaded petrol are available. Getting one that runs on the same fuel as your stove makes life simpler.

White Water Kayaking

Fast and light is the name of the game. A 'Maglight' that takes AA batteries, tucked in the side of your helmet works well. AA's because they are available everywhere, 'Maglight' because it's waterproof, gives a usable light and is light and compact.

Water

Having a supply of drinkable water is essential at every campsite, for drinking and cooking. When you are paddling all day, it is easy to become dehydrated.

If there is no natural source of water at your campsite, you need to carry some with you. If you use a natural source it is unlikely that you will know if the water is safe to drink. To make sure that it is you need to either filter it, treat it with purification tablets or iodine, or boil it. I prefer the latter option, as tablets always leave a strange taste and I do not carry a filter. Abroad, where you may have to kill amoebic cysts, you will need to boil your water for ten minutes. In this country, where you usually only have to worry about bacteria, it is sufficient to bring water to a 'rolling boil'.

As well as water for that night's use, you need to think about water to use during the next day's travelling, and maybe to take to the next campsite. If you are going to collect water to carry, you need to decide whether you treat it as you collect it, or prior to using it. Either way works, as long as you know which carriers contain water that is ready to drink.

There is just as much potential to make yourself ill from contaminated water as there is from poor food hygiene.

Water Carriers

If you need to carry water, there is no need to buy purpose-made containers but there are some advantages. Various drink bottles are available cheaply, and are more durable than empty squash bottles. Look for ones with wider necks for ease of filling. If treating water, mark the bottle clearly with the time of treatment.

My preference is for carriers that will roll up when not in use. The cheaper, clear plastic ones are not so robust and split after a while. It is worth paying a little extra for heavier duty, fabric carriers.

Keeping Kit Dry

It is essential to be able to keep the kit you are carrying dry, whatever the weather and water conditions. On shorter journeys wet kit may just mean temporary discomfort, but on longer trips it is physically draining if you are constantly cold and wet. It will limit what you can achieve on the trip, and may become a safety issue.

Keeping the kit that you are carrying dry requires thought, and practice. Here are a few items that will help:

Drybags

Drybags are produced by various manufacturers, and are sold in most watersports shops.

Photo 16.13   Drybags

Sizes range from 5 litres to 70 litres plus. Several small bags are more versatile than one larger one. Do not over-fill dry bags, you need to be able to fold the top over several times before clipping it shut, in order to get a good seal.

It is important to know what kit is in which bag. Some bags are either partially or entirely made from transparent material so the contents are visible. Alternatively, write on them with a waterproof pen.

As with any waterproof fabric, drybags will deteriorate over time. They will last longer if they are cleaned and rinsed out after use, then allowed to dry completely before being stored.

Portage Packs

Photo 16.14   Portage packs

These are larger, heavy-duty drybags with rucsac type straps sewn on. As the name suggests, they are designed for portaging, when you want to be able to carry all your kit as easily as possible. These make an ideal pack for open boat trips. Although they are waterproof, packing kit in dry bags first should guarantee it will stay dry, and means you can rummage in the bag in the rain without getting the contents wet. The pack size can be reduced for carrying smaller loads, so that there is no wasted space.

Barrels

Photo 16.15   Barrels

These are very popular with open boaters as an alternative to a portage pack. The advantage of a barrel is that it is very durable, and offers a degree of protection to the contents from knocks and bumps. It is easy to pack and rummage around in, and the handles provide good tying-in points. Barrels can be a nightmare on portages unless you improvise a carrying system, and a half empty barrel takes up just as much space in the boat.

BDHs

These are round plastic containers with screw lids, originally manufactured for transporting chemicals. They come in a range of sizes. The larger ones can be difficult to fit through hatches or behind seats, but the smaller sizes are useful, particularly for specific items like first aid kits or repair kits.

Peli Protector Cases

Designed specifically to protect expensive items like camera equipment, these resin cases are extremely robust and offer complete protection from both the wet and from dust or sand. The padded inserts protect against impacts and shock. These cases do not come cheap, but are a worthwhile investment in terms of protecting valuable equipment.

Waterproof Map Cases

Great for keeping maps and charts dry. The other alternative is to laminate them.

Planning

Whatever your choice of equipment, keeping kit dry also needs a deliberate and planned approach. In adverse weather it is easy to unintentionally allow kit to become damp, and impossible to get it dry again. Time spent drying kit is well spent, so don't be afraid to start late or finish early to make the most of the sun!

You can never plan too much! Find out everything you can about the trip, especially if you are going abroad. After all, you can always ignore the information, but it's good to have the choice!

Gaining Experience

Just as paddling skills need to be practised to become fluent and almost second nature, so we need to take time to learn and develop journeying skills such as living comfortably in the outdoors, navigating, and interpreting weather forecasts.

Start with short journeys into areas where you are not committed, and have plenty of options to retreat if things do not go to plan. As your experience grows, so will your ability to undertake longer journeys and to travel into more remote areas. Part of the appeal of journeying is that, no matter what you have already done and achieved, there is always a more challenging trip to plan and prepare for.

Claire Knifton

Claire started kayaking at Southampton University in the late 80s whilst training as a science teacher. She has been an active paddler ever since, having left teaching after one year to work in outdoor education!

Originally from the SW of England, working at different outdoor centres has enabled her to move around the UK and explore a wide variety of our rivers and coastline by kayak and canoe.

Claire is a BCU Level 5 Coach and currently works for Outward Bound in Scotland.

White water kayak specific information contributed by Loel Collins.

17 Open Canoeing

Hauling the canoe up from Loch Hourn had been brutal. We made a food stop just short of Loch Quoich. Martin studied the map and our route from the end of the loch and down the Carnoch. He came out with the opinion that it wouldn't be too bad. I kept quiet. Five years before I had portaged a canoe up the Carnoch. The ground was awful and this time it would be part frozen and snow covered...

With no wind, snow to the waterside and blue skies, Loch Quoich appeared idyllic. Great sheets of fern ice were forming across the surface, thickening to a solid covering as we paddled further. The noise was incredible as the canoe forged through. A tinkling as the ice shattered ahead of us, the rustle and scratch as it ran along the boat. Behind us, a shattered trail and paddle holes marked out our route through the ice. This was a place of frozen and deadly beauty.

Loading the Canoe

To expedition in a canoe is a delight. The canoe is easily loaded. Kit should be contained within dry bags and barrels; indeed however short the trip, we end up with kit to carry.

In very easy conditions the kit may be put into the canoe with no further attachment. Once on the river or on open water, equipment should be attached to the canoe to prevent loss in the event of a capsize. It will come down to two basic systems: lash down or leashes.

Lash Down

Often on a camping trip the kit will completely fill the canoe. This offers a lot of potential additional buoyancy. Kit is laid into the canoe to achieve the desired trim (normally bow light) and then a series of ropes are criss-crossed over the kit to lash it tightly down into the canoe. The canoe can be equipped with eyelets or a series of holes drilled below the gunwale and threaded with 5mm rope to provide a series of attachment points inside the canoe.

In the event of a swamping, it is often possible to keep the canoe upright and continue to paddle. On a big volume rapid or in strong winds self-rescue may be the only option. On open water, we must take into consideration the fact that if a competent paddler or pair swamp, then any canoe coming to their assistance will also be in danger.

Photo 17.1   Kit lashed down

On open water two swamped canoes can be lashed together at the midpoint, and by both paddlers or sets of paddlers leaning and paddling on the outside of the improvised raft, it can be paddled back to shore. Note: both sets of paddlers need to lean outwards to prevent the raft closing like a clam. It is possible to take a rope from the outside of one of the canoes under the pair to be attached on the outside of the second boat. This will prevent the canoes 'closing' but may be difficult to arrange in a real situation.

Pros:

- The canoe is massively buoyant and floats high, making it less likely to be damaged as it washes down a river.

- A skilled tandem pair can keep the canoe upright after a swamping in either open water or a river.

Photo 17.2   Swamped canoe breaking out at the bottom of a rapid

- It gives a solo paddler a chance of paddling out of a swamping.

Cons:

- The canoe becomes very heavy for anyone wanting to 'curl' or 'X' rescue it (see Chapter 6).

- There is a lot more rope around to get entangled in.

> **Note**
>
> *Ropes, canoes and white water are a necessary but dangerous mix. All canoeists should have a knife readily to hand, preferably a knife that can be accessed and used one handed.*

Leashes

Kit is again contained in barrels and dry bags. A length of floating rope attaches from the kit to the boat. In the event of capsize the kit floats clear but is still attached.

Pros:

- With the kit clear, the canoe is much lighter to rescue by 'curl' or 'X' methods.

- Kit is easily moved about the canoe to achieve changes in trim.

Cons:

- Generally there is not enough floatation to keep you and the canoe upright in the event of a swamping.

- Swimming down a rapid with gear on long ropes still attached to a canoe provides obvious entanglement potential.

Avoid:

- Simply clipping dry-bags to thwarts and seats gives no additional buoyancy and grossly hinders any rescues. Bags swing around, catch on the rescuing canoe and generally get in the way.

Some Extra Strokes

In white water or for ease of travel the canoeist depends on efficient strokes. Steering strokes need to be quicker and more powerful. Some are detailed below.

Stern Pry

This is much quicker to perform than the stern rudder. It provides a very quick and powerful steering stroke when the boat needs to be accelerated or the speed kept up.

- Hands should be outside the gunwale. Indicator thumb up. Without changing hand positions on the paddle shaft, the bottom hand should be above the gunwale.

- The paddle shaft should be resting on the gunwale. The paddle will slope downwards at an angle of 30-40 degrees.

- The blade should be behind you and starting from a position where it is pretty well plastered on the side of the canoe.

- Steering is achieved by making a short jerk inward with the top hand.

- The blade should only travel a short distance out from the hull of the canoe. Push it very far and the canoe stalls.

- If you need more steering then make quick repeats of the stroke. Making a bigger stroke slows you.

Photo 17.3   Paddle blade plastered to side of canoe before doing the pry

The short 'J' pairs with this stroke. You really need to develop both at the same time. It is easy to end up thinking that the stern pry is the fastest of strokes but the short 'J' is a quicker steering stroke. However the short 'J' does not have such a powerful correction. The competent paddler will often end up quickly swapping between these strokes in a white water manoeuvre.

Short 'J'

Perhaps the quickest of all the steering strokes, once learnt it puts little strain on the body, wastes little time and allows a stern paddler to match the stroke of the bow. It can be done slowly for easy cruising or kept up at a fast rate whilst making moves on white water, racing or chewing into a headwind.

- The normal power stroke is done, but on the last few centimetres of pull the paddle shaft is run along the gunwale. Initially noisy, this soon becomes much quieter and smooth.

- As the paddle passes the hip, the shaft resting on the gunwale, the blade is turned into a 'J' stroke.

Photo 17.4   Short 'J' position

- All the effort of the steering is done with the top hand pressing inwards into the canoe, levering the paddle off the gunwale.

- During steering the paddle blade will normally be angled rather than vertical. Very importantly, the steering is normally done with a partially, rather than fully, immersed blade.

Once learnt, this becomes the normal cruising stroke for many paddlers. It is very easy on the body. However it does tend to wear paddle shafts rather quickly, but better the wear on the paddle than on you.

Using a Bent Shaft Paddle for Cruising

Learning to paddle with an upright paddle shaft can seem unnatural and awkward. Using a bent shaft paddle makes everything easy again. The blade can be pulled back whilst vertical, but now the top hand is not stacked above the other but slightly further forward. The top hand can now pull back adding more power to the stroke.

The aim as before is to keep the blade vertical during the power phase. The blade exits from the water in the same way as a straight shaft paddle. For cruising this is the natural option. However, for maximum speed or effort, the blade should be clipped out at right angles to the stroke and close to the hip; the power phase is kept very short.

In many general canoes it seems best to combine a 14 degree bent shaft in the bow with a straight paddle in the stern. It is not easy to steer with such a paddle. If you are using a particularly straight tracking canoe it would be worth trying a 7 degree bent shaft in the stern.

Photo 17.5   Bent shaft in use

These are such easy paddles to use in the bow that few paddlers will want to change back to straight paddles other than for rapids.

Sit and Switch

Often seen as the marathon paddlers' method, this still has a place with recreational canoeists. In competition, paddlers will often switch sides every 12-18 strokes. Each side of the body gets exercised, and whilst one set of muscles are working the other get a brief respite.

For the recreational paddler the switch can be used as above, particularly at the start of the day when warming up on the water, when the going gets tough heading into a wind, or just to race another canoe. On the other hand they may paddle for twenty minutes or more before swapping.

If the switch is being done every 12-18 strokes it is best to adopt the marathon technique. Perhaps best if called by the stern paddler so that they can switch to suit the steering. Both paddlers should be stroking in time. The stern paddler calls "hut" during a stroke, both paddlers complete that stroke, do one more stroke and then switch.

In the switch, top hand becomes bottom hand. What was bottom hand slides up to become top hand. The paddle stays upright throughout the switch.

The call of 'hut' seems odd to start with. In reality it is only a grunt on the expelling of breath. 'Hut' is only a way of describing this grunt.

The Canoe in White Water

The canoe is the original white water craft. While the kayak was still a seagoing craft, Native Americans, traders and explorers were paddling the waterways of Canada.

Helmets

This is very much a personal matter in a canoe. Generally, in a capsize the paddler falls out of the canoe with the head being nowhere near the river bed. However there will always be a degree of risk in not wearing a helmet.

You should really consider wearing a helmet when:

- You are inexperienced on white water.
- The river is shallow and fast.
- You are playing on waves and stoppers.
- The water is fast or violent and you could not protect yourself when swimming.
- You are practising rescues.
- Perhaps poling as on occasions the poler may leave the canoe abruptly!

Remember, this is a personal choice.

Tandem

The bow paddler is the boss. He or she is the person who can see, and in most situations is in the position to make powerful changes in direction. Bow and cross-bow draws, rudders and hanging strokes quickly move the canoe on to a new line or into a turn. Big corrections are often the job of the bow paddler. However, it is easy for the bow paddler to concentrate on direction and forget that they also have to apply power.

Communication for Tandem

Rapids are noisy. It is not a good idea to try and discuss the line whilst speeding through this environment. If the rapid is complex or difficult, a plan should be formulated in the eddy above or from the bank. The plan should be discussed and each paddler should be fully aware of what needs to be done. Discussion should take place before, not during a manoeuvre.

In easier rapids or with bolder paddlers, both should be aware of their normal tactics. With an experienced pair, the bow paddler will make decisions and communicate them by his/her actions. The stern paddler's job is to stay behind the bow paddler, a simple concept but it needs experience. If words are used they should be simple, single and loud: "LEFT, EDDY". A stern paddler quickly learns to read the bow paddler. The more they paddle together, the better this non-verbal communication should become.

I once pitched head first out of the back of a swamped tandem canoe. My mate continued downstream blissfully unaware that he was on his own. This blissful state continued until I passed him as I ran down the bank.

One real possibility of confusion would be if the bow paddler intends to start a reverse ferry. Let's say they pull the bow to the right. From the stern the intention will be unclear. They could be intending to power up and head right. It may be they are pulling the bow to the right to initiate a reverse ferry to the left. A very loud shout of "BACK" would let the stern paddler know the intention.

White Water Tactics

Canoeists have a number of strategies at their disposal. They can:

- Travel at the same speed as the water - changes in position are done with draws and pries.

- Travel faster than the current - forward speed allows the canoe to be steered, to cross eddy lines, to punch through waves and stoppers. It also allows fast progress down a river.

- Travel slower than the water - this allows reverse moves to be made, both ferries and breakouts. Travelling slow allows the bow to rise over waves rather than plough into them.

All these strategies will be used by the competent canoeist. The first two are easiest to master and most rapids can be run using these. However, reverse moves, once mastered are powerful tools on harder rivers and create time to think.

Looking Where You Are Going

Vision patterns are key to good paddling. Before leaving an eddy you should clearly identify your next target, whether it be a point on the river, a gap between two rocks, or the place to cross the next eddy line.

As you build up speed in the eddy, focus should be switched between the crossing point in the eddy line and the new target. Even before the canoe crosses the eddy line you should be looking solely at the target. All this causes you to pre-rotate the head and trunk on to the new line, making for far more pow-

erful moves. Everything becomes easier to achieve, and targets are achieved via a single manoeuvre rather than a series of disjointed moves.

Breaking In and Out

This is the critical art for running rivers. Eddies can be places to get on or off the river, or a place to head for to get a look downstream before making a decision on the route down a rapid or whether to portage. Our ability to make eddies is a basis for safe river running.

Going from the current into an eddy is 'breaking out'. Going from the eddy back into the current is referred to as 'breaking in'.

Leaning into the Turn

This lean is best started as you approach the eddy line and made harder (steeper) as you cross it.

As we move from current to eddy or vice versa the influences on the canoe change drastically. This change, in other than the simplest situations, will try to capsize the canoe. The paddler or paddlers counter this by leaning the canoe into the turn. Work out well in advance which way the canoe will turn and then start its lean before you cross the eddy line.

Photo 17.6   Breaking out - lean in evidence

Breaking Out

Under forward speed a number of different things can happen as the canoe approaches the eddy.

- The water can be slowing down as you approach the eddy line, in which case the canoe will start its turn before reaching the eddy. It skids and wallows its way through the turn and into the eddy.

- The water speeds up as you approach the eddy line. In this case the water will grab at the bow and attempt to turn the canoe downstream and down the eddy line.

Fig 17.1 Eddy line and canoe on attack angle

- Current may be consistent all the way to the eddy line. Life is easy but the event rare.

It is normally best to maintain a straight course on an attack angle at the eddy. Imagine an angle running out at 90 degrees to the eddy line. Now point the bow slightly downstream of this angle. Maintain and drive the canoe forward on this angle.

> ### Exercises
>
> *Play with different approach angles because eddies, current and what you want to achieve will vary. See what effect different approaches have. Try starting the turn before reaching the eddy rather than run straight (often necessary when there is little room in the eddy).*

In a solo canoe, steering will need to be done from the rear of the boat. Stern pries, rudders or stern draws will be necessary to control the stern. Resist the temptation to steer with bow strokes, as the stern will continue to skid out of control.

In tandem, the bow paddler can assist a straight run with hanging draws on the appropriate side. The bow paddler must not dither. Correct the angle and then get on with applying power.

The result of this is to cut deep across the eddy line. The canoe will start to turn. The choice is now yours. You can tighten the turn with a bow rudder or jams. You can swing around a hanging draw. You can open the turn by controlling the stern.

This is a more aggressive approach to eddies that many use and there are two issues:

1. Kayakers occupying the eddy may not be expecting you to arrive so quickly!
2. The canoe needs to be leant much further into the turn.

Breaking In

The canoe has to cross from the slower water of the eddy into the current. Speed is built up in the eddy with the canoe facing and travelling upstream before crossing the eddy line. The angle you cross the eddy line will be largely responsible for the speed of turn and where you end up in the current. Angle the canoe to face more upstream and generally the canoe will go much further out into the current before turning. Face more across the river and the canoe will turn more quickly and closer to the eddy line. You need to experiment with this to find the differences.

Very importantly:

- The canoe must be leant into the turn to prevent a capsize.
- Paddlers should be looking downstream to target the turn. Where you look is often where you end up.

Using Low Braces

If the entry to the current or eddy needs more stability, a low brace will provide it. From the brace the blade can be thrown forward into a bow rudder or draw to tighten the turn and finish the move.

Using Bow Rudders

As on flat water, the bow rudder should be placed to slice through the water, and only then should the blade be opened to take the pressure you want and can handle. This can be used coming into or out of eddies. Placed well, the bow rudder also provides stability. If you need to slow the canoe, use a brace-cum-backstroke before using a bow rudder/draw.

In a solo canoe the stroke can be reached forward to help initiate the tighter turn. As pressure dies the blade can:

- Be turned straight into a power stroke to drive the canoe forwards.

- Be turned into a 'C' stroke to keep the speed up in the turn. This can be finished with the Indian stroke combination (see Chapter 5). This is a real delight as the canoe does not stall and momentum is maintained.

- Put together any other combination you need or desire.

In a tandem canoe the bow rudder and hanging draw are identical. Again use the stroke to control or tighten the turn.

The stern paddler can attempt to control the stern; a stern hanging draw will speed up the turn, a stern rudder will slow it. All the time the crew leans the canoe into the turn. The bow rudder used by the bow paddler provides the stability. The stern paddler can do little bar lean, with the possibility of an air brace to impress any other paddlers!

Photo 17.7   Tandem breakout - bow rudder

Using Cross-bow Rudders

This is much the same as with bow rudders. The solo paddler will need to reach further forward to initiate the turn. In tandem the stroke can resemble a cross-deck hanging draw.

The solo paddler will often finish the move with cross-deck forward paddle strokes before going back onto the on side.

Photo 17.8   Solo paddler using cross-deck bow rudder

In tandem, the stern paddler can use a low brace to provide a massive amount of stability as well as increasing the turn.

Photo 17.9   Tandem cross-deck

Use of Hanging Draw as Keel Line

In both solo on and off side bow rudders, the blade can be moved back to provide a hanging draw. This provides a 'keel line' for the canoe to swing around with and it stops the tendency to slide across the eddy.

- Enter the eddy (or current) and throw in the bow rudder (or cross-bow).

- As the canoe begins to come around, move the blade back to a hanging draw position.

- The canoe arcs around the turn.

- If you need to tighten the turn, move the blade forward again into a bow rudder.

Bow Jams for Tandem

Bow jams are a powerful and bold way for tandem canoes to break in or out. Going into an eddy, the bow paddler waits until the moment they wish to turn, and then slides the blade of the paddle down the side of the canoe on the outside of the turn. Whilst holding the jam in place, he or she must lean away from the paddle and into the turn. The stern paddler should throw his or her weight over the gunwale and onto a brace on the inside of the turn. This weight throw is what (hopefully) will keep the canoe upright. With a confident pair this is the most powerful of turns.

Carving the Stern

When doing a breakout (and a break-in), as the turn takes hold, the stern of the canoe starts to skid. This can be partially controlled by radical leaning of the canoe. Two strokes help to slow or control this skid.

For the stern or solo paddler who has the paddle on the inside of the turn, a stern hanging draw (draw element of the stern rudder) will hold the skid. The turning moment is transferred into forward motion and the canoe will go deeper into the eddy. It is best not to cancel out the turn, but just to lengthen it to make use of this transference of energy. When you want to tighten the turn, take the paddle out and allow the skid to tighten the turn.

With the paddle on the outside of the turn, a stern rudder is used braced against the side of the canoe. This will try to trip the canoe, therefore the blade is only partially submerged and the paddler's weight is thrown to the inside of the turn.

Quartering Waves

Photo 17.10   Diagonal run into eddy, cutting corner of large wave

Large waves and stoppers can easily swamp a canoe. A diagonal run at speed can be used to aggressively cut the corner of a wave or stopper. There are no half measures here. Speed works. At the last moment the downstream gunwale can be raised to stop water spilling in. This can make for a very powerful and dramatic entry into eddies beyond the wave. Do this slowly and the wave can easily capsize the canoe.

This tactic can also be used to cut across the side-walls of a big downstream 'V'. Go slowly in crossing the edge of the 'V' and you will be swept into the wave train.

Use of Hanging Draw in Micro-eddies

Behind smaller rocks there will be an eddy that is too small to get a canoe into. However they are very useful in manoeuvring the canoe. Normally, for a hanging draw to work you need to be travelling faster than the current.

* Aim to just miss the eddy.
* Plant a hanging draw in the micro-eddy. Place it in almost parallel to the direction of travel and then open it up to a pressure and pull you want.

Photo 17.11   Hanging draw in micro-eddy

* The canoe should slide sideways and across the downstream end of the eddy.
* Rather than side-slipping, you could use the paddle further forward and initiate a turn.

Big side-slips or turns can be done with little expenditure of energy.

Ferries

A ferry glide can be used to cross from one side of the river to the other, eddy to eddy. It can also be used to make a move out into the current before turning downstream.

For first practice, use an area with weak eddy lines. Facing upstream, maintain a position on the river. Then angle the nose to one side (if directly upstream is 12 o'clock, try angling to 11 o'clock). Maintain forward power. The canoe should slide across to one side, back to 12 and then try 1 o'clock. These are only starting angles. In weaker currents a large angle is effective, whilst in powerful water it may be necessary to keep a fairly tight angle. For tandem paddlers it will be easier to learn if the bow paddler moves back in the boat.

Photo 17.12   Tandem crew ferrying above rapid

As the water speeds up it is more and more important to lean downstream.

In tandem both paddlers can help maintain the ferry angle, although the stern person can do most small corrections. For solo, most corrections must be done at the stern, bow strokes are ineffective.

Solo

Ferry is easiest learnt with the paddle on the side the canoe is moving to. Corrections are best done with power strokes and stern draws to push the bow one way and stern pries to move it the other. With the paddle on the outside of the move, corrections are often necessary using stern pries and rudders to pull the nose back upstream.

Photo 17.13   Solo paddler leaning off a stern pry

By building up speed in an eddy, and exiting with a hanging draw and a ferry glide angle on the canoe, the solo paddler can move a good distance across the river for little expenditure of energy.

In tandem boats, the bow paddler using a hanging draw in the current can do the same move, and the stern paddler uses a stern rudder/pry and leans into the move.

> **Exercise**
>
> *Try different combinations of angles, speed and paddle strokes to ferry glide.*

Surfing

Surfing can be done as an efficient cross-river move or just for the pure buzz. The problem for a solo paddler will be in exerting both control and power. For the tandem pair the problems will be communication and trim. In most cases the bow paddler may need to move back, to stop the bow burying in the oncoming water.

Photos 17.14a-b   Stern rudder and lean solo, practised on rope and then on wave

The canoe is paddled up the eddy and onto the shoulder of the wave. Too far out and the back of the wave is often too steep and fast to climb over. A slight diagonal on the canoe will cause it to move out.

The canoe will want to turn downstream. The solo or stern paddler will need to resist this by using a stern rudder/pry on the opposite side.

Once on the wave, the nose is turned upstream by use of stern rudders/pries. To turn towards the paddle, stern hanging draws are used. These are most powerful if done just behind the paddler and with the paddle shaft fairly steep.

Photos 17.15a-b   Stern hanging draw on rope and on wave

Reverse Ferries

There is no doubt that it is easier to reverse ferry with the weight forward in the canoe so that it is bow down in the water. However this makes any forward speed difficult to control. A mix of forward paddling and reverse paddling makes a very powerful combination for running rapids. In a loaded boat or in a difficult rapid it is impractical to keep shifting yourself or the load. In the end you should be aiming to keep the same trim but be able to reverse ferry when necessary.

Solo

To learn the skill start with a bow heavy boat. This means there is far less pressure on the stern and control is far easier.

- Try the manoeuvre using reverse and cross-deck reverse strokes.

- Play with the angles (as with forward ferries) to see what is most efficient.

- A reverse 'J' is one of the most powerful strokes used to control the manoeuvre.

Tandem

- Move the stern paddler forward to unweight the stern.

Photo 17.16   Tandem with stern paddler in middle

- Both paddlers need to understand the angles they are attaining. Agree beforehand.

- The bow paddler may be in a better position to control the angle but in powerful water it will take both to do this.

- If you need to change the angle, do it quickly and then get on with reverse power.

Once you have mastered reverse ferries with a bow heavy canoe, start doing reverse moves without changing the trim. It will need powerful steering/draws and pries to hold the ferry glide position. The control strokes must be executed quickly so that each paddler can apply reverse power.

Photo 17.17   Reverse ferry, stern heavy

Important

In both reverse ferries and setting in and out of eddies it can be hard to control the angle if the canoe is stern heavy. If the angle wavers then water can easily pile up on the stern and take it the wrong way. Seldom will strokes be able to correct this once the water piles up.

Quickly accelerate the boat forwards; three or four powerful strokes should free the stern. Re-attain the angle and reapply the reverse power.

Setting In and Out of Eddies

On rocky rivers it may not be such a good idea to spin the canoe in an eddy turn. 5-6 metres of boat arcing across a river take up a lot of room. Setting into an eddy avoids this broadside approach. Also it makes for a neater entry into a narrow eddy.

Setting Into an Eddy

Method 1 Solo

This works when the eddy is caused by an obstruction and you can run close to the eddy line.

- Aim to just miss the top of the eddy. Get as close as possible.

- Have the paddle in the outside hand (on the opposite side to the eddy).

- Slow the canoe down as much as you can without losing control. The canoe can still be stern heavy. Too slow and the current will grab the stern and swing it around.

- As the stern of the canoe comes past the top of the eddy, do the most powerful reverse strokes you can. Do not cross-deck. The stern must be smashed across the eddy line and into the eddy. Power, not finesse is the key.

- Only when the canoe is properly in the eddy can you use cross-deck strokes to straighten it up.

This method will work tandem with a couple of key points:

- It is best if the stern paddler has their paddle on the outside of the move.

- The bow paddler must resist the temptation to pull the bow into the eddy. Allow the stern to initiate the move and then the bow puts in powerful reverse 'J's to drive the canoe backwards and the bow outwards. It is this angle that helps drive the canoe into the eddy.

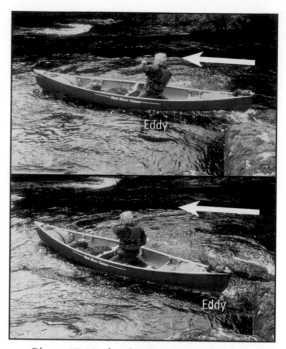

Photos 17.18a-b   Setting in, stern heavy, big reverse strokes

> ### Note
> *When learning to do this manoeuvre it may be worth moving forward in the canoe to become bow heavy. This will give you more time to learn the strokes before moving back into a stern heavy trim.*

Method 2 Solo

This is basically a reverse ferry that ends in an eddy. Much easier if the move is started some way above the eddy and you take a diagonal line downstream and into the eddy.

All the normal reverse strokes can be used. In addition a reverse scull/reverse 'J' stroke can be used on the outside of the move to help slide the canoe diagonally sideways. Run the paddle along the gunwale in a reverse scull (towards bow only) and, as it gets to the front, pry off the gunwale with a reverse 'J' to hold the angle.

The reverse ferry can be used to work around the inside of a bend. This works well if the water slows close to the shore. The tail of the canoe will be in this slower water and the ferry effect holds the boat in position.

Setting Out of an Eddy

Imagine yourself in a small eddy, little wider than the canoe. You are facing downstream. You need to get out wide and remain facing downstream. You are trimmed for forward travel and don't want to trim stern heavy.

Method 1

Solo with the paddle on the outside of the eddy:

- Set a very slight reverse ferry angle.
- Start sculling out towards and over the eddy line.
- As the blade crosses over into the current it should get grabbed by the water and become, effectively, a reverse hanging draw. This, and the stern being on a ferry angle, starts to pull the canoe out into the current.
- As the canoe slides out into the current it will try to spin. This must be resisted.

Photo 17.19   Boat crossing eddy line, reverse hanging draw in evidence

- Move the reverse hanging draw quickly forwards. This pulls the bow out into the current. The ferry angle, combined with the strokes, should throw the canoe across the river, all the time facing downstream.

Photo 17.20   Moving out using bow draw

Method 2

Solo with the paddle on the inside of the eddy.

- Set a slight ferry angle on the canoe.
- Move out to the eddy line using pries, cross-deck sculling or reverse sculling.
- As the canoe reaches the eddy line, do a series of powerful reverse strokes on the inside of the move.
- As you cross the eddy line, slam the blade forward and into a powerful reverse 'J'. Hold the reverse 'J'. If this is done in the current it should prevent the canoe from spinning. Once again you are left facing downstream.

An awkward move to learn but a real delight once mastered, it makes for a powerful reverse move across a river. This is a valuable part of the repertoire.

This is a hard manoeuvre to master tandem. Try different combinations at bow and stern. Both paddlers must work hard to maintain the angle.

When it all Goes Wrong

Occasionally it is all going to go wrong. We end up swimming. Canoe, paddle and paddler are off on separate journeys down the river. Now consider that a cubic metre of water weighs one tonne. So our swamped canoe can weigh upwards of a tonne and may be moving at 6-8km per hour. If a car were rolling down a hill at this speed you would not consider stepping in front of it. To get in front of a flooded canoe and then be stopped by a rock before the canoe sweeps down on to you is potentially lethal. The force of impact is bad enough but in the worst case the canoe can get wrapped around the rock and victim. The Americans have a particularly apt name for this: 'Bear Trap'.

If in any doubt at all, get clear of the canoe. At the least, swim on the upstream side of a canoe.

Swim Lines

Having pointed out the dangers, it still makes sense in many cases to self-rescue both the canoe and ourselves. Swim lines give us this possibility.

Method 1

Twenty to thirty metres of floating line are attached to the stern grab loop of the canoe. A bag is situated right in the stern of the boat and in behind or on top of the air bag. The line is stuffed into this, with the clean end protruding above the air bag ready to grab.

Photo 17.21   Swing the canoe in on a swim line

Method 2

A piece of shock cord is used to fasten a throw bag on to the rear of the canoe. A karabiner is used to clip the bag to the rear grab loop. In the event of a swim the clean end of the rope is grabbed. Some people have a throw bag ready on both ends of the canoe.

Rescuing by Curling in the Current

Rather than attempt to shunt a capsized or flooded boat to the bank, it is often better to perform a very fast curl rescue midstream and then have to deal with an empty (light) boat (see Chapter 6). Pick your spot carefully! Get swimmers clear before you attempt this. Swimmers should have either swum to the bank or at least swum until well clear of the rescue. Once emptied the canoe can be towed to the shore. Use the rescued canoe's painter to make a towline. Take the line once around a thwart and kneel on the end. Do not under any circumstances tie the rescued boat to yours, even with a quick release knot.

Poling

Too often we end up travelling on British rivers in low water. Weed and shallows make travel with a paddle frustrating and inefficient. The pole brings efficiency and elegance (well sometimes).

The Pole

The optimum length for a pole is 11-12 feet. Lightweight glass poles, which split into two sections, are available and are good for downstream travel and light work. A $1^{1}/8$th diameter aluminium pipe sealed at both ends is perhaps better for trips where prolonged poling is envisaged. A spruce pole, shaped

and with its end copper bound, is the height of luxury.

Photos 17.22a-c   Curling in the current

Poling Downstream

In normal British travel this is by far the most useful aspect of poling. Few people will do upstream journeys.

As a learning progression (solo) try:

1. Sit in the canoe and use the pole like a kayak paddle.

2. Stand in the canoe and do the same.

3. Paddle with the pole on one side only.

4. Try cross-bow rudders and any other strokes with the pole whilst standing.

All the above are part of poling and not 'just' a teaching progression. As you go from shallow to deep water you need to be able to paddle with the pole and not keep swapping from paddle to pole and vice versa.

Stance

For the travelling poler, your feet should be spread both side to side and fore and aft. It can help to brace the rear leg against a seat or thwart; this diagonal stance lines up your body for the most effective use of muscles.

Angle of Thrust

The hypothetical ideal would be to use the pole horizontally and push off a vertical wall directly behind you. Since nature only provides a river bed beneath you, a compromise must be made and a pole angle between 30 and 45 degrees is the range for optimum thrust. Past this angle, more effort is going into lifting you from the canoe rather than propelling you forward.

Propulsion

In shallow water a series of short, quick jabs pushes the canoe forward.

Steering

This is achieved by using the pole as a rudder.

Windmilling

As the water gets deeper it is hard to get the pole to the river bed. Then it is time to start windmilling the pole. As the canoe travels forward, one end of the pole is dropped in ahead of the person. As it comes vertical the pole drops to the river bed. Wait. The canoe travels on the pole, drops below 45 degrees and then you thrust. Steer with a rudder. Now drop the leading end into the water ahead of the canoe. Each time use the opposite end of the pole. This is elegant and efficient.

Poling Upstream

For an adventure or real challenge you can try going up rapids using the pole. Again the pole is kept low, below 45 degrees.

As the speed of the current increases, using the pole as a rudder is no longer effective. As an exercise use a section of relatively slow moving shallow rapid. Face the canoe upstream and hold it stationary in the current. Things are much easier if the canoe is very light in the bow.

The feet are the key to twisting the canoe from side to side. Plant them wide and on a diagonal across the canoe. Flex the knees. Now by pushing with one hand and pulling with the other, as well as twisting with the hips and knees, it should be possible to twist the bow one way and then the other. This is the basic control method.

Photo 17.23   Showing stance and twisting action

In shallow water a series of short, fast jabs will keep the momentum going. As the water gets deeper it may be useful, once you have purchase on the river bed, to climb the pole hand over hand before throwing the pole forward before the next plant.

Snubbing

Very occasionally you may need to thread your way downstream through a maze of rocks. The river is too fast and shallow for a paddle. It is possible to use the pole to effect a whole series of reverse ferry moves and travel down the rapid slower than the water.

Photo 17.24   Snubbing down a rock-infested rapid

The canoe needs to be bow heavy. This is achieved by moving any load right to the front of the canoe, and then standing right behind it. The nose of the canoe must be down but you can still be standing in a relatively wide part of the canoe.

The stance should be diagonal and with the forward knee braced against kit or seat. The pole is kept very low and with the knees bent to absorb any shocks. Speed can only be taken off slowly with a series of jabs. Don't allow the pole to be pushed up, keep the angle low. Steering, as with poling upstream, is achieved by flexing the legs, twisting with the hips and knees and utilising a push/pull on the pole.

Holding the canoe stationary against the current, you can put the boat at an angle to the current. The boat now starts ferry gliding. When you reach the desired line, straighten the canoe and head on down.

If necessary it is possible to swing the pole across the canoe and in front of the body. This makes for very powerful corrections. There is a risk: get the pole stuck in under a rock and, as the canoe moves forward, you will be swept out of it and into the water.

Lining and Tracking

In our paddling, as in Canada, almost anything is preferable to carrying the canoe and gear. So when it gets windy or we need to move upriver, tracking is an option, and occasionally we will be able to use a rope to line a canoe down a rapid, rather than walk round if we don't fancy paddling it.

Tracking into the Wind

Paddling into a headwind can be exhausting. If the shore is clear it can be easier to track the canoe into the wind. Using floating rope, the section is attached at the bow and stern of the boat, making a big loop. Depending on conditions and depth, 10 to 18 metres of rope will do the job. Gear needs to be moved to make the canoe stern heavy.

Either get someone to hold the canoe at an angle to the shore or place it in the water at the correct angle but not really afloat. The puller moves off along the shore to the limit of the loop.

The canoe is at a ferry glide angle and ropes are taut. The puller takes a few quick steps to make the canoe bite into the wind and water. At this stage the boat should move out from the shore and into deeper water. The puller can then walk along the shore towing the canoe behind them. You should even be able to stay dry.

> ### Safety
>
> *The rope is an obvious danger. Either the whole length of the rope should be let out or, if coils are taken, care must be taken not to let it tighten around the hand. Being dragged down a rapid by a laden canoe is not fun! Be very wary of loose rope on the ground. A knife should be readily to hand.*

Lining Down a Rapid

Carrying a canoe and kit should be a last resort. Imagine arriving at a rapid that you do not wish to run. It may be possible to use a rope, and line the canoe down the side of the rapid or at least take it down closer to the point you wish to carry around. The canoe is afloat but you walk down the side, controlling its progress.

In easier flows it is possible to do this with a bow painter or a longer length of floating rope attached at the upstream end of the canoe. If a throw line is used, the bag end should be attached to the canoe, leaving the other end clean. Kit should be placed in the downstream end of the boat. The boat is shoved out into the current and allowed to float down with the current. As necessary it is pulled back to the bank or into an eddy.

As the current increases, pressure builds on the upstream end of the canoe. This can make the canoe unmanageable or quite easy to flip. Swamped and with a tonne or more of water on board, the canoe is easily pulled from your grasp and is off on its own. This is avoided by using a bridle to attach the rope beneath the upstream end of the canoe.

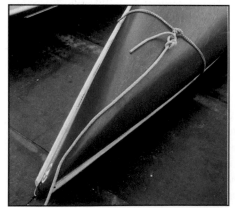

Photo 17.25   Bridle - separate piece of rope

A bridle can easily be made by tying a small overhand knot in a length of rope. The knot is placed under the upstream end of the canoe and the two ends of the rope are taken around opposite sides of the canoe and attached to the seat (clove hitches are ideal). The lining rope is then attached to the overhand knot.

the upstream end. A second rope is attached to the downstream end of the canoe.

Photo 17.27   Tracking upstream

Photo 17.26   Bridle made from lining rope

Separate off a metre and a half of rope (approximately) and then tie an overhand knot at this point. The loop of the overhand knot should also be a metre and a half. The knot is the centre point under the canoe. The loop forms one half of the bridle and is attached in the canoe. The single rope is the other half and goes around the other side.

Kit is again in the downstream end of the canoe. The canoe is shoved out and allowed to drift down. It is now much harder for the current to grab the upstream end of the canoe.

A few things to try:

- Let the canoe drift past a 'target' eddy. Then give the rope a strong, quick pull. This sets a 'ferry' angle and it should drift up and into the eddy.

- A partner can go on down to a target area. As the canoe jolts shoreward, the 'T' grip of a paddle can be used to snag the line and pull it up to the hand.

- A boat can be lined down to the lip of a stopper and then, by pulling on a downstream rope, it can be pulled smartly through. The stopper would otherwise hold the canoe.

Tracking Upstream

Generally two ropes are used. Again the upstream end of the canoe is light. A bridle is attached under

- It helps if the ropes are different colours.

- Some canoes will need the downstream rope attached to a bridle as well.

- If throw bags are used, they should be attached at the canoe, leaving clean ends at the bank.

- 15 to 18 metres gives plenty of flexibility.

- An empty canoe floats too high and will not allow the water to get a grip on it to take it out.

The idea is to get the canoe out into the current and, by allowing the bow to be further from the shore, set up a continuous ferry glide.

Getting the canoe started is often difficult so:

- Set a ferry angle on the canoe whilst it is next to the shore. This can be done by having someone hold it at the correct angle, or by having it just grounded in the shallows.

- Move as far upstream as practical whilst leaving the canoe in place.

- Take the slack out of the ropes but don't move the canoe.

- Put the ropes in one hand and turn to face upstream.

- Run! 5 or 6 quick steps should throw the canoe out into the current.

- Stop, adjust the ropes and then move on up.

- Keep the upstream end further out than the downstream end. This way there is a constant pressure of water trying to take the canoe away from you.

You can track with a person on each rope but it requires a lot of co-ordination.

Tracking can go wrong. In very powerful current, even with an upstream bridle, the canoe can be swung around and control is lost. Perhaps best is to release the upstream rope and hopefully swing the canoe to shore with the other rope.

The Canoe on Open Water

Paddling Downwind

Solo

This is nice and easy for the solo paddler. They move their weight sternward. The bow becomes lighter, presenting a greater surface to the wind. The whole canoe acts as a weather vane and turns downwind. The steering becomes easy. As the wind picks up and waves build, the canoe will start to surf. Everything becomes fun but the canoe becomes less stable and it is well worth kneeling to keep the weight low.

Tandem

Once again the weight shift is critical. Either the load or bow paddler must be moved back in the boat.

Photo 17.28   Solo boat running downwind

Paddling Upwind

Now things get a little more interesting. Working on the same principle as above, it would seem obvious to put the weight forwards and make use of the weathervane effect. However there is one other effect to take into account. With the bow deep in the water, the slightest move off course causes water to pile up on the opposite side and push the canoe further off course. Steering can become a real nightmare.

Tandem

An experienced crew should have little need to put the weight forwards. Only if the bow is very light should weight be shifted to get a more level trim. By frequent switching of sides a higher stroke rate can be kept up. A canoe catches a lot of wind so it is often better, when travelling along a lake shore, to do hard bursts of paddling and take rests on the shore.

> **Note**
>
> *Particularly with a heavily laden boat, tandem paddlers can ship water in over the bow. It may be necessary to take power off as the canoe reaches each wave. Attacking the waves at a slight angle and not head-on can help.*

Solo

With a lot less power being generated, life is much harder for the solo paddler. As the wind picks up it is worth dropping the bow until eventually the trim is neutral. Pressure is put on the steering, but good firm short 'J's and stern pries allow a high stroke rate to be kept up. Frequent swapping of sides allows respite to different sets of muscles. If you are being forced into longer and longer steering strokes it is worth swapping sides to power the canoe back onto line.

As a final resort, weight can be shifted forwards to put the canoe nose-down. Steering and elegance are forgotten and forward travel is achieved by swapping the paddle from side to side. With two to three strokes on each side the canoe swings about behind the paddler. It looks untidy but achieves its purpose.

Wind from the Side

Solo

There are two solutions to this problem:

1. The paddler moves towards the stern, which allows the wind to push the bow around. By paddling on the downwind side, the paddle stroke pushes the canoe back the other way. The real trick is to balance these forces exactly. Instead of steering with the paddle, the canoeist simply does a power stroke. Steering is achieved by varying the power or by moving forward or back in the canoe, hence exposing more or less of the bow to the wind. As the wind gusts you move forward, as it dies you move back. In a stong wind keep the weight very low in the boat and your power stroke should become more like a sweep to stop you tripping over the blade. (See Fig 17.2 overleaf).

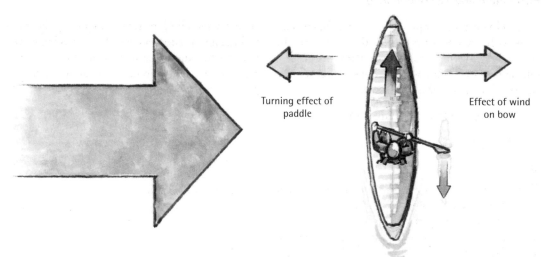

Fig 17.2   Interacting effects of wind, direction of travel and paddle strokes

2. The paddler moves to the bow and paddles on the upwind side. The stern blows downwind and the paddle compensates in the bow. There is an advantage in a strong wind in that you have the paddle on the upwind side ready to brace into wind and waves. The disadvantage is that if all gets too much, you have to swap your position before being able to run downwind.

Tandem

I have never come up with a neat solution to this one. There are too many variables. Try paddling on different sides to find the best combination. It may be efficient for both to end up paddling on the same side, but as the wind strengthens it would make the canoe less stable.

Open Water Rescues

Paddling Swamped Boats

This has already been dealt with in the section on lash or leash. With strong winds, heavily laden canoes and big waves it may not be practical or possible to do any form of rescue. In this case lashing swamped canoes together and leaning outwards allows progress to be made and a real chance gained to make the shore.

All in Rescues

Any rescuer is vulnerable in a canoe. It is too easy to make a mistake or have one of the victims capsize you. Now everyone is in the water.

All canoes used on open water should have buoyancy; this enables a number of options.

Method 1

- Both canoes are left upside down.

- One is dragged across the other at right angles. Painters make this really easy.

- The top boat is now flipped upright. This is not that easy, and with inexperienced people in the water with you, may not be possible.

- As an alternative take a length of rope or a long sling. Attach it to the mid thwart and throw it up and over the upturned canoe.

- One person takes this 'flip line' and gets ready to pull the canoe over.

- A second person is on the opposite side to help with the initial upward move.

- On a command both work to flip the canoe. Be warned; the canoe flips quickly and heads for the puller. Duck!

- Now one person can steady whilst the other gets into the dry boat.

- Rescue continues with an 'X' or curl rescue.

Method 2

This depends on the flooded canoe having sufficient buoyancy to support a person.

- One canoe is left upright although flooded.

- The second canoe must be upside down.

- The upside down canoe is dragged, at right angles, across the flooded one. It can be difficult to get the bow across the first gunwale.

- One swimmer climbs into the flooded upright canoe, stands and then flips the top canoe upright.

- Rescue continues with an 'X' or curl rescue.

17.29   Canoes at right angles, person climbing in before flipping top boat upright

Paddling on the Sea

Canoes were used on the Great Lakes of North America. They are at home on big, open water. However canoes are vulnerable to swamping in big waves.

Many tidal sea lochs are little different to being on a large, inland lake. However, once we get out to sea we can encounter tide races, overfalls and conditions such as wind over tide. Although great journeys have been done on tidal water, canoes are not the craft to learn seamanship in. Remember, however skilled you might be, the boat is the limiting factor.

Further Reading

Path of the Paddle, Bill Mason, 1984, Van Nostrand Reinhold Ltd., Toronto, 0-904405-18-4
Song of the Paddle, Bill Mason, 1988, Key Porter Books Ltd. Toronto, 1-55013-082-X
Paddle your own Canoe, G. & J. McGuffin, 1999, Boston Mills Press, Ontario, 1-55046-214-8
Canoeing a Trailside Guide, G. Grant, 1997, W.W. Norton, New York, 0-393-31489-8
Beyond the Paddle, G. Conover, 1991, Old Bridge Press, Ontario, 0-921820-29-1

Videos

Path of the Paddle, Solo Whitewater and Double Whitewater by Bill Mason
Solo Playboating by Kent Ford - White water specialist canoes but very useful for stroke technique

Websites:

www.acanet.org - American Canoe Association
www.crca.ca - Canadian Recreational Canoeing Association
www.gorp.com - GORP (a good gateway site)
www.RayGoodwin.com - Ray's own site

Ray Goodwin

Ray Goodwin has paddled throughout Europe, North America, and Nepal. His British canoe trips include: the Circumnavigation of Wales, the Irish Sea Crossing, a North to South Crossing of the Scottish Highlands and a trip from the Outer Hebrides to the East Coast of Scotland.

Ray is a BCU Level 5 Coach in Canoe, Inland Kayak and Sea as well as holding a Mountain Instructor's Certificate. He has gained a considerable reputation as a Coach running his own business, Ray Goodwin Coaching.

18 Canoe Sailing

In spite of the thick drizzle it was good to be back on the water, continuing the journey along the Great Glen. The previous day had involved running down the river and paddling back along the canal, but now 10 miles of wide and open loch was ahead of us. We set off under sail with a following wind. Progress was initially gentle, but it gradually quickened as we moved into the main expanse of the loch where we were exposed to more wind and wave action. Soon it was clear that reefing down would be sensible, so we landed on a shingle headland to reduce sail. On returning to the water our speed remained very satisfying and care was still needed to avoid broaching whilst surfing on the bigger waves. As the fetch increased, the front of the canoe started to bury in the bigger waves, at times taking on water that needed to be bailed out. Some anxious minutes passed trying to decide whether more defensive tactics would be required before reaching shelter. The conditions proved to be just manageable and, with relief, we slipped into the calmer water provided by the inlet leading to the canal lock.

Introduction

Any object floating on the water is affected by the wind. Canoes are no exception. In even a light breeze, if you don't paddle and are unaffected by currents you will eventually end up on the down-wind shore. When paddling a canoe, moving against the wind involves more effort than moving with the wind. Even moving across the wind, at right angles to it, has its problems. This chapter will start to explore how canoeists can exploit (rather than suffer!) the wind, which can be seen as a free source of motive power.

Basics

The simplest form of using the wind with a canoe is going downwind. Improvisation to achieve useful assistance is straightforward. Any sheet of fabric or plastic such as a jacket or survival bag can be held up to catch the wind. It is easier if there are two people in the canoe and the person at the front holds the 'sail' up while the stern paddler steers. Some people use a specially made but simple 'sail' which can be held up between two paddles. It may be more fun to 'raft up' with another canoe to make use of the extra stability as well as provide more hands to hold everything, but progress will obviously be slower due to the extra weight to be moved.

Photo 18.1   A simple downwind sail made from lightweight ripstop fabric

Principles of Sailing

No sailing craft can sail directly into the wind, and even the most highly developed performance yachts sail no closer than about 45 degrees to the wind. However, this still leaves many options open for sail-ing craft. By taking a zigzag route an upwind course can be achieved.

The general principle of sailing a canoe is that the more effective you want the set-up to be (e.g. the closer to the wind you want to sail or the faster you want to sail), the more sophisticated and well designed the equipment needs to be. Many canoe-ists understandably prefer to keep weight to a mini-mum and therefore try to double up on uses for any equipment. Some simple rigs can be created from the two halves of a poling pole and a shelter tarp, which together with a few lengths of cord can pro-vide a useful downwind rig. The way that the 'mast' is mounted in the canoe is critical to the success of any arrangement, as it needs to be strong enough to withstand the substantial levering forces exerted by a sail full of wind. It may be worth considering rig-ging a piece of cord as a 'stay' or 'guy line' from the stern of the canoe to the top of the mast to help cope with the strain.

A stable but fun way of getting started is to use this 'square rig' on a simple two-canoe 'catamaran' using two two-piece canoe poles. One half-pole can be used as the rafting 'beam' lashed across the canoes, two halves can be lashed together to make an 'A' frame mast and one can be the 'yard' to hold the sail up.

This simple 'square-rig' can be made to sail across the wind, to some extent, by angling the sail and

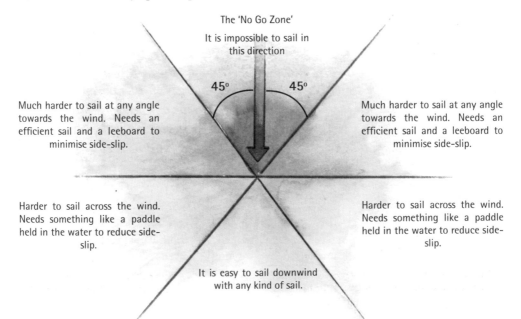

Fig 18.1   Sailing possibilities relative to wind direction.

providing some means of reducing the tendency of the canoe to side-slip, that is to be blown sideways across the water by the wind. In its simplest form, a spare paddle can be held or lashed against the side of the canoe to act as an improvised leeboard.

Photo 18.2   A simple downwind rig using a 'tarp' and the two halves of a poling pole

Developments

To sail at right angles or closer to the wind, the canoe rig must have two well-designed features.

Firstly, the sail needs to be shaped so that it adopts an efficient curve, to channel the wind and drive the canoe, rather than just a flat sheet that merely catches the wind and drags the canoe along. This is commonly achieved using a 'fore and aft' rig. One

edge of the sail is attached to the mast with the sail tensioned towards the rear of the canoe, either by means of a rope direct to the back corner of the sail, or by the lower edge of the sail being fastened to a 'boom' (another shorter pole). The 'boom' is controlled by a rope.

Photo 18.3   A simple downwind rig on a canoe 'catamaran' using a 'tarp' and two poling poles. An 'A' frame rig is made from three half-poles and one half-pole is used to brace the canoes together

Secondly, all boats that aspire to sail across or towards the wind must have a hull design or fittings that reduce the tendency to get blown sideways. Very few canoe hull-shapes grip the water

The airflow with a simple downwind sail is turbulent. It works but it is not very efficient.

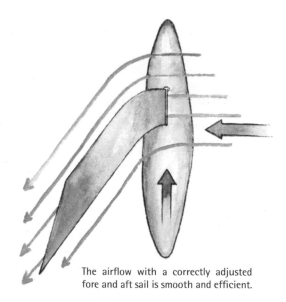

The airflow with a correctly adjusted fore and aft sail is smooth and efficient.

Fig 18.2   Airflows over different types of sail rig.

Photo 18.4   A well developed rig with lee-board able to sail at 45 degrees to the wind

Phot o 18.5   Mast mount - thwart with hole for mast/socket screwed and glued to the floor

Photo 18.6   A leeboard and its mounting

Photo 18.7   A plywood canoe with a built-in casing for a daggerboard

sufficiently to sail well across or upwind without the addition of a leeboard. This can be in the form of a plank of wood, preferably shaped into a streamlined cross-section, which is lashed, clamped or bolted to the side of the canoe and needs to be about 3% of the sail area. This is larger than a spare paddle would provide unless the sail is quite small.

Some canoes, which are specifically adapted for sailing, incorporate a centreboard or daggerboard, similar to those found in sailing dinghies.

Balancing the Forces

There are two basic situations where various forces need to be considered and balanced out to achieve success when sailing a canoe. The first is the simple but crucial matter of stability to prevent capsizes. With the relatively narrow hull-form of canoes, it is understandable that most people assume that adding a sailing rig will feel very tippy. In practice, sailing canoes used in appropriate wind and wave conditions are perfectly manageable and feel much the same as any small sailing boat. The canoeist is able to move their body weight away from the centre line of the canoe far enough to provide sufficient balancing force. When sailing a more powerful rig in a good breeze it may be necessary to sit up on the gunwale, but for most purposes canoe sailors just move across the canoe as required. Sitting right down on the bottom of the canoe is often the most effective, reassuring and relaxing position.

The other 'balancing of forces' to consider, this time at the design-and-build stage of a more sophisticated rig, is that of how the sail and leeboard are combined to work well together. The way that the canoe and leeboard resist the tendency to be blown sideways is technically termed its 'lateral resistance'. The mid-point at which this lateral resistance is balanced is termed the 'Centre of Lateral Resistance' or CLR. This is a combination of the canoe's basic hull shape, together with the effect of the leeboard, and the rudder, if used. The sail must be fitted to the canoe so that its 'Centre of Effort', or 'CE' (where the power provided by the sail is centred), *is slightly in front of the CLR,* when viewed from the side. Although this may sound complicated, it is important to get it right, or the result will be at best awkward and arduous to use, and at worst dangerous and uncontrollable in a good breeze. In practice, provided a few rules are understood and followed, good results are easily achieved.

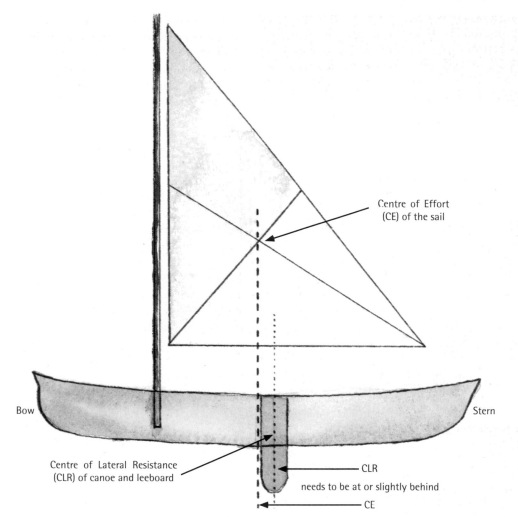

Centre of Effort
(CE) of the sail

Bow

Stern

Centre of Lateral Resistance
(CLR) of canoe and leeboard

CLR
needs to be at or slightly behind
CE

Fig 18.3   Where to fit the sail relative to the canoe and leeboard

Steering: Paddle or Rudder?

For many canoeists using the wind as an additional source of power during a journey, the paddle is the obvious and only choice as a means of steering the canoe. This is easy enough to achieve by the use of stern ruddering technique. Many sailing canoes have a tendency to turn up into the wind and therefore the stern rudder would be best applied on the downwind side. Given that holding the paddle for any technique, including steering, normally requires both hands, the issue of controlling the sail tension needs consideration. Tying the rope to the canoe is best avoided as the ability to let go of it immediately is essential to reduce the chance of capsize in a strong gust. When sailing two-up the jobs can be shared, one steering, the other controlling the sail. When sailing solo, handholding the rope as well as

the paddle can be made to work. Although awkward at first it just needs some organisation and a little practice.

More sophisticated rigs usually incorporate a rudder and tiller mechanism. Although this increases the weight of the canoe, it provides much more control and is far easier than a paddle to steer with for sustained periods.

Types of Rig

For the canoeist who wants to sail, the choice of rig design is wide. It will depend on the performance required, the load to be carried (people and/or gear), the likely waters to be used and, to some extent, the canoe hull design. Most 'general-purpose' or 'family' canoes are great for sailing as they are stable, a reasonable size (4.5 to 5 metres long) and with only slight rocker. Neither fast touring nor racing canoes, which can be very tippy, lend themselves well to sailing, unless rafted together. Canoes designed for rough-water rivers with pronounced rocker for easy turning will not be good for sailing either, as their straight line speed and directional stability is limited.

The rig itself should be designed and built to be as low as possible for lateral stability whilst providing enough headroom for the canoeist. 'Simple but effective' is the best approach with good design, materials and construction being important in providing a canoe/rig combination that works well and avoids frustration. Although they can and should be kept simple, several features of the rig and its fitting to the canoe must be strong enough to cope with the considerable forces encountered when sailing. These include the mast step, the leeboard attachment and the rudder mounting, if used. The shape of the sail chosen, whether it is a simple triangle set on a mast and boom, or four sided set on mast boom and yard, is less important than being able to raise and lower it while on the water. It is also important to be able to reduce its size ('reef') to cope with stronger wind or other tricky situations.

How Large a Sail?

The sail area needed to usefully drive a canoe is not very large because the total weight of a canoe, gear and canoeist is relatively small in boating terms. Depending on the wind strength and adventurousness of the canoeist, sail areas of between 1 to 5 square metres work well. Sails and rigs for canoes can be bought from a few specialist suppliers, they can be home-made from plans, or sails from other boats or sailboards can be adapted to suit.

Fittings

Many canoeists are reluctant to modify their canoe in any way that would permanently affect its use for paddling. But it is quite possible to ensure that any additional features and fittings needed for a sailing rig are neat and discreet. However, the strength that is needed in some key fittings sometimes seems to conflict with this need for unobtrusiveness.

Mast Step

The mast fitting needs to be very strong. The (usually wooden) 'socket', into which the foot of the mast fits, must be firmly and permanently attached to the bottom of the canoe either by adhesive, or

with screws or bolts through the outer skin of the canoe. Some canoeists are reluctant to make holes in the hull of their canoe, fearing leaks.

However, by using the right sealant/adhesive (such as 'Sikaflex' from some canoe specialists or a yacht chandler), a mast socket can be bonded and/or screwed in place with confidence. The mast can be held in place at gunwale level in a few different ways. An existing thwart can be used, by adding a 'U'-shaped hoop through which the mast can pass down into the floor socket. Alternatively a special thwart with a hole for the mast can be made and bolted in. Some canoes may be insufficiently stiff to withstand the side forces that a mast and sail exert on them, and some diagonal bracing will then need to be added.

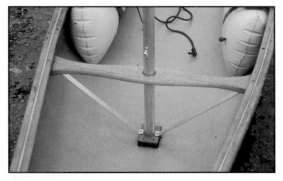

Photo 18.8   Mast mount with diagonal bracing to avoid the canoe flexing

Leeboard

A leeboard can be fitted in a very simple way such as with a length of cord tied round a thwart.

Photo 18.9   The simplest way to fit a leeboard (inside view)

A more sophisticated and adjustable result will be achieved by means of a pivot bolt and wing nut on a purpose-built leeboard bracket.

*Photo 18.10   The simplest way to fit a lee-
board (outside view)*

Rudder

A rudder can be mounted with small dinghy fittings bolted to the end of the canoe.

*Photo 18.11   A neat and effective rudder
and mounting – very little hardware is left on
the canoe when the rudder is removed*

Alternately, it can be fitted by means of a purpose built strap-on mount.

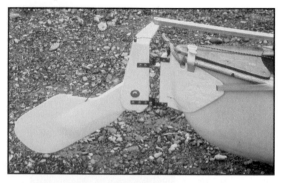

*Photo 18.12   A 'strap-on' rudder and mount-
ing – nothing is left on the canoe when the
rudder is removed and there are no holes in
the canoe*

Conditions and Safety

In choosing where and when to go sailing in a canoe, it is probably best to be guided by your answer to the question, "Would I be able to paddle the canoe here and in these conditions?" After all, if something goes wrong you may have to paddle back anyway. Many sheltered stretches of inland water such as ponds, small lakes or reservoirs and even some canals and slow-moving rivers are great places to experiment with sailing a canoe. Some people find that repeated paddling on a familiar stretch of water becomes tedious but sailing there can bring a whole new dimension to the rewards offered by paddlesport.

Wind Strength

Choosing the right sort of wind strength, especially when trying sailing for the first time, is important. Too much wind can be worrying and things may happen too fast to keep up with, while too little wind can result in frustration and confusion. What weather forecasts describe as light winds, Beaufort Scale Force 2 to 3, (between 3 and 12 mph), are ideal for learning and experimentation, (for more detail see the web-page: http://fp.ocsguk.f9.co.uk/ocsg_windscale.htm).

Extensive bodies of water such as large lakes and lochs can be good for sailing canoes, especially once some experience has been gained, but the potential for serious mishap must not be underestimated. Wind strength can increase, waves can build up quickly and the unwary canoe-sailor can be vulnerable, caught out on open water, far distant from the shore, shelter and safety. Even the assumed reassurance of other canoes nearby may not be of any real use as canoes under sail can travel at very different rates and therefore easily become separated. Even if another canoe is close by, the extra bits and pieces of the sailing kit can get in the way, making conventional rescue techniques impractical. Therefore the canoe sailor should ensure that self-rescue is possible, well thought out and practised.

Self-rescue and Buoyancy

Plenty of supplementary buoyancy, usually in the form of air bags, is essential to make self-rescue feasible. Some successful methods, once the canoe has been righted, include: first baling some water out (while still outside the canoe) before climbing back in; or climbing back in and then baling out the water, provided there is sufficient (that is, loads of) buoyancy. Some people improvise a temporary out-rigger with, for example, a paddle and an airbag to provide enough stability to re-enter the canoe.

Spares and Repairs

As with any canoe expedition, remote from assist-ance, the need to carry appropriate spares, tools and gear should be considered carefully. An 'incident bag' containing a few lengths of cord, some spare nuts, bolts and fittings relevant to the canoe and rig is well worth carrying to save a long paddle home should something fail. A spare paddle is particularly important when sailing; if you are paddle steering and drop it, in an instant, you lose your ability to steer and make progress! Take spare clothes as the clothing necessary to stay comfortable and warm is often more than that required when paddling, as you are not working as hard.

Further Reading

Sail your Canoe, Bull J, UK, Cordee
Canoes Under Sail, Bull J (no ISBN number and privately published by Solway Dory, 2 The Avenue, Grange-over-Sands, Cumbria, LA116AP. Tel: 015395 33878)
The Lines of Sailing Canoes, Bull J, UK, Solway Dory
American Red Cross Handbook (Chapter 14), 1985, USA, ISBN: 038508313
Canoe Rig: The Essence and the Art: Sailpower for Antique and Traditional Canoes, Bradshaw T, Wooden Boat Publications, ISBN: 0937822574
Open Canoe Technique (Chapter 16), Foster N, Fernhurst, UK, ISBN: 1898660263
History of Canoe Sailing, Bull J, UK, Solway Dory
The Clyde Canoe Club, Poskitt J, UK, Solway Dory (Early recorded activities and adventures. 1874-1876 A compilation of newspaper and journal articles written by canoe sailors of the time about their racing and cruising exploits.)

Websites:

Open Canoe Sailing Group (a UK based club for canoe sailing) - ocsg.org.uk
American Canoe Association Sailing Committee - www.enter.net/~skimmer
Open Canoe Sailor International Site - www.users.globalnet.co.uk/~johnbull
Solway Dory - Sailing canoes, rigs, plans, books and accessories - www.solwaydory.fsnet.co.uk
Tyrone Boats Sailing canoes, boat builder, kits and plans (Northern Ireland) - ws4.u-net.net/~tyrone
Selway Fisher. Plans for building sailing canoes - www.selway-fisher.com/
A site on how to set up a canoe for sailing - homepages.apci.net/~michalak/1jun01.htm#SAIL AREA MATH

Keith Morris

Messing about in boats is very much a part of Keith's life, starting as a child when his family bought a tiny dinghy. Shortly after, he tried a friend's kayak on the Severn near Worcester, where he lived. Since then he has paddled and/or sailed as many boats as he can, both in his professional and recreational life, in Europe and the United States of America.

A BCU Level 5 Coach and Royal Yachting Association Senior Instructor, he was RCO for Cumbria for 9 years and is a founder member and past Chairman of the Open Canoe Sailing Group, cur-rently acting as its Training Advisor and Website Author/Manager. He has worked in Outdoor Education and Training throughout his career and at present is Technical Services Manager for a manage-ment development company based in the Lake District.

19 International Canoe Sailing

"After sailing a canoe anything else is like kissing your sister." - Bill Kempner

Introduction

Sailing can be at local, national and world level. Canoe sailors are extremely friendly and helpful. There are winter training events to help new and older sailors hone their skills.

Sailing canoes can cost from a few hundred to a few thousand pounds. The low cost ones are not usually much slower and can be a real bargain.

In 1865 John Macgregor paddled and sailed his canoe across Europe before writing the book that inspired the birth of recreational canoeing. From that moment, paddling and sailing began to separate and each has become more specialised to improve performance.

Sailing canoes became bigger, to carry more sail, and developed differently in the UK, US and in Sweden.

International competition first started in 1884 though events were infrequent. In 1933, Britain's Uffa Fox and Roger de Quincy ingeniously decided they could build a sailing canoe that would conform to both the British and US rules, and challenged for the New York Cup, which they won.

The result of the 1933 meeting was the adoption of the 'International Rules', which have formed the basis for international competition since then. At first the dimensions allowed considerable development, but in 1971 it was restricted to become a one-design hull. The sail area totals 10 square metres, giving the canoe its full name, the International 10 square metre Canoe, or IC.

The International Sailing Canoe has been for many years the fastest single-handed sailing boat around an Olympic course. An IC can achieve speeds of 16-17 knots (19mph).

Boat Description

Hull

The hull is designed to a one-class rule for even competition, and built to minimum weight for performance; it is strong and durable. Modern canoes have been built from different materials including wood, glass-fibre and carbon, and kevlar reinforced sandwich laminates. Top performance lasts for many years and they are usually very well looked after.

The canoe retains its distinctive and fast canoe shaped stern.

Sails

These are usually a jib and a mainsail that total 10 sq metres, but recently some ICs have fitted an asymmetric spinnaker to improve off wind performance. They are raced in a subdivision of the class, called an AC (asymmetric canoe).

Photo 19.1   Out on the seat

Seat

Perhaps the IC's most distinctive feature is its sliding seat. This places the canoe-sailor off the gunwale to balance the wind's power. The seat provides a huge righting moment in heavier winds, which in turn develops speed.

When tacking or gybing (which is when the IC changes direction so that the wind comes from the opposite side of the sail), the seat is thrown across to the opposite (upwind) side.

Foils

The IC holds its track on the water by a daggerboard or centreboard. The former is by far the most popular, and usually faster option unless the sailor is sailing in shallow waters.

The IC is steered by a rudder, which is held in a cassette in the stern.

Controls

Controls are very much a personal choice, and can be simple to control the position and tension in the sails, and the position of the daggerboard, or extremely sophisticated, to control the angle and tension in the rig, slide the seat carriage forward and aft, and much more.

The rudder is steered by a tiller extension, so that it can be operated from the end of the sliding seat.

There are no restrictions on controls so all canoes are personalised, but essentially most controls will be brought to just in front of the sliding seat for the easiest access.

How to Sail the Canoe

Believe it or not, the canoe is not too difficult to sail, if you are reasonably fit, and can get your timing whilst tacking and gybing. The main difference between the IC and dinghies is speed. It is at its best in Force 3- 4 winds, and if on flat water on a reach it is almost unbeatable by any sailing dinghy. Manoeuvring through a corner is the hardest part, as speed and timing are essential if it's windy.

Tacking

In light wind tacking, (that's going upwind) you have much more time to come in from the seat, uncleat the jib, pull the seat across to the other side, whilst steering the canoe across to the next tack, which automatically begins the cleating of the jib on that tack. The wind will fill into the jib giving you some support to go onto the seat, pulling the jib fully in, and then moving further out on the seat whilst hauling in on the mainsail. Sounds a lot, but it can take less than 3 seconds for the complete manoeuvre.

Photo 19.2   Beating to windward (tacking)

Gybing

Raise your daggerboard/centreboard, leave about 15cms down, hold the mainsheet and tiller in your downwind hand, and squat in the centre of the boat. As you bring the IC to run downwind, un-cleat the jib and get the mainsail to come across whilst starting to slide the seat upwind, (swapping hands with mainsheet and tiller as you go). Then, depending on the wind strength, move to lean or sit on the seat. Trim the sails, balance the IC and blast off again. Being out on the end of the seat is sensational and comfortable.

Capsizing

Tacking or gybing is the most common cause of capsize, though a mistake can usually be corrected quickly and the capsize averted. A canoe can be brought back up quickly, by getting on to the dagger/centreboard, and as it's a closed deck boat it doesn't flood. During recovery, the IC will sail off quite quickly as it's completing being righted, so during racing a capsize is not always a disaster.

Where Sailed

Due to its speed, the IC is at its best on an open stretch of water, with low land and minimal trees, hills or buildings to deflect the wind's direction. Canoes are sailed regularly at several inland sites (usually attached to large lakes and reservoirs) and coastal clubs.

Few paddlers have tried the IC, which is a great shame. The exhilaration develops with the wind's strength; it can be docile and balanced, and it can be wild and hairy, depending on the wind and the sailor's skill. I'm a paddler who had never sailed before, and took up IC sailing in my thirties. I can say that I wish I had started younger. It's a canoeing experience for the slightly extrovert of all ages from teens to the sixties, rich in history and thrills. Unless there are extremely light winds, an IC is always a challenge, hence the quote at the beginning of this chapter, and that is its enduring attraction.

Great Boats to Get Started With

The Class Association can be contacted through www.intcanoe.org, and will give you up to date information on all aspects of the class, second-hand boats and where they are being sailed. BCU members who become IC sailors will be sent the excellent Class Association's newsletter 'The Sliding Seat'.

Websites:

www.intcanoe.org - To contact the International Sailing Canoe Class Association

Graham Mackereth

Graham started canoeing when he was 15 years old with a £12 Granta Kingfisher double. He and his scouting friends started building and racing their own boats, and he designed and built his first boat in the summer holidays of 1967. Before long he was competing at international level in marathon, sprint and wild water racing.

In 1971 he started up Pyranha and, although in 1972 he was a part of the Munich Olympic Team, he decided to retire from serious competitive paddling. However, his competitive instinct remained so he took up sailing an International Canoe, an activity where he has had some success and a great deal of enjoyment.

His passion for design has found success and an outlet in a number of ways, World Championship winning slalom designs from 1977 to 1985 (mainly in co-operation with Albert Kerr and Richard Fox), expedition designs that started with Mike Jones' 1976 Everest Expedition, and currently pushing the limits with freestyle and advanced white water designs.

20 Sea Kayaking

I'm setting out across an oily calm sea with a group of friends. We have a few days off work and have decided to try to get to Mingulay yet again, our previous attempts having been curtailed due to the weather conditions.

As we cross the sound of Barra the only sounds we hear are the water dripping from the paddles and the distant call of the oystercatchers on a nearby island. Then it happens... there is an explosion within ten metres of us. A Bottlenose Dolphin surfaces, blows then disappears. We stop, looking around for another glimpse of this wonderful creature, and suddenly the whole sea comes alive. A school of about sixteen adult and young dolphins are cavorting around us, some are completely clear of the water but most are content to come straight towards the kayaks then dive underneath us. As they swim below we can see them in the crystal clear water. We slow down for a better look at them and they move away into the distance, but when we start to paddle again they are back.

Transport to Survive

The word kayak means 'hunter's boat' in Inuit. The boat's primary purpose was to hunt animals on inland lakes, rivers and the sea. A look at the native Greenland and Alaskan kayaks reveals a wide range of designs. Each has evolved as suitable for the region that it comes from.

The range of commercially available specialist sea kayaks is also huge and, with many manufacturers competing for the top sales, competition is fierce.

Sadly, most sea kayaks are available in one size due to the design costs. What this means is that if you are smaller or larger than the person the kayak was designed around then it will not perform in the same manner.

Where Can Kayaks Go?

It is more often the experience, expertise and nerve of the kayaker, rather than the limits of the vessel that dictate what is possible. Numerous circumnavigations, crossings and exposed coastlines have all been kayaked successfully, and undoubtedly more will be ticked off in the future (see Chapter 1).

Types of Kayak

The traditional kayak was for a single person, and most still are, although in Scotland double kayaks have been in use for many years. In the rest of Britain doubles are going through a period of revival.

Photo 20.1   Composite, hard chine hull

Photo 20.2   Polyethylene, slow, stable design

Photo 20.3 Folding sea kayak

Most kayaks are now made of fibreglass, plastic or kevlar, although some enthusiasts still design and manufacture their own kayaks using the 'stitch and glue' plywood method or canvas with an internal wooden framework.

Folding sea kayaks are also going through a period of revival, in part due to the portability of these craft and increased access to travel. Imagine a serious sea kayak that can be carried on an aircraft in a duffel bag to some remote part of the world. The frames and longitudinals (lengthways supports) are generally manufactured from aircraft-grade aluminium, which is then covered with a hi-tech flexible material such as 'hypalon'. Some designs utilise an inflatable tube around the gunwales to tension the skin. The disadvantages of this type of kayak are cost and the amount of care required when launching and landing.

Kayak Design

The dominant forces acting on the kayak are wind and wind-generated waves. A kayak should move forwards and track in a straight line. Constant corrections to keep the boat heading on course waste energy that could be used to keep the boat moving ahead, and reduce the distance travelled for the energy expended.

As with people, not all sea kayaks are created equal. Long, narrow kayaks are fast and unstable; short, wide-bodied kayaks are slow and stable. That is a reasonable rule of thumb to use in beginning a discussion of sea kayak design. The kayaks that influenced our designs of today were built from wood covered with skin. This meant that tight curves and concave shapes could not be achieved. A few thousand years of aboriginal development, updated with new designs and materials technology, have evolved kayak designs that avoid the extremes and provide well-balanced performance.

The majority of sea kayaks are between 4.5 metres and 6 metres long and between 53cm and 81cm wide. They tend to curve slightly from bow to stern (rocker), as this makes for a kinder ride, and they generally have an upward-curving bow which lets water be moved sideways rather than have the kayak plunge below the surface. The front deck is usually peaked, which allows water to run off before it hits the paddler in the chest.

A sea-touring kayak is defined by function more than form. Most of us prefer a boat that will paddle easily, will be kind to us when the water gets rough, and is suited to our style of paddling, body size, and equipment storage requirements.

Hull Shape

Sea kayaks of all shapes and sizes have been outstanding successes, with performance differences more often a function of paddling conditions and the height, weight and ability of the paddler (see Chapter 2).

Manoeuvrability

Manufacturers design long hulls for sea kayaks because longer, narrower boats are faster and track better (tracking is the boat's ability to go in a straight line). A sea kayak hull of similar design more noticeably resists turning than a shorter hull of similar width. If you paddle a shorter kayak and then a longer kayak back to back, you will notice that the bow of the shorter boat moves off course more readily with each power stroke than the bow of the longer touring kayak.

The bottom shape of a kayak is the performance factor, affecting a kayak's ability to go straight or to turn. The keel, the bottom profile of a kayak from bow to stern, is not a straight line, but is shaped like the rocker in a rocking chair. Most boats will have the ends of the keel (at the bow and stern) from 80mm to 150mm higher than the middle. The middle serves as a pivot point, allowing the boat to turn. Boats with plenty of 'rocker' turn easily, boats with very little 'rocker' track well. As ever it is a trade-off: boats that track are harder to turn, whereas boats that turn easily are more difficult to paddle in a straight line.

Speed

The friction or hull drag created by a long boat will soon sap the strength of most recreational paddlers, so the theoretical maximum speed is never reached. Most recreational paddlers cruise at no more than three knots. Conclusion: theoretical maximum hull speed is not that important for most people.

Cockpit Size

Photo20.4   Traditional small cockpit

Traditionally sea kayaks had small cockpit openings so that spraydecks wouldn't collapse under the weight of a large wave. Modern neoprene materials have allowed designers to incorporate the larger 'keyhole' style cockpits into their kayaks.

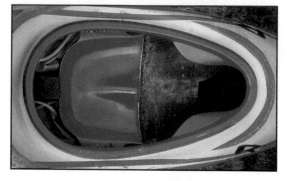

Photo 20.5   Keyhole cockpit (easy to get out of)

Body shape

It may be hard for guys to accept, but women enjoy some anatomical advantages when it comes to paddling sea kayaks. More of a woman's body weight is distributed below the waist in comparison to a man, giving her a lower centre of gravity in a boat.

As a result of this lower centre of gravity, many women may fit comfortably into the narrower, low-volume, high-performance boats that would be too tight or unstable for taller, more top-heavy men. The narrow hull also provides an easier reach for paddles, and the greater hull efficiency can offset any strength advantage a male paddling companion might enjoy. So it turns out that women are more likely to be a natural fit for the higher-performance hulls that some larger men covet but cannot fit.

Materials

Composite

The majority of the sea kayaks available in Britain are of the composite variety, carbon-fibre, kevlar and epoxy being the top of the range, and GRP or fibreglass being the most widely used. Carbon-fibre and kevlar are specialist materials and as such require special manufacturing techniques. They give a high strength to weight ratio with regard to impact damage, however the abrasion resistance is less than that of a GRP kayak. These space age materials are also very expensive and are more likely to degrade due to UV light. These kayaks are lighter, stiffer and faster than the ones described below.

Rotomoulded Polyethylene

Polyethylene sea kayaks made their debut in 1984 with the 'Aquaterra Chinook'. A few companies are producing top quality designs and these are gaining in popularity due to the forgiving nature of their construction. They are harder wearing than their corresponding composite kayaks, although not quite indestructible and are substantially cheaper.

Colour

Colours are an important choice for any sea kayaker. Research carried out by various bodies including the Coastguard, RAF and RNLI has found that the most visible colours are alternate bands of light and dark. You may have noticed that all hazards at airports are painted alternately red and white.

Choice of colour is a combination of personal preference and safety. Most sea kayakers would prefer to have a kayak that is a subtle colour that blends in with the surroundings. However, the same kayaker would also want his kayak to be highly visible when crossing a shipping lane or if a rescue became necessary.

Hatches

I can't think of any modern sea kayak that does not have fitted bulkheads. These create watertight compartments which, as well as buoyancy, also provide storage space. To access this space some type of waterproof hatch is needed.

The three most popular are:

The VCP Round or Oval Hatch

Photo 20.6   VCP hatch

The Kayaksport Design

This is similar to the VCP but has larger openings and a slightly more flexible cover.

The Gaybo/Vynek Type

This is like a small cockpit with a neoprene deck that fits over the top. The neoprene is sometimes protected with a hard cover, secured in place with a webbing strap, to stop most water hitting the neoprene.

Hatch Systems

The vast majority of sea kayaks have a three-hatch set up, with the front and rear hatches used primarily for the storing of equipment that is not likely to be used when at sea.

Photo 20.7 The Kayaksport design hatch

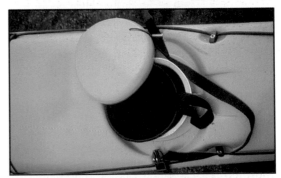

Photo 20.8   Neoprene deck hatch

Photo 20.9   Three hatch system

The third, which is situated behind the cockpit, can be used for items that may be required throughout the day's journey. Due to the small internal volume of this area it would not be too much of a disaster if this filled completely with water.

Top Tip – Hatch care

Regardless of the type of hatch cover fitted, all should be tied to the kayak with a short length of cord. This will ensure that in the event of dropping it in the briny the contents of Davy Jones's locker are not swelled by your equipment. As we know, all plastics and rubber are subject to UV degradation; hatch covers are no different. A good idea is that when you are not using your kayak, remove all the hatches, clean with fresh water and store in a dry dark place. This will ensure a longer life for these expensive items and also enables the kayak to dry out. Perhaps once or twice a year it is also advisable to coat the hatch covers with a silicone spray.

Decklines

Most sea kayaks nowadays are fitted with decklines that go around the edge of the boat. These enable a swimmer to hold onto something secure if they are in the water. They are invaluable when performing any type of rescue, as a wet kayak is unbelievably slippery. They also provide a strong tie-in point to prevent deck accessories like pumps or maps being swept into the water.

Pump

Although a sponge or a bailer is a reasonable way to remove water from a kayak, neither is entirely practical whilst at sea. Pumps for sea kayaks come in many forms. Perhaps the simplest is the stirrup type, which is held and operated in a similar manner to a bicycle pump. These are cheap and portable, but the major drawback is that both hands are used when emptying your boat, and most stirrup pumps do not float! Some manufacturers offer a deck-mounted pump that can be either front or rear deck-mounted. For the front deck-mounted pump a removable handle, tied to the kayak, enables a back and forth movement. This is probably the most effective hand-operated pump as it is possible to pump whilst holding onto your paddle and perhaps supporting yourself. Pumps fitted to the rear deck were the norm until a few years ago. They were very awkward to operate by yourself.

Electrically operated pumps have been around for a few years but have not really caught on due to the weight of the unit and battery life. They can how-ever remove a large amount of water easily and, if the spraydeck is replaced, it is possible to paddle whilst the kayak is emptying.

Compass

For most of the kayaking that we do a simple orienteering type handheld compass will suffice. A deck-mounted compass is invaluable if you are likely to be carrying out any type of open crossing. These, however, are expensive and are also vulnerable to damage. There are several types available, with the choice being one of economics. The mounting position is critical; if it is too close to you the constant looking down will, more than likely, upset your stomach and leave you feeling queasy. Too far away and you will struggle to read the degrees. Somewhere around the front hatch would appear to be the optimum position for most paddlers.

Photo 20.10   Compass fitted well forward to avoid sea sickness!

Rudder/Skeg

Rudders are fitted to approximately 15% of all British sea kayaks. The rudder should not be considered to be an additional turning contraption, more of an effort-saving device. Unfortunately many rudders fail at the most inappropriate time and paddlers who have come to rely on them find that they do not necessarily have the skills required to manage their kayak.

Retractable Skegs

These are now fitted as standard to many sea kayaks and are probably the best compromise between a fixed skeg and rudder. For most people, the skeg is used as an on/off control. However with a bit of thought it can be used to assist turning. If you are paddling along and the conditions worsen (usually the wind increasing) the kayak may try to turn into the wind with the skeg in the fully up position. If the skeg is then put into the fully down position the kayak is most likely to turn away from the wind. This is due to the pivot point of the kayak being moved towards the rear of the kayak. The trim of the kayak or how you pack your equipment has a similar effect.

From this it can be seen that the retractable skeg is a variable trim control, and the best way to find out the limitations to its use is to get out and use it. What we are trying to achieve is straight tracking with little or no turning effect due to the weather. An important point to remember is that as the weather conditions change or you adjust your heading to them, then the skeg will probably also need adjusting to keep the kayak going in the direction that you want. During high wind turns, the skeg can be put to good use to allow the kayak to turn into or away from the wind.

Once afloat it is imperative that all rudders and skegs are checked to ensure that they are fully operational before you proceed. As a result of their exposed position on the keel of the kayak, skegs are likely to become jammed with small stones or

clogged with mud after launching. Fastening a short length of cord to the skeg can be a great help in enabling a skeg to be freed off when afloat.

Photo 20.11   Short line attached to skeg

Paddle Design

A Bit of History

Our sea kayaking forefathers, the Inuit, used what was available to them to make all their equipment. It has long been believed that Inuit paddles were made the shape they were due to the size of the pieces of driftwood that were strewn along their shores. We

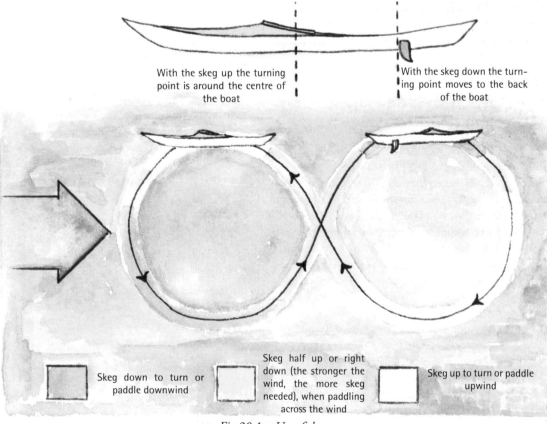

With the skeg up the turning point is around the centre of the boat

With the skeg down the turning point moves to the back of the boat

Skeg down to turn or paddle downwind

Skeg half up or right down (the stronger the wind, the more skeg needed), when paddling across the wind

Skeg up to turn or paddle upwind

Fig 20.1   Use of skegs

now know that this is not the case. A lot of the timber that fell into the major rivers of the north was carried by the currents and ice and deposited all along the Arctic shorelines. Driftwood could be collected by the indigenous peoples and used in the manufacture of a variety of different pieces of equipment. The paddle was one of these pieces of equipment, and evolved over millennia into the classic long, narrow shape that we are familiar with.

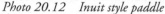

Photo 20.12   Inuit style paddle

There are several reasons for the distinctive narrow blade shape:

- It was easier to manufacture.
- It was less likely to split or break.
- It presented less area to a headwind.
- It gave less of an outline for the hunted animal to see.
- It was less noisy when hunting.

The main reason though was probably one of control; this type of paddle could be gripped at any point along both the shaft *and* the blade.

The paddle was required to perform a large number of specific tasks. It was needed to right the kayak after a capsize, stabilise the kayak in rough seas or when hunting, to assist a fellow kayaker to right his craft and, of course, for propulsion. Clearly, the Inuit had to use his piece of driftwood for much the same things that we would use our carbon, asymmetric, wide bladed, feathered, modified crank, lightweight paddles of today.

Asymmetric Blades

There is a vast array of blade type and areas available, with asymmetric designs being the most popular. The blade area in some cases, especially in smaller paddlers or women, does need to be reduced and some manufacturers are now responding to this need.

With a few exceptions, the majority of sea paddlers in Britain use asymmetric paddles for sea kayaking. There are a few reasons for this:

- The blade shape is more efficient than symmetrical blades.
- It reduces the twisting motion associated with symmetrical blades, (which can cause wrist injuries).
- It enters and exits the water cleanly.
- It is possible to co-ordinate kayak and paddle colour.

One disadvantage of using an asymmetric blade is that, because of its thin profile (thickness), it is very unforgiving if the blade angle is set incorrectly by the paddler. For example when sculling or rolling, the blade can have a tendency to dive sharply. This can cause problems for some paddlers when trying to master certain strokes.

Length

As a rough guideline, and if we follow the Inuit kayakers before us, the usual upstretched arm (when standing up), with hand curled over the top of the blade is a good starting point, although there is now a trend to go even shorter. Using a paddle that is too long will reduce the stroke rate and the angle of the shaft to the water but will also put more strain on all the joints of the arm, possibly leading to injury. The antithesis is too short a paddle; the result then would be a high paddling action with an increase in stroke rate. Although this places less strain on the joints per stroke the increased rate may mean that injury is as likely as with a long paddle. A short paddle will also make turning and supporting strokes slightly more difficult due to the decrease in leverage.

Wings

Wing paddles (specialist racing blades) have not yet caught on in recreational sea kayaking; perhaps this is due to the amount of time required to master the technique and also their unforgiving nature in certain stroke work. They are, however, quite frequently seen at sea kayak races.

Shaft

There are now probably as many shaft types and materials as there are blade types, the Lendal modified crank now becoming the favourite in some form of flexible carbon-fibre material.

Feather

Feather (relative angle of the blades), and to some extent whether there should be any at all, is under continuous debate. Whatever feels comfortable, use it! Lendal use 70 degrees as their 'standard' feather and I have used 60 degrees for a long time.

Latest Developments

In recent years there has been incredible progress made in paddle design and construction technology.

The variable length and feather joint by Lendal is very handy and allows the angle of feather to be easily changed whilst on the move. The even newer Paddlok system brings portability and enables blade changes with no loss of efficiency and performance.

Do not be led completely by what experts or your friends have... experiment and see what works for you.

Packing a Kayak

When going to sea it is important to ensure that you have all the things you will require for your trip to hand as when you are out at sea you cannot land and gain easy access to any items needed. An often-overlooked aspect of packing is that of trim.

Trim affects the kayak in the same way that the retractable skeg does; too much weight at the stern will cause it to turn downwind and too much at the bow will cause it to turn upwind.

Loaded or Empty

The first thing that most people will notice when sitting in a laden kayak is the increase in stability; the second is how much more effort is required to get the boat up to cruising speed. More important than this though is how much effort is needed to stop the thing. The extra momentum created by this added weight is something to consider if attempting Eskimo rescues or indulging in a spot of rock hopping.

Ballast

If your kayak is 'twitchy' when packed for a day trip, you may find it helpful to add ballast. Different types of ballast that can be carried are sandbags, lead sheet or off-cuts in a BDH container, or water bottles.

When adding ballast or packing a kayak for a long trip, the bulk of the weight should be kept:

- in the middle of the kayak
- away from the ends
- as low as possible

- close to the centre line of the kayak
- securely fastened in place

Adjusting Trim

If you were intending to run downwind, and there is a possibility of landing on a surf beach, pack the bow lighter than the stern . This will help the kayak keep on course in a following sea and give more buoyancy in the bow to help stop it burying. This assumes that the weather will not change and your planned trip will not change either. It is usually best to load the kayak in such a manner that it is 'neutral handling' (does not turn into or away from the wind). Then, if plans or weather change, you will not be struggling to control an unwieldy boat.

Stuff on Deck

Many sea paddlers have also developed the habit of loading gear onto the decks of their kayaks until it looks like a bulk carrier! This can play a huge factor in the handling characteristics of the kayak. Moving it from one part of the kayak to another, or better still removal, may be just what is needed.

Adjusting trim will not rectify poor design characteristics of a kayak but it can go a long way to help.

Personal Equipment

Comfort

Choice of personal equipment is very important, as you will probably be wearing it for long periods of time. Comfort is of prime importance to the sea kayaker and most tend to wear layers of fleece or fibre-pile tops and trousers, or salopettes. Unfortunately the majority of these are not windproof so it is a good idea to have a pair of windproof trousers available for when you land. Many people still prefer to wear a long john type wetsuit, which does not interfere with the paddling action and will not chafe the tender underarm area.

Footwear

Some form of footwear (see Chapter 3) should be used, due to the mess that our shores are in with the likes of broken bottles and discarded plastics.

Foul Weather Gear

Care should be taken in the choice of protective clothing. A dry-cag which keeps all the water out is not the most comfortable thing to wear all day, especially if the weather improves and necessitates its removal.

Paddling Jacket

A paddling jacket that seals well at the cuffs is a good idea on rough days. This should stop that horrible rush of cold water that always finds its way to the warmest, driest part of you should you lift your arm above your head. A hood that is adjustable and can be tightened around the face is also very handy.

True Story

A good friend of mine was out with a group of friends. He stopped and started to take off his dry cag. Just when he got it over his head, he capsized. You can imagine the scene, an experienced paddler, whom everyone knows can roll first time, is upside down. What his friends did not realise was that he was trapped and didn't have his paddle. Someone eventually decided that something was not quite right and paddled over to see what was happening. When they reached the kayak they could see the poor victim hanging from the cockpit, trussed up like someone in a straightjacket. He was very quickly pulled up the right way but it took him a long time to recover from the lack of breath. The paddler who pulled him out of the water said that he had gone blue and had stopped struggling. Beware!

Trousers

Wind and waterproof trousers or salopettes are a good idea unless you enjoy sitting in a pool of water all day. Even if you do not wear them whilst in the kayak it is a good idea to have them handy for when you come ashore.

Drysuits

If there is the chance that you will be spending a substantial amount of time in the water a dry suit could be a good investment, although there will probably be a build up of condensation on the inside. Using a breathable drysuit may help this problem, although to work correctly the outside of the garment has to be dry. Cost is the limiting factor here.

Buoyancy Aid or Lifejacket

A buoyancy aid is probably more suited to the sea kayaker as it provides more than just additional buoyancy. A few pockets for storing the items that could be required throughout a day's paddle such as flares, first aid kit, small repair kit and some energy bars are handy. Some paddlers have taken to wearing an inflatable type lifejacket. This, although unrestrictive, does not give any insulation to your body.

Other Items

A warm fleece hat and a sun hat should be carried to cope with our changeable weather. Other items that should be kept handy include:

- Sun glasses
- Sun block cream
- Lip salve
- 'Pogies' or 'palmless' neoprene mittens (in winter)

Spraydecks are covered in Chapter 3.

Planning a Trip

When planning a trip on the sea there are very many factors to be taken into account:

1. Let someone know what your plans are. The coastguard will not automatically search for you if you fail to report a safe arrival. It is the responsibility of the shore contact to raise the alarm with the coastguard if they are concerned for your safety.

2. Take into account how weather, tide and the nature of the coastline interact. What hazards will this combination create? Can you avoid them, or are you prepared to deal with them?

Potential hazards include:

- Offshore winds
- Lack of access and egress
- Prominent headlands and points
- Dumping surf (See Chapter 21)
- Wind against tide
- Tide races and overfalls

Map or Chart?

Ignoring tidal streams (for the moment), most coastal navigation on simple waters can be done using a 'Silva' type compass and an appropriate map. Large-scale OS maps show lots of information of use to sea kayakers; this includes obvious landmarks, structures, and roads as well as the lay of the land.

1:25,000 Maps

The 1:25,000 series serves well where detail is required (harbours, estuaries, etc.) One side covers about 20km, which in a sea kayak amounts to about three hours paddling. If you were to use these maps it would mean that you would need to carry a map library for a good day's paddling.

1:50,000 Maps

The 1:50,000 series shows less detail but covers a larger area. Such maps are very useful for getting around in general, allowing the identification of coastal features even when travelling at a good cruising speed. Access and egress points are obvious, as are escape routes, telephones, toilets and more.

Keeping Track of Your Position

Before looking at charts, bear in mind that a good navigator is constantly aware of the surroundings. Most navigation can be done without the compass in good weather. A good navigator absorbs details of the situation and compares this with the map, keeping the two matched. Look out for natural features, have an idea of your speed, the state of the tide, the strength and direction of the tide streams, the effect of the prevailing weather conditions and the time taken to complete each leg. The compass is a true and trusty tool, but failure to keep track of where you are is inexcusable. Remember why you went out; it is easy to follow a strict compass bearing and become oblivious to what is going on around you.

Transits

Transits are a useful way to establish your position and to assess your rate of drift in a tidal stream or strong wind. (See Fig 20.2)

Nautical Charts

A chart is essentially a map for seagoers, consequently much more emphasis is placed on matters relating to the sea.

Charts show details of:

- Buoyage
- Lights and Transits
- Traffic arrangements
- Coastal features (coastline, landmarks, and prominent features)
- Seabed features (form, depth, type and hazards)
- Tidal streams and direction (at various states of the tide)

Large vessels the world over make great use of Admiralty charts produced by the Hydrographic Survey of Her Majesty's Royal Navy. Small craft (yachts and especially kayaks) often operate differently from very large vessels, so a form of chart dedicated to small craft users has evolved. They are sold as yachting charts, but are of great use to sea kayakers. A good example is the Imray series (Imray, Laurie, Norrie and Wilson); these make good use of colour and some are even waterproof. Recently, Admiralty charts have produced a small craft series of charts in much the same format. These charts show all you would find on the Admiralty charts, with insets of harbours and key areas in lots of detail. They also list useful suppliers of food, fuel and spares, telephone numbers, VHF channels and some access and egress

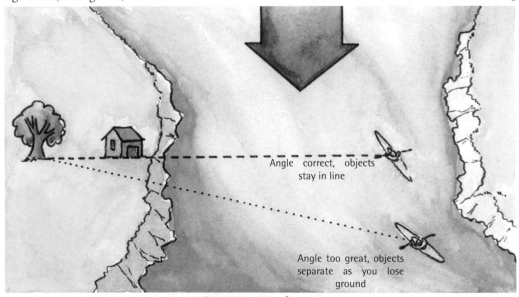

Angle correct, objects stay in line

Angle too great, objects separate as you lose ground

Fig 20.2   Use of transits

information. On the back of these charts is an 'aide memoire' giving lots of useful information normally found in a nautical almanac.

Pilots and Guidebooks

Most charts and tidal stream atlases are lacking in detail when it comes to what happens close inshore. Admiralty and yachtsman's pilots and canoeing specific guidebooks(where available) are very useful to paddlers as they cover the areas where we spend most of our time.

GPS

The Global Positioning System (GPS) provides anyone using a small satellite receiver with information on the current location of the receiver, twenty four hours a day, every day of the year, anywhere in the world. It should not be seen as a replacement for existing navigational skills but more of an add-on backup piece of kit. This said however, these units will enable the sea kayaker to accurately plot their position, route, distance covered and speed.

Tides

Tides are the periodic rise and fall of the sea due to the gravitational forces of the moon and sun on the oceans

of the earth. Generally speaking, tidal cycles contain two high tides and two low tides each day. The time between high and low tides is about 6 hours.

How do the effects of the sun and the moon affect tide? The gravitational pull of the moon tugs on the surface of the ocean until its surface mounds up and outward in the direction of the moon. When the mound of water has reached its highest point it is called high water. On the side of the earth opposite the moon, the centripetal force caused by the earth's rotation produces another mound of water and high water on the far side of the earth. Somewhere in between these two high tides, are two low points on the surface of the ocean, these are low waters.

The moon appears to rotate around the earth each day, however it is the earth's rotation that gives this appearance. The moon actually orbits the earth in an elliptical pattern, taking 27.3 days to complete one orbit. The length of time that it takes for the earth to rotate around, so that the moon is in the same position, is actually a little over a normal 24-hour day. It is 24 hours and 50 minutes or a tidal day. That is why the tidal cycle starts approximately 50 minutes later each day. So if you know that low water is at 0800 today you can estimate that it will be at 0850 tomorrow. As the earth rotates, the moon's gravitational force continually mounds the

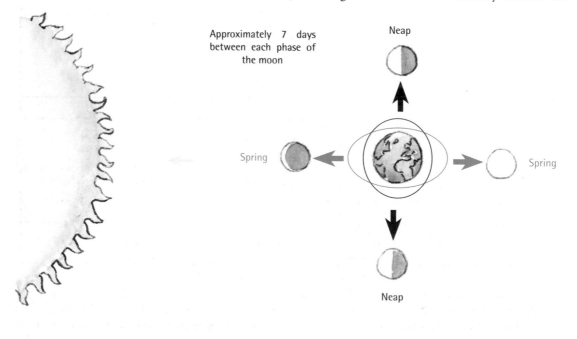

Fig 20.3   Relationship between the moon and 'Spring and 'Neap' tides

Source	Detail	Time	Notes
Radio			
Radio 4 LW	198 KHZ	00.48 05.35	Inshore waters
Radio 4 LW	198 KHZ	00.48 05.35 12.01 17.54	Shipping forecast
Radio Scotland	92.4 - 94 FM	Details in press	Good outdoor activity forecast
Local radio stations	Details in press	Details in press	General forecasts and small craft warnings
VHF			
HM Coastguard	Initial announcement CH 16 then 10 and/or 73 and exceptionally 67	As below every 4 hours starting at:	Inshore waters forecast as Radio 4
Swansea		00.05	
Thames		00.10	
Clyde		00.00	
Yarmouth		00.40	
Solent		00.40	
Brixham		00.50	
Dover		01.05	
Shetland		01.05	
Stornoway		01.10	
Pentland		01.35	
Falmouth		01.40	
Tyne Tees		01.50	
Forth		02.05	
Liverpool		02.10	
Portland		02.00	
Holyhead		02.35	
Oban		02.40	
Belfast		03.05	
Aberdeen		03.00	
Milford Haven		03.35	
Humber		03.40	
Telephone			
Marinecall	09068 505 3 + local number in telephone book under 'Weather' in business section	As required	60p/ minute
HM Coastguard	Local to area available in telephone book	As required	Inshore waters and strong winds forecast for your area
Fax			
	09065 200 5 + local number in telephone book under 'Weather' in business section	As required	£1.50/ minute

Table 20.1   Weather forecast sources

water and that fluid mound moves around the earth. The shape of the coastline and depth of the water influence the actual height of the tide.

Two other terms used in relation to tides are 'spring tides' and 'neap tides.' It was mentioned pre-viously that both the sun and the moon affect the tides. The sun's effect is less than half that of the moon, but when these two bodies are in alignment and pulling in the same direction they cause higher high tides and lower low tides called 'spring tides'.

On the other hand when the Sun and Moon are at right angles to one another with the moon pulling one direction and the sun pulling another there is somewhat of a cancelling effect and you get lower high tides and higher low tides called 'neap tides'.

Flood and Ebb

The rising water produces the flood and the fall of water the ebb.

Slack Water

There is a short period when the water is almost at a standstill, this is known as slack water. Slack water does *not* always correspond with HW and LW.

Range

The difference between high and low water is called the tidal range. For instance, if the water depth at high water is 4.9 metres and at low tide is 1.8 metres, the range would be 3.1 metres.

Calculations

Although there are irregularities in some parts of the world, as a general rule the following can be predicted using publications such as Tide Tables, Sailing Directions and Admiralty Pilots:

- Times of high and low water and depth of water at each of these times.
- Set (direction) and drift (distance covered) of strong tidal streams, including their maximum 'spring' rate.
- Times of slack water.

Further details on tides and information regarding calculating times of high and low water can be found in Sea Kayak Navigation (see Further Reading).

Weather

The weather probably has more effect on the sea kayaker than any other water user. Wind in particular can slow our progress to less than a snail's pace or it can throw us before it. It is therefore useful if we know where we can obtain a forecast and also interpret what it means. There are many good texts on weather theory. (See Further Reading)

Table 20.1 is a list of weather sources that are suitable for sea kayakers. Perhaps the easiest place to get a forecast from is the Internet, with many sites having suitable information. Television is also a good source as is the radio. Newspapers are fine to get an overview of the situation, but if kayaking away

from civilisation not a lot of use. Telephoning your local HM Coastguard is a good means of obtaining a forecast; it is also a good idea to ask if there are any strong winds forecast (Force 6 and above) as this can sometimes be left out of the general forecast.

Weather Forecast Sources

See Table 20.1

Equipment

The equipment that is carried does not vary too much whether you are intending to go out for a day trip or for a multi-day tour. You should always have close to hand and available at short notice the following:

- Map and Compass
- Some form of shelter
- Basic First Aid kit
- Basic repair kit
- Hot drink
- Whistle
- Towing system
- Spare food
- Flares
- Spare paddles

Elsewhere in the kayak the following should also be carried (for when you are ashore):

- Lunch, both food and drink
- Comprehensive First Aid kit
- Comprehensive repair kit
- Torch
- Dry warm clothing and shoes
- Money for phone, food or drink

All equipment carried should be kept dry, (See Chapter 16).

Wildlife

The best way to see wildlife is to travel in small groups, keep your eyes open and the noise to a minimum. Interesting things seen on a regular basis are basking shark, otter, grey and common seal, porpoise, dolphin and many species of whale, as well as a huge variety of sea and coastal fringe birds. (See Chapter 12)

Handling a Sea Kayak

Forward Paddling

It is important to be able to paddle from one place to another with the minimum expenditure of effort. Sea paddlers need to acquire a good working model of forward paddling and then develop the expertise to be able to modify it in the light of changing conditions.

When paddling into a headwind, whilst towing an incapacitated paddler, or having to push against a tidal race off a headland, it is necessary to have a paddling style which delivers maximum power. At other times, for example in strong winds or in a following sea, it is necessary to modify the forward paddling style. The ability to modify forward paddling is a skill that evolves with practice and experience.

There is no one method of paddling forward which will work in all situations, so always beware of the coach who is too prescriptive when it comes to technique. Forward paddling is one of the easiest strokes on which to receive feedback as regards its success. If you are moving forward then you have got something correct. It is more important to think about how much more effective your stroke can become. A more effective stroke will conserve energy and preserve your reserves, so that if the conditions deteriorate, (an approaching storm, increasing tidal streams, an injured paddler to tow), you have the reserves necessary to reach a position of safety in an appropriate physical and mental state.

Most paddlers use a backrest to provide support for the lower back. Beware of the large plastic ones, as they inhibit movement whilst sitting in the kayak (see Outfitting Your Kayak, Chapter 4).

Different Gears

It is useful to compare forward paddling to driving a car with a manual gearbox. Drivers use the gears to gain optimum performance from the car in terms of acceleration and for cruising over a long distance. Most paddlers lack the equivalent of a gearbox. Most of the time cruising is taking place in the equivalent of third gear, which is generally inefficient.

There are times though when it is indispensable to be able to vary the range of forward paddling techniques. One example is when having to cope with moving water. To make progress it may be necessary to paddle hard against the flow. Although technique is important, times do arise when the answer is short

bursts of power. Headwinds produce a similar effect although it can last for a much longer period of time. A third example is when a tow is necessary. The added weight of the paddler and kayak can dramatically increase the power required.

As with all other skills the only path to progress is quality practice. Too frequently with forward paddling, sights are set too low.

Paddling in a Following Sea

A following sea is probably the most difficult in which to maintain good group control. Novices and more experienced paddlers react in totally different ways. As the back of the kayak starts to rise, the natural tendency of the novice is to start reverse paddling; it is their way of maintaining control. The more experienced paddler will accelerate off down the face of the wave with shouts of joy, looking for the benefits of a free downhill ride.

Wait until the stern of the kayak starts to rise, then increase the stroke rate and lean forwards slightly. The kayak will then start to surf down the face of the wave. As the wave passes underneath and the bow starts to rise, ease off the paddling rate until the next wave starts to have an effect on the kayak.

Once the kayak starts to accelerate it is necessary to maintain directional control. Therefore, after the final power (forward paddling) stroke, instead of lifting the blade out of the water close to the hips, allow it to extend backwards into a stroke that is a hybrid between a stern rudder and a low brace.

During a journey with a following sea it is often difficult to hold a course, the kayak naturally wanting to broach. In this situation surf to the left on a number of waves then to the right on the same number. Great care is needed to ensure people have sufficient room to surf without collisions; it is also important not to get split up and lose group control or communication.

Stern Rudder (Steering)

The stern rudder is probably one of the most fundamental strokes in sea kayaking. Sea kayaks have momentum on their side, especially when loaded, so it can be used for fine, delicate manoeuvring or for powerful course changes and correction to great effect.

There are two versions of stern rudder:

1. The basic but more powerful version is where the blade is trailed towards the back of the

kayak, held vertically just below the surface and outwards or inwards pressure is applied to give the desired effect. This is ideal at lower speeds or where greater leverage is required, perhaps to check broaching.

2. The paddle is held in the same way, but tilting the top of the blade from the vertical outwards or inwards by about 30 degrees creates the turning effect. This works well for subtle control and is very effective at high speed, for example when surfing. In reality we probably use a combination of these strokes. Extending the effective lever by moving our hands along the shaft and placing the blade nearer the stern can have a marked effect.

Many paddlers feel unstable when they turn around to look behind them. Combining the stern rudder and a trailing low brace can give all the support they need, especially in choppy conditions.

Combining the stern rudder with edging can be a very potent technique and should be encouraged.

Turning

Sweep strokes to turn a sea kayak are applied in the same way as for any other kayak, the main difference being the length of the boat and the increase in water resistance. There is no way to overcome this resistance but we can do a few things that will enable us to make turning a bit easier:

1. If we examine the waterline we will see that by edging the kayak over, there will be less of it in the water, almost like having more rocker.

2. Why not extend your paddle? For too long we have been loath to move our hands from their original position. The kayaks are long and the paddles have more length than we would normally use.

Photo 20.13   Increasing leverage of paddle

Edging to Assist Turning

By edging a sea kayak we are generating the same assymetrical forces on the hull as for other craft. One difference is that, because of the length involved the turning effect can be quite dramatic. Some kayaks respond to more edging than others. This is due, in part, to the weight of the paddler and in part to the design of the kayak. Generally, edging the kayak to the left will initiate a turn to the right. Edging to the right initiates a turn to the left.

Perhaps a better way to visualise this is:

- To turn left, raise your left knee and lower your right knee.

- To turn right, raise your right knee and lower your left knee.

If you keep your body in a slightly forwards position you will find that the kayak will turn in a tighter circle.

Photo 20.14   Increased rocker obtained by tilting (edging) the kayak

High Wind Turn

In certain conditions, with some kayaks there comes a point when they will suddenly turn off downwind, and no amount of edging and extended sweeping will bring the kayak back to head into the wind. It can be very frightening to suddenly realise you have no control over your kayak and are being blown out to sea. The basic skills we have taught so far will get you out of trouble if applied in the correct sequence.

If the kayak will only run off downwind, *Stop!* Back paddle with full power. Once speed is gained, edge the kayak onto your stronger or favoured side, allow the keel to bite and induce a sharp turn, keep the power, sweep and edge until the stern is starting to point downwind. At this point, keeping the same amount of edge, reach forward and apply a very powerful extended lever sweep stroke on the downwind side. When all speed is lost, reapply the sweep stroke on the same side but change the edge to the opposite side. Continue with the same edge, sweep, and power method until control is regained.

Draw Stroke

The draw stroke is a close quarter manoeuvring stroke. Due to the variations in sea kayak design, hull shape, keel and the amount of equipment carried, you will need to experiment to find the balance point of your chosen boat. Once found however, tight spots (as often found in caves) can be negotiated with ease if the draw is applied anywhere in the arc from the bow to the stern.

Photo 20.15   Tilt towards the draw stroke

I would advise edging the kayak in the direction of travel as much as possible without allowing water to pile up on the back deck.

Bow Rudder

Using the classic bow rudder in a sea kayak with any forward speed is guaranteed to have shoulders popping out of joint all over the place. This said, applied with care, subtlety and cunning it is the fastest turning stroke available in a sea kayak. Used in a quadrant from opposite the hips to the area of the feet, it can have a varying effect on the kayak, from drawing the kayak sideways when opposite the hips, to creating a turn when moved further forward. Only the individual will be able to feel the effect it is having on the kayak and then fine tuning it to the specific need at the time.

Try paddling forward to gain some speed. Apply the draw opposite the hips, the blade feathered into

the water and feel the effect on the kayak. Try again, but this time slowly move the blade and the body forwards to a comfortable position, move back again and note the effect. Now try the same exercise but this time open up the blade angle slightly and note the change in behaviour of the kayak. This subtlety of control is one of the keys to mastering the sea kayak. As with the draw stroke some paddlers may find the length of the paddles cumbersome, just slide the hands down the loom to find a comfortable reach.

Bow Rudder and Edging

Combining a bow rudder with a radical amount of edge produces what is probably the fastest turning sequence for a moving sea kayak.

Paddle forwards and gain speed, perform a powerful sweep stroke on the right side. At the end of the sweep stroke apply edge to the right, keep the edge angle set and move your body forwards. Now apply a bow rudder on the left side, regulate the amount of turn with a combination of edge and blade angle; try to keep in balance by attempting to pull the blade through the boat. As boat speed dies, turn the stroke into a compound stroke by pulling the paddle back into a forward paddling stroke. Keep the edge on and start on the sweep stroke if more turning is necessary.

Safety

In order to avoid straining your shoulder:

- The kayak must have already started to turn as the result of effective sweep stroke/s.

- Always edge the kayak.

- Don't attempt this at high speed, i.e. when surfing.

Brace and Sculling

High and low braces are performed much in the same way as for other kayaks. Every effort must be made to exploit the low brace to its full potential; the high brace should only be used as a last resort. The size of the kayak and its weight carrying potential could have a devastating effect on the shoulder girdle so the high brace should be avoided if at all possible. If used, a good idea is to keep the elbows bent, low, and in sight all the time; this will ensure a more horizontal shaft and less chance of injury.

Sculling for support has very limited use in sea kayaking. That said however, it is a very good confidence building exercise.

Rolling

Rolling a sea kayak is similar to rolling any other kayak although when laden the process is mostly easier and slower. One thing that tends to happen is that the kayak will sit on its side rather than completely invert. This means that to roll effectively you will probably have to come up on the side you went over on. Again lengthening your lever will help to reduce the effort and increase the efficiency.

Rescues

All the safety considerations mentioned in Chapters 6 and 16 must be taken into account when rescuing a laden sea kayak. Try to minimise the load as much as possible by using the swimmer as an assistant.

'X' Rescue

Probably the most performed of all sea kayak rescues, this involves the rescuer positioning himself at right angles to the victim's kayak. Due to the design of most sea kayaks, when an attempt is made to lift the bow from the water the kayak will turn the right way up. This is a good idea as it allows the kayak being rescued to slide onto the deck.

Photo 20.16   'X' Rescue

Photo 20.17   Slide rather than lift the kayak to ease the strain

The victim can assist by either pulling the kayak over the rescuer's deck, or by pushing down on the end away from that which is being lifted or slid. Anything that reduces the load on the rescuer can only be a good option. With kayaks fitted with bulkheads directly behind the seat, merely lifting the bow will empty almost all the water from the cockpit area. If the bulkhead is fitted farther back or there is no bulkhead then the rescue should be carried out as for other kayaks. (See Chapter 6)

Rafted 'X'

If the rescuer requires a little bit more stability then a helper can come alongside and stabilise his kayak by holding onto the cockpit rim or decklines. The rescue is then carried out in the same manner as the 'X' rescue above.

Photo 20.18   Rafted 'X'

Pump Out Rescue

Perhaps the most successful rescue when a heavily laden kayak is involved is the pump out rescue. The kayak is righted and the casualty climbs in, the spraydeck is replaced and then he can be supported whilst the kayak is pumped out. This ensures that nobody is putting excessive strain on their bodies.

Photo 20.19   Emptying out with a stirrup pump

With any rescue involving pumping out the kayak, it must be remembered that there should be some allowance for air to get in to replace the water removed or the spraydeck will be sucked down onto the legs of the casualty.

Getting Back In

The best method is to approach the kayak from the side, and hold onto the paddles and cockpit rim. Using this in a similar way to the edge of a swimming pool, let your body sink as low in the water as is possible then pull downwards hard; this should get your body clear of the water and you can slide your chest onto the rear deck. If the leg that is nearest the cockpit hooks into it then it is quite simple to get the other one in and by twisting you can then sit upright and be helped to replace the spraydeck.

Photos 20.20a-c   Getting back in the kayak

Stirrup Method

If the casualty is tired, or cannot get out of the water, a 'stirrup' method of re-entry is recommended. By using a length of rope or tape, a loop is made. This loop is tied around the paddle shafts with a suitable knot and the other end hung in the water nearest the casualty. The casualty can then put their foot in the loop and, using the stronger leg muscles, stand up and then lie on the deck and enter the kayak as before.

Self-Rescue

Photos 20.21a-c   Re-entry and roll

There are very many methods of self-rescue, with rolling being the best option. When out of the kayak, perhaps the simplest and the one that requires least in the way of additional equipment, is the re-entry and roll. Hold the kayak on its side, then facing the bow and holding the cockpit rim on both sides, float your legs into the cockpit. During this phase your head will most likely stay clear of the water. Next pull your bottom into the seat; you will capsize and, if your paddle is within reach, it will be possible for you to roll, assuming that you can indeed roll before you try this!

For the non-rollers there are other options including the use of a paddle float; this is essentially an inflatable bag, which as the name suggests, floats the paddle. The kayaker can then use this as an outrigger and climb back into the kayak using any of the methods above. For all the above self-rescues to work when required, they must be practised in controlled conditions.

Photos 20.22a-b   Paddle float in use

Towing and Towing Systems

The ability to tow a tired, injured, or sick companion makes us truly independent. We are able to deal with relatively straightforward situations that would otherwise require the help of the rescue services. This chore can be made more bearable if some thought has been put into the preparation and set up of the system, and if the manner in which it is to be used has been taken into account.

Design Characteristics

The line has to be strong enough to withstand the load of a kayak and its paddler being towed through a tide race or being landed through surf. The line should also float, be rot-proof and be brightly coloured. Ideally it should be adjustable for length between five and fifteen metres. This adjustability is required due to the possible conditions to be encountered. At the clip end of the line there should be some type of float and also a shock absorber. The clip itself should be strong, easy to operate with cold hands, corrosion free and have no place that could snag other line.

Short or Long Tow?

If the towing has to be done into a steep sea then the tow should be as short as possible but still keep the kayaks apart. If there is a following sea a long line is best as it allows both kayaks to be in the same relative position on separate waves. There should also be some method of adjusting the length easily for when conditions change.

Quick Attachment and Release

Most towing has to be undertaken in worsening conditions. Any system used should be able to be clipped easily and quickly and, if necessary, should be able to be released quickly too.

Waist Mounted

A waist mounted towing system is a good idea if it is unlikely you will have to tow someone for any great distance.

Photo 20.23   Waist mounted tow

The system shown in the photo has a wide webbing belt with a quick release buckle. This has a fifteen metre line with an added shock absorber, a float and a stainless steel clip; it is also adjustable for length.

Boat Mounted

A kayak-mounted system is superior because the strain is placed on the kayak. Around where the fittings are located should be reinforced below the deck. A typical set-up would include a corrosion-proof cam-cleat and a fairlead situated on the centre line of the kayak just behind the cockpit (think of a tug). The position of the cam-cleat is important, as it is almost impossible to operate if it is behind your back; the best place would be to one side of the kayak within easy reach. This should be angled so that the line runs straight to the fairlead.

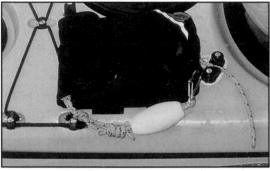

Photo 20.24   Deck mounted tow system

The system shown in the photo has a fifteen metre line with an added shock absorber, a float and a stainless steel clip. It is also adjustable for length.

Types of Tow

A simple straight tow where the casualty is attached to the person doing the towing is ideal and does not seem to slow down the progress if there is a group involved. If casualties are not able to support themselves then a rafted straight tow is suitable. This places more strain on the person doing the towing but works, as long as the distance is not too great or the conditions too severe. If the distance to be covered is longer than you would like to tow, consider changing the tow person and rotating at regular intervals.

Photo 20.25   Towed rescue

Straight Tow

The two kayaks are kept in line with each other and the front boat tows the other. The person being towed should lower their skeg, if fitted, as this assists directional stability.

Anchored Rescue

A straight tow can also be used to hold a person performing an 'X' rescue off a cliff, when otherwise there would be the likelihood of being washed or blown onto it, or anywhere the wind or tide would carry them towards danger and make matters worse. Another use would be to help someone get through a surf break safely and in a controlled manner.

Rafted Straight Tow

As above except the kayaks being towed need to have their bows secured together otherwise they will tend to separate. The best way of achieving this is to pass the towline clip through the forward part of the deck line of the supporter's kayak and clip onto the casualty's toggle. The person being towed should lower their skeg, if fitted, as this assists directional stability.

Safety Equipment

Sea kayakers aim to be independent and self-reliant. That said, if all else fails we need the means to summon help. What equipment you choose to carry will depend on the nature and location of your paddling. A set of flares is the absolute minimum.

Flares

A variety of flares are made with the small craft user in mind. There are three basic types available:

- Smoke flare (daytime use)
- Pinpoint flare (night)
- Rocket or parachute flare

Distress flares are coloured red or orange, and white flares are for illuminating an area for search purposes or for collision warning.

The question is not what to carry but when to use the type you have. We must also take into account the type of paddling we are intending to do. Are we going to be in an area where there is lots of shipping activity or is it somewhere remote, with few houses and even fewer boats?

Parachute Flare

A parachute flare is probably the first flare you would use. This fires a rocket to about three hundred metres which then burns a bright red flare for about sixty seconds that descends slowly by parachute to the sea. If you are in conditions of low cloud or are under a high cliff the possibility of your flare being ineffective is great.

Pinpoint

A pinpoint flare would be your next choice at night when you spot your would-be rescuer. Set off this flare on the downwind side of the kayak and hold it by the plastic handle at arms length. This type of flare gets very hot; the metal tube enclosing the magnesium will glow red due to the intense heat. It will burn for approximately sixty seconds.

Smoke

Smoke flares are used when a rescuer is close during the day. Again set this off on the downwind side of the kayak. The flare does not get particularly hot but the smoke smells and tastes foul; it also stains everything it comes in contact with. The smoke produced is very dense and the burn time is roughly sixty seconds.

What to Carry

A good arsenal of flares for a typical sea kayaker would be one each of the above. In addition there are compact mini-flare kits available that have either six or eight shells that fire about two hundred feet into the air. These have been proven to be successful more due to the bang than the red light produced.

Most flares are now water-resistant; this allows the flare to get splashed but not submerged completely for weeks on end. A good idea is to keep your flares on deck in a waterproof bag which is tied securely to the kayak. *At least one flare should be kept on your person in case you lose contact with your boat.*

VHF Radio

VHF radio is in general use by the nautical population for general communication and distress use. It is also possible to get up to date weather forecasts from the coastguard. The main limitation to the use of VHF is one of reception; with most handheld sets the operating range is 'line of sight'. From a kayak, the range to another kayak is around 8km, to a large vessel about 30km and to a coastal station situated at 100m above sea level approximately 45km. The main benefit of the VHF is that even if your call is not heard by the coastguard, there is a good chance it will be heard by a boat in the vicinity. In addition, coastguard stations can direction-find, making rescue chances greater, and narrowing down the area of their search. Everyone who goes to sea has a duty to others to respond to any distress call.

Mobile Phone

Mobile phones are becoming widespread as a means of communication amongst sea kayakers. Unlike with VHF, your distress call will only be heard by the person you are calling. If your signal is weak, you are 'up the creek without a paddle'.

This said, mobile phone companies are installing more communications masts and the coverage is substantial. In short, these must not be relied upon to summon the rescue services.

Advice from HM Coastguard: "If a mobile phone is all you have, use it".

EPIRB

The Emergency Position Indicating Radio Beacon (EPIRB) is an emergency signal transmitter developed for the mariner in distress. The most basic EPIRB alerts the rescue services by sending a signal to an orbiting satellite. This is the great advantage of this system, for even in the remotest area in amongst mountains the transmitter still has a line of sight to the satellite and range is not a problem.

Satellite Phones

Although still fairly expensive and not an actual rescue device, satellite phones may well become an affordable and popular device in the near future.

Further Reading

Navigation, Weather and General Interest

Sea Kayak Navigation, Ferrero F, 1999, Bangor, Pesda Press, 0-9531956-1-9

Coastwise Navigation, Watkins G, 1986, London, Stanford Maritime Ltd, 0-540-07282-6

Using GPS, Dixon C, 1994, London, Adlard Coles Nautical, 0-7136-3952-0

The Seamanship Pocketbook, Ferrero F, 1999, Bangor, Pesda Press, 0-9531956-2-7

Instant Weather Forecasting, Watts A, 1995, London, Adlard Coles Nautical, 0-7136-3752-8

The Skywatchers Handbook, Ronan C & Dunlop S, 1993, Leicester Bookmart Ltd, 1-85648-119-0

Survival at Sea, McClean T, 1989, London, Century Hutchinson Ltd, 0-09-174017-7

Sea Kayak Specific

Sea Kayaking, Dowd J, 1988, Vancouver, Douglas & McIntyre Ltd, 0-88894-598-1

A Practical Guide to Sea Canoeing, Jeffs H, 1986, Capel Curig

The Complete Book of Sea Kayaking, Huthchinson D, 1976, London, A & C Black Ltd, 0-7136-3835-4

Travel Narratives

Dances with Waves, Wilson B, 1998, Dublin, The O'Brien Press, 0-86278-551-0

Blazing Paddles, Wilson B, 1988, Yeovil, The Oxford Illustrated Press, 0-946609-59-4

The Last of the Cockleshell Heroes, Sparks W & Munn M, 1992, London, Leo Cooper, 0-85052-297-8

Argonauts of the Western Isles, Lloyd-Jones R, 1989, London, Diadem Books Ltd, 0-906371-03-1

Historical Design

The Skinboats of Greenland, Peterson H,

The Bark Canoes and Skin Boats of North America, Adney E & Chappelle H, 1983, Washington DC, Smithsonian Institute Press, 1-56098-269-9

Baidarka, Dyson G, 1986, Seattle, Alaska Northwest Books, 0-88240-315-X

Historical Travel

Watkins Last Expedition, Chapman S, 1953, London, William Heinemann Ltd

Kayak to Cape Wrath, Henderson J, 1951, Glasgow, William McLellan & Co Ltd

Quest by Canoe (Glasgow to Skye), Dunnett A, London, The Travel Book Club

Environment Related

Rocky Shorelands, Packham C, 1989, London, William Collins Sons & Co Ltd, 0-00-219842-8

The Seashore, Fitter R, 1984, Glasgow, Harper Collins Publishers, 0-00-458824-X

Guide to the Identification of Whales, Dolphins and Porpoises in European Seas, Evans P, 1995, Oxford, Sea Watch Foundation Publication

The Grey Seal, Anderson S, 1988, Aylesbury, Shire Publications Ltd, 0-85263-947-3

The Common Seal, Thompson P, 1989, Aylesbury, Shire Publications Ltd, 0-7478-0017-0

Videos:

Over and Out - by Gordon Brown

Websites:

Inshore Waters Forecast - www.meto.gov.uk/datafiles/inshore.html

Shipping Forecast – www.meto.gov.uk/datafiles/offshore.html

Weather - www.onlineweather.com

Satellite Images - www.meteo.oma.be/IRM-KMI/imapro/meteosat.html

Animated Synoptic Charts - www.ecmwf.int/services/forecast/jmenu/index.html

OS maps online and local weather - www.multimap.com

Gordon Brown

Gordon is a Level 5 Coach (Sea and Inland Kayak) and runs his own sea kayaking business, Skyak Adventures, based on the Isle of Skye. He has guided on rivers in Nepal where he ran the first International Whitewater Safety Kayaker Course for paddlers supporting commercial rafting. He has trained both British and American Special Forces and produced Over and Out (a sea kayak rescue video). He has been a member of the SCA coaching committee for the past 15 years and is also on the Level 5 development team.

From his youngest days Gordon was always to be found playing around water, whether by the sea when on holiday or the local river when he should have been at school. His first kayak, a homebuilt wood and canvas Skua was to cement his love of the sea.

21 Surf

... Be patient, wait for the right one, then... Go for it!
The exhilaration of the speed, the power, the spray, the roar of the surf. The rush of flying
down the line on a clean shoulder, tapping the energy source of nature.
Decisions blur into actions.
Paddle hard, be bold!
One more turn... then breathe again - Wow!

Introduction

The boom in paddlesport and the year-round search for challenging paddling have led to a huge increase in the number of paddlers who launch out into the surf. Surf canoeing, in its continually evolving form, is becoming one of the most challenging and expansive elements of our sport.

The understanding that surfing is a sport in its own right, not merely a place to go when the rivers are dry, has had huge implications for both paddlers and other surf users. The key to this change has been the general swing from the green wave type of surfing to the accurate riding of a shouldering wave, in essence, surfing in exactly the same way as other surf users do.

Although competent boat handlers will, with input, quickly make the transition to surf, there is a different set of techniques and skills required to surf accurately, and thus have credibility amongst the surf community.

This credibility has made massive leaps in the recent past. The top paddlers are holding their own, not just on the small wave beach breaks, but paddling the more challenging conditions of points, reefs and larger surf locations around the world.

The development of boats has greatly assisted this accuracy. The relatively small, flat-bottomed play boats are now closer to a surf board than ever before.

These advances allow the true form of surfing to be realized, riding the shoulder of a peeling wave, using all the available potential energy to carve and slash the boat in all directions. The combination of freestyle, white water skills and the finesse and timing of a board surfer is now the world of surf canoeing.

Equipment

As in all paddlesport, the change in equipment design and construction has opened up areas of performance previously impossible. Modern boaters can maintain good speed to carve bottom turns, pull aerials, flat spin and cartwheel, all this whilst still retaining the true essence of the sport that is riding a peeling shoulder.

Boats

Almost any craft can be surfed, allowing paddlers of all abilities to enjoy the thrill of riding surf. That said, some designs and constructions are better suited to accurate surfing than others. This chapter will deal with the generic sport of surfing. Some of the cutting edge moves seen today are only accessible to a select type of design, such as a composite boat, ski, playboat with a hull that is flat-bottomed and hard-railed, or a dedicated surf boat with its super-light construction and fins.

Much has changed since the introduction of the Mirage and Dancer in the early eighties. The modern composite and plastic surf craft show a remarkable similarity to the original surf shoes and surf skis, which themselves attempted to bridge the gap between Malibu surf boards and kayaks.

There are a couple of relatively simple principles you need to apply in order to understand which boat to surf or what your boat is best designed for:

1. As a displacement craft with only the paddler's effort to propel it, longer and less rocker would be the best solution.

2. As a planing hull, drawing its speed from the potential energy stored in a wave, a relatively short, flat-bottomed and hard-railed craft will allow the paddler to spin and manoeuvre on the critical part of a wave.

3. The shorter the boat the easier it is to spin but the harder it is to carve.

4. The shorter and slower the boat, the nearer it must stay to the pocket, so as not to risk stalling and losing the wave.

5. Smaller, slower boats with flat bottoms are harder to paddle out through the surf.

Paddles

Paddles have remained similar to standard kayak paddles, with most surfers using a similar design to that of freestyle, river or slalom paddlers. The length, feather and foil characteristics give plenty of power to take off on a wave, and the feel necessary when applying more subtle strokes. Although there are often no solid objects to cause damage to the paddle, a strong construction is best. It is possible to damage them, particularly when capsizing in powerful breaking surf.

Personal Equipment

The personal equipment needed to be comfortable in a surf session is very much down to personal choice. Initially, a paddler's 'normal' gear will suffice. However, the possible extremes of both winter months in Britain and summer abroad will mean a range of equipment is usually needed.

Keeping Warm

For this cool, windy country, the modern 'steamer' with its super stretchy rubber and either no zip or small back zip is ideal. Couple this with the convenience of only having one item to dry, and it is no wonder that it is the preferred choice of many all-year surfers. The addition of rash vest (designed to stop you getting a rash), gloves, boots, hood and occasionally a windproof, will allow paddlers to be comfortable on all but the severest of days.

As in other aspects of the sport, there are hundreds of possible variations in gear, ranging from one piece dry suits to short arm and legged wet suits used in warmer waters.

The overriding consideration for any standard of paddler is comfort. Bear in mind that we are operating in an environment that will give you a thorough soaking even before the first run.

Buoyancy Aids

The decision of whether to wear a buoyancy aid is a polarized one.

There are pro's and con's depending on your experience, conditions, the craft you are in/on and your role within a group. Buoyancy aids are the same as worn in other areas of paddlesport. There are however, times when experienced surfers, especially ski riders wearing full steamers (which themselves provide considerable buoyancy), will choose not to wear buoyancy aids, preferring the freedom this allows.

Buoyancy aids should be worn unless you are sufficiently experienced to choose otherwise.

Helmets

Helmets provide protection from other surfers, rocks, groynes and other obstructions found in surf zones. They are the same construction as those worn on a river, giving good forehead protection and often warmth.

Helmets come into a similar category to buoyancy aids and are not always worn, particularly on a sunny day out on a beach break. However, when paddling on reefs and point breaks or with other surfers around, it would be foolhardy not to wear one.

Spraydecks

Spraydecks need to be especially secure as the forces in a breaking wave are significant and will pop a poorly fitting spraydeck. Coincidentally this is also the most common excuse for swimming in the surf!

Miscellaneous

There are other subtle tools, such as wax for paddles and cockpit rims, Vaseline for neck seals, and ear plugs to limit 'surfer's ear' in the winter (see Headwear, Chapter 3).

Environment

The term 'surf' is an ambiguous one that can mean many things to many people. Understanding that it does not have to be windy to have perfect four foot swell pumping into the beach, needs a developed understanding of how swell is created. This knowledge then needs to be combined with the complex factors that mould and affect swells, as they complete their journey to shores around the world.

For any given ability level there are perfect surf conditions. Being able to track these conditions down will give you a much more enjoyable surf session and allow the learner to improve faster. Understanding the parameters that mould the 'surf' is a critical part of surfing. Experienced surfers will go to great lengths to find the best surf on any given day and will normally consider the following variables:

- Size of swell predicted
- Direction of swell predicted
- The history of the swell
- The local or micro wind pattern
- The site options
- The tide pattern
- Seasonal factors

Size, Direction and History of the 'Swell'

The information on the above comes in two basic types:

1. The raw data of observations and measurements.

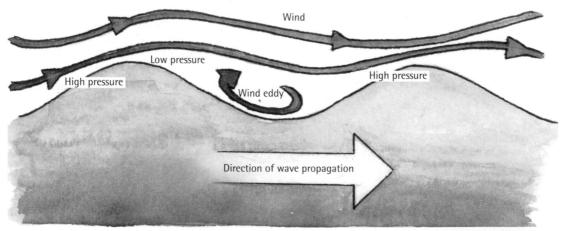

Wind

Low pressure

High pressure

Wind eddy

High pressure

Direction of wave propagation

Fig 21.1   Jeffreys' 'sheltering' model of wave generation. It is mainly the differences in pressure created by wind eddies that drive the waves along.

Fig 21.2   Simplified version of Significant Wave Height and Mean Wave Direction, similar to those provided on the 'net' (see Websites at end of chapter)

2. The synthesis of this raw data by various agencies is used to produce swell predictions (of varying accuracy).

It is much easier with the technology of today to gather both types of information. The internet and its many surf-related websites cover everything from surf prediction to video camera shots of your local break. For the less experienced, it is far easier to use another person's forecasting skill to decide where to look for surf. As your experience increases, the normal pattern is to take on the task of predicting the size, timing, and direction of swell yourself.

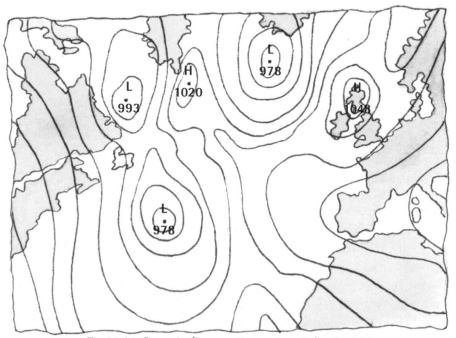

Fig 21.3   Synoptic chart covering same period as Fig 21.2

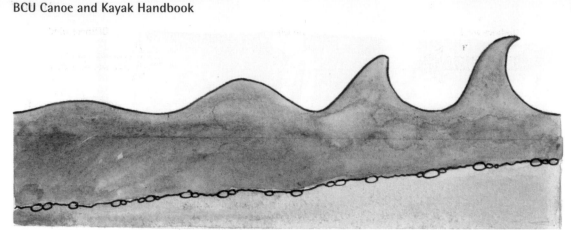

Fig 21.4   The effect of shallowing water

Swell Generation

Wind acting on the surface of the sea creates waves, which in time become a 'swell'. There is a complex and interesting scientific explanation of this process. The simplified version above will suffice for a starting point in the understanding of surf prediction. The wind agitates the surface of the sea to produce waves, travelling from the area of creation in the direction in which they are pushed by the generating winds.

From this point, the waves go through a process termed 'metamorphosis' which will include such effects as:

- Swells joining together to create larger, more regular ordered swells.
- Swells opposing each other to create smaller confused swells.
- Wind increasing or decreasing the wave's speed and size.
- Depth, current and tidal interference.

The British Isles usually receives swells generated by Atlantic low-pressure systems. These 'lows' rotate in an anti-clockwise direction and are roughly circular in shape. They also move in a similar way to that of a spinning top on a table, tracking one direction or another depending on influencing factors, i.e. other pressure systems.

The isobars on the chart represent points of the same pressure reading.

The closer the lines in a pressure system are together, the stronger the wind that is generated.

The result is that any wind generated is not usually acting on any particular area of the sea for very long. Thus, rather than circular, the ideal low-pressure shape is closer to an oval or ellipse stretched across the Atlantic, roughly west-east, with closely packed isobars indicating strong winds. This will generate a swell heading toward the coast of Britain. The technical term for the section of a low generating swell in the right direction for a specific region is 'active fetch'. Being able to interpret isobaric charts and wave buoy readings, to predict swell moving toward a specific area of coast is the core skill in wave prediction.

The same low-pressure could also generate swell for the east coast of Britain, with the active fetch being in a north-east to west orientation.

The internet now is an invaluable source of information and a basic search will reveal sites giving swell sizes and wave buoy readings for the entire globe.

The Effect of Shallow Water

When a swell enters shallower water it undergoes a process of profound modification.

A swell will normally 'feel' the seabed at a depth of approximately half of its wavelength or, more usefully, at anything from half its height to twice its height.

The Effects of Wind on Swell

The macro-weather that generated the wave does not necessarily follow the same track as the swell. This explains why it is possible, on those magical days, to have large clean waves hitting the beach with no wind and the sun shining.

From a surfer's point of view there are three types of wind: no wind, onshore and offshore. All of these are okay, provided they don't rise above a gentle breeze (Force 2/3). If they blow much harder, the effect on the waves will be significant.

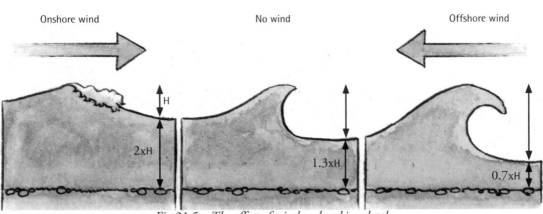

Onshore wind No wind Offshore wind

Fig 21.5 The effect of wind on breaking depth

On westerly coasts, onshore winds are common because the generating wind often traces the exact same path as the swell it has produced. On occasions it will be beaten to the shore by the swell, and on others it will be windy before the swell arrives. It may even have been replaced by another pressure system or have tracked farther east, both scenarios producing offshore wind.

Offshore Winds

Offshore winds are an experienced surfer's dream. Up to a specific strength for any given swell size, an offshore wind steepens the wave to give cleaner and often faster rides. Offshore winds will cause the surf to break much more violently, creating the drawbacks of more serious wipe-outs and a much more committing paddle out.

Onshore Winds

Onshore winds will push the wave over, hurrying it up as it feels the bottom and begins to break. The more gentle, spilling action this creates can provide a much more amenable learning environment for the novice surfer.

If the wind strength is beyond Force 4, on or offshore, it can effectively make the surf unusable, creating a frustrating situation where the long-awaited swell has arrived, but due to the 'local' weather cannot be ridden. This sort of surf is often referred to as 'blown out'.

The Swell Meets the Land

By the time a swell arrives in sight of the coast, it may already have been further affected by such things as the tidal stream, the shallow nature of the water it is travelling in, or changes in direction to clear headlands or islands.

The perfect break would have several features in common:

- Very deep water close up to the shore.
- An aspect that works on swells from a variety of directions.

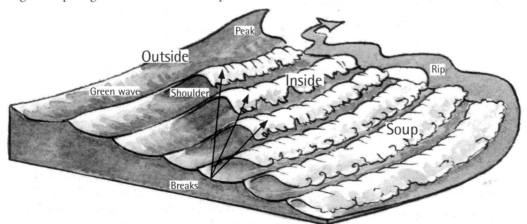

Fig 21.6 Surf layout and names

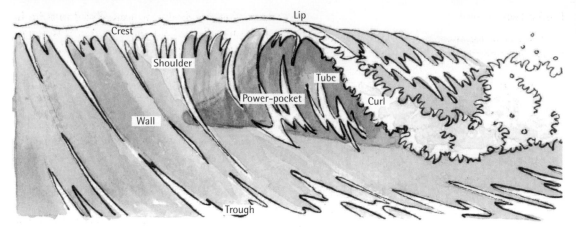

Fig 21.7   Anatomy of a wave

- A bottom shape that produces a wave that breaks to a regular and predictable pattern.

Our island is blessed with a measure of the above.

The sea adjacent to our shores is not significantly deep (Ireland is much better). The west coast does collect a significant amount of swell. There are a lot of changes in profile to our coastline, giving countless reefs and points, interspersed with a significant number of good quality beach breaks.

The Surf Zone

Once the swell feels the bottom and begins to break, there are a range of features and sites that need to be identified:

Outside

On a messy day this may not exist, but on clean days this is the term used to describe the area beyond which the waves are beginning to break. This is usually a safe place to sit and assess the situation.

Inside

This is the term for the whole of the breaking surf area.

Shoulder

The best part of the green face to ride, which is where it gets steeper just before it breaks.

Left / Right Hander

This is the term used to describe the direction of the breaking wave. It is used in reference to the direction you would surf in the pocket (away from the break).

Section

This is the breaking part of the wave.

Pocket

This is the steepest part of the wave, just next to the broken water.

Secondary or Reform

Once the waves have broken, there is usually a second break much closer inshore. This makes an ideal spot for warming up or hiding on big days, when the main wave is too big or the paddle out too difficult.

Soup

This is the large area of broken water close inshore.

Rip

Rips describe areas where the water flows from the beach back out to sea.

Sets

The number pattern of larger sequences of waves.

Choice of Site

The choice of break is the most important surfing decision.

Beach, Point or Reef Breaks

All of the above types of break have pros and cons; much will depend on the ability of the surfer and the conditions on the day.

Beaches

Beaches have a profile in all three planes:

Profile One

They can be bay or crescent shaped, straight, or in the broad form of a headland.

Profile Two

From water to foreshore they can slope evenly, but most commonly are steeper toward the high tide and low tide marks where the tide pauses, with an even angle in between.

Profile Three

They will never be flat. The surface of the beach will slope to the left or right, with troughs and banks created in various positions. This changing profile is the product of the water thrown up the beach returning to the deep water, carrying sand as it goes. Rivers and streams assist in this process, by providing deep channels to hasten the water's escape seaward. The shape of a beach is never constant and many beaches change shape significantly after a winter of storms.

The Effect of Tides

In surfing, when the tide is flooding (coming in), it is generally referred to as 'on the push'. This usually brings larger waves due to the positive or pushing effect of the tidal stream and the waves travelling in the same general direction.

The ebbing tide, conversely, can have a detrimental effect on the swell. It has the capability to completely flatten small swells. Tides are covered in Chapter 20.

Wave Size and Character

When looking at waves at a distance from the car park or cliff top, it is very difficult to judge the size. It is even more problematic at low tide and without some form of scale to judge them by. Arguments about wave size have been going on since surfing began. For all practical purposes the surfer's measurement is the most useful, since this is the measurement the surf lines and internet surf pages use. If a board surfer rides diagonally on a face, and the wave crest behind is level with his head it would be considered 4 feet. This is because the bottom and top section of a wave are not generally regarded as a usable part of the wave, and hence are not included in the measurement.

This '4 foot' wave will be a different matter altogether for a kayak paddler, for whom, sat in the trough in front of it, this would be considered a large wave! It is not relevant that the measuring system most commonly used does not flatter the paddling world, (it doesn't sound good in the pub after a ses-sion, telling everybody you were forced to swim in 2 foot surf). Even if the ego is at risk, it is important that we, as a community, have a benchmark for understanding the surf line forecast. A clean '2 foot' wave is a perfect learning environment.

Character

The character can describe many things, including: the speed, direction and reliability of the shoulder, the steepness or hollow nature of the wave's profile, the wavelength, the spilling or sectioning nature of the shoulder, or the speed and thickness of the swell. Unlocking the realities of the wave's character will allow the paddler to begin to understand what will be possible in terms of manoeuvres on any given day.

A good tip when assessing the characteristics of a wave, is to look at the pattern of the foam left by a breaking wave. The shape and degree of lateral development of this foam cone tells us a lot about the wave's character.

Another trick is to locate a pocket or shouldering section, and count the number of seconds it lasts before meeting another section or closing out. If you cannot count beyond five it might be worth considering other sites.

Photo 21.1   Paddling out

Technique

The techniques of surfing a shouldering wave form a logical sequence:

1. Paddle Out
2. Wave Selection
3. Take-off
4 Run
5. Finish

These elements are combined in various proportions, on different days, according to the conditions.

One day the take-off will be the defining element needed to enjoy the day, on another it will be the wave selection, on another the run itself.

Paddle Out

This element actually begins next to the car, whilst changing facing the sea. By observing the patterns in the sets of waves, counting the times of the sections, and by assessing the patterns, the surfer can make the paddle out and consequent ride easier, and safer. As with sea paddling, the craft of surfing can be split into decisions and preparation on the one hand, and the physical application on the other, something often forgotten in the haste to get afloat. Having assessed the swells, and decided on the position which will allow you to be safe and able to select the waves you want to ride (and it is rarely straight in front of the car park), it's time to plan a strategy to get you there. An experienced surf paddler will make their journey to the 'outside' as economical as possible. Surfing is amongst the most physically demanding disciplines of our sport, particularly when repeatedly paddling out through large breaking waves. To economise on effort during the paddle out is a good strategy. A strategy for getting the surfer 'out back' in some of the more challenging waves is also considerably safer, both physically and mentally. Here are some of the more commonly used tactics for a strategic paddle out:

- Using a rip to the side of the area being surfed.
- Changing direction to avoid the most severe sections.
- Holding station in front of the breaking section before sprinting through to the outside in a lull between sets.
- Knifing the hull of the boat through the white water.
- Trimming vigorously to avoid possible back looping.
- Rolling under waves.

With the modern playboat design, the possibility of a back loop is actually more common than a few years ago. Their flat hulls and low boat speed make them easy prey for the approaching wave. As the surfer approaches the steepening wave, a couple of sprint strokes, followed by a lifting of one knee so

as to present a narrower profile (knifing the hull), should allow the breaking wave to wash over their boat. Combining this sequence with a vigorous weighting of the front of the boat (trimming vigourously) and a paddle stroke just as it clears the wave, should see you safely through.

If your strategy has been judged correctly, you should not have to paddle through more than a couple of these sectioning waves at most. If it has been a straight bash out in front of the car park, the chances are it could be many more. On a big day, it may mean that you don't make it out at all.

Having made it 'out back', it is time to consider which wave to catch in order to ride back in.

Wave Selection

When positioning for a wave, the surfer uses 'transits'. This involves lining up two objects on the shore, and by keeping them in line, keeping the same position.

The foam cone left by a previous wave on the surface is another good guide to where the shoulder can be found.

Once established in the best position, it is best to sit in an orientation which allows you to continually scan both seaward for waves, and shoreward to assess your drift and the pattern of waves you have let go.

Be Patient

The art of wave selection and positioning for the take-off are still the two most important factors in successful surfing at *all* levels.

All surfers pick poor waves for a variety of reasons. However, experienced surfers show greater consistency in their positioning and selection of the best wave for that particular day.

When looking out to sea, check for lines in the wave rather than isolated peaks. On seeing a wave that seems a likely candidate, move the boat left or right to be as close to the shoulder as possible. In the case of a green wave, move toward its steepest point, usually where there is the most shadow, in readiness for it to break. The trick is to be as close to the breaking section as possible. Assuming all is going well, it is now time to execute an accurate *take-off*.

Take-off

The take-off can be straight down the wave, or angled across the wave, depending on the type of wave being ridden. Point toward the shore, armed with the knowledge that your chosen shoulder is going to break left or right. Just before it arrives, put in three to six power strokes, accelerating the boat vigorously and leaving the last stroke to push the boat toward the direction you wish to ride the wave. On this last stroke, add a hip thrust to give that last bit of momentum, then lean forward and commit your shoulders and torso to the ride down the wave and so into *the run*.

Photo 21.2   Take-off

The Run

Having 'taken off' it is time to put together your run. This contains two basic elements:

1. The 'choreographed' elements, i.e. the part of the run you have already decided to complete, irrespective of the wave's character.

2. The 'reactionary' element, which is where your manoeuvres now need to take into account the wave and your speed and position on it.

The choreographed section of your run will almost always include a bottom turn followed by a top turn, or a diagonal run high across the face of the wave.

Photo 21.3   Diagonal run high on face of wave

Bottom Turn

The carved bottom turn is one of the most satisfying of all paddlesport skills, combining the thrill of speed and the subtlety of timing and body position.

Photo 21.4   Bottom turn

The sling shot effect of the boat being launched out of the turn with maximum speed and good position on the wave is the perfect starting point for a good wave ride, and once mastered, can be repeated many times in one run.

A skilful bottom turn is produced through the subtle use of timing, trim and edge control. The messages that the body sends to the boat are always the deciding factor; the paddle plays a limited roll, mostly triggering the actions rather than being the root of them.

This related sequence of:

wave selection - take-off - bottom turn

is essential if you wish to be set up, (high on the shoulder of the wave and travelling at speed), in the best position to pull off spectacular tricks.

'Old school' manoeuvres might include:

- Loops
- Pop-outs
- Pirouettes
- A roll on the face of the wave

The cutting edge manoeuvres can be anything from a large and growing repertoire, such as:

- Slashed top turn
- Re-entry to the pocket
- Aerials with and without rotation
- Blunt
- Pocket spins

- Regains
- Cartwheels
- Paddle out take-offs

Finish

The end of the run should not come as a surprise to the surfer who should dictate the finishing point, rather than let the run dribble to an undignified end.

This finish might be a pop-out, or more simply a carve and pull out over the broken water.

The broken water does not have to signify the end of the run, especially in the modern playboat. Cartwheels and other broken water manoeuvres can significantly prolong the run. Alternatively, on seeing the wave closing out in front of them, the surfer can carve a bottom turn, use the momentum created to pull over the top of the lip, and immediately begin the paddle out.

If the surfer is caught in the broken water sideways (bongo), straightening the boat so that it faces the shore, then turning hard in the direction in which the wave has been broken the longest, will usually allow the boat to be punched through the soup. This leaves you facing out to sea and ready to paddle out again.

Etiquette

In the surf environment there are rules of engagement. They are not exclusive to paddlers, they apply to all surf users. It is important that we become responsible members of the surf community, respecting both the rules and common courtesies to surfers on their local break. There will always be other waves.

Fig 21.8 Dropping in!

This is a very important element in surfing. It is basically the 'rules of the road', the code that allows any 'surfer' to co-exist on a surf break without creating conflict.

Everybody has a right to surf, but that does not mean we can stumble around the ocean ruining the enjoyment of other surf users through ignorance.

The full code of conduct can be found in the BCU Surf Yearbook and on its web page (see websites at end of chapter).

To summarise: the rider that has positioned him or herself nearest to the breaking section of the wave has the right to ride the wave without interruption or interference. The act of *'dropping in'* (getting in the way of someone who is already riding nearest the break) is the single most significant cause of friction in the line-up on surf breaks.

Although the rule is simple in principle, a wave that breaks erratically or has a peak that moves about will mean that more than one surfer will usually attempt to take-off. It is then critical that all other surfers not on the shoulder exit the wave immediately, leaving the surfer who was on the shoulder first to ride the wave unhindered.

Waiting Your Turn

The other main issue, particularly from the perspective of kayak surfers, is the one of waiting your turn, or being even-handed about the number of waves you attempt to catch. On most breaks, a form of rotation establishes itself within the surfers waiting to take-off.

Paddlers are able to exploit the speed that paddles can give them off the wave and catch the wave further out than other surf users. Resist the temptation to catch waves before the peak has formed, and be courteous to other surfers.

Board surfers may only be able to catch the one big wave of the set. Imagine how they are going to feel, if you have already caught two or three and you then beat them to the break on the big one! If a board rider is in a great position to take-off, earn some 'brownie points', give way and catch the next one.

Paddling Back Out

Try to paddle around the area where the waves are being caught and ridden, not straight out through on-coming surfers.

Rescue and Safety

Most of the rescues involve the same logical decision-making generic to all paddlesport in challenging environments. It obeys a few simple principles: protect the casualty, stabilise the situation, formulate a simple and logical plan with contingencies if circumstances change.

In the sea, care will usually have to be taken that swimmers do not come into contact with rocks, or are taken into a worse situation because they are out of their boat. On occasion, this may mean that to go out to sea, outside the effect of any rips or breaking waves, before finding a safe place to come inshore, would be the most sensible course of action.

Dumping Surf

Dumping surf is created where the beach shelves steeply instead of gently. Instead of breaking gradually, the wave breaks in one powerful 'dump'. The only thing to do is avoid it.

Sometimes a perfect break can turn into dumping surf as the tide rises or falls toward its high or low tide point and the nature of the beach changes. Beware!

Rolling

Predictably, the end result of any of the surf manoeuvres incorrectly performed will be a capsize. Rolling in the surf is particularly demanding. This makes it a tremendous medium in which to hone that basic technique learnt in flat water or the pool. There are many similarities to other moving water environments, the principles being:

- Brace the lower body hard, so as to avoid being unseated before you have a chance to roll.
- Stay compact, so as to avoid paddles being ripped out of your hands or possible injury to your shoulders.
- Wait a few seconds to see if the wave will let you go and wash over you. This would leave you with, in effect, a flat water roll.
- Start the roll from the position you capsize in.
- Try to roll with the wave.
- Once upright, prepare immediately for the next wave that is going to hit you. Either paddle toward it or prepare to ride the broken water back into the beach.

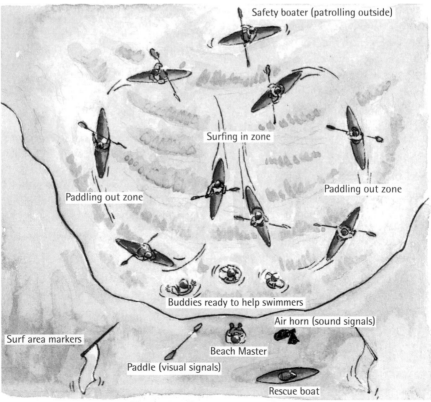

Fig 21.9 Supervising a surf session

It is fair to say that surf is a very demanding environment to roll in and that swims are common, even for the most experienced surfers.

Swimming In

When swimming into the beach, push the boat in before you (to avoid being run over and injured by your own boat). As passing waves give your boat a push, hang on so that they tow you towards the beach.

Rips

Rips will take swimmers out to sea faster than they can paddle in. Fortunately the area of water affected by a rip is generally a very narrow strip. If you find yourself in a rip, you should swim at right angles to the rip (parallel to the beach) until you get out of the rip; you will then be able to swim in towards the beach.

Competition

Competitive surfing has been around since the 1970s. Competitors at that time were primarily kayak paddlers with craft such as the KW7, Comanche and Snipe. A popular performance craft, which originated from California, was the Surf Shoe. This flat-bottomed craft allowed the paddler to surf much more accurately given the extra boat speed. Then came the Zappa complete with centre fin. The paddler sat on this like a ski but pushed against footrests and stayed on by gripping a centre tree with the knees.

The late 1970s and early 1980s saw the introduction of the surf ski from Australia and South Africa. This heralded a boom in competition with younger paddlers being attracted by this cool craft. By the mid-eighties, with ski competitions being held worldwide, paddlers understandably wanted to compete on the world circuit. The BCU, along with other major bodies, had cut sporting links with South Africa because of Apartheid. To overcome this, ski paddlers made the decision to split from the BCU and form the British Wave Ski Association (BWSA).

This was almost the death knell for kayak surfing. Numbers had been decimated by the move, and it was left to a core of paddlers to keep competitions on the calendar.

A New Era

A new era dawned in 1989 when Californian paddlers expressed an interest in attending the Home International. They brought with them a number of craft not seen in this country. From this, an inaugural World Championship was held in Santa Cruz in 1990. The following year saw the official start to the World Championships with Scotland hosting the event in Thurso.

Modern Designs

Boat design generally, but particularly boats suitable to carve and edge their way around a surf wave appeared on the scene. The combination of these new surf craft with improved understanding of the sport at recreational level spurred on the ambition at a world level. Local competition numbers increased, with paddlers becoming fitter and more serious about their sport. Manufacturers designed a variety of boats, leading to a change in the manoeuvres performed. World competitions have since been held in California, Costa Rica, Scotland and Brazil.

Competition Seasons

Local competitions are held throughout the country. (See your yearbook for details). They are held primarily from March to June and September to November.

Home Internationals are held bi-annually and are hosted by the home countries in turn. World competitions are held bi-annually (alternate to H.I.) and are held either in March or September.

OK, so you know where they are. What have you got to do?

How It All Works

You have to enter in advance if you don't want to pay extra for a late entry. Prices and addresses are found in the yearbook. At present there are two main classes: High Performance and International Class, each with their different craft rules. The Surf Yearbook will give all the technical information. There are also Junior and Ladies sections.

The Heats

The heats are normally 20-minute duration with four paddlers in each heat. Each paddler wears a different colour bib for identification. If numbers permit, the early rounds are seeded.

The three highest scoring waves for each paddler are totalled at the end of the heat to give positions. The two highest scoring paddlers from each round move onto the next until the final heat, where first through to fourth positions are decided.

The Flag System

For timing, a flag system is operated on the following principles:

- Red flag - no surfing.
- Green flag - heat in progress.
- Green and Yellow flags - 5 minutes left in the heat. This is also the signal for the paddlers in the next heat to begin their paddle out.
- Black flag or all flags up together - leave the water immediately.

Judging

Judges are usually drawn from the experienced paddlers and work on a rotation system. Three judges are the norm. A chief judge oversees the whole competition to ensure continuity of judging. Paid judges are normally secured for World events.

How to Convince Them That You Are the Best

Judging is subjective, with scores being given for artistic interpretation.

Each wave is scored out of 20.

In short, if you position yourself correctly on a good wave, perform some radical manoeuvres in the pocket and perform some acrobatics at the end, you are going to score well. Don't forget though, you still have at least another two rides to go.

Paddlers for international teams are selected from their ranking positions at domestic competitions. Some teams may have additional criteria to fulfil.

Further Reading

All about Wave Skis, Shackleton R, 1985, Surfside Press
BCU Surf Yearbook, published annually, BCU Surf Committee
Longboarder's Start-up, Werner D, 1996, Tracks
Stormriders Guide to Europe, Fitzjones O and Rainger T, 1995, Low Pressure Publishing

Websites

www.bbc.co.uk/weather
www.coldswell.com
www.a1surf.com
www.the-watershed.co.uk/bcusurf/index.htm
All contain many links into web cams, forecasts, wave buoys and actual beach conditions.

Ian Coleman

Ian is a senior lecturer in Physical Education at University College Chichester and holds coaching and assessor qualifications in three disciplines. Although originally hooked by sea paddling, the perpetual search for new challenges has led to river and surf paddling. This blend of disciplines has meant travelling to some of the most notable paddling venues around the world, from the notorious Skukamchuck wave in British Columbia to Ireland's classic Inch Reef and from the serene Maidens on Skye to the challenging upper Otz valley.

22 Reading White Water

The river banks began to close in and we were soon enclosed in a beautiful gorge. Each drop provided a new challenge with just enough difficulty to get the juices flowing, and between each drop was a clear pool, providing time for me to appreciate the magical landscape of glistening, sculptured rocks, along with lush green foliage of the ferns and conifers. A curious stoat also made an appearance, darting in and out of the rocks on the river bank, further adding to the enchantment of this Tolkien-like landscape.

In the distance I could hear the rumble of something more serious ahead. We continued cautiously, taking it in turn to negotiate each bend until the source of the rumbling was reached. It was an enormous triple-stepped fall, which definitely required closer inspection.

From the safety of the bank we could clearly see the awesome power of the falls. "It will probably go when it's lower," said Chris. That was all the excuse we needed!

After the portage, the river provided a high volume exhilarating, roller coaster ride all the way to the take-out. With aching arms and beaming faces we carried our boats to the car, tired and satisfied. It was a magnificent day.

What Is a River?

To read white water we need to appreciate the key elements that influence how it behaves. These are:

- Gradient
- Geology
- Precipitation
- Soil and vegetation

Gradient

The steeper the gradient, the faster the river will flow. Some guidebooks will indicate the gradient of a river to give you a better understanding of what the river will be like in nature. Seven metres of drop over 1km for example, is shown as 7m/km.

Geology

The rocks that form the river bed have the greatest influence on how the water behaves. Because of this, there are many rapids that appear when there is a change in the rock type. Transitions in rock type will often alter the gradient and therefore change the nature of the river.

Photo 22.1   Low Force on the River Tees is the result of the river crossing a band of more resistant rock.

Precipitation

The more it rains, the more water there will be available to drain into the rivers. Snow will also affect the level of the river when it melts. If it melts slowly the river level will rise gradually, with the opposite being true of fast melting snow. Fast melting snow and rain together will often produce flood conditions quickly. Hydrologists measure the amount of water in the river (channel) in Cumecs. 1 Cumec is 1 cubic metre of water travelling in one second. In the USA they use CFS, where feet are preferred to metres.

Soil and Vegetation

The soil and vegetation surrounding a river greatly affects the rate at which the precipitation soaks through the ground and into the river. Well-drained land, like farmland, causes the precipitation to end up in the rivers quickly. Forestry and moorland areas on the other hand, tend to release or discharge precipitation more gradually, acting like a sponge. The size of the area around a river that will deliver precipitation into it is called the catchment area. The bigger the catchment the more water is available to end up in the river. How the river will rise and fall can be displayed using a hydrograph, shown below. It shows how flow rate, measured in Cumecs, will change over time for a given channel.

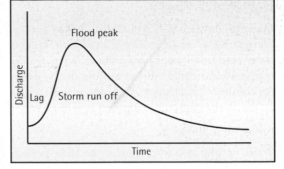

Fig 22.1   A river in a well-drained area rises quickly, but also falls quickly too. This river won't stay in condition for long.

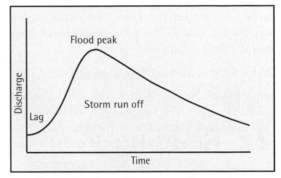

Fig 22.2   A catchment area of a more vegetated valley tends to hold more water in its soil. This river rises and falls more gradually.

The time between the rain falling and the peak flood is called a 'lag'. The quicker the land can release the water, the shorter the lag. You can expect the shortest lag times near towns where most of the ground is covered with tarmac and concrete!

Simple Anatomy of a River

Being familiar with the most common terms will avoid confusion at a later date!

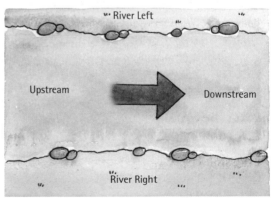

Fig 22.3   River anatomy

How Water Works

Water flows when it is pulled downhill by gravity. Fortunately, on earth gravity is a constant, making water behave fairly uniformly wherever you go. No matter where I paddle abroad, surrounded by different cultures and languages, I am always happy to get on the river where everything feels familiar again.

A River is a 3D World

Water flowing in a river tends to be fairly predictable. The patterns of water we can see on the surface are caused by the rocks below. These patterns tend to give us a good indication of what is going on underneath. As paddlers we like to stay on the surface, but the key to a greater understanding lies with the fact that we must always appreciate that a river is a three dimensional medium.

Water Flow in a Straight Section of River

On a straight section of river with a fairly regular profile the water will flow along it smoothly. The river bank and bed will cause friction, so the flow will be greatest in the middle just below the surface.

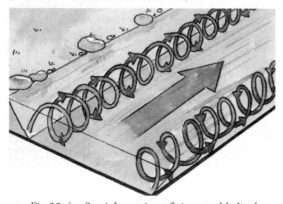

Fig 22.4   Straight section of river and helical currents

The action of the water flowing over the bedrock creates corkscrew or helical currents. In a boat on the surface it is possible to gain a little respite in the slower current here. However, if you are trying to swim to the bank with a swamped boat, you will find that below the surface these currents will tend to push you back into the main flow! Therefore, if you are aware of them you can overcome them with a bit of extra effort.

Water Flow at a Bend in a River

The laws of physics mean that at a bend, the water will always be forced to the outside of the bend,

accelerating the flow and increasing the erosive power of the river.

Photo 22.2   The main flow of water at a bend

The inside of the bend is usually shallow with a gently shelving bank and slow current. The outside of the bend however is often quite different, where the erosive power of the river has scoured away at the banks and bed, creating a fast, deep channel. Sometimes the outside bend of the river can be undercut and jammed with river debris such as exposed tree roots and dead branches. This is definitely a place to avoid as a swimmer, because the water will flow through the debris and the swimmer may not!

Constrictions

When the same volume of water is forced through a smaller gap the water will speed up. This could be caused by the water flowing between two rocks at or close to the surface. Alternatively, the whole river becoming narrower and shallower due to a change in the geology can cause an increase in flow rate. You can expect fastest flows when a constriction is accompanied by an increase in the gradient.

Photo 22.3   The Serpent's Tail on the River Dee. The whole river is funnelled through a gap and there is also a sudden change in the gradient assisting the acceleration of the flow.

Reverse Currents

Water usually flows downhill. In some cases however, water will flow in the opposite direction to the main flow. This happens in two ways:

As water flows around an obstacle, the friction created makes the water spiral. This has the effect of 'back-filling' any gaps as the water continues on its journey downstream. These are called eddy currents.

Photo. 22.4   Eddy (arrow indicates current)

As water flows over an obstacle it picks up speed and energy. This energy is then dissipated by some of the water being forced back to the surface and then being re-circulated.

The technical term for a vertical reverse flow of water is a 'hydraulic jump'. From a paddler's perspective there are two main types of 'hydraulic jump':

1. Surface stoppers (known in the USA as 'holes').

2. Deep or full depth stoppers (known in the USA as 'hydraulics'). (See Fig 22.7)

Water Levels

The more water in the river, the faster the flow and the more power there will be in each of the river's features. As a result, the journey down the river will be faster and reaction times will need to be quicker in order to navigate successfully! Most guidebooks give descriptions at medium levels.

Be aware of rivers in flood. Even familiar rivers change character in flood as features can become awesomely powerful and even span the whole river. The river will be moving so fast that reaction time will be minimal; it will only take seconds for a swimmer to part company from the rest of the group. Paddling flood stage rivers can be extremely exciting but your river reading skills and paddling ability must be first class.

River Indicators

The quickest way to describe the condition of the river is to use an indictor or gauge. Indicators range from measured scales stuck on the riverbank, to natural indicators like rock shelves or shingle banks. Guidebooks will use natural features like this, followed by a comment like, "If the shingle bank above the bridge is just covered, the river is at a medium level".

Photo 22.5   Gauge, note the numbered scale

River level information can also be obtained by telephoning water information lines, which are

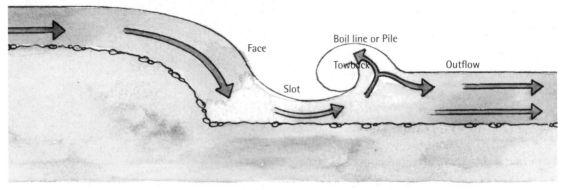

Fig 22.5   Surface stopper

recorded messages that are updated regularly with details of river levels, hazards or access. Dam controlled rivers will have details of when they are releasing and how much water is likely to be released. It is also worth checking out the internet for river information. This facility is well set up in the USA and is likely to continue to develop everywhere.

Experienced paddlers will use these indicators and lots of other information about the river in order to increase their awareness before they get on. The following could be a selection of their thoughts:

- Exposed dry rocks, and the river bed is clearly visible interspersed only by leaping salmon. It looks like you could ride your bike down the river. - A trip to the seaside or go home.

- The river is a high speed, chocolate coloured conveyor of death. - Go home or find another river.

- Weather reports indicate strong winds and heavy rain. - The rain could bring the river into condition but look out for new hazards like farm debris, trees, livestock, etc.

- The ground is very soggy. - Further rain could bring the river up quickly.

- It's already raining. - Is the group good enough if the river level rises?

- Guidebook level indicators show a good level. – We are in for a good day's paddle!

- Water information line gives good river levels. – We are in for a good day's paddle!

The moral of the story is put together as much information as you can before you set off to avoid a wasted journey. Have a contingency plan for another venue in case the river you chose first is too high or too low. You should avoid feeling pressured to paddle a river regardless, just because you made the effort to get there!

Learning How to Read White Water

As beginners, we spend far too much time worrying what the water will do to us. The key to reading white water is recognising what river features can do for us.

Reading white water is the skill of recognising features that indicate what the river is doing, based upon the principles discussed earlier. Remember that water tends to follow similar patterns, so therefore most river features are really variations on a theme.

Eddy currents, for example can be seen on every river in the world. Some are perfect examples where the flow is totally predictable and its effects on the boat can be easily anticipated. These 'perfect' examples form the base line of our understanding. Then it is simply a matter of adjusting to the specific conditions of that particular eddy. This process is then repeated every time we encounter a new feature, making white water paddling an ever-changing physical and mental challenge!

White Water Features

Upstream 'V' Shapes

These handy 'V' shapes point upstream, directly at a rock, which is at or just below the surface.

Photo 22.6   Upstream 'V'

Top Tips:

- Upstream 'V's can sometimes point to eddies behind the rocks they indicate.

- The currents forming the sides of the 'V' can help to push you left or right down the river.

Downstream 'V' Shapes

Downstream 'V' shapes or 'tongues' are created when the water is squeezed through a constriction.

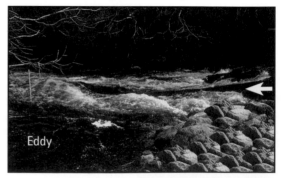

Photo 22.7   Downstream 'V'

The flow is accelerated as described earlier. The 'V' usually indicates the best route, as the channel is deeper and free from obstruction. Some sections of river can be safely negotiated entirely by paddling through one downstream 'V' to the next.

Note that either side of the downstream 'V' is an eddy current which could be used as a rest spot to find the next downstream 'V'. Learning how to do this quickly and efficiently takes time, so read the relevant section in this book for starters!

Top Tip:

- Downstream 'V's can be used to pick up speed for racing, or to punch through stoppers.

Eddies

Eddy currents flow in the opposite direction to the main flow, but are relatively weak by comparison. The eddy current creates a pool of flatter and calmer water called an eddy. These are usually found behind rocks or sections of the river bank that stick out into the main flow. An eddy line or eddy fence is a line of disturbed water visible at the surface that shows the margin between the eddy and the main flow. In more confused water, the boundary between the eddy and the main flow is wider and less clear, forming more of an eddy zone (see Photo 22.4).

Top Tips:

- Eddy currents can be used to gain speed for upstream moves or crossing the main current.
- Eddies are relatively secure places in which to rest or look at the next bit of river.

Rooster Tails

In a rooster tail, the fast flowing water is thrown up by a rock just below the surface, usually where

Fig 22.6   Rooster tail

the river is steep. The plume of water seen from upstream is a good indication of a rock to avoid.

Top Tip:

- Sometimes, wider and flatter rooster tails indicate smoother rocks that can be used as ramps in order to 'jump' something nasty below.

Standing Waves

Paddlers commonly see standing waves as water thrown up by rocks on the bottom. In fact they are caused by fast moving water flowing over a layer of stationary or slow moving water. The bigger the differential between the two bodies of water, the steeper the wave will be. Additionally, the greater the volume of water, the bigger the wave will be. From upstream they are seen as pyramid shapes with points or foamy tops. Those with foamy tops are called 'haystacks' as they were thought to resemble the old style haystacks in fields. Long chains of standing waves or wave trains can give a really exciting but safe ride, so some paddlers call them roller coasters.

Photo 22.8   'Meaty' standing wave

Top Tips:

- Endless fun can be had carving up a well-formed standing wave. However, they can also be used to surf across the river in order to get to the other side more efficiently.
- The crest of a standing wave can give you a great vantage point to scout the river and change direction if necessary.

Stoppers

The basic formation of stoppers has been explained (see Reverse Currents), but stoppers vary considerably in size, shape and personality! Some are harmless and quite playful whereas others can hold boat and paddler indefinitely! Knowing which is which takes knowledge, skill and experience!

No two stoppers are exactly alike but there are key features to look out for. As a result we can identify what some stoppers can do for us.

Surface Stoppers

Surface stoppers tend to be friendlier. Consequently, these are the ones where you will often find boaters playing (see Fig 22.5).

Photo 22.9   Surface stopper

Basic characteristics of a surface stopper are:

- Noisy because all the energy is at the surface
- Shallow ramp angle
- Frothy foam pile
- Shorter towback

Surface stoppers tend to have quite strong out-flows because a lot of the water is flushing through below the surface. Although a boat being buoyant may be held, a swimmer will usually be flushed through quite easily.

Top Tip:

- Small surface stoppers can be used to slow you down and give you time to think. Alternatively, if you can side-surf you can use the stoppers as a kind of eddy to view the river ahead.

Beware

All stoppers deserve respect. Get the skills sorted in the popular, safe stoppers before testing yourself on the unknown!

Deep or Full-Depth Stoppers

Full depth stoppers generally fall into the 'not nice' category. Consequently, they can't do much for us and you won't find too many boaters playing in them.

General characteristics of a full depth stopper are:

- All the water is recirculated
- Quieter, because all the energy and action are beneath the surface
- Longer towback
- Steeper ramp
- Less foam pile

These stoppers are more dangerous because the towback is longer and much more of the water is recirculated back into the slot. Deep, recirculating stoppers are far more likely to hold swimmers.

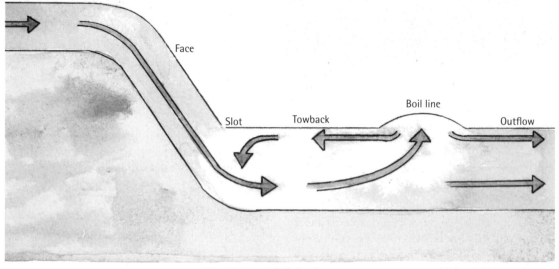

Fig 22.7   A full depth stopper

Top tip:

- If the towback is more than about two metres it will almost certainly hold a swimmer.

Exits

In Photo 22.10 the stopper is angled downstream. All the water is recirculating downstream and there is a clear exit at the downstream end with a strong out-flow. The direction of the recirculating water is called the 'kick'. This type of stopper is open because the kick is directed towards a clear exit.

Photo 22.10   An open stopper

In Photo 22.11 the stopper has no clear out-wash and consequently no clear exit. Both ends are closed in by the river bank and so this type of stopper is closed. These are potentially very dangerous.

Photo 22.11   A closed stopper

Top Tip:

- Gently angled stoppers with clean exits and a helpful kick can be used to propel you across the river without too much effort, in order to line up with the next drop.

An exit in a stopper is an area of weakness in the towback. This is where the out-wash is strongest and it will provide the best way out of a stopper.

The rocks below may be irregular, making the towback weaker. Alternatively, the angle of the rock shelf may be such that a simple chute or down-stream 'V' is formed in the stopper.

Either way, they are very important features to be able to identify before launching into a stopper.

Top Tip:

- Seen from upstream, an exit will be shown by a 'V' of white pointing downstream. The longer the 'V', the better the exit.

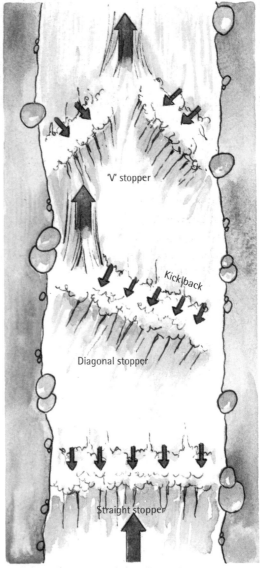

Fig 22.8   Angled and straight stoppers

Smiling Stoppers

A curved stopper with exits at either end has the appearance of a smiling mouth when viewed from upstream. These are friendlier because the water will re-circulate towards the exits downstream, providing a means of escape, even for a swimmer!

> **Beware**
>
> *In flood, even smiling stoppers can be nasty. If in doubt - get out!*

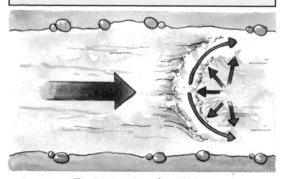
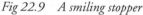

Fig 22.9   A smiling stopper

Frowning Stoppers

A frowning stopper when viewed from upstream will have the exits pointing upstream, giving the appearance of a frowning mouth. The towback will be recirculating back into the stopper making progress to the exits almost impossible, as you will have to fight your way back upstream. The exit will be poor because the out-wash will be weak, due to most of the water being recirculated back into the centre of the stopper.

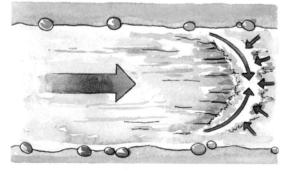

Fig 22.10   A frowning stopper

Top Tip:

- A smiling stopper is like an umbrella with the main flow being the rain. The water will hit the umbrella, stay for a while and then fall off.

- Turn the umbrella upside down in the main flow (making a frowning stopper) and it will hold the water and you for a lot longer! This is why they are called 'keepers' in the USA One such keeper is reputed to be called 'Hotel California' .You can go in but nobody seems to come out!

Pour-overs

Seen from upstream, a pour-over has the appearance of a glassy dome. Consequently in the USA they are sometimes referred to as 'domers'. On the downstream side of a pour-over there will be a stopper, which is usually a 'frowning' type. Even if there is not much water flowing over the rock, the stopper on the downstream side can be strong if the rock creates a steep ramp.

Photo 22.12   A pour-over

Top Tip:

- Generally, most pour-overs are avoided. However, a carefully chosen pour-over can provide a good eddy just downstream of the stopper, if conventional eddies are scarce.

Weirs

Weirs that get regular river traffic often have warning notices. Many do not, so keep an eye for other warning signs. On approaching a weir, the flow of the river will slow and there will be a clear change in the horizon line. Old weirs may have a large mill building next to them but there are fewer clues for modern weirs.

The job of a weir is to allow the river to lose gradient and therefore energy in one go. This is sometimes to reduce the erosive power of the river, or to simply slow the river down and create sections of deep water for river traffic.

Whatever the reason for construction, most weirs are made of metal and concrete. Water flowing over smooth concrete has lots more energy and the stoppers are often full-depth. Even small weir stoppers can have very powerful towbacks. Beneath the surface there may also still be metal parts of the construction left sticking from the concrete or lying on the bottom.

Fig 22.11   Change of horizon line

Some weirs, like Hurley Weir on the River Thames are quite safe to use for paddling and these have become popular venues, particularly during the dry summer months.

In short, any weir that is worth paddling has probably been checked out already. Get information from other paddlers or a guidebook wherever possible. Depending on water levels, all weirs can be lethal and they all deserve the utmost respect. As a general rule, paddle weirs that are known to be safe and leave the rest alone.

Cushion Waves

On the upstream side of any obstacle in the water you will find a cushion of water piling up against it. Some pour-overs will also have a cushion wave on their upstream side. Other cushion waves can be found on the outside bend of the river if the water crashes into a vertical or near vertical wall.

Photo 22.13   A cushion wave

Top Tips:

- With the correct technique, cushion waves can be used to 'bounce off' and redirect you.
- Rocks with cushion waves are not usually undercut and hazardous.

Drops

On approaching a drop from upstream you will clearly see a noticeable change in the horizon line. Drops are created when water flows steeply over a rock ledge or shelf. The main features of a drop are:

- Run in
- Take off or lip
- Descent
- Landing

Photo 22.14   Drop features

When reading a drop it is necessary to look at each of the above features to identify how difficult the drop is. Easy drops will mean that all of the above are straightforward. As each of the above increases with difficulty, so does the nature of the drop. There are often stoppers at the bottom of drops and these should be treated with the same respect as any other stopper on the river.

Top Tips:

- Pick up other clues from the change in the gradient of the land either side of the river. If trees are present you may see the tops of a line of trees sloping downhill steeply long before you reach the drop itself.
- If in doubt, get out and inspect the drop.
- Listen out. Drops can usually be heard from upstream.

Bigger Drops

Drops over 3 metres are called waterfalls as defined by Franco Ferrero in his book 'White Water Safety and Rescue'. He makes the point that these are different from smaller drops in that they require different skills, due to the injury potential of free-falling from this height. Read it!

Double Recirculations

Be aware of these on vertical drops. The water erodes a softer layer of rock, forming a mini-cave behind the face of the fall. Look out for water recirculating behind the fall as well as downstream.

Hazards

Unlike other river features, hazards are not of any use to white water paddlers. They are to be recognised and avoided by either paddling around them or in some cases, portaging around them.

Undercuts

Undercuts are angled rocks or sections of river bank that the water flows underneath. Some are clearly visible from upstream and can be easily avoided. The most dangerous undercuts occur beneath the surface. Their presence is more difficult to detect and they can entrap boats and swimmers.

Photo 22.15   Cushion wave shows that most of the flow probably doesn't go under the rock.

Top Tips:

• Avoid undercuts like the plague.

• The absence of a cushion wave on a rock or steep bank will sometimes indicate an undercut.

Strainers

Strainers act in exactly the same way as a tea strainer. Water flows through easily but larger obstacles get trapped. Strainers made of exposed tree roots and branches often grow as more river debris gets swept

onto them. They will entrap boats and swimmers, and rescue from them is often problematic. Scaffolding or road building materials can also create strainers, trapping building waste and river debris.

Top Tips:

• Keep an eye out for new strainers. Even on familiar stretches of river, new strainers will appear after strong winds or heavy rain.

• Overhanging branches are not as bendy as you think! Don't assume that you can fight your way through. They too can act like a strainer, so they should also be avoided.

Boulder Chokes

A boulder choke or sieve acts in the same way as a strainer. Water will pass through the gaps in the rock, but a larger object such as a boat or swimmer may not. The presence of a boulder choke may be difficult to spot from the river because, unlike strainers, the rocks look as though they belong there! The water is flowing through the gaps in the rocks, rather than over them.

Siphons

Siphons are holes through rocks where the water flows. Small stones get whirled around in small depressions in the rock, called potholes. The stones wear away at the pothole, eventually creating a tube with an entry and an exit. Siphons may also occur in a gap between two rocks. They are a bit like a giant plughole, so they are avoided at all costs.

Top Tips:

• Siphons are easier to spot when the water is missing, so go and have a look when its too dry to paddle.

• Read the section on spotting siphons in 'White Water Safety and Rescue.'

To Paddle or Not To Paddle?

At the end of the day, the decision to paddle a rapid or fall is yours and yours alone. Being aware of hazards and anticipating where they are likely to be is a key part of safe and enjoyable paddling. You should be able to make an informed judgement fairly quickly as to whether you can run it or not. Sometimes, if you are unsure of a drop or rapid, it may be better to walk around it and save your energy for the next section that may be much more enjoyable anyway. Don't forget to still look at the river during your portage; you may still learn a thing or two on the walk down!

Artificial and Dam-release Sites

These are important white water venues, often providing the only reliable source of white water around. They are excellent places to practise white water skills, and most features seen on natural rivers can be found there.

Key points to consider:

- Artificial sites are usually made of smooth concrete. The water will behave slightly differently to a natural river, although it can resemble a flooded river.

- Paddling regularly at these sites can improve personal skills, but continually using the same venue does little for improving reading white water skills.

- Hazards have been minimised and you are usually not too far from help in the event of injury. Be aware that continual use of a site can help develop a complacent attitude when transferring skills to the natural white water environment.

Putting It All Together

If we think of each individual river feature as a letter in the alphabet, then a section of rapids is like a sentence on a page. With only a relatively small number of river features, almost limitless combinations or 'sentences' can be found, making each rapid different from the last and each river different from the next. This is the lure and the challenge of white water paddling.

Being only human means that we like to make sense of this complex and random environment.

River grading systems such as the one below attempt to categorise river features and their respective difficulties. It is by no means perfect but it is the one most widely used and, more importantly, the most widely understood.

The International River Grading System

Variations

There are variations to this system of grading. These variations attempt to take into account more of the individual aspects of a river. Probably the most widely used variation of this system is an adaptation formulated by Terry Storry.

In his guidebook 'British White Water' he attempts to describe the potential danger you may experience if you swim on the rapid by adding letters to the existing number grade. At one end of the scale the letter 'a' is used to indicate that swimming and rescues are easy. At the other end of the scale the letter 'f' is used to describe a rapid where swimming is potentially fatal and rescue is much more difficult.

Other variations found in river guides take into account conditions such as:

- Gradient
- Remoteness
- How continuous the rapids are
- Water level
- Technicality

Many find this additional information useful, particularly when paddling abroad. However, the decision to paddle still remains yours. Good judgements are made using as much correct information as is available to you. Most importantly of all, the correct judgement must be made using your eyes, ears and brain on the river.

Grade 1	Grade 2	Grade 3	Grade 4	Grade 5	Grade 6
Regular stream Regular waves Small rapids	Passage free Irregular Stream Irregular waves Medium rapids, small stoppers, eddies, whirlpools and pressure areas	Route recognisable High irregular waves Larger rapids Stoppers, eddies, whirlpools and pressure areas	Route not always recognisable Inspection mostly necessary Heavy continuous rapids Heavy stoppers, whirlpools and pressure areas	Inspection essential Extreme rapids Stoppers, whirlpools and pressure areas	Generally speaking impossible Possibly navigable at particular water levels
Simple obstructions	Simple obstructions in flow Small drops	Isolated boulders, small drops and many obstructions in stream	Boulders obstructing stream, big with undertow	Narrow passages, steep gradients and drops with difficult access and landing	High risk

Table 22.1   International Grading System

Having Your Cake and Eating It

Trying to read a whole section of white water is a bit like trying to eat a delicious, whole cake in one go. In order to do the job successfully without making a mess or feeling sick we must slice the cake into pieces that we can deal with.

The river can be broken down into 'slices' or 'bite size chunks' that are much easier for our brains to handle. This can be done from the boat or from the bank. Open canoe paddlers have a third option of looking from the boat whilst standing up.

The aim is to gather information so that you can give yourself options. This way you will always have a choice. It may be a choice of route or it may be the decision to get out. Either way, you never want to find yourself running a drop or rapid blind because you had to (i.e. it was the only option).

On approaching a rapid or drop, experienced paddlers' thought processes tend to follow a fairly regular pattern where they rely on gaining as much information as possible from what they see and hear.

To choose the best route we should ensure that:

- We have the best view to spot useful features and potential hazards. This often means having to move from our current position or sometimes getting a view from the bank.

- We recognise what the water is doing and where most of it is flowing.

- We can make the move to the next viewpoint, utilising water features.

- We know what to do in order to avoid the hazard.

- When we reach the next viewpoint we have the option of another viewpoint if we need it.

Conclusion

Learning to read white water is an active process best done on the water. Use this chapter as a reference source to develop your understanding in conjunction with practical white water experiences.

Further Reading

British White Water, Storry T, 1991, London, Constable, 0-09-467770-0
Kayak, Nealy W, 1993, Menash Ridge Press, 0-89732-050-6
Path of the Paddle, Mason B, Revised 1995, Key Porter Books, Toronto
The Playboaters Handbook, Whiting K, 1998, Heliconia Press, Clayton - Ontario, 1-896980-02-3
White Water Kayaking, Rowe R, 1988, Salamander Books
White Water Safety and Rescue, Ferrero F, 1998, Pesda Press, Bangor - Wales, 0-9531956-0-0

Other Useful Books

The Essential Whitewater Kayaker, Bennett J, 1999, Ragged Mountain Press
The Art of Freestyle, Brymer E, Hughes T and Collins L, 2000, Pesda Press, 0-9531956-3-5

Matt Berry

Matt is a BCU Level 5 Coach who lives and works in Staffordshire where he teaches biology. More often than not however, he can be found on the river, either paddling with his mates or working with groups. He started paddling as a young boy with Barking and Dagenham CC way back in the early eighties, when all boats were long and pointy.

In almost 20 years of paddling, Matt has enjoyed most aspects of paddlesport, ranging from polo to marathon and sea kayaking to freestyle, but he is most easily lured by the prospect of paddling a new white water river. As well as spending many a damp weekend in Britain, Matt's passion for new white water has taken him to such places as the USA, Canada, Nepal, France, Austria, Switzerland, Germany and Corsica.

23 White Water Kayaking

Just as this was due to be sent to the editor, I took the opportunity to go paddling, rather than do the spell checking.

I had been on that river more times than I cared to remember. Yet, later that evening, I still sat down in front of the fire enjoying that great feeling of having done something new, always different and challenging. That is what I love about white water kayaking.

Introduction

This chapter is built on the work of two previous chapters, Foundation Kayak Skills and Reading White Water. A thorough and skilful performance of the skills in the foundation kayak technique chapter and a good understanding of the hydrology section are essential before this one can be understood and appreciated fully. Take time to read them before delving into this one!

Having mastered the foundation strokes and gained an understanding of moving water, we can apply ourselves to the three fundamental elements of white water kayaking:

Balance   (trim and edge/lean)

Accuracy } (speed and angle)

Timing }

The term 'fundamental' is, perhaps, a new one to kayaking. I prefer 'fundamental' or foundation to the term 'basic' for the reason that these skills form the basis of good white water performance, and yet are not basic. When learning new skills we need to return to the fundamentals before we can address the sophisticated elements of the more complex techniques. Time spent developing and understanding the fundamentals is never wasted and its benefits returned ten-fold.

Balance

Being able to put the boat on edge and maintain the balance of the boat is a vital component on white water. The idea of achieving balance is a continuum, using edge at one end (which requires a great deal of leg and back effort) and lean (requiring the paddler to extend the body outside the boat) at the other.

A	B	C
Edge	**Dynamic Edge/Dynamic Lean**	**Lean**
More knee lift	*Knee lift*	*Less knee lift*
Less weight on buttock	*Weight on buttock*	*More weight on buttock*

Fig 23.1a-c   The Balance Continuum illustrated

A paddler will need to develop the ability to alter the boat's shape in the water by holding the boat on edge without being off balance. This is achieved by the use of the legs and a subtle shifting of body weight from side to side and from front to back.

Fig 23.1a Edge

The kayaker is sitting upright in the boat, using a single knee to raise one side of the kayak. The edge is achieved by lifting a knee and arching the back towards that knee. An extended period of edging is very tiring.

Fig 23.1b Dynamic Edge/Lean

The kayaker has lifted a knee, and in order to hold the kayak in that position, has subtly shifted weight over the buttock, holding the boat on its edge and maintaining that edge.

Fig 23.1c Lean

The kayaker has now leaned the boat to create an edge by shifting body and head outside the gunwale lines of the kayak. The knees and hips are held perpendicular to the body. This position can only be maintained by gaining support from the paddle; this prevents the paddle from being used for any other purpose and has limited value on white water.

Accuracy

Accuracy is as much in the mind as in the paddling skills and the paddler must aspire to be accurate in terms of boat positioning.

The foundation kayak skills need to be effective and confidently performed. These skills will enable the kayaker to apply speed and set the boat's angle to the current. The kayaker will need both control and power in order to be accurate.

Being accurate also requires an understanding of the hydrology section beyond the simple reading of the words. The kayaker must be able to identify the different wave features on the river and understand their effect on the kayak.

Setting a boat's angle and then being able to apply speed in a series of linked strokes is an important skill. Whilst these elements are examined separately, they form two elements of the same sequence.

Angle

Creating, setting and maintaining the boat's angle to the water feature prior to applying speed is essential; it allows the kayaker to control the effect of the water on the kayak. Setting the angle is achieved with sweep strokes. When combined with dynamic footwork, a dramatic turn can be achieved. The stroke is wide from the boat, blade covered but with the paddle loom close to horizontal.

A forward sweep can be used to set the angle of attack if the boat is in mid-current. If the boat is close to an eddy, a reverse sweep may be more appropriate as this will also move the boat away from the eddy, having the effect of opening the angle of attack into an eddy if required.

New boat angle

Fig 23.2   The use of a forward sweep alters the angle of the boat and maintains forward speed

In large standing waves, setting the boat at an angle needs to be timed so that the boat is turned on the way up a wave. This ensures that the bow is free of the water and the boat can be moved easily.

Fig 23.3   The timing of the forward sweep, when used to turn in standing waves, needs to be practised

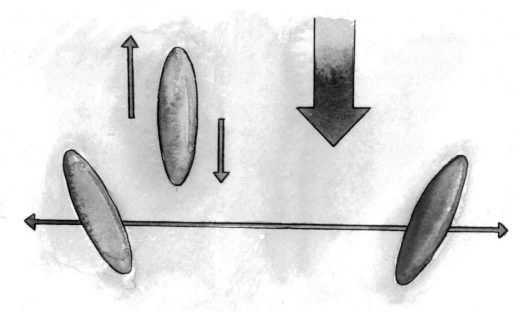

Fig 23.4   Current, upriver speed, dowriver speed, lateral speed

Speed

Speed, when used in relation to a boat in white water, is a difficult concept. The boat's speed is described relative to the moving water in the river. It is described in terms of upstream, downstream and lateral speed.

- Upriver speed is best described as going against the current.

- Downriver speed is best described as moving with the current.

- Lateral speed is best described as the movement across the current.

A The kayaker accelerates the boat towards the stopper to penetrate the stopper at 90 degrees.

B As the boat enters the stopper, the kayaker reaches over the stopper as part of the forward paddling action.

C The paddling sequence is continued as the boat passes through the stopper.

Fig 23.5   Boat accelerated forwards to 'punch' through a stopper

All are combinations of boat speed and current:

- Directly against the current to create upriver speed.

- Against the current and by setting the boat at an angle to create lateral speed.

- With the current to create downriver speed.

An understanding of how to generate speed, (both forwards and reverse) is important because it enables the kayaker to accelerate the kayak in a straight line to penetrate eddies. That speed needs to be controlled so as to match the conditions and the manoeuvre, (i.e. identify and move at a speed appropriate to the conditions). These are all related to and rely on the use of effective power strokes that have minimum turning effect and maximum driving power (both forwards and reverse).

Downriver Speed

Accelerating to the kayak's maximum speed, for most white water kayaks, takes 4-5 effective strokes. Once the boat is at speed, effort can be reduced to maintain speed rather than trying to push the boat faster and faster. Accelerating strokes differ from the cruising and racing forward strokes required in other disciplines. The difference in technique is forced on the kayaker by the design of most modern white water kayaks. White water kayaks tend to be wide and short with limited directional stability; indeed the hulls are designed to enhance manoeuvrability, often at the expense of forward speed. The result is that the kayaker must create forward movement with minimum turning effect, (this is difficult in a short, flat-hulled boat). It requires a very short rapid stroke to 'pull' the boat forwards with limited body rotation. This means that the strokes need to be short, close to the boat and rapid. The blade should be covered but in the surface water. The more vertical the paddle (during the period of most effort), the better. This will necessitate the upper arm coming over the boat which will differ from the technique required in craft with a greater directional stability.

Downriver speed need not be generated simply by the kayaker's effort; speed can be 'carried' by the kayaker by using the hydrology of the river and/or gradient of the water. The natural gravity of the rapid or wave can be used to add speed to a manoeuvre.

Reverse Paddling

Losing downriver speed creates time for the paddler to pick a route down a rapid and enables the kayak

to be positioned in order to set the correct angle to a wave feature.

Photo 23.1 Carrying river speed!

Speed and Angle Together

Setting the angle and then following it with the application of power to create speed goes hand in hand. The paddler needs to be able to continually adjust the boat angle to the current. As the paddler accelerates forward they may feel the need to adjust the angle of the boat to a wave or eddy. This is achieved by 'widening and lowering' the power stroke to provide an element of turning effect.

Photo 23.2 A 'low wide' stroke to turn

Photo 23.3 A vertical stroke for power

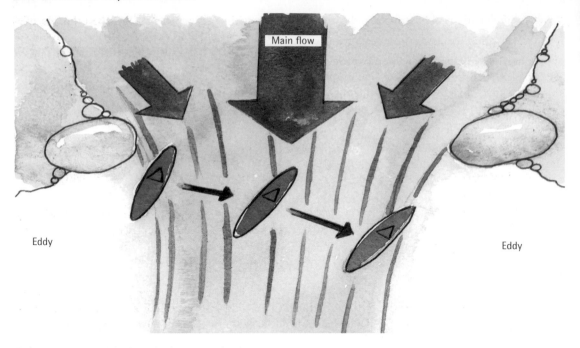

Main flow

Eddy

Eddy

Fig 23.6   Keeping an angle to the current

The two strokes do two different jobs. A stroke that compromises by doing a bit of both will not do enough of either. The kayaker needs to be able to vary the stroke within the paddling sequence without a break in rhythm. Training on flat water enables the kayaker to practise varying the height and width of the stroke to give the required effects.

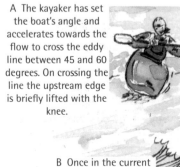

A The kayaker has set the boat's angle and accelerates towards the flow to cross the eddy line between 45 and 60 degrees. On crossing the line the upstream edge is briefly lifted with the knee.

B Once in the current the speed is lost and the boat can be allowed to flatten. The bow can be allowed to face slightly more across the flow.

C As the kayak approaches the desired eddy the bow is allowed to face across the flow to create an angle of entry into the eddy of between 45 and 90 degrees (upstream).

Fig 23.7   Forward ferry glide

Timing

The environment of the white water kayaker is always moving! Just because we aren't paddling, it doesn't follow that we aren't moving! For the paddler this means that strokes, edge and changes of speed need to be timed and paced to maximise effect.

Sometimes a good paddler will know when to do nothing but wait, and the ability to 'float with intention' can be practised. Simply floating over waves and allowing the boat to move as it will within the rapid requires flexibility and a relaxed kayaker. The paddler should attempt to maintain sight on a downstream point so that the head stays passive with the eye line level whilst the body and hips are relaxed, allowing the boat to float over waves and move with the current.

Foundation Manoeuvres

Crossing the Current (Ferry Glides)

Moving from eddy to eddy or within the flow is essential for the kayaker and is refered to as a 'ferry glide'. An understanding of the water movement with a downstream 'V' is important. The current within a chute does not flow in a single direction.

Flow within a downstream 'V' is best thought of as moving towards the bottom of the 'V' (i.e. downstream) and also towards the mid-point of this 'V' shaped tongue of water.

In all ferries it is vital to set the angle of the boat to the current to create a vector, because if you keep an angle to the main flow you will ultimately be paddling parallel to the current and be unable to cross into the eddy.

Crossing the Current from Eddy to Eddy (Forward Ferry Glide)

Moving from eddy to eddy allows the kayaker to inspect rapids without getting out of the kayak, rest, wait, and move within the current.

The High Cross

In fast flows the kayaker can gain speed by using the upstream face of a standing wave to assist in the ferry. This manoeuvre is referred to as a high cross.

Changing Position in the Current (Reverse Ferry)

Once in a rapid, the kayaker may need to reposition the boat, lose unnecessary speed and/or set the angle of the boat to the current as part of setting up the next manoeuvre.

Fig 23.8   High cross

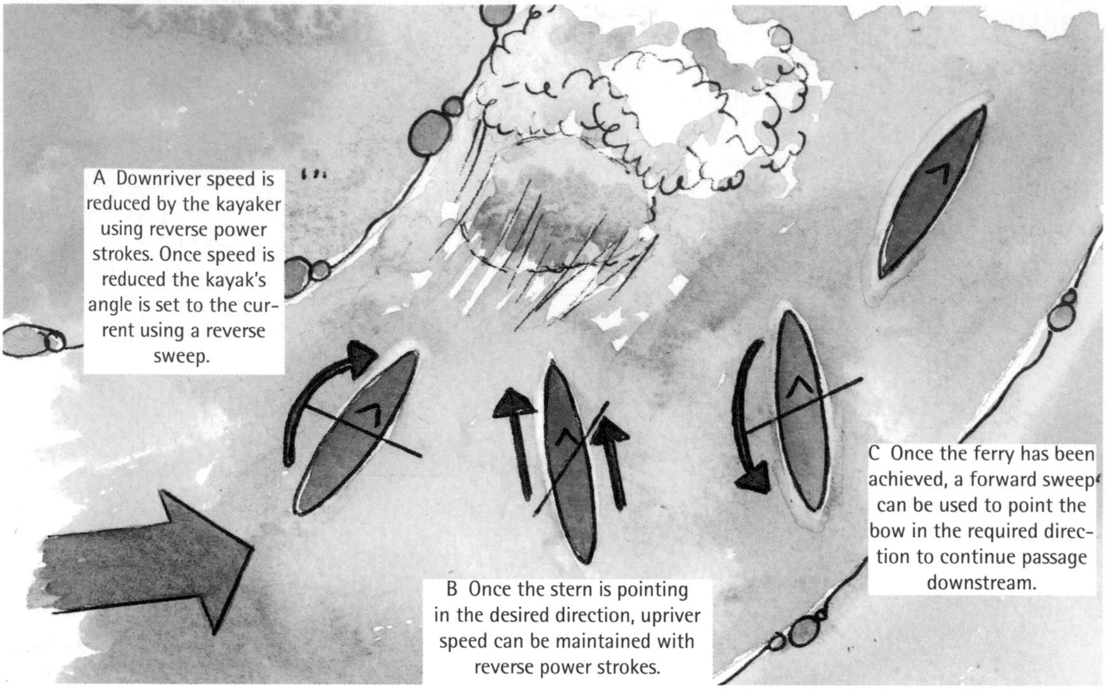

A Downriver speed is reduced by the kayaker using reverse power strokes. Once speed is reduced the kayak's angle is set to the current using a reverse sweep.

B Once the stern is pointing in the desired direction, upriver speed can be maintained with reverse power strokes.

C Once the ferry has been achieved, a forward sweep can be used to point the bow in the required direction to continue passage downstream.

Fig 23.9   Reverse ferry glide

Breaking In and Out

Moving into an Eddy from a Current (Breaking Out)

Moving out of the current is not only a white water technique, it's a safety skill.

The radius of turn achieved in the breakout is related to four elements:

1. Position of entry into eddy. Ideally, a paddler will want to enter the eddy in its upper third. At this point the eddy line is distinct, defined and easier to cross.

2. Speed of entry into the eddy. The boat must be driven into the eddy with positive downriver and lateral speed. This pushes the bow into the eddy as the stern is pushed round by the current. This creates the turn to face upstream and no sweep is required to cross the eddy line.

3. Angle of attack into the eddy. The boat will need to cross the eddy line between a 45 and 90 degree angle (beyond 90 degrees and the boat is effectively ferry glided into the eddy).

4. The stroke used to consolidate the kayak's position in the eddy. A bow rudder can be used here. The bow rudder is placed well into the eddy and converted, (rolled) into a power

stroke to consolidate the boat's position. Alternately, if the eddy is shallow or support is needed because it is turbulent, a low brace is placed well into the eddy and converted into a power (consolidation) stroke.

Problems often arise because people use a low brace turn (a combination of sweep stroke and low brace) in the same form that it is taught on flat water. This sequence is considered easier to perform but actually requires greater judgement. The sweep stroke spins the boat too soon with minimum driving effect into the eddy. The low brace is often mistakenly pushed forwards to create the turn, because the eddy has not been penetrated, acting as a reverse sweep. Inappropriately timed or executed, this in effect 'bounces' the boat back into the current.

On moving water there is no need for a sweep if the angle, speed and edge are correct. The low brace is only applied when the boat has penetrated deep into the eddy and the turn has already been initiated by the opposing currents.

Every eddy is different, and the greater variety of breakout techniques you can choose from the more skilful your performance will be. Choosing the right techniques for the right situation is a question of practice and experience. Find a site with a number of eddies that are different in character and experiment.

C Once in the eddy the kayak's speed is lost. As the kayak turns to face upstream the kayaker can sit up, allowing the boat to flatten.

B On crossing the eddy line, the combined speed of the paddler and river enables the kayaker to dynamically lean the kayak into the turn.

A The kayaker has set the boat's angle to the eddy line and accelerated towards the eddy to cross the line between 45 and 90 degrees (downstream).

Fig 23.10   Breakout using speed, angle and edge; forward power stroke used as consolidation stroke

B As the kayaker crosses the eddy line, the dynamic lean is applied to raise the outside edge. This allows the kayaker to reach deep into the eddy with the bow rudder.

C Once in the eddy the kayak's speed is lost, so as the kayak turns to face upstream the kayaker can sit up, allowing the boat to flatten.

A The kayaker has set the boat's angle to the eddy line and accelerated towards the eddy to cross the line between 45 and 90 degrees (downstream).

Fig 23.11   Bow rudder breakout sequence

Fig 23.12   Break-in using speed, angle and edge, forward power stroke used as consolidation stroke

Moving into the Current from an Eddy (Breaking In)

Once in an eddy, the time has to come when the kayaker needs to re-enter the main flow.

The objective of any break-in is to enter the main current. The same principles apply as in a breakout. The kayaker will need to leave the eddy with speed in order to penetrate the water moving downstream.

Fig 23.13   Low brace break-in sequence

Using Diagonals

Water, within a diagonal wave, always moves to the downstream end of that wave. This can be utilised by the kayaker to create speed and move across the current. It could also have an unwanted effect on the paddler if its influence is not anticipated.

By presenting a large surface area of the boat to the wave, the water has the greatest effect.

By presenting a small surface area of the boat to the wave, the water has the least effect.

Fig 23.14   Using diagonal waves

Getting out of Stoppers

Stoppers occur downstream of drops in the river bed. They are best avoided but need not be a problem if you find yourself in one.

If you inadvertently find yourself in a stopper, it is important to stay relaxed and in balance. Firstly find a relaxed, balanced, sitting position that allows you to look around (edge the kayak dynamically downstream).

Dynamic edge/lean enables you to lift the upstream edge of the boat without becoming tired. This keeps you upright and also enables you to use the paddle to move the kayak towards an outflow and so out of the stopper.

Practice

At the end of the day, there is no substitute for time spent on the river. However, by structuring your practice you will improve faster.

See you on the river.

Exercises

Find a jet of water and vary the amount of angle and speed you use to ferry glide across.

Find a site with a number of eddies that are different in character and experiment.

Try the following:

Break in and out at different speeds.

Break in and out at different angles.

Break in and out using different amounts of edge.

Break in and out at different points on the eddy line.

Break in and out using different stroke combinations.

Vary the combinations of all the above factors.

Further Reading

Kayak, Nealy W, 1993, Menash Ridge Press, 0-89732-050-6
Whitewater Paddling - Strokes and Concepts, Jackson E, 1999, Stackpole Books, 0-8117-2997-4
White Water Kayaking, Rowe R, 1988, Salamander Books

Loel Collins

Loel Collins was formerly the Director of the National White Water Centre, Canolfan Tryweryn and is now the head of the canoeing department at Plas y Brenin, the National Mountain Centre. Loel is one of the UK's leading coaches.

His passion lies in coaching white water skills and exploring and travelling in both kayak and canoe. He has paddled and taken part in first descents in many parts of the world including Papua New Guinea, Pakistan and Iran.

24 Slalom

I started canoeing in 1980 as a 7 year old on the placid waters of the River Wey in Surrey, but it wasn't until 1986, after watching Richard Fox at the Europa Cup in Nottingham and BBC TV's 'Paddles Up', that I was inspired to try slalom. To me the attraction was that slalom combined all the attractive features of paddling – speed, skill and agility, whilst challenging the force of nature down a white water river in a fragile 9kg slalom kayak, all this against the clock.

I never get bored. At every race there is a new challenge, a different sequence of gates and often a different water level, which changes the characteristics of the river. Slalom has taken me to some of the most beautiful places in Britain and the world.

By its very nature, slalom has given me the confidence to challenge any white water through the skill and precision learnt. The combination of mental, physical and technical challenges makes it the ultimate challenge, but the feeling you have when you get it right is like a drug, you need more...

What is Slalom?

Slalom is one of the most spectacular water sports, demanding skill, stamina and courage. The aim is to run a rapid river course marked by 'gates' fast, and without touching the gates. A 'gate' is two poles, suspended over the water. Green and white gates are negotiated in a downstream direction, red and white gates in an upstream direction.

Touching a pole is penalized with 2 seconds added to the competitor's time. Missing a gate costs 50 seconds – game over in serious competition. Each competitor takes two runs, and the times plus penalties are added together; the lowest aggregate score wins. Fast and clean is the name of the game.

Four classes compete: Men's (K1M) and Ladies' Kayak (K1W), Canoe Singles (C1) and Canoe Doubles (C2). This is a sport in which Britain excels, with a successful past and excellent prospects for the future... is this for you? Imagine this:

You are sitting at the start of your first run at the World Championships in the heart of the Alps. You have spent the last two years thinking of nothing else but this race and now you have a minute to go. All those hours of practice will now be put to the test. It's 30 seconds to go and you glance down the course, watching the 40 cubic metres of water per second thundering down a course that drops 6 metres in 400m of length. You have visualised every detail of your run, to negotiate the 18 gates faultlessly whilst guiding your fragile boat between the rocks to the finish. Above all, that key sequence, the one that has already put paid to some competitors' hopes after months of training...

Five beeps from the electronic starter. At the 5th, you're away; your mind is so focused that you can't even hear the water.

The first part of the course has been designed to tear your arms off. On the bank, your supporters are going crazy - but you see and hear nothing of them. You haven't cleared one gate before you focus on the next.

Half the course done, so far no touches. Your arms are getting pumped; your body is steaming despite the chill of the river. Now the key sequence, total concentration. One slip will destroy you. Triumph or disaster is here, and you know it.

You're through! Rising confidence; you push harder still, though your arms feel like lead. You must stay focused; you could blow it even in the last gate. And you are there. The final sprint, 10 metres to the finishing gate. It feels like an eternity.

This is the elite end of the sport and it takes time and progression to get that far but it is possible. At whatever level you choose to compete, you will always find fun, variety and a challenge in slalom.

Why do Slalom?

Slalom can benefit the recreational coach and paddler alike by providing valuable technical skills and other knowledge that can be practised in all forms of paddlesport.

Skills useful to an individual:

- The skill of mental rehearsal used to remember the route through the gates on a slalom course can be used to remember the route down a technical section of white water.

Photo 24.1 Paul Ratcliffe, Silver Medallist, Sydney 2000

- Slalom is an enjoyable way of improving personal skills for a rapid progression up the Star Test Award Scheme. A Division 1 slalom paddler will probably have the technical skill base to go for a BCU 5 Star Award. This combined with leadership and safety knowledge acquired in other areas would help you to achieve the required standard.

- Slalom provides a progressive introduction to white water in a safe and fun environment.

- The methods of physical training will prepare you for all forms of paddling.

Skills useful to a coach:

- Slalom gates can be used to make learning skills more interesting. For example, when teaching a draw stroke on the move it can be hard to develop an understanding of why the stroke is required. By using a couple of offset slalom gates, the application of the technique is made obvious.

- Introducing beginners to slalom gates may help to inspire them to maintain an involvement in canoeing.

- A slalom course can be set to utilise some of the skills that have just been taught.

The Diamond Slalom Challenge leaflet published by the BCU Paddlesport Initiative will provide you with details on how to set gates up and some ideas on how to use them to best develop paddlers' skills.

Getting Started in Slalom

You can do slalom almost anywhere where you can string up some gates, and the techniques learned in slalom will prove invaluable in all forms of paddlesport.

Whether you have canoed before or not, the best place to start is at a local club. Here you will be able to learn the skills required alongside other people in a safe and friendly environment. The BCU website lists canoe clubs throughout the country; also the BCU Slalom Yearbook lists clubs that are particularly active in slalom.

Lots of clubs have a slalom night when their slalom paddlers practise, and clubs also provide an opportunity to borrow equipment to find out what suits you. You can also get lots of practice at competitions. There's always practice time there, and other people to watch.

Reading the Water

The gates are positioned to test your skill in using, and coping with the water. This training is perfect for running big white water rivers. There may be an upstream gate to test your ability to break out into the eddy behind a rock; then a downstream gate on the far side so that you must ferry glide or surf a wave to reach it before the river pushes you past. It takes skill, as well as speed. You must learn to read the water well and use the water to help you.

Competitions

Competitions are held all over the country from March to October and the calendar is published in the BCU Slalom Yearbook.

To enter, send an entry card to the address in the calendar, or just write to the organiser. If you send two envelopes with a stamp and your address on, they will send you the start list before the competition and the results afterwards. You also need to send a cheque or postal order for the entry fee. Often you can enter on the day but it costs more, so entering early is always best.

The Division System

There are five divisions - Premier, and Divisions 1 to 4. Newcomers start in Division 4. When you do well, you get promoted. You build up your skill, and work your way up to bigger water and tougher competition. At the end of each season a ranking list is produced in all divisions so you can see where you are in the National Rankings.

In Division 4, where you start, the water won't be too hard; a rush of water from a weir, or moving water in a stream. By the time you get to Division 1, the water will be getting rougher and the courses

more challenging. You can use any type of boat to race in Division 4, have a go!

A typical weekend competition programme is usually:

Saturday

Free Practice

Team Competition

Sunday

Individual Competition

Prize Giving

Individual Events

In individual events paddlers of all ages compete together, but there are usually special prizes for the best in each age group. Paddlers are awarded points from the result of each race, and ranking lists are produced from these results.

Team Competition

Teams of three boats work together in the team competition. The time is from when the first boat starts until the last boat finishes. The only extra rule is that all three boats must go through an identified gate, the 'team gate', and the finish within 15 seconds. Most people treat the team competition less seriously than the individual competition and have a lot of fun doing it.

What Equipment Do I Need?

To get started you will need the following equipment:

A Boat

Photo 24.2   Canoe Singles (C1) - this is a canoe where a single paddler kneels in the canoe and uses a single bladed paddle

Photo 24.3   Canoe Doubles (C2) - a canoe for two paddlers, both kneel and use a single bladed paddle

Photo 24.4   Kayak Single (K1) - the single paddler sits in the boat and uses a two bladed paddle

Most boats are manufactured from composite materials (diolen, kevlar-carbon & carbon) to keep the weight down to a minimum. For safety reasons all boats must have a grab loop at the front and rear, a footrest and central foam buoyancy in the front and rear. All boats are subject to minimum weight regulations of K1 - 9kg, C1 - 10kg and C2 -15kg. When deciding which boat to buy, you must take into account your weight and the style of your paddling. If you are not sure what you are looking for, the best advice is to ask other paddlers in the club for advice and try out different boats to establish what is best for you.

A Paddle

Both the blades and shafts are mostly made from composite materials (glass fibre, diolen, kevlar-carbon & carbon), which provide a very rigid construction whilst keeping the weight down to a minimum.

There are two forms of shaft, cranked and straight; the choice falls mainly to personal preference as there is no real difference in performance.

Other Equipment

You will also need a spraydeck, a buoyancy aid, a helmet (CE marked) and warm clothing, (see Chapter 3 Clothing and Equipment).

The best thing to wear close to your skin is a thermal with a windproof and waterproof cagoule over the top. Neoprene shorts are good to keep you warm and some form of footwear is a must.

Sometimes you can borrow equipment from a club to get you started or you can buy the equipment. The best place to get bargains is by buying second-hand equipment at competitions or through club members.

The Rules

The aim of slalom is to negotiate the course fast and clean. The most important rules to know are:

- If you touch a pole with anything - paddle, boat, buoyancy aid, helmet or yourself - a 2 second penalty is added to your time. If you miss a gate out, go through in the wrong direction or negotiate a gate in the wrong order the penalty is 50 seconds.

- When you start slalom, you get as much practice on the course as you like, followed by 2 competition runs where your best run counts (the lowest total of time + penalties). As you progress up to the premier division, practice is removed and you have two runs, both of which count and the person with the lowest aggregate score is the winner.

- You must wear a buoyancy aid and helmet and your boat must meet regulations (mentioned earlier).

- At the end of your run, you must wait on the water until the next two competitors finish before getting off- it's your turn to provide safety cover.

Slalom Sites

You can use any stretch of water as long as there is somewhere to string a line to hang some gates. Most training sites are on flat or moving water and suitable for all ages and all levels of ability. On progression to higher divisions the slaloms take place on rougher water.

In recent years the construction of artificial white water courses have become more popular around the world, as they provide a more reliable water supply and consistent racing conditions. The regular sites for training and racing in Britain are:

England

Holme Pierrepont, Nottingham

Washburn, Harrogate

Cardington, Bedford

Scotland

Grandtully, Perthshire

Fairnilee, Borders

Wales

Canolfan Tryweryn, Bala

Mile End Mill, Llangollen

Llandysul, Carmarthenshire

European Racing & Training Venues

La Seu D'Urgell, Spain

Bourg St Maurice, France

Bratislava, Slovakia

Liptovsky Mikulas, Slovakia

Tacen, Slovenia

Training for Slalom

There are three key elements to slalom:

- Mental
- Physical
- Technical

You can argue that some are more important than others but there is no doubt that to make it to the top of the sport, high skills in all three are essential.

Mental Preparation

Mental skills are an important element in slalom as it is essential to have a clear plan of the intended route through the course from start to finish. You will find that at first you will just work on remembering where all the gates are! With practice these skills will improve to the extent that you can visualise every detail of your run with ease.

Physical Preparation

To prepare physically for slalom you first need a good basic level of aerobic fitness. This is best achieved through running, swimming, cycling and long, medium-paced paddles of 20-60 minutes duration.

Once you have a good level of aerobic fitness there are other ways of improving performance in slalom.

Strength is an important component, and although this will improve through regular paddling, it can be enhanced by training in the gym. The most effective way of developing strength in the gym is to keep the exercises paddling-specific, and to use a weight where you can achieve around 3 sets of 12 reps. The use of free weights is more effective than machine weights as it helps to improve muscle stability. Always seek advice to ensure that correct technique is used and an appropriate programme is adopted.

There are other factors that will play a part and become more important the better you get, such as:

- Nutrition and hydration: Keeping hydrated before, during and after exercise is very important, and even being slightly dehydrated can have a big impact on your performance. Eating a healthy, balanced diet is important; cut down on the fats and eat lots of carbohydrates that will provide you with the energy you need.

- Flexibility: good flexibility is an important factor to improve the range of movement, as well as reducing fatigue from training and reducing the risk of injury.

Technical Preparation

Whatever level you are in slalom, the foundation has to be a solid technical base on which to rely, whatever the course that is set. Two of the key strokes that need to be mastered are:

- The bow rudder - essential for fast, tight turns and upstream gates.

Photo 24.5   A bow rudder used to turn in the gate line

- Sweep strokes - key to keeping the boat moving through staggers.

Photo 24.6   An exit sweep from a downstream gate

Advice on technique is available through the slalom coaching manual published by the BCU. This contains detailed information on all aspects of slalom canoe and kayak technique. See the refer-ences section later in this chapter. The golden rule when training technique is to always work on your weakest area, as that will have the most effect on your performance.

Useful Training Aids

Heart Rate Monitor

If you can afford it, a heart rate monitor will help you to target your training, particularly when doing aerobic fitness training.

Video Camera

A video camera is an excellent tool for analysing technical performance. If you have access to one make use of it. Video others at the same time, as you can often learn more from watching others than watching yourself.

Further Reading

BCU Slalom Yearbook, published annually by BCU Slalom Committee
BCU Slalom Coaching Manual, 1995, BCU
To Win the Worlds, Endicott W, 1980, USA, Reese Press
The Ultimate Run, Endicott W, 1981, USA, Reese Press
The River Masters, Endicott W, 1979, USA, Reese Press
Diamond Slalom Challenge Leaflet, BCU Coaching Office
Every Crushing Stroke, Shipley S, 2001, USA, Crab Apple Publishing, 0-9710320-0-9
Every Second Counts, Jayes J, 1992, Wales, Colchester Institute

Websites

www.canoeslalom.co.uk - Newspaper and Information on Canoe Slalom
www.bcu.org.uk - British Canoe Union website
www.hppslalomcourse.co.uk - Holme Pierrepont Canoe Slalom Course
www.members.aol.com/ukslalom - GB Team Results Pages

Andy Maddock

Andy has been canoeing for over 20 years, and worked in outdoor education as a Level 3 Coach whilst coaching the Great Britain Canoe Slalom Team on a voluntary basis. He was then appointed to work full time for the BCU as Head Coach for the World Class Potential Slalom programme in 1999.

He holds the Level 4 Slalom Coaching Award and is still an active slalom and recreational paddler.

25 Wild Water Racing

Imagine your favourite stretch of white water – the waves, the stoppers, the breakouts…
Now imagine you have to get down it as fast as possible. Sounds quite easy… doesn't it?
Now imagine you're in a carbon-kevlar boat that may be damaged if you hit a rock, doesn't
turn corners easily, and is significantly more unstable than your nice playboat.

Alternatively, think of a regatta lake and the two minutes or so you would take to sprint
the course, then add some flow to help you along, and some corners and waves to make
the usual crosswind seem tame. The countdown to start is as regular as clockwork, literally.
Your boat is a bit less tippy, but now you're on your own; no rescue boat nearby, the nearest
competitor thirty seconds behind (and closing!) and the time is ticking away…

That's wild water racing.

Introduction

Wild water racing, or river racing as it is sometimes called, sounds easy on the face of it - get from point A to point B via a stretch of white water as quickly as you can. However, the best wild water racing paddlers have to have the river reading skills of slalomists or playboaters, and the fitness of marathon paddlers.

Getting Started

You can start river racing quite easily in this country, without needing specialist equipment. The racing rules require boats to have maximum length and minimum width, which means that most kayaks and canoes conform. Many people start their racing careers in general-purpose boats, which get a time allowance in Division B to encourage newcomers to the sport.

However, in the late 1980s considerable effort was put into developing a plastic wild water racing kayak which could be used to help those starting off in the sport. The outcome was the Wavehopper, a slightly shorter and thus more manoeuvrable and stable, as well as more durable, version of a basic river racing boat, which is given a 7% time allowance over a standard racing boat to encourage its use. The Executive

Committee bought a fleet of these boats, and made them available for clubs and individuals to borrow. This opened up wild water racing to many people who would not otherwise have tried the sport.

In addition, the Committee may be able to help you to access second-hand boats, as a stock is maintained, especially for junior paddlers.

Photo 25.1   Wavehopper

As with the flat water racing disciplines, most people now use wing paddles. In general, for river racing most people use shorter paddles than for flat water racing. Opinion is divided on the ideal size of blades, although the current position seems to be that you should find the largest blade you are comfortable using for the length of a race. Men in general can use bigger blades than women or juniors.

Other than that, you'll need a CE marked helmet, a buoyancy aid and a spraydeck.

Buying your own Boat

Of course, once you decide you like wild water racing, you may want to buy a specialist carbon-kevlar wild water racing boat, to make yourself more competitive. There is a range of boats to choose from, including a number of designs being imported from Eastern Europe.

A new boat can cost a lot of money, but there is a thriving second-hand racing boat market in this country, allowing you to spend much less and still end up with a good boat. The wild water racing website, www.wildwater.org.uk is a useful source of information.

The make and design of boat is very important. Different boats perform better on different types of water, and with different weights of paddler. You therefore need to choose a boat that will suit you, and the rivers you are going to paddle it on. There is a school of thought, probably started by boat design-

ers, that you should have a different boat for each river, but that might be taking things to extremes. The international paddlers will often select their boat taking into account the venues for that season's international competitions, but most mere mortals whose boats have to last them more than one or two seasons will balk at this. It is probably best to talk to someone who knows a bit about boat design before handing over any money. The discussion board on the website is a good source of information.

Racing

Racing takes place in two divisions, A and B.

Division B

This is the starter division. Races are often suitable for novices to wild water racing, and much of the race course is likely to be gently-moving water, rather than 'white water'. The season runs from January to January, and races take place throughout the year, although mostly during spring and autumn.

Division A

This is the National Championship Division. Races are held on true white water; some part of every race has to be on at least Grade III water.

The classes are: men's single kayak (MK1), women's single kayak (WK1), Canadian singles (C1) and Canadian doubles (C2). There are also separate age categories for veterans, and juniors under 14, 16, 18 and 23.

Times

Classic Division A and B races last between 8 and 30 minutes, depending on the race course, and on your speed. Sprint races, recently introduced to the National Championships, are two runs of approximately two to three minutes duration, almost entirely white water of Grade III, with the two runs added together to give the total time.

The Scoring System

Races are run as a time trial, with competitors started at 30 second or one minute intervals. Points are scored towards the National Championship Series based on a complicated formula that works out the time you would have been behind the winner if the winner had taken 20 minutes to complete the race. This makes all races directly comparable. This scoring system has some flaws, notably that faster water makes for better scores, but is widely accepted as the best way of comparing different races.

Points are scored in Division B on a slightly different system, based on the number of competitors.

What Happens at a Race?

It is easier and cheaper to enter races in advance. The Wild Water Racing Yearbook and the website give details of all races, including the organiser's address, and explains what you need to do to enter.

Photo 25.2   C2 in action

The organiser will send you a start list and details of the race course, including access points and car parking. Races are often in fairly remote places, and can be hard to find, although the distinctive shape of river racing boats on car roofs will help.

It is advisable to inspect any major rapids or falls in advance, and have several practice runs on the river. If you're not sure of the best way down the rapid, arrive early, and ask others inspecting the fall to explain the line to you. Since most people try to inspect, you will usually find someone to tell you the 'racing line', or you can watch the early risers on their first practice runs.

Since everyone wants several practice runs, and almost nobody has a 'captive driver', it is usually possible to hitch a lift from another paddler back to the start to pick up your car. Of course, in your turn, you may be asked to give others a lift up too…

River Reading when Racing

Using the fastest water, avoiding hazards and saving energy are 3 main objectives from your river reading skills. Listed under general topic heading, these are some of the skills you will learn with experience.

Features

When you are paddling the river you will come across many different features that require recognition and decision-making.

Weirs

Here the water often slows as it is 'backed up' on approach. Look for dips in the line forming the weir line, and white or faster flowing water below. Once you are confident of where to go, accelerate to the weir to maintain control and punch through a stopper.

Standing Waves

These can be regular or confused, and of differing pitch (steepness). The latter will decide whether you run down the sides and so avoid being hit in the chest by the waves. Confused waves may require a slower rate to maintain stability. In all cases the idea is to get the boat to run smoothly with no pitching. Whenever possible, the catch of the forward stroke (see Chapter 4 Foundation Kayak Skills) should be planted on the downstream side of the waves.

Rapids

The golden rule when entering rapids is to follow the smoothest and greenest water. This rule is rarely wrong, however always strain your eyes for potential hazards! Shallow stony rapids need a high stroke rate with the body weight shifted backwards. Both these actions assist steering and speed. Recognition of many different parts of the river will make your paddling much smoother as you piece together your routes and race plan. Try to keep concentration; even the flattest pieces could have submerged rocks that you could have spotted. Judge your pace on approaching hazards such as trees, and the angle and velocity required to miss them.

Stability

Always look well ahead for currents and 'tippy bits'; that way you can assess and anticipate the effects they will have on your boat. For instance:

A sharp bend with water running up against a cliff will require extra speed on the inside line or a slight edge into the cliff to support the boat.

Shoot drops and their resultant waves in the middle; here it is generally more stable as the flow is moving in a straight line.

Current at the edges often curls inwards. Place the blade in areas of least turbulence and especially avoid aerated eddy lines.

Manoeuvring

The following can all be used to move your boat to, or stay on, the racing line:

- Cushion waves on rocks
- Eddy lines
- Eddies behind rocks
- Waves and diagonal waves
- Stoppers
- Boils

Photo 25.3   C1 in action

If you are using energy to move the boat with forward sweeps or reverse (negative) strokes, your boat will decelerate and become less responsive. All the features listed above have the effect of displacing your boat laterally without the need for an adjustment in the forward stroke.

Hitting a rock cushion on the right will move the boat right. Entering the bow into an eddy from the right will move the boat to the left. The amount of movement is dependent on your exposure to the resistive effect of the water on the front side of the canoe/kayak.

When a boat is on the crest of a wave, the bow and stern are often clear of the water. With far less resistance the boat can be easily steered using an adjusted forward stroke.

Paddle Stroke Timing and Stroke Rate

Recognition of shallow, deep, small chop (waves), tight rapids and big rapids will all affect where you put the paddle and how often you put it in. Beginners will often try to paddle really fast to stay upright. The tension and lack of control will actually increase in this scenario. Experienced paddlers will slow the stroke down; a well placed blade held for longer in the water adds additional stability. An inappropriate stroke may send the boat in an unwanted direction.

In general, a paddle hitting a rock is an ineffective stroke, so look and delay the forward stroke to avoid them. Good purchase of the blade in the water offers stability and the generation of speed. A high stroke rate into rapids projects the speed required for stability and steering. A high stroke rate out of rapids, using the available current, offers energy-efficient re-acceleration but must be timed for optimum effect.

Relaxation and Mental Rehearsal

Despite the fear and adrenaline surges experienced by paddlers, it is important to remain calm. In a state of panic a high stroke rate is achieved with little thought to efficiency and effects. Inner calm allows the body to maintain its elasticity and stroke efficiency. Stiffness through anxiety makes steering and balance much harder. One way of combating this problem is by doing practice runs on the river. This helps you memorize the stroke sequences and route details. Another highly recommended technique is the rehearsal of the 'perfect shoot' of a scary section. This can reduce nerves and trigger the mind to complete the correct paddle sequence in the race.

International Competition

A number of international competitions take place in wild water racing, including Senior and Junior World Championships every two years, with Pre-Worlds in the intervening years, European Championships, and a yearly World Cup series. Great Britain sends teams to these on a regular basis.

Here, Yael Ford, a member of the Great Britain Wild Water Team, who has competed in several championships, describes her experiences of racing internationally.

"I would describe wild water racing as like a roller-coaster ride, which is why I find it so exciting, but I suppose that applies equally whether you are throwing yourself down the Graveyard on the Tryweryn or a river in Europe that you've never paddled before. But racing internationally is different from at home.

Class C internationals are open races and are quite like domestic races - except for the numbers. An open race in France can start at midday and still be running at 5 o'clock in the evening - even with 30 second start intervals! Not everyone in Europe is a World Champion, so whatever your standard, there will be many other people of a similar ability. Plus, these are opportunities to paddle rivers other than the limited selection available in Britain - so what are you waiting for? Get out there!

Championship Internationals (Worlds or Europeans) are very different. There are periods of intense training in the build-up, until a few days before the event. This is followed by 'tapering' (gradually reducing the amount of training) and resting. We get the opportunity to travel to some fantastic places, only to spend most of the time in our hotel rooms - believe me, it can get very boring! I always feel it is a great honour to be allowed to represent Britain in these events, and give it all I've got for the few minutes of the race itself, even though I may never present a challenge to the medal winners. Finally, we get to let our hair down at a post-race party before returning home, usually the next day.

The World Cup is more important than an open race, but often seen as less serious than a Championship. The World Cup is made up of six races, four to count for ranking. There are two races at each venue, often over consecutive weekends to allow competitors to do a tour. These tours can be the most fun as, over a period of a few weeks, you can really get to know some of the foreign paddlers as well.

At first it may seem daunting seeing so many people at races, but once you've become a 'seasoned' international paddler, these events become a reunion - a place to meet old friends that you haven't seen since last year."

Yael Ford

Finding Out More

If you like the sound of wild water racing, more details are available from the Secretary to the Wild Water Racing Committee, via the wild water racing website. Or just get in a boat and try it…

Websites:

The wild water racing website, www.wildwater.org.uk

Melissa Simons

Melissa Simons first went canoeing on a day trip to a PGL centre aged 9, and has been hooked ever since. She is a regular competitor in divisional marathon races in London and South-East region, and has completed the Devizes to Westminster Race twice. She also enjoys white water touring.

Her interest in wild water racing began when she was a student, when she took part in the Universities Championships in Llangollen for several years, winning the Ladies' Team event (together with Yael Ford) in 1994. Melissa was secretary to the Wild Water Racing Committee between 1999 and 2001, and maintains an active interest in the sport.

Martin Streeter

Martin is currently the Kayak Coach for the British Wild Water Racing Team. He has been involved in canoeing since the age of sixteen, taking part in slalom, surf and river trips with the Adur Canoe Club based on the south coast. Before concentrating on wild water racing, he dabbled in marathon to Division 2 standard and in his younger years made a fleeting visit to slalom's Premier Division before joining the RAF when he was eighteen years old. The RAF has supported him in his kayaking for many years.

Having completed a number of international races representing Great Britain, he turned to coaching in 1996. He still competes in the odd race to represent the RAF and is the current Inter-Service Champion (wild water racing).

26 White Water Safety and Rescue

The Koronigl River in the Highlands of Papua New Guinea had never been kayaked before and we were having a blast, making the first descent. Rob was last to run a particularly long and complicated section and unfortunately got his 'boof' off a ledge wrong and landed side-on in a hole. I'd just run out of film so, as the others snapped away, I picked up my throw bag and set up for a throw. Rob was fighting hard in the hole, but to no avail and was then briefly re-circulated out of his boat. As with the vast majority of throw line rescues, it was a one-shot chance before Rob would be swept down the rapids after the bridge. Not a good scenario!

Thankfully my throw was on target and Rob was soon on the line, heading towards the bank. The locals were going wild, with a number of women wailing at Rob's presumed demise. The photograph of Rob being helped the last foot or so out of the river by a local is now quite well known in canoeing circles.

Introduction

Paddlers are continually pushing the limits of the possible in running white water rivers. Certain key developments can be identified that have allowed major advances in river running, e.g. the introduction of the plastic kayak. The development of modern river rescue equipment and techniques is another of these key steps that have allowed paddlers to 'stretch the envelope', with there being at least a good chance of rescue should it all go pear shaped.

Advanced river rescue rarely involves new advanced techniques but rather relies on advanced applications of basic rescue techniques in extreme situations. These techniques are those that all river paddlers need to understand and master, i.e. the basic use of a throw line and rescuing swimmers from a kayak. It's not rocket science but it may save your neck some day!

River Safety

More important than rescue is safety. If we can paddle in a safe manner, we can go a long way to avoiding the need for rescue. River safety is all about avoiding the need to be rescued. Our priority should be to educate ourselves to be safer paddlers and hopefully keep our throw lines and first aid kits happily tucked away in the backs of our boats. There are many factors that contribute towards a group of paddlers being safety conscious, including:

Paddling as Part of a Supportive Group

The atmosphere in the group should be one of mutual support. More able paddlers should look out for those of less experience. Inspection should be encouraged, not seen as a sign of weakness. If some of the group elect not to run a particular rapid, they should provide safety cover whilst the others run the rapid. Remember: avoidance is better than cure.

Line of Sight

Endeavour to keep all members of your group in sight at all times. Try to keep two eddies between the eddy you are heading for and where the river disap-

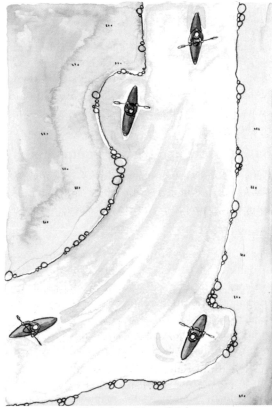

Fig 26.1   Line of sight

pears out of sight. This gives you a margin of error should group members miss the target eddy.

Position of Maximum Usefulness

As a leader, always try to be in a position that allows you to be of maximum benefit. This is a matter of judgement and will be based upon such things as maintaining the line of sight and being in a situation to sort out the most likely incidents. It may be that the position of maximum usefulness is to be on the bank with a throw line.

Be Properly Equipped

Paddle in suitable clothing and use equipment that is in good condition. In Britain white water paddling tends to be a winter sport and hypothermia is one of the greatest potential hazards. Within the group carry a first aid kit, repair kit, spare clothing, bivvy bag, group shelter and split paddles. Carry your kit so that it does not present a hazard in itself. Multiple karabiners and slings clipped to a buoyancy aid can be an entanglement hazard to a swimmer.

Speed versus Safety

Plan to be off the water well before dark, and include a good margin of error. Time is all too quickly lost if an incident occurs.

In winter this may mean aiming to be off the water by 2 p.m. So start early and enjoy that cup of tea in the café rather than trying to find the take-out in rapidly descending darkness! As you paddle, try and increase your time reserve through good teamwork on and off the river and quick decision-making when inspecting.

Less than Three There Should Never Be

Probably the most commonly abused guideline, but when things go wrong it's really useful having some extra people around to pull ropes, go for help, etc.

Choose Your Rivers Carefully

A lot of the thrill of paddling is running new rivers. Guidebooks provide useful information, but too much information can quickly become misleading. Look at the overall grade, length of run, suitable river levels and where the put-in and take-out are. Then run the river as you find it on the day and not as you remember it from the guidebook. Rivers are always changing and the same river is likely to be vastly different at different water levels. Paddle within the skill level of the group.

Clear Communication

Good clear communication is essential. Rivers are noisy so verbal communication is usually impossible. Agree clear and simple hand signals amongst the group before getting on the water. Which signals you use are not so important as the fact that they are agreed amongst the group. I try and use signals that are one handed, so that if needs be I can hold onto the bank to stay in a small eddy whilst signalling.

Below are some commonly used signals:

Photo 26.4   Move in the direction I am pointing

Photos 26.1a-b   One person to come down

Photo 26.5   Pre-arranged paddler to join me

Rescue and First Aid Training

Most river runners these days carry an assortment of karabiners, a throw line and a first aid kit, and wear buoyancy aids fitted with a chest harness. All of these are potentially lifesavers but some can also be lethal if misused. Book on recognized training courses and take your paddling friends with you. It might be your life they save!

Basic Safety and Rescue Equipment

General paddling equipment has been covered elsewhere in the book but there are some items of equipment specific to white water rescue:

Throw Line

Throw lines (a.k.a. throw bags) are the basic tool of bank based rescues. At their simplest, they are a means of storing rope so that it does not kink and tangle and can therefore be easily thrown when needed. Regardless of size, shape or design they should contain floating rope and not have a tied loop or handle on the non-bag end. Beware of very small diameter ropes (5-7mm) as these can be difficult to work with and can act like 'cheesewire' when under load. Commercially manufactured throw lines are available in a variety of lengths between

Photo 26.2   Whole group to paddle down

Photo 26.3   Stop!

10 and 40 metres. Whilst smaller bags are easy to stow in your boat and throw easily they have limited range. Larger bags can be difficult to throw but are invaluable on larger rivers. You can always make a long line easier to throw by removing a few metres of rope from the bag before throwing, but it's much harder to make a short line longer. I would recommend a 20 metre line as a good compromise for general river paddling.

Photo 26.6   Throw bag

Photo 26.7   Different types and sizes

Clean Rope Principle

Many commercially manufactured throw lines come with a handle tied in the non-bag end. This handle presents a potential entrapment hazard should the rescuer let go of the rope. This handle should be removed so that the non-bag end of the throw line is now 'clean rope'. This clean rope principle can be extended to other aspects of rope work in river rescue to reduce any possible entrapment hazards. Rather than being a technique, consider clean rope as a way of thinking.

Tape Sling

A 2-3 metre length of climbing tape is invaluable and can be used for a multitude of uses, from dragging your boat to the river to making a loop around a tree to anchor a throw line to.

Karabiners

Large bent gate HMS karabiners are the most useful for river rescue work. Screwgate karabiners provide more security against unintentional opening and are ideal for attaching lines to chest harnesses. Silt and grit from the river can seize up the screw mechanism, so regular maintenance is required.

Knife

An easily accessible sharp knife, which can be used single-handed, is essential if ropes are being used.

Whistle

A whistle can be used for attracting attention or as a means of communication. As with the knife, this needs to be accessible at all times, particularly when it's you who is in need of rescue.

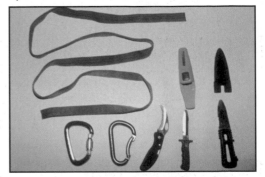

Photo 26.8   Sling, HMS snaplink (right), HMS screwgate (left) and knives

Types of Rescue

White water rescue should be kept as safe and simple as possible. Always try and use as low a risk rescue solution as possible and if that does not work, try a more difficult approach. Safety of the rescuer is paramount. There is no point in attempting an unfeasible rescue only to become a second person in need of rescue!

Talk

The simplest and lowest risk option for a rescuer is for them to avoid all physical contact with the victim and to shout encouragement and advice to the person, in effect helping them to rescue themselves – a 'talking rescue'.

Reach

Slightly higher risk is for a bank based rescuer to reach to the swimmer, i.e. with a paddle or throw a rope to the victim. This could potentially result in the rescuer being pulled into the water but the rescuer should be able to release the rope or paddle before this happens.

Row and Tow

Boat based rescues are the next step up the risk ladder. Commonly labelled as 'row and tow' rescues within paddlesport, this usually means paddling out to the swimmer and towing them back to shore. The potential risk is obvious if we imagine trying to paddle on white water with a panicking victim clawing out our eyes!

Go

Rescues which involve a rescuer, usually attached to a floating rope, swimming out to the victim, making contact and then bringing them to safety are labelled as 'go' rescues and represent a significant potential risk to the rescuer.

Helo

In some countries helicopter rescues (helo) are common but are the domain of the rescue professional and beyond the scope of this book. It should be noted however that, although they can appear slick and quick, they place a large number of people at great risk both in the air and on the ground and consequently are right at the top of the risk ladder.

Fig 26.2   Low-high risk rescues

Rescue versus Recovery

Whilst we try to rescue using the safest and simplest approach, there will always be a drive to keep trying new and potentially riskier methods until the victim is successfully rescued. A clear distinction needs to be made between rescue and recovery. If there is a chance that the victim is still alive, then we are dealing with a rescue situation and the risk assessment made at the time will have this fact as a foundation. If we are dealing with the recovery of equipment or a body, the level of risk that a rescuer can accept is vastly reduced. Equipment can be replaced or recovered on another day, and is not worth dying for.

Unfortunately, the line between when rescue of a potentially live victim becomes body recovery is not a clear one. There are many documented cases of victims being rescued after prolonged periods under water, who have survived either as a result of moving water creating air pockets and/or the effects of immersion in cold water slowing the body's metabolism. This is particularly pertinent to young children.

Self-rescue

The most important person in any rescue situation is you. This is equally true whether you are the rescuer or the victim. Often the quickest, lowest risk and simplest rescue is a self-rescue. Indeed the Eskimo Roll is such an effective and common rescue on white water that we almost forget it is a rescue technique and consider it as paddling! However, even the best paddlers fail to roll on occasions and being able to effectively swim in white water is then a vital skill.

"There are only two types of paddler. Those who have swum, and those who are going to swim." Anon.

White Water Swimming

Swimming in white water can be broken down into two types: Defensive and Aggressive.

Defensive Swimming

In fast moving water, especially when it is shallow our priorities are to prevent injury, avoid entrapment and if possible swim towards safety. This is achieved by swimming on your back with your feet downstream and as near to the surface as possible. This greatly reduces the possibility of your feet becoming trapped between rocks on the river bed. Additionally, if you are swept onto an obstacle such as a rock you can fend it off with your feet as opposed to your head! By doing a backstroke action it is possible to slow your speed down. If in addition you position your body at an angle to the current, so that your feet point downstream and towards one bank and your head points upstream and towards the other, an effective reverse ferry glide can be made to shore. This backstroke action has the added benefit of lifting your head out of the water and making it easier to breathe in rough water.

Aggressive Swimming

On occasions it is vital to get to a place of safety and you need to leave the defensive swimming position, roll onto your front and front crawl aggressively. Normally it is best to keep your feet downstream of your body, however one exception occurs when you are faced with an obstacle across the river at water level, e.g. a log or tree. In this case, turn so that your head is downstream, front crawl aggressively towards the object and then climb up and over the obstacle.

Fig 26.3   Defensive swimming position

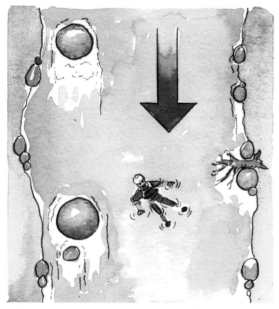

Fig 26.4   Aerial view of reverse ferry

Photos 26.9a-c   Swimming over an obstacle

Swimming over Drops

When swimming over vertical drops, keep in a defensive swimming position until you are over the lip and falling. From then on, it is best to 'ball up' into a tight ball by gripping your lower legs with your hands and tucking your chin into your chest. This

Fig 26.5   Swimming over a drop

has the dual advantage of reducing the possibility of having a limb trapped in rocks at the bottom of the drop, and encouraging your body to be flushed out downstream and not held in a surface stopper.

Swimming with Boat and Paddle

In easier grade water it is often possible to defensively swim to shore and keep hold of your boat and paddle. Endeavour to keep your body upstream of your boat so that, should you hit an obstacle, you will not become pinned against it. Once the difficulty of the river is such that you cannot hold onto your boat and paddle in one hand and swim with the other arm you will need to let go of some kit and concentrate on getting yourself to safety. In big water there is an advantage to keeping hold of your boat as it will provide buoyancy. Generally however, paddles are more easily lost than kayaks so if possible keep hold of your paddle.

Photo 26.10   Swimmer in easy water with kit

Swimming with open canoes is more difficult and it is normal to have a long floating line attached to one or both ends of the canoe. Once capsized, the swimmer grabs the free end of this and swims to shore. All being well, the swimmer will be safely at the river's edge before the line comes tight and they can then use the line to pendulum the canoe to shore. On larger rivers such lines may need to be as long as 40 metres (see Chapter 17).

Rescues from Boats

Rescues of swimmers and equipment by kayakers and canoeists are perhaps the commonest form of rescue on white water. They should not however be underestimated. Impact with the rescuer's boat can result in injury to the swimmer and it is considerably more difficult to paddle white water whilst carrying or towing a swimmer. If you are not 100% sure that the swimmer will not panic, will listen to your instructions, and most importantly of all, will let go of your boat when asked, do not make contact with them. Paddle near them and 'talk' them to shore.

There are a number of methods of carrying/ towing swimmers which are covered in detail in other books. However a few key points are:

- Do not tie or attach yourself to a swimmer or loose equipment in white water. Specialist towlines are available for flat water use but can become difficult to release in moving water. Similarly, chest harnesses are designed for attaching lines to rescuers swimming in white water and are not for towing boats and paddles to shore. Many paddlers will use a nylon tape sling and a karabiner to clip boats and paddles and then hold this in their hand whilst paddling. Do not put such a sling over your head or shoulder.

- Try to keep the end of your boat which has the swimmer as the upstream end.
- Encourage the swimmer to kick with their feet.
- Keep talking to the swimmer throughout.
- If you are going to have to paddle over a drop or through a stopper, tell the swimmer to let go of your boat. You both have a better chance of negotiating the obstacle independently. Once below the drop or the stopper, paddle over to the swimmer and resume the rescue.
- Practise different methods of rescuing swimmers on easier water, so when it happens for real you know what you are doing.

Photo 26.11   Back deck carry for shallow water

Photo 26.12   'Bulldozer' method for deep water

Photo 26.13   Simple tow - easy but slow

Bank Based Rescues

The vast majority of rescues from the bank are throw line rescues to passing swimmers. Even when the rescuer has been pre-placed, you normally only have one chance to make contact with the swimmer before they have been carried downstream and out of reach. Thus the ability to make an accurate first time throw is essential. Other key requirements for a successful throw line rescue are:

- The rescuer being in a position that enables them to throw to the swimmer and land them in a suitable eddy.
- The swimmer being able to hold the line.
- The rescuer being able to hold the weight of the swimmer on the line.

Photo 26.14   Swimmer being 'pendulumed' into the eddy

Positioning

A rope thrown from the wrong place can make matters worse rather than better. There needs to be a 'landing' eddy downstream to pendulum the swimmer into. Make sure you are able to hold the load and are not going to be dragged into the water or injured by falling onto a rocky bank. Being able to choose a suitable position comes with experience and training.

Throwing the Line

Accurate use of a throw line requires practice. This need not be on the river but can just as easily be in the back garden aiming at the compost bin! The most common throws are:

Overarm – 'American Football' Style

Good for accurate mid to long distance throws, especially with smaller throw bags.

Photo 26.15   Overarm throw

Overarm – 'Cricket Bowling' Action

Some people prefer this throw when trying to throw a big bag its full length.

Photo 26.16   Bowling action

Underarm

Excellent for quick short throws or when using a bag that is too big/heavy for you to throw overarm.

Side-arm

Useful when conditions prevent you throwing underarm/overarm i.e. under trees.

The Swimmer

An educated swimmer can make life much easier for the rescuer. Ideally they will be aware of where the rescuers are and be actively looking for a throw line to be coming in their direction.

Once you have hold of the rope, it is essential that the swimmer remains in the defensive swimming position, on their back, feet downstream and holding the rope across their chest.

Photos 26.17a-b   Underarm throw

Some people find that tucking the rope under the armpit on the midstream side of your body can help your body travel through the water, and keeps your head higher out of the water. This does depend on your body shape and doesn't work for everyone.

Photo 26.18   Holding the rope

Holding the Load (Belaying)

Rescuers needs to be ready to cope with the load by bracing themselves. There are a number of options:

Standing Belay

Adopt a low centre of gravity 'Kung-Fu' stance, with body side-on to the direction of pull and knees and elbows bent to act as shock absorbers.

Photo 26.19   Standing brace

Sitting Belay

As soon as the swimmer has the line but before it comes tight, sit down and brace your feet, keeping your knees bent to absorb the shock. Throwing the line to the swimmer whilst they are still upstream of you can provide vital extra time before the rope comes tight.

Photo 26.20   Sitting brace

Reducing the Load

In addition to the above methods of coping with the load, there are a number of methods that reduce the load on both the swimmer and the bank rescuer. After all, if the rescuer on the bank is struggling to cope with the load, the swimmer in the water is even more likely to be struggling to hold onto the rope. Newton's third law and all that!

Methods include:

1. Ensuring that you have enough rope on the bank before throwing the throw line. This allows you to keep letting out rope as the swimmer pendulums to the shore.

2. Moving down the river bank and pulling in the rope at the same time. This method needs clear tree-free banks and obstructions.

Re-throws

There will be occasions when you have time to re-throw the line, having missed with your first throw. Rather than having to re-pack the throw line it is possible to coil the rope and make a quick re-throw. There are a number of methods that, with practice will allow you to make quick, tangle-free re-throws that do not involve having to fill the throw bag with water or stones!

Specialist Rescue Techniques

Buoyancy Aids with Chest Harnesses

The majority of buoyancy aids intended for white water use now come with an integral chest harness. This is a specialist piece of equipment whose use requires prior training. It allows wearers to attach themselves to a floating line and enter the water to carry out a rescue, whilst retaining the ability to release from the line if required. The harness can also be used to safeguard a bank based rescuer on difficult terrain, but it is not a climbing harness. Although undoubtedly an excellent tool for advanced rescues, they do allow us to place a rescuer in a high-risk situation and they need to be used with caution.

Photos 26.21a-b   Vest (left) and Jacket (right) type buoyancy aids with harnesses

In particular, consider the following points:

- Is there a simpler/less hazardous solution to the rescue? I personally would have to think hard about entering a section of river on a harness in which I was not prepared to release the harness and swim downstream.

- Do not use a chest harness for towing kayaks. They are designed to release under bodyweight - not the force of an empty boat.

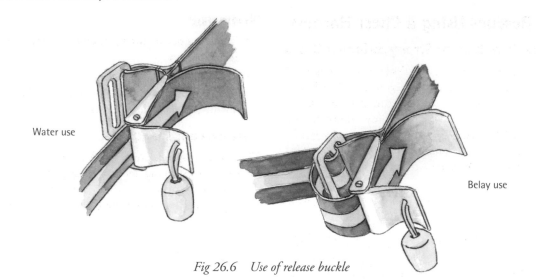

Water use

Belay use

Fig 26.6   Use of release buckle

- Chest harnesses are designed for loading in a river situation, not protecting the user when in a vertical environment, e.g. climbing/abseiling on gorge walls.

- For in-water use the harness should be fastened using the plastic quick release buckle. Only in situations when you anticipate greater degrees of loading (bank belay) should the harness be led through the backup plate before fastening with the quick release buckle.

Attaching a Line

When attaching throw lines to a chest harness, clip the bag end of the line to the harness and ensure that there is no knotted loop/handle on the other end. This follows the 'Clean Rope Principle' and places the wearer at less risk should they end up swimming in the river trailing the line. If possible attach the line to the harness using a screwgate karabiner.

Photo 26.22   Attach the line with a 'screwgate' karabiner

Two snaplink karabiners clipped 'back to back' would be a suitable alternative as this decreases the chance of the rope accidentally unclipping from the harness.

Photo 26.23   Karabiners clipped back to back

Use of a Cow's Tail

A cow's tail is a length of webbing which is attached at the load point on the back of the harness and has a karabiner at the other end which is stored somewhere on the front of the buoyancy aid. This allows rescuers to quickly and easily attach themselves to a throw line. You can't use a chest harness by yourself since you need at least one other person to hold the rope you are attached to. Thus it will always be possible to get them to attach the rope to you and do a safety check before you enter the water. Whilst cow's tails are convenient, it can be argued that anything that makes you stop, slow down and think before making a conscious effort to enter the water is a good thing.

Practise using your chest harness, especially releasing it under load, in a controlled environment.

Rescues Using a Chest Harness

The 'Live Bait' or Strong Swimmer Rescue

In this rescue the rescuer swims or jumps to the victim and holds onto them by means of their buoyancy aid. Both rescuer and victim then pendulum to the bank attached to the throw line connected to the rescuer's harness. This allows unconscious swimmers and those with arm injuries who would be unable to catch a throw line to be rescued.

The rescuer's harness is attached to the 'bag end' of a throw line and the belayer on the bank controls the 'clean end' of the rope.

Photo 26.24 'Live bait' rescue

If the rescuer has to jump into the water they need to have a couple of coils of rope in their upstream hand which is thrown upstream when in flight. This reduces the chance of entanglement in loose rope upon landing.

> **Safety Point**
>
> *Rescues that involve swimmers in the river attached to lines, or lines tensioned across the river, represent a significant risk to other river users. Spotters should be placed on the bank upstream of the rescue to warn other river users of the hazard and to look out for debris flowing downstream that would be a hazard to rescuers. Similarly, rescuers with throw lines should be placed downstream of the rescue to provide safety cover in the event of someone being washed downstream from the rescue site.*

Advantages:

- It is a quick and easy to set up rescue.
- The rescue can be carried out by two people.
- It is ideal for rescuing unconscious swimmers and for use in small pools between waterfalls.

Disadvantages:

- There is a risk of entanglement of the rescuer in excess rope.
- If a rescuer has to jump into the river there is a risk of impact injury when landing; as shallow an entry as possible minimizes this.

Downstream Diagonal

This is a comparatively simple technique that involves a rope being tensioned diagonally across the river. This allows rescuers/victims to clip onto the rope and slide across the current to its downstream end.

Fig 26.7 Tensioned diagonal

The 'bag end' of the throw line is anchored on the 'upstream' bank and the clean end is belayed downstream on the opposite bank (a waist belay is usually best). Note that the downstream end of the rope must be releasable when in use.

The angle at which the rope lies relative to the river depends upon the water speed. On slow rivers it will need to be angled well downstream. It is better to be over-angled downstream than to not have enough downstream angle – 'If in doubt, angle it out'.

By using a 'cow's tail' or by holding onto a sling clipped to the tensioned rope, a rescuer/victim will be moved along the rope whilst maintaining a safe swimming position.

Never tension a line at 90 degrees to the current as anyone attached to it will end up stuck in the main current as the rope forms a 'V' shape.

Should this happen, one end of the rope needs to be walked downstream to create a downstream diagonal line.

Advantages:

- Ideal for crossing from one bank to another, or evacuating from a large midstream obstruction to the shore.

- It can also be used to send a rescuer out to help an injured paddler on a mid-stream rock and evacuate them to the shore.

Disadvantages

- The potential for use is limited by the length of rope available.

- On wider rivers it can be difficult to get the line across the river.

Entrapments

It is possible for paddlers to be entrapped in two main ways:

1. Against an obstruction, e.g. kayaker against a fallen tree or a swimmer with a foot entrapment on the river bed.

2. By a stopper - these re-circulating water features can stop and hold paddlers, swimmers and equipment. Most naturally occurring stoppers have a weakness where swimmers and equipment will be eventually released but man-made structures such as weirs can create uni-

form stoppers with large towback that will trap swimmers and equipment almost indefinitely. (See Chapter 22)

There are a number of possible solutions but the key points are:

- Stabilize the paddler
- Extract the paddler

Fig 26.8   Tag line supporting foot entrapment

Fig 26.9   Tag line supporting vertical pin

Stabilize

Keep it simple. On Britain's relatively narrow and shallow rivers it is often possible to break out behind, (or even wade into the eddy behind) and then climb onto the obstruction. The rescuer is then in a position to simply grab hold of the victim.

A throw line across the river can be held in tension and walked upstream to the trapped paddler where it can provide support. Such a line is known as a Tag Line and can help maintain a trapped paddler in a 'head up and breathing' position.

Once the paddler is stabilized a decision needs to be taken as how best to extract them. The tag line may itself provide enough support so that they can release themselves from the entrapment or a rescuer may need to be sent to help them. When dealing with entrapments it is likely that, once free of the entrapment, the victim will be exhausted, possibly cold and probably unable to help further in their rescue. A pre-set live-bait rescue downstream of the entrapment to collect the victim once released is advisable if manpower allows.

Stopper Rescues

A stopper that is powerful enough to hold a swimmer is a significant hazard for any rescuer. Quick and accurate use of a throw line may recover a swimmer but can be very difficult as the swimmer may only be visible intermittently and there is the added risk of entanglement as the swimmer is re-circulated with the loose rope.

Carefully managed live-bait rescues can reduce the amount of excess rope involved but are a high-risk option. Once the victim is unconscious this may be the only option available.

Photo 26.25   Tag line used in stopper

A tag line across the river can be walked upstream at water level and the swimmer can then grab hold of the tag line. This has advantages over a thrown line in that there is no risk of entanglement in excess rope and it will also provide a degree of support. It may also be possible to clip a buoyancy aid onto the line which will increase the visibility of the line for the swimmer whilst also providing additional buoyancy. Once the swimmer has hold of the tag line, it can be let out from one bank and pulled in to the other to move the swimmer across the face of the stopper, to exit via a weakness or recovery to the shore. Unfortunately, it is often impossible to access both sides of a stopper at water level.

Equipment Recovery

Recovering pinned kayaks, canoes and paddles can be an almost impossible task. Often the most difficult part of the whole process is connecting a rope to the boat or paddle. As we are dealing with equipment recovery and not saving lives we need to limit our attempts to low risk ones. It may be possible to use a paddle, karabiner and tape from your repair kit to improvise a paddle hook. This allows us to extend our reach when trying to attach a rope to a boat.

Photo 26.26   Improvised paddle hook

Once we have a line attached we need to determine two things:

1. What direction do we need to move the boat to free it? (Ideal angle of pull).

2. How far do we need to move the boat for it to release?

As well as getting the angle of pull correct it is vital we utilise the force of the water to help our rescue and not hinder it. If we are pulling in the wrong direction no amount of mechanical advantage and pulleys will rectify the situation. With short modern kayaks we need only move the boat two feet for it to release. Open canoes can be a much more difficult problem; not only do they usually need to be moved further but the forces required can be much greater.

Once a line has been attached to the boat and the direction of pull determined, there are a number of options available:

Tug of War

As the name would suggest, this is simply a matter of getting all available people on the rope and pulling as hard as possible.

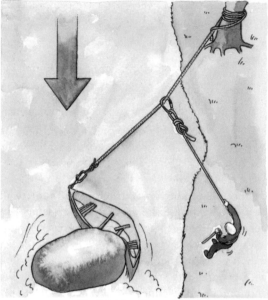

Fig 26.11   Vector Pull

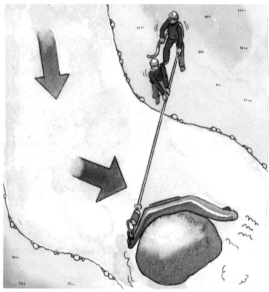

Fig 26.10   Tug of war

Vector Pull

If the above method does not release the boat, if the tensioned line can be tied off with a 'no knot' or similar, by applying a force at right angles to the tensioned line, we can increase the force applied.

3:1 Mechanical Advantage System

If none of the above methods work, a simple mechanical advantage system can be created with a sling and karabiner as an anchor and one overhand knot being tied in the rope.

Using 'prussic' knots we can create more complicated mechanical advantage systems, but these are beyond the scope of this chapter. It should be remembered that the majority of ropes used for throw lines have a polypropylene sheath which has a low melting point and therefore is not designed to be tensioned using prussic knots.

Regardless of which of the above systems is being used, should the system fail there is a danger of the tensioned lines recoiling and hitting the rescuers who are tensioning the system. Hanging a spare spraydeck, buoyancy aid or drybag filled with water

Fig 26.12   3:1 Pulley system

on the tensioned line will act as a damper should the system fail and hopefully prevent injury.

Training

The importance of quality river rescue training cannot be overstated. Even some advanced rescue techniques look easy on the pages of a book and it is not until you try them in the supervised environment of a training class that the problems become apparent. There are three types of training currently available in the UK that will be of interest to river runners. These are the Palm River Safety Initiative, the British Canoe Union White Water Safety & Rescue Course and the Swiftwater Rescue Technician courses administered by Rescue 3.

Palm River Safety Initiative

As a leading manufacturer of paddling kit Palm Equipment International have sponsored the delivery of a one-day course looking at safe throw line work and use of a buoyancy aid chest harness. Palm's support has allowed this course to be provided at a budget price.

BCU White Water Safety and Rescue Course

This is a two-day course aimed at *all* white water paddlers. Unfortunately, as it can be used as a pre-requisite for paddlers wishing to do their Five Star Award it is often wrongly perceived as being only for people operating at that standard. Good white water safety and rescue training is invaluable for all white water paddlers, not just those operating on Grade 4 and 5 rivers. Courses can only be run by approved providers and work to a standard syllabus. Dates of courses are advertised in the BCU Yearbook.

Rescue 3 – Swiftwater Rescue Technician Courses

These in-depth three-day courses are run throughout the world and, although primarily aimed at emergency service personnel and commercial river guides, they may be of interest to some paddlers.

No matter which course you do, it's vital that you keep your skills up to date after your course. Paddlers are generally very good at getting out and practising their boating but how often do we practise our rescue skills?

Further Reading

White Water Safety and Rescue , Ferrero F, 1998, Pesda Press, 0953195600
River Rescue-A Manual for Whitewater Safety, Bechdel and Ray, 3rd Edition1997, Appalachian Mountain Club, 878239554
Swiftwater Rescue - A Manual for the River Professional, Ray, 1997, CFS Press, 0964458503
Whitewater Rescue Manual: New Techniques for Canoeists, Kayakers and Rafters, Walbridge C, 1995, McGraw Hill Professional Publishing, 070677905
Whitewater Kayaking, Rowe R, 1990, Stackpole Books, 0811722848

Websites

Rescue 3 (UK) - www.rescue3.co.uk

Paul O'Sullivan

Paul O'Sullivan has paddled throughout the world including first descents of rivers in Papua New Guinea, Pakistan and Iran. As well as being a BCU Level 5 Kayak Coach, Paul is a Level 5 Raft Guide Trainer and a Rescue 3 Swiftwater Rescue Technician Instructor. Paul is employed as a Centre Director of Canolfan Tryweryn, the National Whitewater Centre in Bala, North Wales.

27 Specialist White Water Canoe

*Living with the immediacy of challenge helps you sort out your priorities in life.
It helps you live a less trivial life.*

Specialist White Water Canoeing (SWWC or C1/OC1) arrived in the UK some years ago from North America where it remains a very popular aspect of canoeing. A hard core of UK boaters have been accepting the challenge of OC1 on rivers of all grades since that time. This chapter will explore the Open Canoe (OC1), but is recommended as highly relevant to closed cockpit C1 boating, where the techniques used are almost identical.

A Definition

The definition of a SWWC has been the subject of many a debate over the years. However, common consent now makes the distinction between traditional open canoes and their white water counterparts by looking at the outfitting and the context they are used in. The white water canoe will be bagged up throughout, (as shown in the section on outfitting in this chapter) and have a saddle or pedestal in conjunction with a strapping system. It will be used to run white water of all grades, with the skill of the paddler being the only limitation.

Boat Design

Boat design has moved swiftly in recent years, being driven by the freestyle scene. You can see from the next three photographs that this progression has led to boats that are equal in performance to most modern kayaks.

Photo 27.1   The Dagger Encore

The evolution of the white water canoe is well documented in the excellent text, "Thrill of the Paddle" by Paul Mason and Mark Scriver. This book also offers an expansion of the content in this chapter and will form an invaluable reference to all OC1 boaters.

Photo 27.2   The Dagger Ocoee

Photo 27.3   The Savage Skeeter

The Basic Strokes

The stroke work in a SWWC has a similarity to that of the traditional open canoe, the difference being that the range of manoeuvres is far more extensive. This allows the craft to be paddled both on technical white water and for freestyle moves in holes/waves. The approach is also different; you could liken it to paddling a canoe with a white water kayak mentality. There are a few fundamental strokes, crucial to making the boat perform.

On Side Power Stroke

- Long catch achieved through trunk rotation (see Photo 27.4a), vertical paddle, top hand drives blade into water.

- Transfer power and correction. Hips thrust boat past blade, stern pry against side of boat and active top hand. (See Photo 27.4b)

Off Side Power Stroke:

- Completely vertical paddle, top hand actively pushes through.

Photos 27.4a-b   On side power stroke

- Length of the stroke much shorter than on side power (6-8 inches). Boat thrust past paddle with hips, recovery by slicing blade in water.

Photo 27.5   Off side power stroke

Support Strokes

- Back of blade projected out from side of boat, head down onto 'T' grip.

- Roll the boat up with hips, keep head down.

- Head, still down, moves across the deck to flatten boat, sweep paddle forward.

(See Photo 27.6)

The 'J' lean can be used to avoid capsizing on the off side.

(See Photo 27.7)

Photo 27.6   Support stroke

Photo 27.7   The 'J' lean

The Carving Effect

This can be used to increase the effectiveness of manoeuvres:

Photo 27.8   Carving

- Set boat on edge (on or off side).

- Move weight forward, alter boat trim to bow.

- Initiate turning direction, using short 'stubby' strokes.

Leaning forward and making it more bow heavy will increase the carving effect.

Setting the boat on a slight carve will allow you to paddle forwards in a straight line with consecutive power strokes and no correction.

Outfitting Systems

Photo 27.9 shows how a pedestal and basic strap system is arranged. It is typical of how a boat may arrive ready outfitted from a supplier. The straps are attached very effectively in Royalex™ boats by vinyl adhesives directly to the hull. In plastic boats such adhesives do not stick well so many boaters will drill their attachments to the hull.

Photo 27.9   Pedestal and strap system

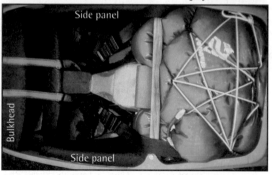

Photo 27.10   Bulkhead and side panels

Many paddlers will want to outfit their own boat or customise their outfitting. Photo 27.10 shows how a bulkhead and side panels of foam have been added. Together with the strap system, it offers excellent boat control. Care should be taken to ensure it is all fixed securely, as losing it on an isolated river will compromise performance and hence safety.

Photo 27.11   Quick release straps

The release system is crucial. You need to be able to exit the boat whenever necessary. Some boaters use central release systems, which release with one pull of a strap. Other systems use two independent releases. There are also systems which incorporate double self-equalising straps. These must run freely and not be prone to jamming if they are to release.

> **Important**
>
> *Any outfitting will affect your ability to exit the boat. You should be quite happy that there is no risk of entrapment before using a customised system. This is particularly so when borrowing boats!*

Other Outfitting

Toe blocks stop your feet slipping back and help transfer power in your strokes.

Knee cradles are very important for comfort and also help control the boat through your knees.

Photo 27.12   Buoyancy bag retaining system

Buoyancy bag retaining systems use a combination of cross-deck lacing and longitudinal straps as shown.

Pedestals and saddles are made of expensive minicell foam. Which style to use is purely a matter of personal preference.

The Open Canoe Roll

I am often asked, "What can I do to help me improve and develop my paddling of specialist canoes?" The answer is usually two-fold: Good coaching to begin with, and, without doubt, a reliable roll. Your commitment, in practice, changes when the implications of a mistake are only a wet head and not a long swim. Note that rolling an open canoe is more difficult than a kayak, and that, unlike in a kayak, we have to start from a bow set up.

Here are some pointers for developing an effective open canoe roll:

- The set up position. It is the screw-roll set. From the set, sweep the blade across the surface of the water to the side of the boat.

Photo 27.13   Set up

- Switch to the back of the blade and get your head down onto the 'T' grip.

Photo 27.14   Head on 'T' grip

- Begin rolling the boat with your thighs and abdominal muscles. Keep the head down on the T-grip until the on-side gunwale has come out of the water.

Photo 27.15   Keep head down

- Force your head down across to the off side to flatten the boat. As you move your head across, sweep the back of the blade on the surface of the water to the front of the boat. Remember: the hips, stomach and head roll the boat; the blade is for support.

Photo 27.16   Roll the boat

Here are a couple of tips for practice:

• Get someone to stand in the water next to you. They will be able to guide your blade through the set up and if your roll fails they can right the boat with you still in it.

• Try mastering a deep low brace first. The action is the same (Photo 27.6). If you do this try the brace on both sides because you will have to concentrate on technique on your less favoured side. That technique should then transfer to your better side. It works with the full roll as well.

A Few Tips on River Paddling

The performance of your OC1 will be just as the manufacturer intended and your ability allows. Until such time, that is, when it gets swamped. The bigger your boat, generally the more water you will have to carry and manoeuvre. To combat this, you can ensure the outfitting system in the boat is customised to allow little space for water. When paddling swamped, it is often only possible to control the direction of the boat by steering. In fact, you should be aware that the increase in weight makes injury when paddling swamped a very real possibility. Steer the boat as efficiently as possible. Use draws and prys at the stern and anticipate where the boat will need to go. Begin the manoeuvre as early as possible. The principle of paddling proactively with a plan is as important in SWWC as it is in traditional open canoeing.

Emptying

Emptying is essential after a swamping, but it becomes a real chore if you have to get out of the

boat to do it. The following photographs show 2 ways of making things a little easier:

Photo 27.17   Hooking with your 'T' grip

Photo 27.18   Using a 'J' lean to empty most of the water

This can be done in an eddy or in the flow.

Self-rescue Line

A self rescue line (SRL) will save many an exhausting mile of arduous chase boating (see Chapter 17).

River Kit

There are a number of essentials to include in your personal kit. Each boater will need to carry a spare air bag. A puncture is almost impossible to repair on the river bank, and its loss will make you a liability to your party due to the effect on your paddling performance. When they are dry, air bags can be repaired very effectively with a seam sealant solution, (just pour onto small holes and let it dry; with a larger hole, use in conjunction with a patch).

Paddles

You will also need a spare paddle. In smaller boats this will need to be a split paddle. Consider investing in a quality spare. The grade of water you are paddling will not suddenly alter just because you break your stick, and your performance will need to match the environment.

OC1 boaters tend to use paddles with blades that are short and wide. This maximises the displacement in shallow British creeks. The length of your paddle will be a personal thing, but as a general rule it will be short enough to optimise your ability to transfer to, and subsequently perform on, the off side. Measure the loom, not the whole paddle. It is the height of the top hand when the blade is immersed that affects performance (try your top hand around eye level).

Dry Suits

Two piece dry systems are rarely watertight. Most SWWC boaters use dry suits. You cannot blame them; they do spend much of the time kneeling in 20 centimetres of water! The advantages of dry suits are numerous with warmth and comfort coming high on the wish list. Take care to remove the excess air when you put one on. Otherwise you will tend to float head-heavy when swimming. There is also a danger of the bottoms filling with water if there is a leak. Good river leaders and experienced paddlers

Photo 27.19   Parting shot!

will be aware of this danger and will conduct themselves accordingly to protect their colleagues.

Dehydration is always a threat to your performance when wearing dry-kit. Try using a hydration bag with a tube. It will sit between your bulkhead and air bag and you can take on water whenever you wish; now you can't do that in a kayak, can you!

Useful Contacts

ken@aftershock2.fsnet.co.uk - Ken's e-mail
info@bcu.org

Further Reading

Thrill of the Paddle, Mason P and Scriver M, Cordee (UK), 1552094510
White Water Safety and Rescue, Ferrero F, 1998, Pesda Press, Bangor - Wales, 0-9531956-0-0

Videos

Solo Playboating, Kent Ford
Drill Time: Solo Playboating II, Kent Ford

Ken Hughes

As a BCU Level 5 Coach in Specialist White Water Canoe (OC1) and a Mountaineering Instructor, Ken has paddled, played and climbed extensively throughout the UK and Europe. His coaching activities include other paddling disciplines and he is an active BCU Course Provider. He has coached members of the GB Canoe Freestyle Team including two British champions, is Regional Coaching Organiser (RCO) for the North East Region and a Lecturer in Outdoor Education.

(Thanks to Ian Duffy, GB champion 1999 and talented OC1 boater, for his help in compiling this chapter - Ken.)

28 Playboating and Freestyle

In the spring of 1997 I was sent a video-tape. It totally blew my mind. Kayakers surfing perfect green waves in the most unbelievable looking boats... but they were not just front surfing, they were side surfing at the bottom of the huge green waves, sliding sideways, spinning 360s, cleans, 720s and more... Amazing, I would never have imagined these moves were even possible. Freestyle kayaking pioneer Corran Addison adapted ideas that had been used in surf skis, and by giving a white water kayak a radically flat hull and hard edges the sport took another leap forward.

After five years off boating, keeping stimulated climbing and mountain biking, there was only one thing I could do... I purchased myself a radical new boat.

Ever since the day it arrived, I've been totally hooked.

Playboating

Playboating is all about having fun in white water. It's about surfing, dipping, getting vertical, falling in... Paddling with your friends on anything from your local weir, rapid, tidal race, or beach to running down melt water in the Alps or Himalayas. All white water paddlers do it. It adds enjoyment and challenges to running the river.

The Boats

You can playboat to some degree in almost any white water boat including open canoes. To have more fun and to make the latest moves easier, specialist playboats are best. Since 1997 the evolution of boat design has moved quickly. Nowadays, play/freestyle boats come in different sizes or volumes, offering paddlers the perfect tool for the job. Modern freestyle kayaks are often converted into C1s. Other boats you may come across include open canoes and squirt boats.

Freestyle Kayak

This craft features a flat hull for planing and easy spins, hard edges for wave speed and carving, slicey ends for easy vertical moves, central volume for stability and balance on end.

Squirt Kayak

Squirt kayaks also feature a flat hull for planing and easy spins, and hard edges for wave speed and carving, but have minimum volume. These babies sink and are paddled vertically from end to end. In the correct hands it is the ballet of paddling, smooth and effortless moves linked seamlessly. It's a pretty tight fit though and hurts your feet!

Photo 28.1   Squirt kayak

Freestyle Open Canoe

A freestyle open canoe features a flat hull for planing and easy spins, and hard edges for wave speed and carving. It is far shorter than a regular open canoe and also has highly rockered ends for easy spins and more predictability.

Photo 28.2   Freestyle open canoe

Outfitting

In order to get the most out of your boat good outfitting is essential. A strong supporting backrest, firm hip pads, secure knees and positive footrests are all essential. The boat needs to be stuck to you,

move with your every lean and react instantly to your actions. To make a C1 from a kayak shell you'll need to create your own foam seat and leg strap system.

Seat Position

You'll need to find the perfect balance position for your seat. Most boats work best with the seat forward. This will make back surfing far easier. Position your seat so that when you are sat still and relaxed the boat is level, with the bow and stern equally above the water. Don't buy a boat that is too small so that the only way to paddle it is with the seat fully back.

Rolling

Before you can really begin to enjoy freestyle you must perfect your rolling skills. Learn to roll on both sides. Learning to handroll is valuable. Having a bomb-proof roll on both sides will remove the fear element from freestyle, allowing you to work on the moves far more effectively. Check out the rolling chapter of this book for further information.

Avoiding Injury

Playboating is awesome fun, but it is hard on your body. It is therefore important not to support upstream if flipping in a hole or on a fast wave. Many playboaters dislocate shoulders in hole or fast wave 'trashings'. Try to lose the reflex action of supporting upstream. High braces and support strokes are not applicable on a fast feature. If you're going to go over, let it go... and use the power-flip momentum to roll lightning fast. When side-surfing in a hole, use a low brace, and use the back of your blade for balance.

The Basic Moves

Surf Front/Back

Photo 28.3   Front surf

Tips: Relax, carve around from edge to edge. Always watch the wave you're sprinting onto. If drifting back, move body weight upstream.

Photo 28.4   Back surf

Avoid: When front surfing do not lean back too far, it affects the balance of your boat. If you struggle to sit relaxed when back surfing, perhaps your seat position is too far back.

Spin

A spin is a full 360 degree rotation of the kayak on a wave.

Tips: Start from a front surf. Move to the top of the wave and, just as you start to glide down the face, initiate the spin with a reverse sweep. Keep your boat level and try to avoid leaning downstream (this will send you off the back of the wave).

Photos 28.5a-g   Flat spin sequence

Try not to stop in a back surf, complete the move in one smooth sequence. Sometimes you'll have to pause whilst surfing backwards; if you find yourself drifting off the wave then a reverse push back stroke often helps you maintain position on the wave. When spinning from backwards to forwards, avoid leaning downstream. Keep the boat flat with body weight forward.

Avoid: Leaning downstream too much... as this will certainly wash you off the wave.

Vertical Ender

The first vertical move to learn. Find a deep hole or pour over, then go get some air...

Photo 28.6   Vertical ender

Tips: Line yourself up at a right angle to the current, paddle upstream into the green water and rocket vertically upwards. Keep your angle straight, using a stern rudder to steer. When proficient at endering, try a pirouette. Line up the same way, but the moment the bow goes down, rotate your boat by changing your stern rudder into a reverse sweep.

Avoid: Common mistakes are caused by not keeping your boat at a right angle to the flow. Remember, keep straight with a stern rudder.

Stern Dip

Photo 28.7   Stern dip

Just getting the back down!

Tips: Find yourself a good eddy line. Start from the eddy with an approach angle to the flow of about 45 degrees. At the point where your bottom is in the current, lean slightly upstream and push the tail of your boat against the flow with a powerful reverse stroke. As the current catches your tail, the bow will rise up.

Avoid: Too much upstream lean will end in a dunking. It will take a bit of practice to find a balanced position. A lot of fun when starting out and a sure way of getting your roll sorted!

Top Tip

Train your weaknesses, not your strengths. You'll find that for every freestyle move you have a strong side. Always practise the most on your bad side.

It's not as much fun, but it'll make you a far better paddler, and if you ever progress to competition, rides with changes of direction and moves both sides will always out-score endless moves in one direction.

Freestyle

The basic moves outlined in the previous Playboating section are an ideal learning tool for more complex linked moves.

Flat Water Moves

Many skills can be mastered on flat water in modern boats.

Edge Balance

Photo 28.8   Edge balance

The ability to balance on either edge of your kayak is important. Most vertical moves are initiated by presenting the edge of your boat to the current. Practise paddling forwards and backwards on edge. Keep your weight forward as this makes it far easier to initiate moves. Good, tight outfitting is important for edge balance.

Double Pump

The double pump is the initiation skill for use on white water. Having this skill wired will help you throw down vertical moves in any white water situation. Edge balance, timing and power are important factors for the double pump.

Photos 28.9a-b   Double pump sequence

Tips: Paddle forwards to get some speed up. Lift your bow up by simultaneously pulling hard on your forward stroke and raising the edge of your boat. As you finish your forward stroke, smash the bow down by changing the stroke into a reverse stroke, pushing down and across your feet. With enough edge, speed and correct timing your bow should slice through the water. This is a tricky skill to learn. Lots of practice is essential. The smaller and 'slicier' your boat the easier this will be; but don't be tempted to downsize your boat especially for this move, you'll need more volume when you paddle on white water.

Avoid: Leaning too far back will prevent you from doing this move. Weight forward is the key. Too little edge and your boat will go flat. Too much and you'll land on your head.

On flat water, effort is required to push the ends of your boat through the water. When you get proficient in white water less effort is required. With the correct positioning and timing the moves become almost effortless. Your paddle becomes a support rather than a power source.

Advanced Moves

Cartwheel

A cartwheel consists of two consecutive vertical ends in the same rotational direction. It is possible to do one or more ends with no paddle strokes. This is termed a clean, or a superclean.

Tips: If initiating on the bow, start the cartwheel with a double pump. Always look upstream at the part of the hole where you want the ends of your boat to chop through. Try to be one stroke ahead, so that your body is pre-rotated and your boat follows through.

Avoid: Try not to throw your weight forward and back. Generally keep your weight forward. If you hit the sweet spot this move will be almost effortless.

Split Wheel

A split wheel consists of a direction change in the vertical plane. Both ends need to be high to score in a competition. Usually performed from bow to stern but can be done stern to bow.

Tips: Always look upstream at the part of the hole where you want the ends of your boat to chop through. For the split you need to stay on one blade. Cut the bow through on a reverse push, but add rotation to the end so that you land your boat flat and pointing completely downstream. As the hole starts to pull you back, change edges so the bow rotates up and over using a forward stroke for balance. When you have mastered this, try to add it into a cartwheel sequence.

Avoid: Try not to throw your weight forward and back. As with the cartwheel, generally keep your weight forward. If you hit the sweet spot this move will also be effortless.

Blunt

One of the most dynamic moves performed on a wave, a blunt is an elevated rotation of the kayak around the bow or stern of the boat. Usually performed on a shoulder of a wave or hole. With a carefully timed bounce to the start of this move it is possible to perform aerial blunts. Blunts can also be performed backwards.

Tips: Watch the part of the wave where you want your boat to rotate around. For a really dynamic

Photos 28.10a-h   Cartwheel sequence

Photos 28.11a-h   Split wheel sequence

blunt, lift your bow with a forward pull, moving your weight backwards; then with perfect timing, transfer your weight forward whilst smashing the bow down with a reverse push. If timed well 'air' will be your reward. Speed and timing are the key to good blunts. Make them high, as in competitions they only score if your boat is elevated higher than 45 degrees.

Avoid: Try not to chop your bow through the green as in a cartwheel. Aim to jump high and barely touch the water with the tip of your boat. Tricky, but awesome when you get it right.

The Loop

The full loop is a really cool move. Difficult, but impressive if pulled off well. The move is basically a linked together front and back ender, where the kayak goes end over end, airborne in a hole, but at a right angle to the current.

Photo 28.13   A loop

Competition

Playboating - a sport that started out as a bit of fun has become competitively very serious. All the boat manufacturers are keen to show whose latest creation is best. Many paddlers are now professionals, training every day for several hours.

Modern freestyle competition venues usually feature a super fast hole with wave diagonals at each side. Wave and hole moves are possible in both directions offering paddlers an exciting and varied challenge. Competitors usually have 30 to 45 second runs on the feature. Top boaters will seamlessly link rides of spins, cartwheels, split-wheels, blunts and clean moves together.

The Rules

Technical judges score levels of verticality throughout the run, scoring 180 degree direction changes with one point for horizontal moves, two points for elevated

Photos 28.12a-e   Blunt sequence

moves and four points for vertical moves. Extra points are awarded for aerials and changes of direction. A variety judge notes the different moves performed, each being worth a multiplier value depending upon move difficulty. The final score is the technical score multiplied by one plus the variety. To score highly a paddler will need to execute many vertical ends combined with perfect examples of many different moves. The harder moves score bigger multipliers, so linking those moves should place the paddler high in the rankings.

Training

As freestyle kayaking is so technical, most training is done in the boat. The key to improving skill levels is hours of experience in different holes, waves and water features. Top freestylers will train for several hours each day, working on technique and learning new tricks.

Strength

Good strength is a key factor. This will develop from many hours in the boat, but a good regular trip to the gym to work out on the weights will increase strength as well. Choose paddling-specific exercises and set yourself a circuit of medium weights where sets of 3 x 10 reps are just possible. Ask gym staff to help you out setting up a paddling-specific circuit.

Cardio-Vascular Fitness

A strong cardiovascular system is also important. Good heart and lungs will aid recovery and enable you to link longer, more dynamic rides. Run, ride a bike or just go for a flat water straight-line paddle in your playboat, all at a medium intensity.

Flexibility

Good flexibility is a key factor. Regular paddling and paddling-specific stretching will increase your flexibility and also aid recovery on those days when your body has been beaten.

Diet

A healthy diet with a high carbohydrate content such as potatoes, pasta, bread and rice combined with fresh fruit, vegetables and lower fat white meats will aid good health and fitness. Hydrate with water, especially during long sessions.

The Future

As skill levels increase, moves will develop. Linking parts of existing moves will provide further variety. New designs will enable more aerial tricks. Events will develop and regular freestyle competitions will incorporate more extreme downriver and slalom events.

I'll see you there...

Further Reading

The Art of Freestyle, Brymer, Hughes and Collins, 2000, Wales, Pesda Press, 0-9531956-3-5
The Playboater's Handbook, Whiting K, 1998, Ontario, Heliconia Press, 1-896980-02-3
Playboating Moves and Training, Jackson E, 2000, Pennsylvania, Stackpole Books, 0-8117-2894-3
Rodeo Boating, Olly Grau

Videos

Searching for the Gee Spot - Corran Addison
Searching for the Pro State - Corran Addison
Playdaze - Ken Whiting

Websites

UK freestyle information and calendar - www.ukfreestyle.westhost.com

Pete Astles

Pete Astles turned to freestyle after spending his formative years in slalom where he made the Great Britain Squad. He is now a member of the Great Britain Freestyle Squad and is also the owner of Peak UK.

Glossary of Terms

The following are some important and commonly used paddlesport terms. Many more key words can be found by consulting the index. There are also a few terms that are included because they are not explained elsewhere.

Back face - The opposite side of a paddle blade to the power face (see below).

Blade - The broad part of a paddle that goes in the water.

Boat - In the context of paddlesport this is used as a generic term when referring to both canoes and kayaks.

Bow - The front end of a boat.

Canoe - A canoe is paddled by a paddler or paddlers who sit or kneel and use a single bladed paddle.

Cockpit - This is the hole in the deck of a kayak or closed deck canoe in which a paddler sits.

Cockpit coaming - The raised edge around the cockpit onto which the spraydeck is attached.

Deck - The top of a kayak or closed deck canoe.

Downstream - The direction the river or stream is flowing towards.

Drive face - See power face.

Feather - The angle at which kayak blades are set to each other. This is usually somewhere between 50 and 90 degrees depending on use (see Chapter 2). Unfeathered means that the blades are set at the same angle.

Flare - This is a design term that refers to how much of a 'V' shape there is in the bows of a boat. A boat with a good deal of flare will tend to ride over waves (i.e. a sea kayak), a boat with little or no flare will plough through them (i.e. a sprint kayak).

Open canoe - A canoe with no deck, in the style of the North American native peoples.

Gunwale - The place where the deck meets the hull, or in the case of an open canoe, where the hull finishes.

Hull - The bottom of a kayak or closed deck canoe.

Kayak - A kayak is paddled by a paddler or paddlers who sit very low in the boat and use a two bladed paddle.

Offshore wind - This is a wind that is blowing out to sea, beware!

Onshore wind - This is a wind that is blowing onto the shore.

Power face - The face of a paddle blade that is pulled against the water.

Reverse face - See back face.

River left - The left hand side of a river as you face downstream.

River right - The right hand side of a river as you face downstream.

Shaft - The narrow part of a paddle that the paddler holds.

Stern - The back end of a boat.

Spraydeck - A nylon or neoprene 'skirt' worn around the paddler's waist and used to seal the cockpit and keep water out.

Tumbleholme - This is an open canoe design term. It refers to the amount a hull curves back in from its widest point before reaching the gunwale.

Upstream - The direction the river or stream is flowing from.

Index

Also Available from Pesda Press

visit www.pesdapress.com